Thomas Anderson

Literature on the Blind

Volume 2

I0084612

Thomas Anderson

Literature on the Blind
Volume 2

ISBN/EAN: 9783742833792

Manufactured in Europe, USA, Canada, Australia, Japa

Cover: Foto ©Thomas Meinert / pixelio.de

Manufactured and distributed by brebook publishing software
(www.brebook.com)

Thomas Anderson

Literature on the Blind

REPRINT, 1895]

OBSERVATIONS

ON THE

EMPLOYMENT, EDUCATION, AND HABITS

OF

THE BLIND

WITH

A COMPARATIVE VIEW OF THE BENEFITS OF THE ASYLUM AND SCHOOL SYSTEMS

" Nothing is easier than to make the blind perform extraordinary feats, by accustoming them to conquer difficulties apparently insurmountable ; but what advantage would such useless employments be to them ? "

Guillié, Superintendent of the School for the Blind, Paris.

BY

THOMAS ANDERSON

LATE MANAGER OF THE ASYLUM FOR THE BLIND, EDINBURGH : AND MASTER OF THE
WILBERFORCE MEMORIAL SCHOOL FOR THE BLIND, YORK

LONDON
SIMPKIN, MARSHALL AND CO.
Manchester—GEORGE SIMMS, EXCHANGE STREET
1837

LONDON
SAMPSON LOW, MARSTON AND COMPANY
LIMITED
St. Dunstan's House
FETTER LANE, FLEET STREET, E.C.
1895

ADVERTISEMENT.

HAVING, within these few years past, been several times requested to give a general outline of the plan pursued at the asylum for the blind with which I had the happiness of being so long connected, preparatory to the establishment of others in this country, and one on the Continent; I have been induced to embody the whole in a more permanent form. An unwonted interest in behalf of the blind has, within these few years, displayed itself, and several munificent bequests have recently been left for the endowment of such institutions. I shall be happy if the following pages do, in any degree, aid the inquiries of those into whose hands these funds have been committed.

I feel happy in having an opportunity thus publicly to express how much I am indebted for all I know on the subject to ROBERT JOHNSTON, Esq., of Edinburgh, to whom these pages are inscribed. Not only have the plans which he suggested secured employment to the blind, to an extent both as it regards production and sale, beyond any institution of the kind in the kingdom, but he was the first in this country who engrafted, if I may so call it, nearly twenty years ago, on the merely mechanical pursuits common to all such establishments, the admirable system of intellectual education which has caused it to stand out as a model to others,—a system in every way fitted to meet the wants of those blind, who have to gain their livelihood by their labour, yet are, at the same time, capable of being instructed in much calculated to raise them in the scale of society. His aid, his counsel, his patient consideration of any proposal I had occasion to lay before him, and his readiness to give me the weight of his authority, made the period I passed in that institution one of perfect smoothness. And it will always give me the greatest pleasure to think of the amicable feeling which existed between the directors and myself, unbroken, as it was, even by a single difference of opinion. To this aid, and to this unity, it is, that, with special reference to " Him who has the hearts of all men in his hand," I owe all the happiness I experienced, as well as the success which attended my efforts in fulfilling the duties then committed to me.

School for the Blind, York,
    August 30, 1837.

OBSERVATIONS

ON THE

EDUCATION AND EMPLOYMENT

OF

THE BLIND.

WITHIN these few years there appears to have arisen a feeling on behalf of the blind, which contrasts strongly with the apathy and neglect this interesting class of our fellow-men had previously experienced. The last ten years has done much for them both at home and abroad; and there are good grounds for saying that the next ten will do as much, if not more. Nothing in the way of an educational institution seems to have been thought of for them until about 1785, when the school at Paris was opened under the auspices of Louis XVI.; and the immediate superintendence of the celebrated Hauy. But, such was the success of this seminary, that an immediate movement took place towards the amelioration of their condition, and the governments of Russia, Prussia, and Austria followed in the same line, by the establishment of similar institutions in their respective capitals.

In our own country the same feeling showed itself by the school at Liverpool being opened in 1791. The asylum at Edinburgh and the school at Bristol followed in 1793. That of London, 1799, and Norwich in 1805.

After this the blind seem to have been nearly forgotten, as it was not until 1828 that the asylum at Glasgow commenced its operations, since which period several have been opened in the United States, viz.:—one at Boston, another at New York, and a third at Philadelphia.

In 1835 the Committee appointed to carry into effect the wishes of the subscribers to a memorial in remembrance of the excellent Wilberforce, opened the Yorkshire school for the blind, while another, combining also the instruction of the deaf and dumb, commenced operations at Belfast in 1833.

No less than *four* others are at this moment projected in our own country—at Manchester, London, Aberdeen, and Dundee. The first will very soon open as an ASYLUM, on a scale fully equal to any. This has been accomplished by the munificent bequest of Thomas Henshaw, Esq., of Oldham, joined to a large subscription by the inhabitants of Manchester. The second will arise from the largest bequest ever made for such a purpose, that of the late Mr. Day, of London, who left £100,000 for the endowment of an asylum for the blind. While the third and fourth are from considerable sums left recently for like purposes. Seeing then that so much is likely to be done it is an important question, how shall these ample means be disposed of, so as to secure the greatest amount of benefit to the blind as a body—keeping clear of the mere show of the continental schools on the one hand, and on the other, the equal error of making no provision for their intellectual training.

It is a striking feature in our own institutions that they are all the result of private charity, while those on the Continent are supported wholly or in part by their respective governments. The American establishments have also shared largely in the funds of the local states—these grants, at least that of Boston, being connected with the right to present a certain number of pupils.

It is, however, to be questioned, whether institutions mainly supported by national funds, are so efficient as those of the other description. While, on the other hand, a grant even to a trifling amount, *in proportion to the number educated* would prove a great benefit. This of course would be accompanied, as in similar cases, with the patronage of so many appointments : and if only such in amount as to prove an *aid*, not an *independence*, could be obtained, the benefit arising to the indigent blind would be very great.*

There is not the least doubt that the institutions for the

---

* The very partial endowments of schoolmaster-ships in Scotland is all that is wanted in the way of proof (to those who object to such grants on the score of engendering evil) as to the truly beneficial results which might fairly be anticipated. They have as much as will keep them from starving, but they must work well and hard if they desire to live comfortably. I merely throw out this as a hint, and would be glad to see it followed up by some one better able to do it. How desirable is it that a few of those many thousands at the disposal of Parliament, should be appropriated to the *help* of those institutions whose aim is to ameliorate the condition of those four classes of suffering humanity, whose claims upon our sympathy no one will call in question, viz. :—the insane—the incurable—the blind—and the deaf and dumb. No one will inflict upon himself that which would entitle him to relief from any such institution, however well endowed, and in this, as it has been well and eloquently argued by Dr. Chalmers, lies all the security possible that such funds would not be abused. "Men," says this distinguished writer, "will become voluntarily poor, but they will not become voluntarily blind or deaf, or maimed, or lunatic. It is thus, that while an asylum for want creates more objects than it can satisfy, an asylum for disease creates none, but may meet all and satisfy all. It is a disgrace to our philanthropic age, if infirmaries, or dispensaries, or asylums, whether for the cure of mental and bodily disease, or for keeping of that which is incurable, are left to languish for want of support, or compelled to stop short, ere the necessity for which they were instituted has been fully and finally overtaken."—*Political Economy*, p. 418.

blind throughout the country have already done much good. Some of them are amply provided for; while others have had much to do to carry on, chiefly from the numbers seeking relief at their hands. Still the benefit conferred on the great mass of the blind is but small, when it is recollected that the number of these amounts to about *twenty-six thousand*. However general this estimate may be (and it is confessedly so, owing to the imperfect data on which it is founded), still it may warrant the assertion that a great deal remains to be done, particularly for that portion of them (forming by far the majority) who must, in some way or other, be dependent on impoverished friends or parishes, viz., the indigent blind.

From the information contained in an interesting article on the education of the blind, in the North American Review for July, 1833, we have some valuable particulars on this subject. The writer says, " In several countries in Europe, the census gives accurately the number of the blind. In the centre of Europe it is about 1 in 800; in Austria, 1 in 845; in Switzerland, 1 in 747; in Denmark, 1 in 1000; in Prussia, 1 in 900; and in France, 1 in 1050." The average of these gives 1 in 890, and if we take the same rate as applicable to Great Britain and Ireland, then the population, being just upon 25 millions, the number of blind will be nearly 28,000.* The first attempt

---

* At the close of the Report of the Society of Arts at Edinburgh on printing for the blind (1836), amongst other suggestions relative to this class the following is deserving of particular attention. " That the ministers throughout Scotland be solicited to ascertain the number of blind persons in their respective parishes—the causes of their blindness—how they are occupied—the age at which they became blind—and how many could read previous to their blindness." A request of this kind, combining with a return of the deaf and dumb, would doubtless meet a ready compliance on the part of the clergy. It would have formed an appropriate item in the New Statistical Account of Scotland, now in course of publication.

made in this country to ascertain the precise number of the blind in a given district, has recently been made by the committee of the school for the blind, York. In the first report of that institution, just published, the indefatigable chairman, the Rev. W. Vernon Harcourt, has laid before the subscribers and the public, not only a report teeming with interest, but has accompanied it with an elaborate digest of about *seven hundred* returns from parishes in the county of York, of the numbers, ages, &c., of the interesting class alluded to. This the reverend author unassumingly denominates a "preface." But, to those who are at all conversant with the subject, it cannot but assume a much more important place, being neither more nor less than a census of the blind in the large and very populous county just mentioned,—indeed, quite a *desideratum.* Almost all the countries on the Continent have a census of the blind—but Great Britain has none : and the document alluded to, emanating from what may now be called a provincial town, is the first of the kind of which our country can boast.

It is not my intention to enter into any detailed account of the respective institutions. But having given my attention to the subject these ten years past, and having carefully observed the practical working of one of the oldest, and confessedly most efficient in the kingdom, though unfortunately but little known—that at Edinburgh,—and seeing there are no less than four institutions of a similar kind in prospect, with means at their disposal commensurate with much good, I mean to confine myself to some particulars whereby to show the vast advantage arising to the blind themselves, as well as to the funds devoted to their benefit, from the adoption of the ASYLUM system, as compared with that of the SCHOOL system.

In the outset of this it is worthy of remark, that the

institutions in England and Ireland are all *schools,* while
those of Scotland are *asylums**—better described, perhaps,
by saying institutions for the *education* and *employment,*
but, with the exception of the junior members, not residence, of the blind. The only explanation I can offer for
this difference is, the necessity our northern friends are
under of taking the most economical mode of doing the
most good ; though they may thereby be obliged to forego
much of that not very valuable eclat, which arises from
the other. And when I state, quoting from the speech
of the Rev. W. Vernon Harcourt, at the first meeting of
the subscribers to the Wilberforce school for the blind,
that "the annual expenditure of the school in London,
exclusive of articles of manufacture, for which there is a
return, is £4000 ; and the annual expenditure of the
institution at Liverpool is £3000,"—the number of *pupils*
being in each about the same—100 to 110 ;—while the
asylum at Edinburgh maintains nearly *a like number of
blind,* as well as the wives and children dependent on
about one-third of the number, which equal that, if it does
not exceed, on much less than £1000, there surely is room
for the inquiry,—What are the principles, the working of
which produce such very different results, bearing in
mind, too, that there is pursued at the northern asylums
constant and most efficient plans for the *intellectual*
education of those under their charge, which have as
yet found no place in the others ?

* In the very excellent article "Instruction of the Blind," in the Penny
Cyclopædia—by far the best I have seen on the subject in the department
of our literature to which it belongs—I was surprised to see it stated
that "the evidence of the fact that blindness is no insurmountable obstacle
to the acquisition of knowledge has not led to a proper system—*asylums*
having been provided rather than *institutions*—places of abode rather
than of instruction." The reverse of this with the exceptions stated is the
correct statement: as, indeed, may be gathered from the interesting particulars contained in the article itself.

Connected as I was for eight years with the asylum at Edinburgh, and having thereby had the advantage of observing the plans adopted for the education of the blind, as well as the no less important modes whereby they may be profitably employed, I trust I shall be in some measure enabled to answer the question proposed.

It is much to be regretted that Mr. Johnston, whose long and active connexion with the institution qualified him above all others to do so, did not come forward at a much earlier period with a development of the views which regulated the charity for which he has exerted himself so much. Had he done so, he would undoubtedly have occupied a place which, in consequence of his blameable reluctance, has been, in a limited degree, occupied by others; while all the institutions of a like kind in the country would have had before them details in every way beneficial to their funds, as well as to the best interests of those under their care. In lieu of any such, we have only the usual newspaper notices of the annual examinations, which took place from time to time. These excited much, but perhaps too local an interest; and being altogether devoid of those pecuniary details which would have brought its economical and truly efficient management at once before the public, these notices served little else than the purpose of the passing day.

It gives me much pleasure, however, to refer to the excellent report made to the directors of the Boston institution by Dr. Howe, in 1833. That gentleman had been sent over to Europe to visit all the institutions for the blind, preparatory to opening one there. In this document he says, he " engaged one teacher from Paris, and another from Edinburgh. The institution at Edinburgh is, on the whole, the best I saw in Europe. It comes nearer than any other to the attainment of the great object of such institutions, viz., enabling the inmates to support themselves by their own efforts. The establishment is not so showy as that at Paris, nor has it the same means* the latter possesses (which receives an allowance of 60,000 francs per annum from government), nor has it printed books for their use. *Still they receive most excellent education,* and learn some most useful trades. The mattress and mat making are carried on by the blind there with great skill and success." Again, he observes, "The asylum at Edinburgh is certainly superior to any in England, and on the whole is so to that of Paris, and were it in place I might detail many curious and interesting processes for facilitating the education of the blind : the general principle, however, is to *combine intellectual and physical* education in such a way as to qualify them for the performance of a useful part in the world ; *and of so storing the mind with knowledge,* that they may have a fund within themselves from which to draw in after life." The writer of the article in the North American Review for July, 1833, formerly quoted, who appears to have visited the European institutions, observes of the one now spoken of—"It is decidedly of a higher order than any other in England ; and it is one of its merits, that the fabrication of the articles we have just mentioned (mattresses, baskets, rugs, &c.) *chiefly* occupies the attention of the inmates, and have quite as good an appearance as any made in the city ; enjoying at the same time a well-merited reputation of being stronger and more durable," they command the highest market price.

To the same purpose the author of the article on the

---

* It is barely able to carry on, from its being so long the only establishment of the kind in Scotland, and has scarcely any capital. Subscriptions are its sole reliance

Instruction of the Blind, in the Penny Cyclopædia, says—
"The whole machinery (of the Edinburgh Asylum) seems
to be of a high order. From its admirable management,
it may be inferred that there exists both the disposition
and the capability to make it all that could be wished as
an establishment for the blind." Who the author of the
article is I do not know. In it, however, he has certainly
furnished us with something approaching to a desideratum
—an account of our own institutions.

I hope to be able to show that these estimates of this
institution are not over-rated, and that the principles on
which it is conducted have done much towards the amelioration of those labouring under the deprivation of sight,
and this combined with the least possible expenditure.

There can be no doubt that in proportion as we economise the funds of an institution, the great body of the
blind are benefited, by aid being extended to a larger
number; but *in practice* this obvious rule seems almost
to have been lost sight of. When to this is conjoined
the great error of mistaking, or fondly representing in
glowing language, the *possibilities of the few*, as the *real
and daily operations of the many*, the amount of hindrance
to their actual benefit has been great indeed.

In short, the question seems all along to have been,
What CAN *they do?* rather than *What* OUGHT *they to do?*
On this point who can read the touching sentiments of
Dr. Blacklock, himself one of the class, without at once
feeling their force? "Were men to judge of things by
their intrinsic value, less would be expected from the blind
than from others. But, by some pernicious and unaccountable prejudice, people generally hope to find them
either possessed of preternatural talents, or more attentive
to those they have than others. Hence, it unluckily
happens, that blind men, who in common life are too

often regarded as raree-shows, when they do not gratify
the extravagant expectations of the spectators, too often
sink in the general opinion, and appear much less considerable and meritorious than they really are. This general
diffidence of their power, at once deprives them both of
opportunity and spirit to exert themselves; and they
descend at last to that degree of insignificance in which
the public estimate has fixed them."

In the following pages I shall make some observations
on the two systems pursued—that of the school and the
asylum—on the employments and results of each—on the
education of the blind—and conclude with some notices
of the pursuits, habits, and peculiarities which distinguish
them.

The design of *schools* for the blind is to instruct young
persons for a few years, and then let them go to provide
for themselves as well as they can. On the other hand,
that of an *asylum* is not only to *teach* them, but to *employ
them after they are taught*—dependent, of course, on their
own wish to remain, and good conduct, as in any other
working establishment.

The first method is founded on the idea that they *can
do as much out of the house as in it*, or nearly so, joined
with the desire to spread the benefit of the institution as
much as possible. The second proceeds on the assumption
that they—at least the *far greater proportion—cannot do
so*, and that the funds of the charity will go a great deal
farther, and much more thoroughly provide for those enjoying its benefit, than the principle of a school can do.

I am quite aware how it "strikes a stranger" when
he enters a school for the blind:—"Well, this is delightful—who would have believed it! How very nicely they
get on!—and such a blessing to be enabled to do for

themselves —how cheerful, how happy!" No feeling mind can look on such a scene without indulging in such thoughts. But, let that stranger—and I would also invite the directors of such institutions—look forward to a few years, when these young people will all have been dispersed to their several villages, crowded lanes, or hovels! Visit them there in the mind's eye—visit them in detail, one after another—and where is the bright vision and glowing anticipations excited by the appearance of the same children when at school? The charm is gone. All the adaptations so well fitted to bring out the feelings described have disappeared, and it is found at last that the excitement and benevolence called forth while perambulating the extensive and comfortable premises of a *school* are one thing, while those called forth by viewing a succession of those very pupils, after they have left the institution, are quite another—perhaps I do not go too far in saying, a melancholy contrast. Some may be inclined to say that the same observation applies to any large school or public charity for education, and that the same reasoning would go to prove the necessity of keeping all children permanently on the funds. I think not. Every pupil leaves school *with those powers entire* which enable him to take his place in the world on an equality with those around him. Not so the blind, even when educated. They labour under a privation which wholly disqualifies them for taking a similar place. By their being trained in schools, they can get nearer it by a step or so ; but by being brought together, and employed within the precincts of an asylum, they can make a far closer approximation. One exception alone can be made, but that is a decided one—I mean as to music. This is the solitary branch which they can cultivate with any hope of *competing* successfully ; but it is one which could be easily grafted on

c

the system of an asylum at very little expense, and with manifest advantage to such an institution. In any remarks, therefore, which I may hereafter make, on the inefficiency of the school system, I would wish the exception now made to be kept in view.

In proof of what I have just said, I shall adduce, from among many others, a case of very recent occurrence, and I do it as presenting a fair average : some may be better, and some worse, but I consider it one well calculated to bring out what is meant.

A girl was sent very lately to a school at the age of fourteen. She had lost her sight when an infant, and her parents, however willing, burdened as they were with four or five children, could do little for her benefit. When she entered the institution she could not put on her own clothes, and of anything like information, or ideas beyond her immediate and most humble wants, she was totally destitute! In a fortnight she could dress herself completely, much to her own delight. Possessed of a lively temper, and good capacity, she soon acquired plain knitting, a little arithmetic,* committed to memory portions of the Scriptures, some psalms and hymns, and was, on the whole, proceeding remarkably well, when, after a year's stay, she was removed, owing to her parents being unable to afford the sum requisite. Being in the town where she resides, a few weeks after she went home, I called upon her. I found her just as might be expected—wholly idle, sitting on a low stool by the fire, in an apartment where she could not move three steps with freedom, and in a locality which afforded not one step of a walk to her with safety. All she had acquired had become nearly useless; and as to fancy-knitting, it was out of the question, in such a place, without means and still more without the help which,

* By means of the Pentagon Arithmetic Board, afterwards to be noticed.

although but little, is still absolutely necessary to enable
one in her circumstances to go on. Not a thing around
her—scarcely an idea of those about her—was suited to
her situation. While in the institution she had acquired
new tastes, almost new feelings, from being able to do
something really useful. But all had passed away like a
dream ; and she was left, I would almost say, worse than
when she was withdrawn from her obscurity. She had
tasted the happiness of being associated with companions
under similar circumstances, all of them delighted at the
new powers which they found themselves possessed of;
they felt they were much nearer to the great mass of
those around them than they had imagined ; and that by
a little care and a little attention, they could reach them
in many things, and approach in all. They had besides
become objects of public attention and approval; they
felt they possessed a place in society, however humble ;
and that the barrier which had so long stood between
them and the seeing world they had heard so much of, was
not quite so insurmountable as they had supposed it to be.
But, separated from the institution, how much of all this
was left to the young person spoken of? Scarcely a shred.
She falls back, in one short hour, from all the comforts
which surrounded her, upon impoverished friends, or, in
all likelihood, sooner or later, on the miseries of the
workhouse! Of her, and of all such, may we not adopt
the language of the reviewer formerly quoted, when
speaking of the failures of the school at Paris?—" The
pupil has drank at the fountain of knowledge long enough
to create a painful thirst for its waters, which cannot be
gratified ; he has lived in ease only long enough to make
penury doubly dreary ; and his mind has been so
elevated as to make a feeling of dependence the source
of wretchedness."

It may be said—" Well, but this girl was only a short time at school. Had she been allowed to remain a few years, it would have been otherwise, and it is not right to draw a general inference from an extreme case."

Had it been either a solitary or an extreme case, I *would not* have brought it forward. I adduce it as an *average* case, and only one among many I know. I have seen several leave the asylum at Edinburgh of their own accord, under the idea that they could do better, or at least as well, out of it. Others had been dismissed for bad conduct. All of them had been many years in the house, and most of them good workmen. One of them, a steady, well-behaved man, having a wife and two children, opened, by the assistance of his friends, a little shop in a large market town. He attempted to carry on the basket and rope-mat making, while his wife aided by the sale of crockery. But he was not six months out of the institution until every endeavour was made on the part of his friends to get him reinstated in his old berth and his 9s. a week, which, after much difficulty (from the crowded state of the house), was at length accomplished. He had, however, lost every shilling, become indebted for rent, materials, &c., and long struggled under the effects of his laudable but ill-advised attempt.

Another young man, also of excellent character, made the same experiment. He left with the same idea in his head as the preceding case. He opened a shop in a populous manufacturing town—the very best field whereon such an attempt can be made. He persevered two or three years, surrounded with difficulties, and unhappily added to them by getting married—a step which is almost sure to follow in the great majority of cases.. After a long struggle, he also made every effort to get readmitted; but, however willing the directors were to accede, the state of the funds, as well as the pressure of applications, forbade compliance.

Another very striking case has just come to my knowledge, which I cannot omit. It is that of a man who spent four years in one of the most celebrated schools, and acquired a knowledge of mat-making and sack-weaving. In an application made to another institution for employment, he says that from the difficulty of procuring material, as well as of finding a market,—although resident for several years past in a populous shipping town,—he would willingly pay ten pounds premium to be admitted to teach or work, receiving only his board and clothing in return—looking for no wages.

Still it may be objected that I have adduced local cases not calculated to go far when brought to bear against a system. To meet this, I shall then quote two testimonies, which will carry with them, I have no doubt, very considerable weight. In the report of the Dublin (Richmond National Institution) school for the blind, for 1833, the committee say, they "have not merely to lament the limited aid received from those places whose industrious blind have been, in so large a proportion, benefited by the institution;—they have also heard with pain, that pupils who had acquired a proficiency in one or *more* trades, and had been discharged from the institution with a good character, and a considerable sum in earnings, have been suffered, on returning to their homes, *to languish for that support and encouragement* to which they were so eminently entitled; *their funds have been gradually exhausted, and too frequently they have reappeared in Dublin,* to add to a mass of poverty already excessive ; a result the more to be regretted as it is believed there are few provincial towns where one or other of the trades taught in the institution would not fail to secure a livelihood, were a friendly countenance shown to the blind proficient." And what is it that brings relief to the committee under this melancholy picture of the result of their endeavours ?— "It is, however, hoped," they continue, "that amongst the first measures devised for the relief of the poor of Ireland, this class, so deserving of public commiseration, will have that full care and provision to which it is so justly entitled"; which, in other words, expresses a hope that these "proficients" will be provided for as paupers.

Again, at a meeting held in Manchester, in March, 1834, relative to the erection of the asylum there, now so soon to be opened, the committee state in their report that they "have been informed that the trustees of the Liverpool institution *have long felt the want of an* ASYLUM for such blind persons *as were unable to obtain their own livelihood;*" and farther state, that having "proceeded to procure the regulations of the schools or asylums for the blind, established at London, Liverpool, and Edinburgh, the result of the information derived from these sources of information was, A CONVICTION ON THEIR MINDS, that it would be inexpedient, at present, to connect *a school of instruction* with the intended asylum;"—assigning as reasons for this opinion, "the abundant facilities" of the school at Liverpool—"the *great expense* which must be incurred in the appointment of masters for the purpose of teaching trades, and the *positive loss* to the institution with which they are attended."

A very prevalent argument in favour of the school system is, that there is a *succession of pupils* received, taught, and dismissed, enabled to provide for themselves : while, by the other plan, the whole good of the institution is centred in the favoured few who can, once for all, gain admission : therefore the great body of the blind are left out. This is much more plausible than correct. By

observation, it is ascertained that from seven to ten per
cent. per annum leave (in one way and another), or die out
of an establishment of the kind, *thereby making room for a
corresponding number.* Were asylums only a little more
numerous, and the system of *employment* rather than the
system of mere tuition adopted, this ratio would be found
beyond the demands of the blind. It must also be kept
in view, that by the former system nearly three times the
number will be provided for, as compared with a school;
*supposing a proper field be chosen for the ready disposal of
their work; and that the articles manufactured be sold at a
price not higher than they can be had elsewhere.*

As an additional corroboration of these views, I would
adduce the evidence of the author of the article in the
North American Review already referred to. He has
drawn as glowing a picture as the most imaginative could
desire of the aspect of the Parisian institution. All is
represented (for he speaks from personal observation) as
delightful — joyous — sportive — and interesting. One
would almost be inclined to think that the picture had
been thus highly coloured that it might stand the stronger
out in contrast with the succeeding paragraph. But that
I may not be accused of giving a partial view of his
observations, or only that portion of them which tends
to support my own sentiments, I shall transcribe the
whole :—

" In the institution for the young blind (between the
ages of ten and fourteen), there are one hundred of these
interesting beings, and a more delightful spectacle cannot
be imagined than a view of its interior. You see not there
the listless, helpless blind man, dozing away his days in a
chimney nook, or groping his uncertain way about the
house ; but you hear the hum of busy voices,—you see
the workshops filled with active boys, learning their trades

from others as blind as themselves,—you see the school-room crowded with eager listeners, taught by blind teachers. When they take their books, you see the awakened intellect gleam from their smiling faces, and, as they pass their fingers rapidly over the leaves, their varying countenances bespeak the varying emotions which the words of the author awaken. When the bell rings, they start away to the play-ground,—run along the alleys at full speed,—chase, overtake, and tumble each other about, —and shout and laugh and caper round with all the careless heartfelt glee of boyhood. But a richer treat and better sport awaits them; the bell again strikes, and away they all hurry to the hall of music; each one brings his instrument, and takes his place; they are all there—the soft flute and the shrill fife—the hautboy and horn—the cymbal and drum—with clarionet, viol, and violin;—and now they roll forth their volume of sweet sounds, and the singers, treble, bass, and tenor, striking in with exact harmony, swell it into one loud hymn of gratitude and joy, which are displayed in the rapturous thrill of their voices, and painted in the glowing enthusiasm of their animated countenances."

What can go beyond this? The most enthusiastic advocate for the school system could not wish for a description more calculated to obtain a verdict in its favour. Let us, however, carefully mark what follows:—

" Such is the scene which presents itself to the delighted visitant of the Parisian institution; and he comes away with a feeling of unqualified admiration for that spirit of humanity which, guided by science, is there accomplishing so much in defiance of the apparently insurmountable obstacles of nature. But he who goes again, and again, and examines not only the foliage and the flower, but waits for the season of the fruit, finds his admiration

dwindling into doubt, and feels at last the painful conviction, that all this *display is of comparative little good*,
and that *not one-half the benefit* that might be derived
from such splendid means ever accrues to the unfortunate
inmates. He asks the question—How many of those who
leave the institution at the expiration of their time are
enabled to gain their own livelihood?—and is startled at
the answer, ' NOT ONE IN TWENTY!' What then? Must
they relapse into their former inanition? Must they take
their places by the highwayside, and beg at the corner of
the streets, with the pangs of dependence sharpened to
torture by increased sensibility? Alas! *it is as bad as this
with many.* And how is it proposed to remedy this evil;
how do they hope to prevent the glimmering which the
blind here catch of happiness, from being followed by a
futurity doubly dark and wretched? Why, instead of
looking for the cause of the evil,—instead of suspecting
the *system*, and correcting *that*,—they propose to establish
a place for the permanent reception and support of those
who come out from the institution, and who cannot provide for themselves. This," concludes the reviewer, " is
very like educating men for the almshouse." *

Never was there a juster view taken of the glittering,
unsubstantial, and delusive system under consideration,
whether to be seen at Paris or in England; and while I
would acquit our own institutions of a like kind from
much of the Parisian leaven, consisting, as it does, according to the writer just quoted, in making all go through
the same routine of work and music, there is also, on the
other hand, a far too near approximation to it in some of
recent date. The remedy proposed, as above, is the very
thing wanted; but it by no means follows that the asylum

---

* North American Review, July, 1833.

is to become an almshouse. Whether it does so or not, depends solely *on the way in which those so to be provided for may be prepared for it.* If by the tinsel, so strikingly set before us by this animated writer, then let us share in the melancholy tone of his climax; but, if they are really brought up to that which is identified with the daily wants of an immense metropolis, or of a busy, stirring, district of country, in place of those which are forced upon the sight-seeking visitor, then would there be ample reason to hail the opening of an ASYLUM for the blind in the French capital. If it is even near the fact that NINETEEN-TWENTIETHS of the inmates are not benefited, in what stronger language can we state the uselessness of the system there pursued? But how does the reviewer propose to remedy "the system" of which he so justly complains? "It is alleged that (in the British institutions) the pupils, being all indigent, must depend solely upon the labour of their hands for their livelihood; but we maintain that this is a *false* (wrong?) *view of the subject,* and we shall endeavour to show that, on this principle (which has been followed hitherto in all the institutions), FEWER blind persons will be made competent to their own support than might be by following *an opposite one.*" In short, he sets aside handicraft occupation, as that in which the blind cannot *compete,* and presses their being instructed in "music, mathematics, and languages," as affording the desirable field whereon they may gain a competency. — "Manual labour," he concludes, should be considered as the *"dernier ressort,* the forlorn hope of the blind, and such only should be put to it, as cannot expect to attain excellence in the occupations" he had already recommended. He laments the little prospect they have, even in this way, of providing for themselves, as "machinery defies competition;" but they must be sanguine indeed, who can ever hope to see

the blind (as a body) succeed in gaining even a niche in
that world of talent, which with its intellectual machinery,
is more than commensurate to meet all the demands
upon it for "music, mathematics, and languages,"—the
machinery intellectual appears to me on the one hand
just as destructive of these hopes respecting the blind as
the machinery mechanical is on the other,—while, in
addition to the mere circumstance of the *supply* being, in
our day, beyond the *demand*, it cannot be denied that,
foolish and cruel as the feeling may be, there does exist a
strong prejudice against the blind *as teachers*. This, I
believe, no one will deny, however much it may be
regretted.

If this fact of the *constant change* occurring in an asylum
were more kept in view, it would do away with much of the
idea, that only a limited number of the blind are benefited.
I have little doubt that the number of such institutions
will increase: and that, ere long, we shall see every city
and large town in the kingdom having its Blind Asylum,
just as they can at present boast of their Infirmaries.

But here, let it be strongly impressed, that every such
institution ought to be strictly in proportion *to the probable
demand for the work the blind can furnish.* To erect an
asylum in an inconsiderable town where little can be sold,
would be a waste of funds. No doubt it might become
rich, and have no difficulty whatever in supporting its
inmates, but I am speaking of doing so, in such a way,
as to make the blind nearly support themselves. Now,
looking at London and Edinburgh, as to population, the
former ought to give employment to TEN such asylums as
the one at the latter, and that at a low estimate. Thus at
least ONE THOUSAND blind would be constantly employed
and educated in the Metropolis alone,* and if as many of

---

* The school there contains about 120 pupils.

these had wives and children dependent on them as there are at Edinburgh, then, at least another thousand human beings would be creditably provided for. This is no theory. The thing is done, and has been in existence many years. But I shall recur to this point afterwards.

By the nearest estimate which has yet been formed (as before stated), of the total number of blind in the United Kingdom, it is thought to be about 28,000 of all ages. Allowing that one-fourth of these are unfit from age to do anything, and another fourth under the age of ten, we have then 14,000 remaining. But from this amount, we must deduct, say, three thousand who are in the middle and wealthier classes, therefore not objects for such institutions ; still we have to find tuition and employment for the very large number of ELEVEN THOUSAND. And is there not ample means in our large towns to meet this demand? There certainly is, if proper attention were but turned to the subject. At least, a very great deal more might be done than has yet been effected. The Metropolis itself presents by far the most important field. To this moment it remains almost unoccupied, while, as before stated, it could in all probability find ample and *constant employment* for ten times the number of those at present under tuition, at the school in St. George's Fields.

Again, in the populous and busy districts of Yorkshire, for instance, at Leeds and Hull, highly favourable situations might be found for the employment of the blind of the county : while in Manchester, it is probable that a system somewhat akin to that advocated in these pages, will soon be made ; and, under the direction of gentlemen so thoroughly acquainted with business, as that community boasts, the best results may be confidently expected—results which *cannot* be looked for from the school system, however well conducted.

These, and such like districts, present very peculiar facilities for the object in view, in respect of the great demand for all kinds of heavy basket work used in the mills, as well as the domestic baskets in constant demand. Rope and twine spinning is another branch of business which would of itself employ many hands. It forms a principal item in the sales of the Asylum at Glasgow, and from specimens put into my hands lately by Mr. Alston, the spirited treasurer of that institution, the *finish* is equal to any in the market. An equally extensive branch wholly unknown in schools is MATTRESS making. This alone gives employment, at the asylum in Edinburgh, to not less than about thirty of the inmates—the sales of this article alone amount to nearly £2,000.

When visiting one of the most celebrated schools, I was surprised to see that there were but two or three hands employed on baskets for domestic use, a branch which constitutes by far the greater part of any basket maker's business. The reason assigned was, " They had no demand for such — visitors purchased what they thought curious, and easily carried." But I found, on further inquiry, that an additional reason existed, in the fact that the price charged was beyond that at which such articles could be procured in town. This of course shuts out the great body of the population from ever entering the institution *as customers*. They may come as visitors, and *then*, as they wish to see the inmates at work, a purchase is made as a preliminary to their request being granted. Experience has proved that common, useful, and therefore always saleable basket work would find a ready market. I have seen no less than nineteen persons employed in an asylum on this kind of work, while very little of the curious or fanciful was to be had at all—the loss being so much greater upon it.

A fact which came lately to my knowledge will illustrate the practical evil of charging articles at a higher price than usual:—A lady much interested in the prosperity of one of our most celebrated schools, knew that there was a large accumulation of flour sacking on hand. Desirous to promote a reduction of the stock, she ordered a quantity of it—(into Yorkshire, I believe). She did all she could to effect a sale, at the price at which she purchased them, but in vain. She pleaded the quality of the article (for it is a well-known fact, that articles manufactured by the blind are very stoutly made), and backed this with what she deemed an unanswerable argument, viz.: that it was for the good of a charitable institution. But this was of no avail. She could dispose of none of them. I had this from herself. Now, if the institution had such difficulty in meeting a market, aided as it was by the local influence of its fair patroness: what was the shadow of hope held out to an obscure pupil, whose time had been consumed in making the article, that *he* would succeed in gaining a living by following the same occupation when he left the school?

Another instance of the same kind is as follows: A young man was sent to the school above alluded to— remained some years, acquiring a knowledge of rope and twine spinning, and returned home "to do for himself." But his patroness told me, that it was more difficult to provide for him on his return than before—for he could not follow the occupation he had acquired without a little capital, *and the constant assistance of a seeing person*— finding this to be the case, he got quite unhappy. In short, his wants were increased, while his means were stationary, and he soon found that what he could perform very well at school, he could do very little in at home, still less find a ready market.

There is no description of work indeed which has been usually put into the hands of the blind, but is now made by machinery at such prices as to render anything like competition on their part utterly hopeless—hopeless even to those who have their sight, if they persist in what formerly might have been every way available. Much was open to the class I speak of in 1790 and 1795, which has long ago been taken out of their hands, by improved machinery. And, since the peace, the beautiful baskets imported from the Continent, not only command a market from the excellence of their workmanship, but also from the extremely low prices at which they can be had—even after the heavy import duty, and still more expensive charges of freight and carriage are paid! No basket maker will now engage in what is called " French work," because of these insurmountable difficulties. Why then teach the blind, *as a means of obtaining* THEIR *livelihood*, that which the regular tradesman has long ago given up?

I am anxious it may be kept in view, that while I thus reason, and adduce the instances above mentioned, it is the *system* of schools which is opposed, not the *management* of them. The same results would arise in whatever hands they might be placed. I think no one can look at the reports of our various institutions of *that* kind, and those of the *other*, without at once seeing the truth of this. The former have to surmount all the difficulties, and sustain all the losses consequent on employing a succession of *learners ;* the latter, though always burdened with many who cause a great loss, have on the other hand many who work nearly for their wages.

I do not know a better light to place this in, than to show at one view the numbers, and amount of sales of the London, Liverpool, and Bristol schools, and the asylums

at Edinburgh and Glasgow. From the reports of these
institutions for the years stated, they stand thus—

	Report for	No. of Pupils.	Sales.
London	1832	112	£1,345
Liverpool	1836	108	1,820
Bristol	1835	40	1,000
* Edinburgh... ... { Average of ten years, 1822-32 }	—	80	3,200
Glasgow	1836	60	2,500

Wherever the public are excluded—unless a purchase
is made, or an order given—we cannot look for sales equal
in amount to those institutions where a different rule
obtains. The reason assigned for such a rule is, that from
the numerous parties visiting the school—the time of the
pupils is much broken in upon. The experience of the
institution at Edinburgh, and I believe, I may add, that
of Glasgow too, is quite opposed to this view of the
matter. The directors of the former (for of it I can speak
positively) found it of the greatest consequence to the
prosperity of the institution, that there should be no restriction. Any one, of whatever station in life, was made
welcome to go over the premises during the hours of work,
without any stipulation—as to purchase or order. The
directors found this to be the best advertisement they could
have. And, as to taking up the time of the inmates,—
they invariably found, that the idea of strangers being
at all times admissible, was an incentive to application.
They were never busier than when visitors were on the
premises. All were at their posts. If idleness ever went
on, it was just at those times when visitors were not expected. Thus the "good will" of the *community* was
cultivated, and not the comparatively casual "custom"

---

* I take the average of these ten years, because I have them before
me. At present the numbers are rather less, but the sales continue much
the same.

of those who came merely to gratify curiosity, and charitably burdened themselves with "something, however small,—made by the blind." This could be gratified only to a limited extent, the articles made there being more for *use* than *show*.

The expenditure necessary to carry on the London and Liverpool schools, as stated before,* is fully triple that of the institution at Edinburgh, while by the reports of the Glasgow asylum, it would appear that there they go still closer than their eastern neighbour, carrying on the work so as to pay itself. May I be allowed to say, that the rule followed out there, combined with the extreme economy in every department, appears more reconcileable with the strictest *pecuniary* considerations, than with the *philanthropic* view of the matter? The rule alluded to, as laid down in "Statements relative to the Glasgow asylum," 1835, is—"they (the blind) are allowed the same rate [of wages] that other workmen are allowed for the same kinds of work. It being ascertained that a man can make seven or eight shillings per week, he receives that as his weekly wages. At the end of every four weeks a statement of his earnings is made up from the work-book, and whatever he has earned over that sum is paid him; and as a reward to industry, *he receives one shilling per week of premium;* but if the weekly amount of work be not kept up, or the work be badly done, there is no premium allowed." †

This rule will no doubt go a great way to secure industry and good work. But are these confessedly desirable ends not obtained at rather a high rate in the eye of philanthropy, seeing the rule seems to visit upon the blind their privation, as if it were their fault? It seems to

---

* p. 6.   † p. 25.

say,—" You labour under the loss of sight, but you shall
be allowed like wages as those paid to workmen who have
their sight, with a shilling premium on every seven or
eight wrought for,—finding out of that, as they do, house
rent, coal, food, clothing, &c." Is it not a well-known
fact that weaving, and such like trades, are now paid at
such a rate as to afford the scantiest supply to the most
industrious engaged in them, even when working unusually long hours? And can it be supposed, that *the
blind* can earn such wages, when paid at the *same rate*, as
enables them to be even on a footing with their more
favoured neighbours? That *some* do so, there can be no
doubt, but to reason from extreme cases, *or such as are
not applicable to the mass*, leads us sadly astray. A constant reiteration of the *pecuniary* aspect of affairs, does
not appear to be all we have to look for from an institution formed for the amelioration, and relief, of one of the
heaviest calamities to which human nature is subject.
Might not this great and valuable end be better secured,
although at the sacrifice of a few hundreds per annum?

Still, a glance at the above tabular view will at once
show that there is something else than mere locality,
which causes such very different results between the
schools and the asylums: and when it is considered that
the Glasgow one is only in the tenth year of its age, the
amount of sales, the number of returns, as well as the
education they receive, reflect high credit on those in
the direction of its affairs.

It has many times surprised me to hear it said—"This
or that person at such and such a school can make so many
of these little baskets in a week—they sell for so much
a-piece—and the demand is constant." From this an
argument is drawn that the same, or nearly the same,
could be done by him or her out of the house. But it

ought to be remembered that the public have the *institution* in their eye—not the solitary inmate who makes the article. The former has a power of attraction, which the latter never can hope for. It has a status and an eclat which its members in vain attempt to carry with them. They sink into their own individual place, deprived of all the simple but excellent machinery which enabled them to do so much as they did : and those who would most cheerfully aid in every way *an institution*, cannot be brought in all cases to listen to the unknown and almost unbefriended blind. The question is not simply how much work a person *can make*—a far more important one is, *how much can he sell?* The aggregate of privation to be relieved is presented at one view in an establishment, whereas a unit of that aggregate, isolated from the attracting mass—in some fifth-rate street, some dark lane or alley, can only drag out a precarious subsistence, indebted in too many cases to parish aid. This is no fanciful representation. It is too true, as very many existing examples can bear witness.

But leaving generalities—always to be avoided—a closer view may be taken. And when reference is made to the report of the school at Liverpool, let it be kept in view that it is altogether the *principles* of that description of institution which are the subject of examination—not the management. I have no feeling but that of respect towards those who have so long and perseveringly laboured in that field of genuine philanthropy—certainly none but a wish, in all sincerity, to do good.

Taking, then, the report for 1836, we find that
the sales of work of the hundred and eight
pupils amounted to £1,820
And of accounts due for goods sold........... 50
                                          _____
                                          £1,870

Dividing this sum by the number of inmates, we have a trifle above SEVENTEEN pounds as the result of the labour of each, and that at a price fully above the market, with the very great advantages arising from *abundant capital, a dense population, adaptations, arrangements, superintendence, and concentration of public attention* ON THE INSTITUTION. From this sum the pupil, supposing him to have left the school and able to sell as much, has to find materials, rent, and expense of manufacture. What, then, is the pittance left? Or, what can a solitary pupil do, dissevered from the above-mentioned aids?—as essential to him as, in the great majority of cases, they are beyond his reach. It is a serious mistake to speak of charitable feeling doing everything, or almost anything, in such a case. If a school sells five shillings' worth, an asylum selling at shop prices will sell the double of that,—and if I mistake not, enough has been shown to prove this: while the loss upon the latter will not be nearly so great as that on the former, the workmen being so much better qualified to produce an article in shorter time, and of better quality.

There are also some valuable branches of manufacture which can be carried on in an asylum, which cannot make any part of the tuition of a school. This is a matter of great consequence, and has been little adverted to. The remark applies to the female as well as the male blind. Sewing, for instance, is useless to a young woman, as a means of obtaining her livelihood, after leaving school; but it can be turned to good account as a branch of employment in an asylum. I allude particularly to the manufacture of hair, wool, lea grass, and cotton mattresses, and straw palliasses. This branch forms no item in the details of any institution, except that at Edinburgh—and to a small extent that at Glasgow. It furnishes employment to fully one half of the entire number at the former, while the amount of sales under this head does not fall much short of £1600 a year. The sewing and binding of the covers of these, the repairing of others, as well as all the domestic sewing required, furnished constant employment for twelve or sixteen girls. This they did with great neatness and expedition. During the busy season for this description of work, the institution had more the appearance of a large upholstery concern than anything else. But no part of this work would have found its way into the hands of the blind, had they been unconnected with the asylum. However well they might sew in the house, the exercise of their abilities would never have been required out of it.

Again, at Glasgow, sacking and twine spinning form the staple articles of manufacture, the sales of the first *alone* amounting last year to £1136, and of the second to £408. It is by comparing facts of this kind, that we are to arrive at what should form the engagements of the inmates of an asylum for the blind. The articles just alluded to—mattresses, sacking, and twine, and I may add, basket work, and rope mats,—are as well finished as any in the market, are always in demand, and repay their cost better than almost any other description of work.

In addition to the weaving of striped Holland, ticking, and canvas for the covers of mattresses, there are also at the Edinburgh institution a few looms employed on sheetings, diapers, and towellings. The excellence of the loom and horse-hair manufacture is acknowledged by everyone. The yarns used are of the very best description, as anything of the kind, of an inferior quality, could not be made use of by the blind, from the frequency of breaking, knotting, &c. The weaving department is carried on under the care of only two overseers, who have the charge of warping the webs and seeing them properly put in; while the blind assist in "dressing" them, and carry on the remainder themselves. The blind not only help each other, but in many cases become excellent teachers of the younger members. This, however, cannot be carried into effect in a *school*, as the time of the pupil in that description of institution is expected, and ought, to be devoted to his own advancement; while, in the other case, he is entirely at the disposal of the directors.

The branches of business just mentioned, particularly the mattress making, would be quite unsuitable to teach a pupil at a school. However well a young man might be able to go on while there, his acquirement would become nearly useless to him on leaving. He is unable, from the want of capital, to take a single step in such an extensive matter. Difficulty would surround him on every side. Indeed, turn his attention to what you will, the same, or nearly the same may be said. Many are apt to think, that people will not grudge to pay him a little more for anything he can furnish, on account of his privation; and that work would be put up with from him, although not quite so neatly finished as it might have been by others. It is not consistent with fact—that such arguments would go far in practice. Charity will not do much for him. It may induce a few purchases, while the feeling is novel, but it soon finds the level of all such excitements.

Another reason of the economy of the asylum over the school system is, as before hinted at, that the latter has all its work in the hands of apprentices, and this ensures the necessary but expensive oversight of masters for the different branches. The pupil just leaves at the time he is beginning to be useful, and when by his proficiency he is doing a great deal towards his own maintenance. As an illustration of the opposite system, I would mention the case of a man who has been ten or twelve years employed at Edinburgh. He lost his sight after being married—supports his wife and three children on 8s. 6d. a week; having also a suit of clothes once a year. He is an excellent diaper weaver, and returns by his work 6s. to 6s. 6d. per week. Thus, he and his family cost the funds only 2s. 6d. or 2s. a week,—whilst, at the same time, he receives the most valuable aids in everything religious, moral, and instructive; without a single restraint being laid upon him, more than there is on any man working in a large manufactory.*

I come now to speak of a class which has been little, if at all, thought of by the promoters of our schools for the blind,—a class which, *of all others*, one would have thought should have been provided for in the first instance. I allude to those *who have been visited with loss of sight after being married, and having families.* I know of no cases which call for relief with claims equal to these. Rendered sightless by the providence of God, at a period of life when

---

* Speaking of what they have as wages and clothing, reminds me of an arrangement with regard to coals and potatoes, admirably fitted to secure to the inmates the *best article* at the *lowest price.* Mr. Johnston, secretary of the institution, observing that they were exposed, as all such in similar circumstances are, to the wasteful practice of buying both these articles of daily consumption in small quantities,—living, in fact, " from hand to mouth,"—adopted the plan of every man " underwriting " himself, in the month of August or September, for so many tons of coals and so many bushels of potatoes, according to his anticipated winter wants. The list was regularly taken round the premises by the overseer. signed by him, and sent in to the secretary. To this was added the probable consumption of coals for the institution, and the whole was contracted for, to be delivered at the respective houses of the parties. These were *not a gratuity.* Immediately on the season commencing (October), every man on receiving his wages from the hands of the manager, paid 6d. or 1s. (according to the quantity he had ordered) into the hands of the " collector," a steady man, blind too, who thus, " sitting at the receipt of custom," received

all his habits and ideas have been fully formed, *what can a school do for such a one?* Its routine and confinement, especially if reading at spare hours has not been introduced, dissociating him from all to which he has been accustomed, would go far to paralyse everything like exertion on his part; but enable him to alternate his hours of work with the kind attentions of his family; give him the indescribable pleasure of thinking that he is still earning their bread; and you place him in circumstances than which no plan could go so far towards ameliorating his distressing privation.

It affords me much pleasure to observe, that the committee of the school at London have of late acted in a limited degree on this plan. By the noble bequest of £10,000, left by the late James Tillard, Esq., they have been induced to retain a certain number of good workmen *permanently,* their support to be wholly chargeable on this fund. In the report for 1833, it is stated, " A few of those instructed in the school have been kept upon a

---

from each the appointed payment, assisted by another, also blind, whose duty it was to *see* that none passed without depositing their weekly quota in the hands of the cashier. Thus sixty or seventy payments were made every Monday evening (for *that* was our pay day)—the cash was regularly balanced *by themselves*—and remained in the hands of the collector until it amounted to ten pounds, when it was paid over to the credit of that particular account.

Thus, also, they had among themselves a funeral society—the weekly collection for it was made precisely in the same way. They conducted their own meetings, having a committee of their number to manage its affairs, " the clerk," who recorded their " resolutions," being the only seeing person concerned, but concerned only as the recorder of their operations.

Circumstances such as I have just stated may appear trifling to some: but I mention them, because the design of these pages is to show how much the blind may be enabled to do for themselves when employed *in a body.*

permanent establishment, on a supposition that their earnings are sufficient to maintain them, and that their skill is necessary to enable the institution to keep up the credit of its manufacture." How they have found this to succeed, I have not learned. They will, I have no doubt, very soon find the advantage of such a plan.

It is due to the London school to notice an excellent feature in their plan—that of permitting the work of those who have been taught there, to be sent to the institution for sale. But, considering that it is the Metropolis, the amount of such sales is of very limited extent, being, by Report 1832, only £237.

But, on the prospect of institutions of the asylum description increasing, may not the following be suggested—that a portion of the ground be laid out at some little distance from the main building, for the erection of 20, 30, or 40 cottages, each suitable for a family? These might form three sides of a square, while the manufacturing portion of the establishment would, at a little distance in advance, form the fourth. For these a small rent should be paid, such at least as would pay the interest on the cost of the erection. This would remove the married men from under the irksomeness of those rules indispensably necessary, where numbers are congregated together. The young *may* be bent, and most needful it is that they should be so (quite as arduous a task with the blind as with the seeing), but grumbling and discontent are sure to follow where the same measures are applied to those grown up. We may build palaces, and provide an ample table, but what is that to the class I speak of, accompanied as it *must* be by rules of uniformity, galling to people who have had a house of their own over their head all their lives? By the other plan, they enjoy the feeling of independence. Their pittance, their endeared articles of furniture (and where is the married, the widow or the widower who has not such ?), and should they have a child who ministers to the comfort of their declining years, would anyone interdict this solace residing with them ?

A bit of garden ground, however small, would be a great acquisition. " What ! " some perhaps will be disposed to say, " a garden for the blind ? " Yes, for the blind. They enjoy everything we enjoy, and if any one witnessed the care in watering a few plants,—their anxiety in watching the progress of vegetation,—and their delight in the development of a fine flower, they might be inclined to change their opinion. But, it is only as a solace I speak of it—a place of retirement in which, after a day's work, they would heartily delight. The entire of these cottages might be under the general superintendance of the institution, as to exterior regulations, regarding cleanliness, &c. A premium to the best kept would prove an incentive to laudable efforts. The possessors of them would be entirely under the rules of the manufactory, as to hours for work and meals; while a chapel on the premises, and the pastoral care of a chaplain, would at once constitute a community of no small interest to every benevolent mind.

Whether such a plan may be realised or not, the class of blind I have now been considering deserves the especial notice of those in the management of such institutions. They have a large, very large claim upon our sympathies, and their situation has been almost overlooked. They constitute not less than one-fourth (if not a third) of the blind.

From the adult, however, I turn to the young. Pupils, ere they are admissible to schools, must have reached their eleventh or twelfth year at least. It has often been asked me, why not take them in younger ? This can only be answered by saying, that the design of the institution, as well as of the parents, and others sending children, is to have them qualified as soon as possible *to gain their own livelihood.* To accomplish this, they must be received at such an age as promises to secure application and progress; and if *that were all,* the choice would be well. But it has often occurred to me that, where funds would admit of it, a most interesting department of an *asylum* would be a nursery for children under such circumstances, taking them in so early as four or five years of age. It is melancholy to think how many become incapable of instruction, and how many more never reach mediocrity, from the total want of the early care befitting their situation; or of any arrangements by which to call forth their powers. These lie dormant in the great majority of cases, while in the meantime, not only awkward habits of body, having no necessary connection with blindness, are acquired and strengthened beyond remedy, but the mind is also left to vegetate in ignorance—"no man taking care for it"—not from want of will, but from not knowing what should be done in such cases; meanwhile the "natural heart" remains in full operation, and is getting rooted in evil. In youth, they are too often the objects of ridicule and trick on the part of thoughtless companions, and thus, that feeling of inferiority is engendered in their minds, which is so apt to beget the worst feelings. Some become very listless, from sheer inaction. I have in my view many instances of all these. Had such been placed in early life under proper management, carried gradually forward from one thing to another, in education and work, many would have been rescued not only from bad habits, but fitted much more thoroughly for filling a respectable place in their own world. When children in these circumstances have reached the age of twelve, fourteen, or sixteen, it is no easy matter to bring them into habits of thought, and action, so dissimilar to all they have been accustomed to. *If introduced, however,* in childhood to companions in similar circumstances, and engaged in pursuits adapted to their privation, a rich harvest of benefit would undoubtedly ensue. Their hands would get gradually initiated into what they were afterwards to use daily, *and a vast advantage would be gained as it respects moral training.* One girl at present under my charge laments, sometimes even to tears, that she was not sent to any kind of school at an early period, so that her memory might have been brought into exercise. That faculty, and her reasoning powers, are of the very weakest description; while, as to all kinds of domestic engagements,—making beds, dusting, washing-up, brushing shoes, &c., there is not a more active girl in the house. Wherever a blind child is, let it be sent to school—any kind of school—at the usual age. It is sure to learn—and learn much too. Parents are too apt to sit down with their hands folded, and say, "We can do nothing." This is a great mistake, and in many cases has led to grievous results. I believe the reader will, ere this, have discovered that all I aim at is an infant school for the blind—combined with something introductory to their future handicraft engagements.

It appears to me an error, in establishments for the blind, to say a boy or girl shall not be admitted until they have reached a specific age. In place of this, if they show good capacity, it would be well to lay aside the rule in their case. Many are quick, observant, and inquisitive to a remarkable degree, and show a decided taste for music or other pursuits at a very early period.. Of this Saunderson was an eminent instance. Such are certainly ready to take their place in an institution. While, on the other hand, all above a certain age are excluded without any experiment being made as to their capabilities. An examination, and a few weeks' trial, ought to be made of any candidate, and let the result decide. By this means the benefits of the charity would be greatly extended. I have instances before me which will be mentioned afterwards in support of this opinion.

I would shortly advert to a rather prominent feature in institutions for the blind, viz.: the desire to carry forward the pupil at any sacrifice, to accomplish such pieces of work as may call forth the mere surprise of the passing visitor. If this is bad in an asylum—where it is very little practised—it is far worse in a school. The time of a *pupil* ought to be considered most sacred, and as much as possible appropriated to the acquirement *of that which he will be able to perform and* FIND A READY SALE FOR *on his leaving the institution.* Experiments on the capabilities of the blind ought to be left to those institutions where the time of the inmates is entirely at the disposal of the directors, and where failures would not fall upon the pupils after they are done with their course of tuition. To excite surprise is an easy matter, and one, I regret to say, too much cultivated. Everything which is attempted merely for the purpose of display, losing sight of the real benefit which the blind ought to reap by being put in the way of performing work *for which there is a demand, irrespective of mere curiosity,* is little else than waste of time and means. This applies as much to education as to work; and now that some attention seems about to be awakened in our schools to the culture of the mind of the blind, let us carefully guard against having the glittering filigree and partly-exploded scheming of the Continental schools foisted upon us.

I have already noticed that it was at Edinburgh the

first attempt was made in this country to introduce a *useful* system of education. That institution stood alone in this respect until 1828, when the asylum at Glasgow opened, following the former in all its details, and employing, for some years as its schoolroom teacher, a young man named William Lang, who had been taught at the first-named asylum under Mr. Beath, formerly mentioned; and of whose improvement on the Arithmetic Board I shall have occasion to speak afterwards. It is to be hoped that something will soon be done in the same way by the schools in England, whereby to bring out those powers which are so active in the blind.

The means adopted at Edinburgh were the teaching the younger portion particularly spelling, grammar, arithmetic, geography, and a general view of the solar system, by means of a very large globe and beautiful orrery. Joined to this, the directors, at the suggestion of Mr. Johnston, engrafted on the whole a system of *regular* and *extensive reading*—a means of instruction which, to a community placed in such circumstances, cannot be too highly appreciated. I advert to this feature more particularly, as it was altogether unseen by strangers—its effects, and the delight it imparted, could only be known by those in constant contact with the inmates. The reading took place after work hours, was furnished by the institution purchasing a share in a subscription library of about 12,000 volumes, and placing the choice of the books to be read entirely in the hands of those who were to hear them. The asylum paid the reader (one of the overseers), furnished the schoolroom with fire and gas, and added a newspaper twice a week. The attendance was entirely optional. Many of the inmates were married and had domestic concerns which prevented them availing themselves of it; but, if they did not enjoy it directly, they did so indirectly, by the interesting materials furnished for conversation and remark. Many otherwise heavy hours, which would have been given to idleness, were thus enlivened. A tone of information and remark was imparted which at once struck on the ear, as coming from a well-informed mind—a tone far above their situation in life. The reading provided by the institution produced a desire for more, and latterly a considerable number of the inmates united in procuring the services of another of the overseers, who with themselves devoted only twenty minutes to their breakfast and dinner, returning to the schoolroom or workshop, where a favourite volume was indulged in, until the bell again rang for work. These they procured with great ease from the various congregational or mechanics' libraries with which the inmates or overseers were connected. Chambers' Edinburgh Journal was a weekly treat, furnished by the kind consideration of the publishers gratis, and was given by the blind listeners to the sighted communicator of its pleasing or instructive contents, as a reward for his labour in reading it to them. This was perhaps the easier settled, as it belonged to the blind only collectively.

During the whole period of my incumbency there, I never saw any books brought in for reading, but such as were of standard character. I am not, to this moment, aware of any orders, or injunction being in existence against novels, romances, or plays. But, although there had, they could not have been more practically obeyed than they were. Robertson's Scotland, Charles the Fifth, and America, Hume and Smollett's England, Captain Basil Hall's Travels, History of the Knights of Malta, Laing's History of Scotland, and many other such like works, will give an idea of the good taste and judgment with which the selection was made—and made, it is to be remembered, altogether by themselves. The book to be read next, was regularly *voted in* at a meeting convened for the purpose.

But the foundation for the enjoyment of such a course of improvement was laid in the educational course adopted. The general knowledge of geography they had acquired by means of a large globe about thirty inches diameter, adapted for their use, and various maps raised in the same way, gave an interest to everything they heard, which could not have existed otherwise. And those who, from their advanced period of life, could not be expected to "go to school," yet were highly benefited by the quality (if I may so call it) and flow of conversation induced on those around them. The religious instruction of the institution was also amply provided for, although, I am sorry to say, from the very slender funds at command, by no means so amply remunerated. The chaplain spent half an hour every morning and evening, immediately before and after work, in singing, reading a portion of the Bible, and prayer. On the afternoons of Saturday, a regular service took place; and Monday morning was devoted to a catechetical examination of the younger branches as to the duties of the preceding Sabbath, accompanied by the repetition of the Catechism, the Psalms, Hymns, &c., which they had committed to memory during the preceding week. On these services all the inmates were, by the rules of the house, required to attend; while on Sunday every one went to his own place of worship, the institution providing for the accommodation of the junior members in a neighbouring church.

As connected with the instruction of the inmates, I must not pass by an excellent old man, named John M'Laren, who had spent his years from boyhood in the institution. Some notices respecting this singular individual found a place in the Saturday Magazine for October, 1836. A hard day's work never prevented him getting the youth of the institution into his "workshop," in rotation, to teach them to commit to memory portions of the Scriptures, Catechism, Psalms, and Hymns. This he did every night for an hour and a half from the ample stores of his early-loaded memory. He never tired, and very seldom, indeed, was he to be found from his post. He entered the asylum early in life, and his companions observing his great extent of memory, sent him to an evening school, that he might teach them what he himself had acquired. The directors afterwards marked their sense of his valuable services by an annual remuneration. John continues these services to this day, although years are now pressing upon him. Neither newspaper nor book will tempt him from his evening avocation: the "reading-room" is a place unknown to him. He gets hold of the youth whose "turn" it is to come under his care, and sitting down together, the monotonous murmur of the oft-repeated passage falls upon the ear as you pass his humble place of instruction. He had a very handsome silver snuff-box presented to him by the directors, bearing a suitable inscription, as a mark of their sense of his exemplary conduct and services.

I dwell with the greater pleasure on the subject of education as conducted at the institution referred to, as the whole of it, including the teacher's salary (himself blind), and the allowance to "the reader," did not cost the funds more than *thirty pounds a-year!* For this very trifle the great majority of that house, consisting, at one time, of one hundred and twenty individuals, were in mental cultivation raised far above their condition. May the hope not be indulged, that some one or other interested in our far wealthier establishments in the south, will set about doing something towards rescuing those listless hours which,

E

after work, are too often given to conversation and plotting, not the best calculated for the peace of an institution or the morals of the younger members? And this is the more to be desired, as all the schools have the inmates boarded on the premises, perhaps with very limited play-grounds. There lies a heavy amount of responsibility when so much good can be done at so little cost.

On the opening of the school for the blind at York, reading an hour in the evening to the pupils—all between the ages of eleven and sixteen—has been adopted with the greatest success. When they came in, the ignorance of the greater part was deplorable. An ignorance not arising from their blindness, but from no instruction of any kind having ever been imparted, seemingly from the idea that their privation precluded everything of the kind. Two of them, about fourteen years of age, could not count beyond thirty. When they came to "twenty-nine," they said, "twenty ten"! Two girls could not put on their own clothes at the age of thirteen and fifteen. In a fortnight or three weeks, they were delighted beyond measure that they were not only able to do that, but also make beds, wash-up dishes, brush shoes, and dust rooms. As to the reading resorted to at first, it was of the most humble kind. The very simplest of Æsop's store had to be selected,—many of even these were beyond their comprehension. Sleep was a frequent visitor ere the hour was done. But after a little perseverance, a *show* as it were of otherwise good understandings took place, and the delights of Robinson Crusoe, Prince Lee Boo, and for Sunday reading, the never-to-be-worn-out Pilgrim of the inimitable Bunyan, opened up a new world to them. Twice has that work been so read, and the pleasure of hearing one and another saying during the second perusal, "Well, how much better I understand that now than when read before!" was by no means small. Hannah More's delightful narrative Tracts formed another great step in their mental progress. Berquin's Children's Friend, and several volumes of that excellently got up "library" of the Kildare Street Society, afforded delightful occupation for many happy evenings. The enjoyment was much increased by all being invited and encouraged to make any remarks, and ask the meaning of words or phrases they did not understand. Many times the little audience avowed that "the reading hour was far the shortest of the day,"—playfully "that the watch *must* be wrong," and many times cough down the warning of the clock at the half hour, when "good night" followed.

As a class, the blind are just like their seeing neighbours, and the great bulk of them must be provided for by the every-day kind of work, which can be procured for them. In view then of extending education to them, apart from mere manual labour, there is reason to fear that more may be attempted than is befitting their condition in life. I do not know a greater error than wasting a child's time on pursuits which there is not the least expectation he will ever find practically useful. One in a hundred may perhaps show superior talent. Let that be pursued, and a little additional expense would not be grudged in such a case—but evidently to graft a system suited for such rare cases on the routine of an institution, would be increasing the expense,—wasting time,—and pandering to that insatiable thirst for the marvellous which has been so well depicted by Blacklock in the extract already given.* In this, as in everything else, the "golden mean" ought to be well studied, avoiding on the one hand the total want of provision for the mind which unhappily exists in our

---

* Page 10.

E 2

own institutions,—and on the other, that which is threatening to make an inroad upon us of late, the showy, nicknack, and unsubstantial style of those on the Continent. More nonsense, undue expectation, empty gasconade, and discreditable quackery, have resulted from this consideration being thrust aside than many pages could tell. Well might Wood say, when speaking of some who consulted their own popularity at the expense of those under their care, "That the craving appetite for popular applause is not always peculiarly delicate, or fastidious in the choice of its food, and rather than remain unsatiated, will too often be content to prey on garbage." *

Many things may be, and have been got up, very suitable for the *wealthy* blind, conducive perhaps as much to their amusement as anything else ; but the necessary apparatus for teaching arithmetic, geography, &c., are both simple and cheap,—while *reading to* them, whatever their age, or state of mental progress may be, is to be had to any extent for a mere trifle,—*and this* (combined with the exercise of that faculty which seems to have been bestowed upon them in double measure, viz.: memory) *will always form the great instrument of their instructions, in a moral and religious point of view.* In saying so, I am well aware of what has been, and is now doing in the way of printing for the blind, by means of letters in relief— whereby they may read by the finger. The first attempt of this kind was made at the institution at Paris. The works put into the hands of the pupils, viz. : prayer books, grammars, dictionaries, and selections—amounted, in 1832, to about forty volumes.† The character used was the

---

* Account of the Edinburgh Sessional School, p. 46.
† North American Review, July, 1833.

Italic, which, although not so well fitted for the purpose as some others, was still read, it is said, with ease by the children. The volumes were however large and clumsy. The first attempt of a like kind made in this country was by Mr. James Gall, of Edinburgh, who in 1830, I think, printed several introductory books, and in 1834, these were followed by the entire Gospel according to St. John, in one volume, quarto. Mr. Gall, with the laudable intention of facilitating the progress of the blind, adopted a modification of the Roman character, taking away the circles, and substituting angles, so as to make the letter easier felt. Whatever opinion may be formed of the practicability, or rather the amount of ultimate benefit the blind may derive from this mode of imparting instruction, it is due to Mr. Gall to say, that for perseverance, industry, indefatigable prosecution of his views in a field entirely new, and amidst many difficulties, much praise is due to him. But, on the other hand, I feel bound to say that his statements as to the results of his labours, contained in his "Literature for the Blind," * and a smaller work published lately, are marked by an imaginativeness, a kind of rainbow colouring, unworthy the soberness which ought to distinguish matter-of-fact details. Representations such as I allude to, are sure to lead to disappointment. But these remarks apply just as much to the statements of others who have started in this pursuit, as to Mr. Gall; and may perhaps be

---

* Mr. Gall speaks of his *inventing* a "Literature for the Blind." There seems to be a mistake in such a definition of his labours, as the literature for the blind can be no other than the literature for the seeing *made available to the blind.* This is one of many of the "fog islands," to use a nautical phrase, to which writers on this subject have of late been leading the way. Mr. Gall is too much a man of business to confound type letter with literature, although there is an inseparable connection.

attributed to the enthusiasm almost inseparable from ardent minds when expatiating on a favourite subject.

We have a remarkable instance of this in the case of music printed in relief, which "had its day" at the Paris school about twenty years ago. It is one of those instances which strikingly shows how much groundless anticipation may be indulged in, and positive assertions made, respecting a favourite, although manifestly a visionary, scheme. To show this the better, I will place the glowing representation, evidently drawn from publications on the subject, on the one side, and the matter-of-fact result on the other :—

"It (the Paris Institution) teaches the blind to read music with their fingers, *as others do with their eyes*; and it does this with so much success, that although they cannot at once feel the notes, and perform them upon the instrument, yet they *are capable* of acquiring any lesson *with as much exactness and* RAPIDITY *as those who enjoy all the advantages of sight.*"—*Ency. Brit., Article Blind,* 5th *edition.*	Dr. Guillié, SUPERINTENDENT of the Paris school, in his "Essay on the Blind," London, 1817, says, "Music was formerly printed in relief; but we have ceased to make use of it, as it was very expensive, and of NO USE; *the scholar* COULD NOT *read with his fingers and perform at the same time.*"—P. 118.

The reason assigned by Guillié for the failure of this experiment is one so very obvious, that it is surprising any attempt of the kind was made. Supported as the school at Paris is, by a munificent grant from Government, it was all well enough that anything which promised fair should be tried. But music read piecemeal, to be played in the same fashion, could not but come to the ground, wearing out as it must have been to the pupil, however delicate his touch might be. It is not upon *that* the question depends. If a pupil has any musical ear at all, he will carry off a piece of music in an incredibly short space of time, as all acquainted with the subject well know, and of which I will give some examples afterwards. But the failure of the French seminary has not prevented the repetition of the experiment, as a " Selection of Psalm Tunes and Chants, in raised characters, for the use of the Blind," was lately (1836) published by subscription by the Rev. W. Taylor, of York. However, as the obstacles which prevented the earlier attempt proving successful still remain in undiminished force,—" the pupil not being able to read with his fingers and perform at the same time,"—it is to be feared the blind will still be indebted for their progress in this delightful science to the more obvious and incomparably better plan of teaching them by repetition, as Guilliè acknowledges they found themselves, after all, obliged to do. It may be presumed that any one making an attempt of the kind must have been unacquainted with the work of Guilliè, although it is one well known to, and to be found in the library of, most of those at all conversant in the education of the blind.

That music " generally forms a prominent part of the education of blind persons," as we are told in the preface to the work alluded to, and " that every effort should be made to render their acquirement of it as easy as possible," are positions which no one will deny. But that these desirable ends are to be attained, or advanced in the least degree,—nay, are they not positively retarded ?—by any such means as " music printed in relief,"—however " legible to the touch," are positions which will be admitted by none who have had the most elementary experience in the matter. In saying so, I do not for a moment pretend to dispute the " advantages of music " to the class alluded to, nor that " it adds to their natural cheerfulness, and makes many an hour glide pleasantly away ; "—neither would I refuse to hear any one "dilate upon the gratification it affords them," and yet it is not to be admitted for a moment that any, or all of these put together, would form "an apology" for *such* "an attempt to serve our fellow-creatures, who have so large a claim upon our sympathy," distinguished as it is by all that ample experience has pronounced to be utterly "useless."

No doubt "each [musical] character must be fully explained to the pupil, and its use, value, &c., well understood;" but this can be done incomparably better than by the plan above alluded to, by the notes being cast in lead a little larger than the usual size used in printing, and fixed on a board if for a school, as is done at Liverpool and Edinburgh,—or, if for a private pupil, by the notes, rests, sharps, flats, &c., being pricked out on a sheet of paste-board ; a mode, by-the-bye, as simple as it is economical, and equally applicable to maps, plans, elevations, and mathematical diagrams. It is remarkable how simple the materials are whereby to convey to the blind much that has been considered exclusive to the seeing. The wall of separation crumbles away, little by little, and it often strikes the mind how small a portion of what was once esteemed insurmountable has been left standing. Were the blind to study music only by the futile instrumentality of this "cast-off" suit of the French school, they would run every risk of remaining in double darkness with regard to this delightful science. Every hour a poor pupil spends upon it is an hour lost in time, temper, and acquirement.

Dr. Guillié well observes,—"It is not to be supposed that because music printed in relief has been thrown aside, that therefore the blind are not taught music by *principles*." Thorough bass, for instance, is, I believe, as readily studied by the blind as by the seeing. This is done by means of " Tansure's Musical Board," * and " Cheese's Common Pin Musical Notation ; " both fully described, and figures given of them, in the Encyclopædia Britannica, 5th edition, 1817, article " Blind." The board is nearly three feet long, about eight or nine inches wide, and has two staves with ledger lines, above, between, and below. These are raised upon the surface of the board about one-sixteenth of an inch ; the top of the stave lines being flat, while that of the ledger lines is round. It is pierced all over with little holes, upon and between the holes, so as to receive the pins, which represent the notes. But the drawing of it above referred to will enable any joiner to make it. Some slight alterations have, I believe, been made on them ; but those now in use are, substantially, the invention of those they are here ascribed to, and have been in use in one of our institutions for nearly twenty years. Mr. Cheese used the common pin,—twisting the tops of some—striking off the heads of others—and, in short, forming, by similar means, all the musical characters in use. " These," he continues, " are kept in a box in the same style as a printer keeps his types, each different compartment of which must be marked with the character it contains." This gentleman's ingenuity led him to metamorphose his humble aids into no less than *thirty-two different forms!* But thorough bass may be studied with not above one-third of that number,—the mahogany board forming the entire expense. He proposed (and I believe used) an oblong cushion, whereon to set up any little piece of music he wanted, stretching a bit of thread across to serve for the stave. Of the board being really serviceable there can be no doubt, for it has been long in use.

---

* Originally described in his " Musical Grammar."

Exaggeration, one would think, had really been called in of late to do its utmost on this and kindred topics. Printing for the blind, so as to be read with the finger, must take a large share of this: and, without at all saying that they cannot be taught to read slowly by such means, I do not hesitate to say, from the experience of four trials made during these five or six years past, that to the *working* blind *as a body*, it will rank with the "music printed in relief" for them—"*useless.*"

It is not attempted to be said that the cases are parallel. The reason of failure in the latter was quite decisive of itself, viz.: that "the pupil could not read music and play at the same time,"—apart altogether from one which I am confident held as good, had not the other settled the matter—that the music *could not* be read with the finger in the usual, or near the usual sense of the words "reading music."

Allowing, however, that *some* of the young blind may attain to read about half as fast as a tolerable reading child at school—speaking of this as an average rate—yet, what is to become of all this acquirement when the pupil's fingers become gradually hardened by his employment in basket and mat making, weaving, rope and twine spinning? Does it not almost amount to a certainty that his finger sight will follow his eye sight, and thus his time is not only wasted, but a *second infliction* comes upon him, and dashes all the hopes with which he had been inspired!

No one can contemplate such a result without painful feelings. But it is one which appears to me never to have occupied the place which it demands in the question at present abroad on the subject. In any observations I make, I trust it will not be thought that I am impugning the motives of those who have stepped forward in this matter,—but I cannot help thinking that a great deal too much value has been attached to the trifling progress yet made, and that a sweeping general conclusion has been arrived at from the narrowest possible data. As I am not the inventor of any arbitrary alphabet, nor even the proposer of any one founded on our own Roman, while at the same time I have seen something of the working of those already out, I may perhaps be considered as the more unbiassed in the opinion I hold. I shall shortly state what has come under my own observation.

Printing for the blind was first introduced at the school at Paris, about forty years ago. That institution has continued all along, I believe, to use the *Italic* character, and their doing so has been assigned as the reason of so little good being done. But from ample testimony it would appear that the pupils there read as well as any, and that the number of works in their library, as before stated, was, in 1832, about forty. Mr. Gall, of Edinburgh, was the first in this country who directed the attention of the public to the subject. In 1831 he published some elementary books in what may perhaps be called the angular Roman character—the common Roman with all the circles turned into angles. When these books came out, he requested that some of the boys belonging to the asylum at Edinburgh might be allowed to take lessons from him. This the directors immediately, and with pleasure, granted ; and I think, three, if not four, of out sharpest youngsters were under his care twice or three times a week. No restriction as to time was laid upon him—he had them quite at his own disposal—and they continued with him for some months. But, even with Mr. Gall's own attention—and, I am sure, when I say so, every security is given that all that perseverance, kindness, and ardour in a favourite pursuit could do was done in their case. Yet, the result was nothing more than their being able to make out letter by letter and a few short words, some of them scarcely that. As to anything like "*reading*," in the common acceptation of the word, it was out of the question, Mr. Gall himself being judge. I am sure that gentleman will bear me out in saying, that a fairer specimen of what the *working blind* are could not have been found. They were boys of excellent parts, varying from fourteen to twenty years of age, and had been shorter and longer in the institution, so that even a variety of *finger delicacy* might have been reasonably expected amongst them. They were tried under his own eye—without limitation as to time,—and I will leave it to Mr. Gall to say to what the result amounted.

In every point of view I consider this to have been worth some dozen of subsequent experiments. Not only because, as I have just stated, Mr. Gall was the sole and unrestricted superintendent of it, but because the youths *were in those very circumstances*—working indigent blind— in what four-fifths of their companions in privation are to be found: and if printing is to be of any use at all, it ought to be so to them, else we are pursuing a phantom.

When the Gospel according to St. John appeared in 1834, many benevolent individuals who had subscribed for it, offered their copies to the directors for the use of the schoolroom. This was gratefully accepted, and to leave nothing undone, they directed a second trial to be made under the care of Mr. Robert Mylne, the teacher at the asylum—himself blind. Six boys were daily engaged on it, for as many months, and yet with all the attention possible, the result was not one whit better than the first one. Both teacher and taught were tired out of measure. They often averred they could get the gospel by heart in half the time, and I don't doubt it. Mylne himself was very desirous of benefiting by this mode of instruction, and took a copy of the work home with him, but although able, like the others, to do a little, yet it was nothing when compared with " reading."

Thus, then, there were only *five* or *six* ever engaged on this study at the institution alluded to, while the number of inmates amounted to 110, or thereby. Yet, in a report published by the Society of Arts at Edinburgh, it is stated at page 6,—"Mr. Gall has obtained ample testimonials from the directors of the Edinburgh, Glasgow, and London asylums, as to the efficiency of his alphabet, and *his success in teaching the blind* TO READ by means of it in these institutions." Confining myself, of course, to the first-mentioned, I cannot but express my surprise that any such statement could have been made, when not more than *six* were at any time engaged in the pursuit, and the result being as I have stated it.

I consider the value of these experiments to be far beyond any which have been made with pupils who have never been engaged in *skin-hardening work*. Such a boy was brought to Edinburgh from the Belfast school in the summer of 1835. This boy read slowly but correctly. But this did not, and does not yet, shake the opinion I had formed. He had never touched a bit of work, nor had he done so up to the month of March last, when I heard of him, so that I cannot consider him as any proof of the real value of printing in relief to the working blind. If, after five or seven years' application to the usual avocations of an asylum, he retains his acquirement, he may then be adduced in favour of the system. Extreme cases, however, whether for or against, ought always to be avoided.

Another trial, such as I have just detailed, took place

at the London school. It was commenced by Mr. Gall himself, as detailed in his "Literature for the Blind," and carried on so far, but was soon after relinquished by the directors. As the reasons have not appeared before the public, I can only state the fact.

Mr. Gall's publications were also adopted at the asylum at Glasgow, and by the reports of the examinations, promised to realise all the hopes which had been formed of them, when, about six or eight months ago, they were relinquished for a character which was recommended some years ago by the late Dr. Fry of London to the Society of Arts at Edinburgh. This Mr. Alston, the treasurer of the institution, adopted, and in consequence of liberal subscriptions, he was enabled to set up a press in the establishment, and has printed several works in the character alluded to, viz.: the Roman capitals. These are beautifully executed, and Mr. Alston has succeeded in publishing them at a price far below what the most sanguine could have some time ago anticipated. It is to be feared that his Ruth and St. James are too small, or perhaps too close for the great bulk of the blind. The introductory book of fourteen pages, issued lately, appears superior in every respect—the character is both large and sharp.

The character, however, does not seem to me to have so much to do with the matter as has been represented. Those enjoying sight are too apt to think that what appears so nice to their eye, must therefore be the best for the blind. This by no means follows; and so far as *experiment* goes, Mr. Gall's triangular Roman is as good as Dr. Fry's capitals. The former has been ranked amongst the arbitrary characters. This I think a great mistake, if not an approach to injustice, as any one looking at it only a few seconds can read it with ease. Under the idea that so much depends on the character, we have no less than five different characters out already,—a course which, if persevered in, must tend to hurt the very cause so many have at heart. There is Gall's, the Bostonian, the Philadelphian, Lucas', and Fry's. Would it not be advisable to make a fair trial by one of these, rather than incur such a heavy expense, in publishing so many, *four-fifths of which must ere long be thrown aside?* The last mentioned has all along appeared to me the best (with a few slight alterations), both as to the letter itself and the smaller space it takes up. But, either way, I may be allowed to express my fear that the whole will become useless by the hardening of the skin under work.

In this opinion I am joined by men who, although they have never appeared on the subject, have had far longer experience in matters relative to the blind than any yet before the public. With one solitary exception, the whole has originated, and been carried on by those not practically acquainted with the blind, as an *indigent* and *working body.* Much undue anticipation also has been raised by promulgating that reading has been accomplished in such and such *institutions.* By this mode of speech we are led to suppose that all, or nearly all the inmates, if not *reading*, are at least engaged in the pursuit of it. The very opposite is the true statement—it is a mere fraction who are so engaged. Six or eight were all whose attention were ever turned to it at Edinburgh, where there were *a hundred and ten*—and something of a like kind holds true in other cases. To speak of this as benefiting the blind in these institutions is using language extremely liable to mislead. But, admitting there were a greater number engaged in the study, much may be maintained and carried on *in an establishment* which would prove altogether useless out of it—and such appears to me the difficulties attending reading in this manner, that however successful an inmate might be *while within the walls of the institution*, it would be no proof that a really practical use would be made of it on his leaving.

A great deal too much importance has been attached to what the blind have said, when specimens of printing have been put into their hands. In their present circumstances of entire ignorance as to what reading is, how can they be judges? Besides, dependent as they almost all are, more or less, on those who have interested themselves in their behalf, and influenced by that feeling which inexperienced persons must ever feel towards a superior or teacher, how can an unbiassed opinion be looked for from them? I have seen even "the horn book" welcomed for a day or two. They hear what is said of it—"this is to teach you to *read*," and, associating this promise with all that they understand by the term, as well as being quite pliant—naturally so—to what they well know to be the views of those who take their opinion, they go in with the current. The best proof of this is, that no alphabet is out, but it has had the approval of those blind, to whom the proposers of that particular form of letter had submitted it. This appears to me no criterion at all, and is a description of proof very little to be relied on.

I have one remarkable feature to notice in connexion with this, viz.: the *extreme dislike of the blind to reading by the finger*. This has been the case in all the experiments which have come under my own notice, and in one I have heard of. I know it is said that this is no criterion—that everything new presents difficulties, and must be disliked. But this is not the case with all the other studies of the blind. Arithmetic, geography, grammar, that generally tiresome employment, committing to memory by repetition, and all kinds of handicraft work, are pleasures, and anxiously sought for. Exclusion from any of these, in the great

majority of cases, might be converted into punishment ;—
but nothing of the kind can be said of the other. An
arithmetic board or a map has been frequently borrowed
from me to fill up part of the play hour, or to communicate
to a companion the accession of knowledge which the
borrower has just acquired,—but as to *borrowing a book*,
I never once heard of it.

The positive dislike of the blind to this study seems to
me to arise from a cause which has not been accounted
for, viz. : the strong contrast which they perceive to exist
between, not only the *rapidity* with which they hear us
read, but the endless *variety* which we can at all times
command. This they can never hope for,—nor indeed is
it pretended to by the promoters of printing in relief.
The hackneyed phraseology of "reading with the fingers
as others do with the eyes,"—"reading with as much ease
as those who enjoy the blessings of sight,"—"reading with
the book under the bed-clothes,"—nay, to outdo all other
bombast, we are told, "they can read with a stout glove
upon the hand, or with a piece of linen laid upon the
book" !—will not stand the test of experiment as it regards
the mass. Indeed, ideas of this kind, combined with a
volume of such recently published, are so abundantly
ridiculous, that they are only fit for the nursery, or that
much-abused personage,—"the discerning public." One
wonders how such crudities can be put forth by sober-
minded men. The blind, therefore, contrasting their
own slowness, and circumscribed limits, with our speed
and ample range, feel that they are not only immeasurably
behind, *but will always be so* in this respect, and even those
in a superior walk of life, who have anxiously applied
themselves to the works already out, do so far more as
an amusement than anything else. One blind gentleman,
who is much interested in everything of the kind, told

me lately, that his St. John just served to bring known passages to his recollection.

I have had several communications on the subject from individuals practically acquainted with it. The first is from a gentleman who has anxiously promoted this method of instruction, and given much of his attention to it. In a letter, dated March 25th, 1836, he says, " The expense of books for the blind will prevent their coming into general practice, and nothing but a national exertion can do it. *After all, many of them will not take the trouble, and the young must be kept to it,* or they will not do it of themselves." I may mention that at the time this was written, Mr. Gall's books had been a considerable time in use, and extremely well reported of.

The same gentleman writes me again, August 5th, 1836 :—" I observe what you say about the education. I am decidedly for teaching the young, but my fear is that the old will not learn, and as the young grow up, and are put to a trade, I fear they will not then be able to read, as the ends of their fingers will get hardened with work, and thereby lose the acute sense of touch they possessed in early life. I think Dr. H., of B., has great merit in what he has done, *but it is worth nothing* IF, in due time, they are not taught to gain their livelihood by their own industry."

Again, October 11th, 1836. After speaking of the progress some pupils had made with Gall's books, he continues,—" The books will soon give way with the fingering, and it is to be feared that attempts to make them portable will hurt the general benefit. As to those who must be sent to trades, time must settle that ; but my own opinion is, that a large type will be required."

From another gentleman, equally interested in the matter, I have the following, relative to a school lately established in another part of the empire :—" The pupils there read with the greatest fluency, and some are engaged as Scripture readers in the cottages of the poor. Thus the blind, in their perambulations, are welcomed into the cottages, not to increase revelry by the tones of the violin, but to cultivate devotional feeling by the word of God. In the school for the blind here (Edinburgh), not connected with the asylum, children of all ages are taught in an exceedingly short space of time, and they read at least equally well with children of the same standing at school who have their sight." I may mention that the school here spoken of (at Edinburgh), whatever the number might have been at the date of the letter, had very lately, as I am informed by a friend, only *a very few* little ones attending it, in the midst of a population of 200,000; and when Mr. Gall's system had been before the public of the Scottish metropolis for *five years* at least, the "Gospel according to St. John" was offered at half the original price, since reduced, as I see by advertisement, to six shillings.

From another correspondent, *well acquainted* with the school spoken of in the first paragraph of the above extract, I have the following; the dates nearly correspond: —"The school at —— is not doing well. The number there a short time ago was fifteen blind. At present they are eight or nine. They were taught many things; such as reading, writing,* geography, astronomy, Euclid, &c.

---

* By means of stamps, whereby a blind person pricks through on a sheet of paper *each successive letter* as he goes on,—the character being the same as that used by Mr. Gall. I do not see how a process so slow, tiresome, and perplexing, as this must be, can, in fairness, be called "writing," as in all Mr. Gall's publications it is. We might nearly as well speak of printing being accomplished by each successive type being used and restored to its place in the "case," ere another could be brought into operation. *Facility* ought, in my opinion, never to be lost sight of—the blind being enabled either to read or write. Acquirements, as well as doings, should be called by their right names.

Looms were erecting a few days ago, but prior to this,* no work was attempted but sewing and knitting. The children there could read more rapidly than any I have yet met with—but, *they hated it!* I believe they uniformly do so. I was always aware the superior progress of these pupils in reading was chiefly to be attributed to their *idleness!*" My correspondent, by using the word idleness, means nothing more than that there was no handicraft work, such as is usually carried on in institutions for the blind.

On the other hand, in the Appendix No. 10, to a little work recently published by Mr. Gall, we have "an address written and signed with the writing stamps, presented to Mr. Gall, by the pupils of the school at Belfast, accompanied with a handsome copy of the Bible." This document says :—"Permit us to convey to you our deep sense of the unspeakable benefits you have conferred upon us. We can now read and write. Our solitary hours, which were formerly employed in brooding over our deprivation, are now spent in drawing holy comforts from the Word of Life, so that to us who sat in darkness, light is sprung up. For these blessings, Sir, we are, under God, indebted to your exertions. We cannot express what we feel,—we cannot repay what we have received," &c. A suitable reply follows.

From these confessedly very discordant testimonies, the reader will form his own opinion. The whole of my own experience, up to the day, corresponds exactly with what is stated in the extract respecting the school at ———— "They hated it." However strong this language is, it is strictly true, so far as I have seen—and I speak not only from what was before narrated as having taken place at

---

* The school had been in operation about eighteen months.

Edinburgh, but from my later observation of eighteen pupils following it out for nearly as many months—with one solitary exception, they "hate it." The dislike indeed arising from its tediousness—I would almost say its hopelessness—must be greatly increased where, as at Edinburgh and York, *reading to them* is amply provided for. Two hours a day are spent in the former, and one in the latter, in this happy method of combining amusement with instruction. But in proportion as that is pursued, the other will come into unhappy contrast.

The above paragraphs were written, when happening to take up a volume of the Christian Observer for 1835, I met with the review of Mr. Gall's "Literature for the Blind." It is there stated that at Paris this mode of instruction (printing books in relief) had also failed, and been given up. The reviewer says,—"The conductors of the school at Paris began to print with great zeal, but the objects of their benevolent solicitude reaped little benefit from their labours, and the scheme at length *died away, and was forgotten.* Similar attempts were made in this country, but they shared the same fate." The reason assigned is, " the rounded forms and too intricate shapes of the letters (the common italic), which were not adapted for easy discrimination by the sense of feeling." If this is the case, it adds one more to the amount of failures ; and, as the French began it long ago, had plenty of money at their disposal, and have always been distinguished by a keen pursuit of the *curious*, it carries with it the more weight. But to any one who has really engaged in the practical part of the matter, this throwing the cause of the failure on the shoulders of the character will not do. It lies just where it has been already placed, in the sense of touch becoming obdurate by work, combined with its tediousness

—its circumscribed range—and its unsuitableness to the great majority of the blind, from the necessity they are under of doing something to maintain themselves.*

I cannot quit this subject without saying that the elementary works both of Mr. Gall and Mr. Alston are distinguished for their simplicity. The latter has adopted some of the excellent little works of Mr. Charles Baker, of the institution for the deaf and dumb at Doncaster. Although these were written with a special eye to his own charge, yet, the ignorance in which the blind are too often allowed to remain, makes them as suitable for the one class as the other. I may here add, that while I have taken a different view of the subject under consideration from the promoters of this mode of instruction, I trust it is with a feeling of unmingled respect for the motives which pointed to the amelioration of the condition of a class of our fellow-men who have, as yet, even with all our institutions for their relief, had little done for them as a body. I speak particularly of the indigent blind. Whatever may be thought of the general question, great praise is due to both, for the perseverance with which they have contended against every difficulty.

---

* Appended to the report of the Society of Arts at Edinburgh, there is a communication from York. The writer says (page 15)—" Would it not be advisable for blind persons, especially those who do much rough work with their hands, to wear constantly upon some one finger a leather preserver (such as the finger of a glove) to keep it always in a delicate state to read or examine anything which requires nicety of touch?" When will idle *ingenuity* cease to be identified with *utility ?*—and at what an easy rate may such theorists gain notoriety! The thing is impracticable. A basket-maker working with a finger-stool has been tried, and, as might have been foreseen, has failed ; not to mention half-a-dozen other such items of ingenious trifling, plausible enough, and gaining much commendation when exhibited in a drawing-room by means of pocket models, but altogether useless when brought into practice.

ARITHMETIC is a study peculiarly suitable for the blind, and now really enjoyed by them, from the extreme simplicity of the " slate "—for so we call it—by which they are enabled to accomplish it. And it is somewhat remarkable that they are indebted to those labouring under the same privation as themselves for this beautiful appendage to the schoolroom. It was commenced by Saunderson a hundred and twenty years ago—improved by Moyes about 1790—farther improved by M'Beath at Edinburgh about twenty years ago—and received its last (one would think the last of which it is susceptible, so far as arithmetic is concerned) from the hand of a young man named William Lang, many years an inmate of the asylum at Edinburgh, where he received his education, but at the time he proposed the alteration alluded to (about ten years ago) of that at Glasgow.

The first idea of such an aid to arithmetic occurred to the celebrated individual first mentioned in the above enumeration, who, although blind from early infancy, rose by force of genius and laborious study to the professorship of mathematics at Cambridge. It is worthy of record that he was aided in gaining this appointment by the exertions of Sir Isaac Newton, who held him in great esteem.* He filled this office for a period of twenty-eight years, with the greatest credit to himself and benefit to his pupils. The board he constructed for himself was filled with square spaces, cut to a little depth. Into each of these squares he inserted *two* small pins, and the relative position of the one to the other—one of them with a larger head being

---

* I have much pleasure in possessing an excellent portrait of this extraordinary man. It is engraved by Vanderbanck, after a painting by ——, 1719. He is habited in his official robes, and has in his hand a small armillary sphere, seemingly in the act of examining it.

placed always in the centre—denoted our ten figures. Thus, *each* figure required two pegs to represent it; and it does not appear that he thought of any simpler method. But it was a beginning.

The next improvement made upon the board was by Dr. Moyes, who, about 1790, and ignorant of what had been done by Saunderson, formed one to work with *three* pegs, screwing them into the holes in the same way as a violin peg. This was a great step, but he also remained satisfied with what he had done.

It would appear from statements made in the North American Review for July, 1833, that the Paris institution had not even availed themselves of Moyes' advance, but had gone back to the use of *ten* symbols—in short, just our own figures raised on the end of a type. These are arranged in boxes, and, when in use, are taken out of their "case," and inserted in the board. When the pupil has finished an account, his time is then wasted in " distributing " all his figures ere he can begin anew. Fifty or sixty movements of this kind must be a sad affair. " This method, however," says the reviewer, who had just returned from a survey of our European institutions, " has been much simplified* by a contrivance of one of the pupils of the Edinburgh asylum, where they use but *two* types instead of *ten*—a matter of no little importance to a blind person, even as compared with Moyes'. This is done by a point being raised on one *corner* of the little square peg, which, being capable of four positions, gives four figures. The other end of the peg has a similar point on the *side* of the square, denoting, by change of position, other four; thus, eight figures are represented by one peg, while the remaining two are on a second one. Still, two divisions,

---

* This was done twenty years ago.

to keep the pegs apart, has to be resorted to, and so far is a hindrance."

The last and I may say greatest improvement was made upon it in 1829 by Lang. This young man was received at an early period of life into the institution at Edinburgh, where he had an excellent education, both mental and mechanical, and with some others, his companions in blindness, went to the asylum at Glasgow on the opening of that establishment in 1828. He for several years continued to fill the office of teacher; and the successive notices of the results of his labours, as detailed in the reports of the annual examinations of his pupils, were highly flattering. Several suggested improvements in the board, but, as Mr. Alston, the treasurer of the institution, informed me lately, Lang's at once recommended itself from the extreme simplicity which distinguished it. This was nothing more than turning the *square* hole into a pentagon—or five-sided figure, and thereby at once reaching that most desirable point, viz.: having the whole TEN figures on ONE little peg!—five on the one end and five on the other; the point in the *corner* representing the odd numbers 1, 3, 5, 7, and 9, while the point on the *side* represents the even numbers 2, 4, 6, 8, 0. Two points on the side have been adopted at the Boston school,* and a

---

*On the opening of the school at York, a trial of six months was made of a plan whereby a piece of cork served the purpose of a slate, while another piece held an assortment of figures. These were formed by means of bending the head of the common pin into *five* different positions, and then striking off the heads of those meant to represent the *odd* numbers, while those with the heads *on* represented the *even* numbers. The figures were "sorted" on one of the pieces of cork, there being a row of ones, twos, threes, &c.—ten rows;—the other piece serving, as I have said, for a slate. When in use, the figure was sought for on the one piece, and stuck into the other, and when the operation was finished, they were all put back again into their own row,

line in place of a point on the side, by which a readier apprehension is given of what the figure is. This I find aids the beginner much, as by telling him to keep in mind that the *even* line (or ledge) on the one end show the *even* numbers,—while the end with two points being *uneven*, are the uneven numbers. Three children were adding five and six figures by this means, one in less than an hour—the two others in an hour and a half. This change has been adopted at the school at York, where Lang's board has called forth the admiration of every visitor.*

By this admirable idea the necessity of having *any* division of pegs, or figures, is done away with; and now the pupil taking up any one which comes in his way has the figure he wants, and by the average practice of children at school, he can calculate as readily with it as the seeing can with the pencil. This has been proved. And when done with a sum, in place of wasting time by " sorting off," *i.e.*, replacing each figure in its respective receptacle, all he has to do is to turn the board upside down, and they fall out. A sharp little fellow on doing so one day, said to me, " Why, Sir, I'll have my count rubbed out before you have yours ! " I was accompanying his operations on a common slate. I may truly say of Lang's board, what

---

preparatory to a new one. But this, consisting, like the Paris plan, of TEN *different* symbols, presented such difficulties to most, and was so tedious to all—besides being very expensive, the corks soon becoming so perforated as to prevent the pins standing upright, and costing from 1s. 6d. to 2s. 6d. a-pair,—that I requested Mr. Alston for one of the boards used at Glasgow, which was immediately and kindly complied with. This I took the liberty of recommending to Mr. Taylor, as a substitute for the other; and its adoption has been accompanied with corresponding facility and pleasure to the pupil.

* North American Review, July 1833.

Arithmetic Board,

for the Use of the

BLIND.

as improved by William Lang,

formerly an inmate of the Asylum at Edinburgh and now of that at Glasgow.

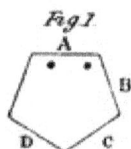

Fig 1.

Improved Peg.

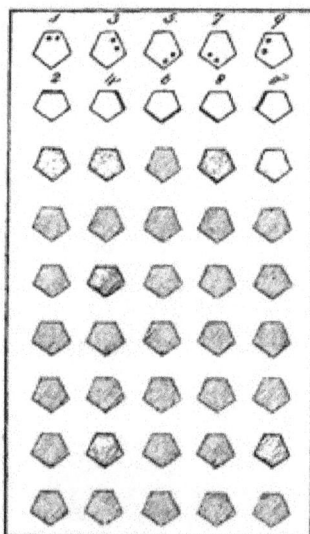

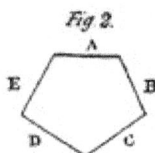

Fig 2.

Glasgow Peg

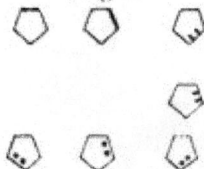

Fig. 3.

I have often said to visitors, that it has, to the blind, macadamized the road to arithmetic.

As this board might be extremely useful to many who are not near schools, and can be procured for a mere trifle, and last a life-time, I will shortly describe how it is used, and give the sizes and prices of those I have lately had made. The diagrams one and two show the form of the hole, but much enlarged. The sides, as marked, may be called A, B, C, D, and E. When the little peg is put in, having the end up with the two points on it, as at A, it represents *one*,—turned round, so as to stand at B, it is *three*,—at C, *five*,—at D, *seven*,—and at E, *nine*. Then turning up the other end with the slightly raised ledge upon it, and inserting it in the same order, we have the even numbers *two, four, six, eight*, and NOUGHT,—not *ten*, as I have often to impress on my young charge, for we have to use *two* figures for *ten*, as well as the seeing. To illustrate this, I have put down a sum in multiplication, which I have no doubt will be at once understood, and enable any one, giving it ten minutes' thought, to teach it—were it but as a matter of amusement to some blind neighbour. Figure 3 shows how the sum 245 would stand in the board: the multiplier 3 is under 5, and the answer is 735. Where the seeing use a line under a sum preparatory to casting up, this is accomplished by the blind leaving a row of the holes unoccupied. The same in division—the divisor and quotient is separated from the dividend by a hole being left between. Thus with these few pegs, *any* sum in hundreds may be expressed, just by turning round the peg, or upside down. The facility to the teacher is not one whit less than to the pupil.

The size, as well as the weight of the board as used at Glasgow, has been greatly reduced; those I got made lately not being larger or heavier than a common desk slate, although necessarily a *little* thicker—while those who are curious in very small ones, may have them so as to go into a vest pocket, or a common card-case. I have one of this description only five inches long, and three wide, containing *ninety-six* holes in it. For real utility, however, the common size we use is far preferable. These weigh only fifteen ounces, measure ten by six and a half inches, and contain 204 holes, price 4s. They are made of wood, covered on the top with a white iron plate. I have had smaller ones made, quite large enough for beginners, six inches by four and a quarter, containing seventy-seven holes, weight, *five* ounces, price 2s. 6d.— These last I have more than once been requested to get made in mahogany as a drawing-room curiosity, and to add a short historical notice, which was pasted on the back.

In conclusion, on this part of my subject I may be allowed to express my surprise, that the humble individual whose name has now been connected with the improvement just described, has never had any mark of approbation bestowed upon him; while both medals and money have been awarded to others for inventions in aid of the science alluded to—arithmetic—which every practical man knows will not stand a comparison with the pentagonal board. For myself, I am happy in being at full liberty to say all I think of it, having had nothing to do with it, either in the way of invention or suggestion. Knowing its value, I recommended its introduction into the school at York; and gratefully acknowledge the relief it has afforded both to my pupils and myself.

In addition to arithmetic, GEOGRAPHY has proved one of the most delightful studies the attention of the blind can be directed to. It partakes more of a recreation than anything else; and from the interest it imparts to everything they hear read, it is pursued with the greatest avidity. It is not for the purpose of "showing-up" a young person labouring under such a privation, as being able to place his finger upon this, that, or the other place. Not at all. But as reading *to* them, whether in an institution or out of it, will always prove the best means of imparting instruction to them, a general knowledge of this science is almost indispensable. It makes everything alive to them—it is soon acquired—and once obtained, it needs little revision, if any. Their delight in resorting to a map to "see" whereabouts such a place is—teaching each other with all readiness, and now and then coming, as they have often done to me, and borrowing a map "to look at it," affords the strongest proof how heartily they engage in it. In the education of those in better circumstances, I would esteem an intimate knowledge of geography, by globe and map, to form one of the most important branches of their education, and certainly to hold a place prior to that of the exact sciences. What is the reading of even a newspaper to them without it?

In the close of 1835, circumstances led me to think on some plan whereby to avoid the tedious operation of glueing on small cord round the coasts and boundaries of a common map, so as to adapt it to the blind. This had been the practice previously followed. Besides the expense of time and labour, it did not furnish me with a *different feeling*, whereby to denote rivers,—a desideratum in such matters; and any which had yet been in use in this country afforded no idea of mountains or chains of mountains, without which a map is far from perfect. Glue and sand were tried without success, and also a composition of paint. But these gave way to one of the simplest, quickest, and cheapest methods I could wish for,—so much so, that in course of a few hours a common map may be prepared for the use of the pupil. This plan was described in a paper inserted in the Penny Magazine for October, 1836, and I have now sufficient proof that the finger of the pupil, after twelve months' practice, makes no impression whatever on the raised line.

This was accomplished by pasting the map upon a sheet of thin pasteboard; or, what I have found to answer quite as well, cartridge-paper, and pricking through, by means of a bluntish pricker, a succession of small punctures, which, on the right side of the map, appear raised, and guide the finger round the boundaries of counties, islands, &c.; mountains were still easier denoted, by pressing the handle of the pricker into the back of the map, a quire of paper being placed under it to serve as a cushion; and the rivers were raised in like manner by pressing hard into their course *the side* of the pricker, indenting thereby a continuous line. I had a composition put into my hand by a young man, a chemist in York, which, with care, answered remarkably well; but, if the finger of the pupil is the least wet, or even damp, the composition rubs off. For those who would take care, this could be used successfully; but for a school something less liable to being defaced is requisite.

Embossed maps for the blind have lately been printed, both at Boston, United States, and at Edinburgh: but from their extreme scantiness of information they convey scarcely any idea, particularly those published at Edinburgh; which, from their smallness of size, render it exceedingly tantalising to the pupil. There is only the capital of each country marked in either, although the Boston one is four times the size of the other. They are both maps of Europe. The latter has had the sea done in parallel horizontal lines, as *feelable* as small wire, which presents a very rough surface, while the land is quite smooth. Would *vice versa* not have been more appropriate? In a sheet map of the same quarter, prepared as described above,—there are not less than a hundred and ten places indicated, besides rivers and mountains; and the sea being rendered, as a little boy said, "just as smooth as glass," by being highly varnished, while the land is done over with what I may perhaps call a blind varnish—quite dull and roughish,—the distinction between land and water is of the most marked description. The capitals are denoted by a roundish headed brass tack,—towns of greater or less note, by the heads of three different sizes of the common pin. For schools it is necessary that the map should be glued on thin board; but for any one in the better walks of life, they may be kept in a portfolio.

Having occasion for a map which would embrace the whole geography of Scripture—both Old and New Testaments,—and not being able to procure one to my mind, I constructed one of two sheets of pasteboard, by *embossing on the* REVERSE SIDE with the handle of a hammer, using the handle of a much smaller one for finishing off the niceties of the coasts. This, when finished, had all the appearance of having been laid down with a thin coat of plaster, and from the action of the instrument, the land had a roughness conveyed to it which realised every expectation.

I am the more particular in these details, as they may be useful to those near the blind. I believe many would be glad to devote both time and trouble to a relative so situated, if they knew how to be of use. There is far more within their reach, even with the most simple materials, than they have been accustomed to suppose.

In addition to a few maps, a large globe is indispensable for an institution. That at the asylum at Edinburgh, the first of the kind ever constructed in this country, is thirty

G

inches in diameter. The land and mountains are roughened and quite raised from the "level of the sea," while little pegs denote the principal cities. It has a semicircular meridian notched on the side at every ten degrees,—by this the latitude is easily found: while by a similar mark, every fifteen degrees is distinguished on the equator, and thereby the longitude reckoned. An excellent appendage to this is a board with the heights of mountains marked; and another having the comparative lengths of rivers laid down upon it. I have found a few pieces of willow answer excellently for the last, choosing for the longest river the thickest willow, and flattening it at the embouchure somewhat in proportion to its real width.

I shall now shortly consider WRITING for the blind. When speaking of this acquirement, I could wish I was spared the necessity of saying that things should be called by their right names. With the exception of the facsimile contained in the report of the institution, 1833, at Boston, United States, of the writing of three blind girls, I have never seen anything that approached to what we usually call *writing*. In that term, *facility* ought, in my opinion, to be included as well as the mere fact of certain letters being formed. Thus stamping *letter* after *letter* by means of stamps, each having a letter of the alphabet upon it, has been gravely talked of as "writing." "Stamps," it is said, "with the letters set with pins, are used by the blind to press through the paper, and in this way they are able to write a long letter upon a sheet of paper,—write the address upon it—and forward it by post, with as much accuracy as if they had been addressed in the common way." Let anyone analyse this process—by thinking of a person destitute of sight, sitting with a box containing the twenty-six letters of the alphabet on stamps--ten figures and stamps--and as many more for commas, periods, &c., in all about forty-six different stamps. They wish to *write* a letter, and commence with the words, "Dear father." The letter D is groped for, found, pressed through the paper, and returned to its place; e follows with the same accompaniments, and every successive letter brings with it the same routine of "toil and trouble"; and we are soberly told of this as constituting "writing"!

Nay, by another process, somewhat different, but not less wearisome than the above, the same fertile imagination assures us, "in sober seriousness," that it would not be difficult for the blind to write the Lord's Prayer "*upon a piece of paper, not larger than a square inch!*" and, "that there is no doubt the blind may yet exhibit specimens of penmanship which might be fairly entitled to comparison with the productions of accomplished writers!" Anything like comment upon such "entertainments," so much akin to our nursery reminiscences, would be out of the question. It would be well if they even stopped there; but a farther stretch of the same amiable enthusiast proposes a plan whereby the blind pupil is to read printed music *with his tongue*, while his hands are occupied with the keys!!

As I have in view, in these pages, the prospect of institutions for the blind doing something towards such an education *as is befitting the station of their pupils or inmates*, I shall here quote the experience of the Paris school, as recorded by Guilliè in his essay formerly referred to. The doctor allows the "*practicability*" (p. 91) of this art being taught, but adds, as a winding-up of the whole, as follows:

"The writing of the blind is never very regular, because they cannot keep a line with a uniform base; the tails of the letters go beyond that line; nor can they appreciate the dimensions of our letters written with a pen, nor form an exact proportion in the form of them. But still their writing is legible, *and sufficient for their wants.* They do not write very fast; but, as they are never in a hurry, slowness is to them a trifling inconvenience." (P. 100.)

If such is all that could be said of the results in an institution confessedly abounding in such like "curiosities," pursued, too, with a pertinacity worthy of a better cause; what are we to think of the time of young people being wasted in an acquirement so difficult to be attained, and, under their circumstances, so evidently of no practical benefit? I say so, even with the Boston report before me, for, until we are told in *what time* such and such lines were written—by what means—*and to what extent the handiwork of these children promised the realization of their being able to do for themselves,* AFTER *leaving the school,* I am confident that any favourable opinion must, in the minds of practical men, be suspended.

I allow much may be done in the way of amusing that class of the blind who are not dependent, by getting up numberless pursuits, which would be altogether unfit for the indigent blind. And I venture to think this is one of them. I have seen, within these few months, the genuine writing of one so taught, and I can truly say it has no claim to any such designation, and can only wonder how any one could suspend his credit as a teacher on such a result. Even those who have had their sight, and lost it in after life, can scarcely sign their name legibly after a few years, of which I have seen several instances. If stamps are to accomplish anything, the plan proposed by Mr. Craig, of Edinburgh, is far preferable to those spoken of above. He had only *seven* stamps, each of which, having a character upon it—suppose a V—was capable of four different positions, representing the four first letters of the alphabet, and so on of the rest. Still, this *looks* more simple than it will be found to be in practice, as the stamper does not require the letters *just as they follow alphabetically.* If he requires a, g, o, he has to resort to three different stamps: he has to get them—use them—and replace them in succession: the combining of four letters on one stamp aiding him nothing at all, unless he could use them in the order in which they are combined.

In conclusion, on this part may I be allowed to make one or two general remarks? Institutions for the blind have chiefly in view those who, from their situation in life, must do something for themselves; and it is this class I have chiefly had in view in the remarks I have made. When I speak of educating them, it is not with any intention of withdrawing them from the main object of their being sent to an establishment of the kind. *That* must be the first care—the other may be superadded more in the way of recreation than anything else. To speak of introducing algebra, and mathematics, and printed music, and other such like pursuits into an institution avowedly established for the *indigent* blind, or even those in the middle ranks, appears to me setting up a toy-shop rather than anything else—ministering far more to what I do not hesitate to call a pitiable craving for the notoriety of a name, than to the real benefit (whether present or prospective) of those whose sole attention ought to be directed to the great purpose for which they were sent: with such a limited time devoted to education as may raise them from gross ignorance—imbue their minds with sacred truth—and furnish them with such means of mental enjoyment as may cause their leisure hours to pass swiftly by. To surprise visitors is one thing—to benefit the blind is another and a very different: and this portion of these pages cannot be better closed than by reiterating the words of Guillié which appear on the title-page:—"Nothing is easier than to make the blind perform extraordinary feats, by accustoming them to conquer difficulties apparently insurmountable; but what advantage would such useless employments" (and, let me add, *studies*) " be to them ? "

I come now to what I promised at first, viz., to conclude these observations with a few notices respecting the habits, modes of thinking, and expression of the blind. They certainly are, as a body, the most habitually cheerful of mankind. How it comes to be so, I cannot tell, and I have no wish to theorise. I cannot designate the blind, as is almost universally done, " the unhappy," " melancholy," " pitiable," and so on. I know nothing more erroneous, or more opposed to the feelings of by far the greater majority. They cannot endure such terms themselves, and strangers should be on their guard against using them in their presence. I know a fine young girl, who lost her sight a few years ago at school, who immediately leaves the room when such misplaced expressions are uttered. Strangers visiting an institution invariably see them to great disadvantage, as then the whole are instantly quiet, —the cheerful song or chorus breaks off in the middle,— the stream of gaiety and instruction running in conversation, whereby, indeed, as much is conveyed to the junior branches as they gain in the schoolroom, and is a most excellent preparative to their entering on its pursuits,— is instantly hushed, and they appear more like so many automatons than anything else. This, combined with the usual feelings with regard to their privation, naturally begets expressions, in their hearing, of commiseration, which never fail to give pain, and even sometimes to excite their ridicule on the mistaken party leaving the room. Some schools have, therefore, adopted the plan of having printed labels up throughout the premises, warning visitors against doing so.

I remember a lady walking round a school to view the different kinds of work in the hands of ten or twelve girls. She, by half articulated ejaculations, showed what was passing in her mind, but I believe none of us were prepared for the astounding climax which followed, when turning round to me she said, in the hearing of all— " Well!—*poor* things!—do they *ever speak?*" The effect was almost instantaneous, and I was glad to get her outside the room door, to allow vent to the burst of laughter which immediately followed her exit. "Poor things!—do they ever speak?" became quite a bye-word among them afterwards.

"The world to them is not less an enchanting scene than it is to us, provided they have occupation. Were they not continually reminded of their inferiority by our officious and unnecessary expressions of sympathy and compassion, they would not feel it. They look upon the want of sight as a loss of advantage, and not of enjoyment." *

Romping, jumping, laughing, and screaming, are as delightful to them as they can be with boys and girls who see. The cross-bow, bow and arrow, trundling each other in a wheelbarrow, spinning tops,—and to those who have a glimmer of light, marbles and a kind of cricket, such as secures at least both healthful exercise and plea-sure—all afford ample amusement to the first mentioned, while there is no want of the usual boyish plotting and mischief. The girls also enjoy their play hours very much, and contrive to stand in as much need of the needle as their more favoured sisters of sight.

"Well, Jane," said I to a little girl of twelve years of age, whose frock seldom but showed signs of rough usage.

---

* North American Review, July, 1833.

"Well, Jane, this will never do, why you would require a new frock every week." "Aye, aye, Sir, just what my mother used to say,—she would need to get a *leather dick* for me," was the animated reply,—at the same time giving a bound away, as if not much inclined to turn a new leaf.

It is a remarkable fact that the blind scarcely ever hurt themselves, either on furniture or in play. At Edinburgh, they were constantly walking about the crowded streets. There were four or five "messengers" whose business it was to carry home all the goods sold—baskets, mattresses, rope mats; and not only did they do this with the greatest exactness, but they were daily in the habit of going to all parts of the city, Leith, Portobello, and environs; to take measurements for bedding. I have many times had the dimensions of two, and even three beds brought me,—all on memory,—with a precision not exceeded by the most expert workman, including the exact allowance of so many inches to be cut out for the bed-posts.

I had occasion one evening (when at Edinburgh) to send out one of these blind men with a mattress. I gave him the bill with it, that he might receive payment. He returned with the account and mattress too. "I've brought baith back, ye see, Sir," said he. "How so?" "Indeed, Sir, I didna like t' leave 't yonder, else I'm sure we wad ne'er see the siller—there's no a stick of furnitur' within the door!" "How do you come to know that?" "Oh, Sir, twa taps on the floor wi' my stick soon tell't me that!" Having to send the same man to Portobello,* towards evening, I warned him (rather inadvertently!) that if he did not make speed it would get dark. "My word, Sir," said he, laughing, "I wish I

---

* Three miles from Edinburgh.

had a shillin' for ilka time I've been in Portobello i' the dark."

Illustrative of this, the following beautiful lines, which appeared in the Saturday Magazine for June, 1835, will, I hope, not be unacceptable. I have never met with anything of the poetic strain so genuinely descriptive of the feelings of those labouring under this privation—they are true to the very letter. The idea conveyed in the two lines in italics is, of itself, a gem :—

THE BLIND BOY.

FROM A SPECIMEN OF PRINTING IN RELIEF, FOR THE USE OF THE BLIND.

THE bird, that never tried his wing,
Can blithely hop and sweetly sing,
Though prison'd in a narrow cage,
Till his bright feathers droop with age;
So I, while never bless'd with sight,
Shut out from heaven's surrounding light,
Life's hours, and days, and years enjoy,
Though blind, a merry-hearted boy.
That captive bird may never float
Through heaven, or pour his thrilling note
'Mid shady groves, by pleasant streams
That sparkle in the soft moon-beams;
But he may gaily flutter round
Within his prison's scanty bound,
And give his soul to song, for he
Ne'er longs to taste sweet liberty.
Oh! may I not as happy dwell
Within my unillumined cell?
May I not leap, and sing, and play,
And turn my constant night to day?
I never saw the sky, the sea,
The earth was never green to me;
Then why, oh, why, should I repine
For blessings that were never mine?

Think not that blindness makes me sad,
My thoughts, like yours, are often glad.
Parents I have, who love me well,
Their different voices I can tell.
Though far and absent, I can hear,
In dreams, their music meet my ear.
Is there a star so dear above
As the low voice of one you love?
I never saw my father's face,
Yet on his forehead when I place
My hand, and feel the wrinkles there,
Left less by time than anxious care,
I fear the world has sights of woe
To knit the brows of manhood so.
I sit upon my father's knee:
He'd love me less if I could see.
I never saw my mother smile:
Her gentle tones my heart beguile.
They fall like distant melody,
They are so mild and sweet to me.
She murmurs not—my mother dear!
Though sometimes I have kissed the tear
From her soft cheek, to tell the joy
One smiling word would give her boy.
Right merry was I every day!
Fearless to run about and play
With sisters, brothers, friends, and all,
To answer to their sudden call,
To join the ring, to speed the chase,
To find each playmate's hiding-place,
And pass my hand across his brow,
To tell him I could do it now!
Yet though delightful flew the hours,
So pass'd in childhood's peaceful bowers,
When all were gone to school but I,
I used to sit at home and sigh;
And though I never long'd to view
The earth so green, the sky so blue,
I thought I'd give the world to look
Along the pages of a book.

Now since I've learned to read and write,
My heart is fill'd with new delight;
And music, too,—can there be found
A sight so beautiful as sound?
Tell me, kind friends, in one short word,
Am I not like that captive bird?
I live in song, and peace, and joy,
Though blind, a merry-hearted boy.

PARK BENJAMIN, OF BOSTON, N. AMERICA.

I have many times observed how lightly, even jocularly, they have adverted to their own privation. It may indeed be questioned if the majority consider it any privation at all. Standing for a few minutes after prayers to have a little chat, became quite a practice with the girls at York; it was with difficulty, indeed, I could get them prevailed on to go to bed. One of them, a girl of strange mental peculiarities, slow to the last degree in acquiring everything—still, inactive, sleepy—yet at times showing by her playful, sometimes quaint observations, that there was an activity within, took up a book laying at my hand—turned her face up towards the gaslight above my head (which she only *knew* to be there by report), and playfully observed as she whirled over the leaves, " Dear me, Sir, what bad gas that is, I can't see to read a word by it ! " The same girl, standing near the fire, heard a companion trying to decipher some of the letters of the book in relief. " Let me see," says the latter, " what's this—b, i, t, t, e, r,—bit—what does that mean ? " " Sit a little nearer the light, my dear," said her fireside companion—" sit a little nearer the light, I know you don't see very well, Jane." The tone of this, indicating as it did—genuine playful mischief—struck me much.

" Now, now, Mr. A.," said a little romp, as pretty a child of eleven years of age as one could wish to see, as she laid hold of a letter on my table, and popped it up to her face, " now for all the secrets in this! " I told the same little one to tell a servant to bring me a candle. The latter (improperly) committed it to her care. On seeing her with it, I said it was wrong in her to take it. " O, Sir," said she, laughing—"haven't I seen my way with it?" " O, ho," said a spirited boy, as he heard me telling of something disagreeable I had seen in town—" I beat you there, Mr. A.—I never see anything that vexes me, you never heard me grumbling about that ! "—laughing at the same time with all the hilarity imaginable.

A young man, at the Edinburgh asylum, born blind, was at all times the essence of cheerfulness. He was one of our most correct "messengers," and a good collector of accounts, of which from the amount of our annual sales we had many. He, as well as several others, could easily take from four to eight of these at one time. Coming along the passage whistling—he was always whistling— he began to grope about for his hat, which not finding on its usual peg, he cried to a companion, whose foot he heard not far off, " Willie, come here, man, and look for my hat, ye see better than me." The one was as blind as the other.

The ardent thirst of the blind to *see sights* is a feature no less extraordinary than it is true. The great bulk of them express every desire, and make every endeavour to gratify this (to us) unaccountable propensity. When his Majesty, just deceased, was proclaimed at Edinburgh, the united request of the inmates of the institution was, to give them liberty *to go and see the procession.* Having only recently entered the establishment, I was exceedingly puzzled ; and acting on the safe side, as I thought, I at first gave a negative. I was assured by our excellent and indefatigable overseer, who had been a considerable time in the house, that there was nothing to fear, " they would take care of themselves," and that nothing but discontent and grumbling would ensue if they were denied their request. To get the burden off my shoulders, I hastened into town, to Mr. Johnston, our secretary; I found him in the Parliament House, just at the moment *the procession was forming*, stated my dilemma, and immediately had for answer, " I would not like to be you, if you don't agree; you had better give in, they will manage themselves, depend upon it." A general " deliverance " ensued. They got " good places," whereat to witness the whole; some, I think, went even down to Leith, to secure a " stance," and for days afterwards, what each " saw " and heard was ample matter for conversation.

By the kindness of Professor Jamieson, as many as chose to avail themselves of it were permitted to visit and examine the larger objects in natural history, in the splendid rooms on the ground floor of the University of Edinburgh—lions, bears, deer, &c. This proved a great treat to about twenty-five, who on two successive mornings spent nearly two hours in examining all they could lay their hands on. They were delighted beyond anything I can describe. The cameleopard, whose towering head none of them could reach, was an object of great interest; no less so some idols from Hindostan, while a mummy secured in a glass case was an object of incessant inquiry, and its un-come-at-able situation brought out many expressions of regret.

Five or seven of the same body went one morning out to the rural village of Roslin, seven miles from Edinburgh, to *view* the beautiful chapel there. One of their number a man of the most cheerful disposition, born blind, and who got joined " for better for worse," with a helpmate under like circumstances—endeavoured to procure a "stance" in a window for a shilling, on occasion of a public procession ! How this couple could manage may surprise many; but still more so, when they learn that they also had a boarder—one of the asylum folk—under like circumstances. I can safely say, that had the marriages of the blind turned out nearly as well as this one, it would have been much to their advantage. Their house —and I have entered more than once wholly unexpected by them—was a picture of tidiness and comfort. She had three as pretty children as one could look at, but they all died. She washed, cooked, marketed, in short did everything for all. I have often seen her walking out with a baby in her arms, and always as if going to church,—so clean and tidy—the neat net-bordered cap of the little one "whipp'd up" by her own hands. It was said that his excess of good temper and pleasantry would have been to her an acquisition of which she stood in need.

The recognition of a person by their voice is common to the blind. It is astonishing how this enables them, at a long distance of time, to welcome an old friend. I was passing along a street in Greenock (sixty-five miles from Edinburgh), when I observed about a dozen persons, young and old, assembled round some one sitting on the low wall of some rails. I stopped to see the object of their curiosity. It was a blind man—stout, healthy, and hale, about forty-five years of age. He had a large label hung round his neck, telling a heart-rending story of his being struck blind by lightning on his passage home from the West Indies. His hat was in his hand receiving the trifle of the credulous passer-by. Now, his tale was " truth," but by no means " all the truth." I instantly recognised him as some years before one of my own "crew" at Edinburgh, who, for some acts of unruliness, and finally for getting married once more than he should have done—he said in "a frolic,"—had been expelled the institution. He had travelled a great deal since that—far into England—yet the moment I uttered the words, "Well, Andrew, my lad, how d'ye do?" he popped up his head, exclaiming, "Bless me, Mr. A.———, is that you?—how's a' wi' ye?" I am certain that he derived far more comfort from the information that I was just on my way to the steamer to leave Greenock, than from the trifle slipped into his japanned nor'-wester. Apart from his misdeeds, he was a straightforward, active man,—a capital " messenger,"—and, on the whole, as useful as any we had in the establishment. He was one of two or three I always employed if I wanted a letter or message delivered speedily. I have many times sent one of them to Leith—five miles going and back—and had an answer in an hour and a quarter, or an hour and a-half! Nothing diverted their attention.

Walking along the street at Edinburgh, I observed two of the asylum urchins before me. I saw one of them come bounce against a passer-by. The *other* did the same immediately after—then again the first—each collision being accompanied by a smothered laugh. I at once saw what they were about. Coming up close behind them, I heard the one say to the other—" Noo, Jamie, noo—it's your turn next!" "There," says Jamie, as he directed his whole weight against a coming footstep, while the credulous sufferer soothed his sorrows with—" Poor things—they're blind!" and passed on. Much to their astonishment, they, on their return, found they had not been unobserved.

It has often occurred to me how it should happen that no expression of desire to *see* anything ever escaped their lips. I never heard one of them say—" I wish I could see that as you do." A boy lately went up to the top of the Minster Tower (at York.) He had many times asked me to let him go. He went, and was quite delighted. But next morning he came to me, saying, "I wish, Mr. A———, I had taken your advice yesterday. It was *so* dull and misty—now this is a delightful, clear morning!" Ghosts, too, and goblins are fully as much the object of their anxiety and aversion as among the inhabitants of the nursery. The idea of Charles I. appearing without his head some night, they believing he had been beheaded in the Manor House, York (his Northern palace, now the school for the blind), was constantly in their mouths, and required no little argument to allay their fears. They many times, as told me, popped their heads beneath the bed-clothes to avoid his Majesty's visits!

On the beautiful eclipse of the sun last year, a few felt afraid, while the greater number, particularly those who had the least glimmer of light, got amply provided with pieces of smoked glass to view the phenomenon. They watched it the whole time, reporting progress to their less favoured companions, who surrounded them for information. These, amongst the blind, are technically yclept "blinkers," and are not accounted as belonging properly to the *right* sort—the totally blind.

One or two, who filled honourable places in the asylum at Edinburgh, I cannot pass unnoticed. The first I shall mention was an old man, named John M'Laren, who, as before spoken of, aided in the instruction of the young. He has now spent the long period of forty-six years in that institution; and, when his character and extraordinary usefulness are considered, it is difficult to say whether he has most benefited by the institution, or the institution by him.

John was, I believe, born blind, or, what amounts to the same thing, became so a few days after his birth. His parents were poor, and how his earlier years were employed, I know not; but by the time he had attained his fifteenth year (1793), the asylum at Edinburgh was projected, and a very slender beginning having been made, John was amongst the few who entered it on its being opened. On this circumstance, the old man now dwells with peculiar pleasure. "I cam' in a bit callan' (a little boy), an' noo, ye see, am grown an auld man amang ye," he has many times observed to me, when chatting of years gone by,—and this he does with a peculiar elevation of the head, habitual to him when speaking of anything he deems important.

Like all his fellows in the institution, he works nine hours a-day, principally at a machine for teasing hair, wool, and cotton—a process which causes a great deal of dust; but of this I never heard John complain. When his day's work is over, he betakes himself to another employment, in a way which cannot be too much commended, and which has been of essential service to the interests of the institution—the teaching of the young as spoken of before.

There is one peculiarity in his mode of teaching, namely, that he never will take in hand more than one pupil at a time. It has been more than once argued with him that the same repetition would do for one, or ten, or twenty. But no—John does not comprehend such an innovation, and must be allowed to proceed in his own way. At seven o'clock, he searches about for the urchin whose "turn" it is that evening (the younger, and therefore, more unthinking portion, are not very fond of the engagement, but that is nothing to John), and having laid hands upon him, conducts him to the "Machine-room," the apartment where the old man and two others work during the day, and sitting down together, there

H

they may be heard conning over the oft-repeated passage of Scripture, or verses of the Psalms.

None of the "readings" going on in the house move John from his purpose of Scriptural instruction; he allows it all to pass by as a thing of nought. When he is absent, and that is rare indeed, it is to hear some evening sermon. He cares little about anything but his Bible. Upon subjects connected with that he is quite at home—on almost every other subject comparatively uninformed. His memory, however, takes one singular direction; he picks up and stores in it—it may be supposed almost involuntarily—the merest trifles, and these he can refer to for years back with precision. A question arose as to which of two men came first into the asylum, one of whom had died. John, as in all such cases, was applied to, and, without the least hesitation, he replied, " Ou, Sir, this was it;—David cam' in first, for he cam' in about eleven in the forenoon, an' William about twa in th' afternoon; an' it was an unco wat (wet) day, just seven years past the ninth o' last April ! "

This is one of a hundred such registrations, which might be quoted. In the same way, he has chronicled all the texts from which the annual sermons for the institution have been preached, the clergyman who officiated, the sums collected, to a halfpenny, and the state of the weather on the day the collection was made. So long as that mode of aiding the funds continued (for an annual examination has of late years been resorted to in lieu of the sermons), John was invariably mounted in the desk, to act as precentor, or clerk, in raising the tune. He has a good voice still, and, every morning and evening, at family worship in the institution, he performs in the same way.

One source of great anxiety to John is the state of work in the institution. He is always sad, and makes many observations and inquiries, when "it is slack;" but when a revival comes, which it always does about March, from that to October being the busiest period of the year, his spirits get up, and he works with all his energy. Some of his waggish companions, knowing his foible, frequently annoy him with pretended doubts as to the stability of the institution.

The asylum has for many years had the furnishing of the door-mats for the light-houses in Scotland. The order is generally received about the beginning of April, but, being later about three years ago, some of them put it into his head that there was to be no more of these orders, "as they had *seen* by the papers that a certain economical member of the legislature had been overhauling these spendthrifts,—the Scottish Light-house Commissioners,—an' so, Johnnie, be assured, there's an end to our gude yearly orders!" The poor old man believed this, and every time he could get hold of the overseer as he perambulated the premises, his inquiry was,—" Dinna be offended, Sir, but hae ye heard onything o' th' order yet? Sure that man might hae let that bit thing escape." His joy on hearing that the order had at length been received, was in proportion to his former depression.

One anecdote more, and I have done.—A distinguished party visiting the house, were accompanied by Professor —— (of Edinburgh). The Professor knew John to be one of the "lions" of the institution, and, wishing to exhibit him, asked him to repeat the *nineteenth* verse of the sixteenth chapter of Isaiah. John, with his usual elevation of the head, and evidently with a feeling that he could wish to spare the learned gentleman, replied,— " Eh Sir, I wud wi' pleasure, but there's only fourteen

H 2

verses in it." It was quite evident, from the *appearance* of the querist, that the question was not put with the intention of catching John : and the Professor heartily joined in the laugh raised by the quaint manner in which the answer was given.

It is gratifying to have to add that the directors, appreciating the merits of this extraordinary man, made him an annual allowance for his almost self-imposed labour in teaching, but he had been engaged in it for a long period ere it was known to them. In addition to this, he had a very handsome silver snuff-box presented to him, with a suitable inscription on it. This heir-loom John only exhibits on " field-days,"—namely, two or three anniversaries still celebrated in the asylum. Of this token of approval John is justly proud, and on these occasions it makes the circuit of the table, every one enjoying a pinch.

But John M'Laren is not altogether singular in the Edinburgh asylum. There are among his companions men who, during nearly the same period, have gained an honourable livelihood by their industry,—supporting wives and families (most of them having such before they were deprived of the blessing of sight) respectably, though necessarily on slender means, a credit to themselves, and the excellent institution which has enabled them to do so.

I cannot close this notice without remarking the contrast which this case presents to one recorded in the Penny Magazine for May, 1833, of " Blind Alick, of Stirling." Both men were born in like circumstances of extreme poverty,—both were noted for astonishing memories,— both exercised these memories on the same invaluable treasure—the Bible. But there the parallel ends.— Unremitting industry, both in manual labour, and in communicating to others rising around him the words of salvation, supporting himself and wife creditably by that industry; esteemed for his valuable qualities by those placed over him, as well as by his companions and fellow-workmen; distinguished no less for his scrupulous sobriety and respectable appearance on the Lord's-day—mark the one case. While the other, we are told, becoming a kind of wonder, an object of mere curiosity, " lived an easy sort of mendicant life," as the account informs us, eking out a precarious livelihood by the charity (if such it could be called) of the curious visitor, spending his days in idleness, and by the notice which recently appeared in the newspapers of his death (which happened about April last), not particularly distinguished for his temperate habits.

The next prominent character in the institution alluded to was the teacher, David M'Beath, prominent as to situation and acquirements, but the very reverse as to bodily appearance. He was quite a dwarf, standing only about four feet six inches, a mere morsel, as all his make was in exact keeping. He looked more like a boy of ten or twelve, and that a very thin one. But he was a walking encyclopædia. He had lost his sight very early in life, became an inmate of the asylum, and was at first engaged in handicraft work. But his great extent of knowledge, and a happy mode of communicating it, pointed him out as one well fitted to convey to others what he had acquired himself. He therefore was fairly installed as preceptor, and an excellent one he made. He continued in this office for about twenty years until his death (which was sudden) in 1834. He taught spelling, grammar, arithmetic, geography, history, and writing on twine—the latter an invention, the credit of which he shared with a companion who succeeded him in the schoolroom, until he again was replaced lately by one of their own pupils, a smart boy, who is in view of becoming teacher in a projected institution in the north. As I have already stated, Dr. Howe, of Boston, engaged one of M'Beath's pupils to go there on the opening of the school for the blind; while another went to the New York institution, and three or four to the Glasgow Asylum. One of these, William Lang, I formerly spoke of as the improver of the arithmetic board. Unhappily the other, a young man of good family, and inferior to none of his companions in talent, did not turn out so well, and had to be parted with. M'Beath's instructions were all given orally, and, from the abundant stores of an unrivalled memory, never failed to make his instructions interesting to the tyros who excelled him physically as much as he did them mentally.

This was, indeed, a source of some annoyance to him. "Boys, whether blind or seeing, will be boys," and the science of "putting old heads on young shoulders" is about as difficult in a blind asylum as anywhere else. Visitors were constantly in the habit of taking the teacher for the taught—a boy—a mere child. Had he not been placed in a situation which daily, and sometimes several times a day, exposed him to the dreaded, though kindly-meant expletive, "Well, you are a very clever boy—how old are you?"—his Zacchean infirmity would have been of little consequence. But, assailed by this mosquito query,—while, at the same time, his sense of politeness (for that, and his corresponding address, were strongly marked) never would allow him to slur a question kindly meant, as he well knew,—he always endeavoured to shape a middle course, by sticking closely to the "standing" answer, "Nearly thirty, ma'am,"—giving, at the same time, his watch-key such a twirl as bespoke to those who knew him the infliction he was undergoing. And one-half of it was yet to come, as immediately on the party clearing the threshold, and sometimes scarcely that, his ear detected the titter and suppressed ebullition of fun indulged in by his "rank and file." "Order, boys!" "I wish you'd keep quiet, boys!" too often added to the evil, for they knew as well as any that ten years added to the "thirty" would have been nearer the mark.

We had one poet amongst us in the same institution, a very quiet, industrious young man, who lost his sight early in life. His name is Alexander Letham. From amongst many others, the two following little pieces have appeared in more than one of our periodicals. They bespeak a well cultivated mind :—

ANECDOTE FROM PARK'S FIRST JOURNEY IN AFRICA.

"WHATEVER way I turned, nothing appeared but danger and difficulty. I saw myself in the midst of a vast wilderness, in the depth of the rainy season, naked and alone, surrounded by savage animals, and men still more savage. I was five hundred miles from the nearest European settlement. At this moment, painful as my reflections were, the extraordinary beauty of a small moss in fructification irresistibly caught my eye. I mention this to show from what trifling circumstances the mind will sometimes derive consolation, for though the whole plant was not larger than the top of one of my fingers, I could not contemplate the delicate conformation of its roots, leaves, and capsula without admiration. Can that Being, thought I, who planted, watered, and brought to perfection in this obscure part of the world, a thing which appears of so small importance, look with unconcern upon the situation and sufferings of creatures formed after His own image? Surely not. I started up, and, disregarding both hunger and fatigue, travelled forward, assured that relief was at hand, and I was not disappointed."

VERSES ON THE ABOVE AFFECTING INCIDENT.

BY ALEXANDER LETHAM,

An Inmate of the Asylum for the Blind, Edinburgh.

AH! lovely flower, what care, what power,
In thy fair structure are displayed
By Him who reared thee to this hour
Within the forest's lonely shade!

Thy tender stalk, and fibres fine,
  Here find a shelter from the storm;
Perhaps no human eye but mine
  E'er gazed upon thy lovely form.

The dew-drop glistens on thy leaf,
  As if thou seem'st to shed a tear—
As if thou knew'st my tale of grief—
  Felt all my sufferings severe!

But ah! thou know'st not my distress,
  In danger here from beasts of prey,
And robbed of all I did possess,
  By men more fierce by far than they.

Nor canst thou ease my burdened sigh,
  Nor cool the fever at my heart,
Though to the zephyrs passing by
  Thou dost thy balmy sweets impart.

Yet He that formed thee, little plant,
  And bade thee flourish in this place,
Who sees and feels my every want,
  Can still support me by His grace.

Oft has His arm, all strong to save,
  Protected my defenceless head
From ills I never could perceive,
  Nor could my feeble hand have staid.

Then shall I still pursue my way
  O'er this wild desert's sun-burnt soil,
To where the ocean's swelling spray
  Washes my longed-for native isle.

THE OTHER IS AN "ADDRESS TO THE SUN."

GREAT refulgent orb of day!
  O! what joys thou dost impart!
O! how sweet thy cheering ray
  To the eye and to the heart!

See the lark with transport rise
  To salute thy early beam;

Whilst thou, in the eastern skies,
  Smil'st on mountain, wood, and stream.

Sweetly thou unfold'st to view
  Nature in her rich attire;
Giv'st the rose her lovely hue,
  And the ruby all its fire.

Yet the scenes thou dost display
  Cannot to the human breast
Lasting happiness convey—
  Earth is not our place of rest!

Lasting joys are only found
  Far beyond thy golden sphere:
There unfading flowers abound—
  There the sky is ever clear.

There a brighter sun doth shine,
  Which shall cheer the spotless soul
With resplendent beams divine,
  Long as endless ages roll!

Amongst the pupils of the school at York, there is one who though of only eighteen months' standing, has shown promise of no ordinary kind—mental, mechanical, and musical. He is just sixteen; came from the neighbourhood of Malton, and is, I believe, "the son of a widow." He comprehends everything, so to speak, at first sight. Possessed of an excellent memory, great perseverance, an ardent thirst for everything new, without at all leaving former acquirements behind, he makes such progress as leaves all his companions at a distance. Basket-making presented no difficulty; and now he is turning out such work of the "fine" description, as would do credit to an able and long standing workman. In geography, a map with eighty to a hundred and fifty places marked upon it, including rivers, mountains, bays, cities, and towns, is only the work of a few hours' lesson. He has thus "at his finger's end," Europe, England, Scotland, Ireland, Palestine, Yorkshire, and a general map of Scripture geography, from Rome to Babylon. In arithmetic, he is quite master of the four simple, and two compound rules (two hours a week). He, as well as his companions, have their memories brought into exercise daily, by committing a verse of the Psalms, immediately after prayer. Thus, in the period above - mentioned, they have acquired twelve Psalms—about three chapters of the Bible—Watts' Catechism of Old and New Testament names—one half of " Milk for Babes "—a Child's Catechism—about fifteen metre Psalms and Hymns—and have just finished the Church Catechism. The memory has always appeared to me the great substitute, whereby Providence has made up to the blind their privation—and the instrument, which those having the direction of their education ought to bring into constant operation, cautious at the same time to direct it towards the best end.* This youth is no less distinguished for his progress in music.

---

* While I speak thus of memory, its exercise should ever be accompanied (as in the case of all children) with familiar explanation and constant development of the understanding. If models too are of such great benefit to the seeing in their education, much more so are they to the blind. Witness the delight of the party who visited the museum. Seeing an old sailor, with the help of his faithful dog, pulling along a fine large model of a three-decker, I procured for my pupils—at the small cost of sixpence and a morsel of bread and cheese—a delightful hour's amusement, in examining all the details of this pretty representation of the wooden walls. A considerable number of shells which I had collected afforded great delight, and made their first step in conchology. A whole evening was spent in joyous delight, when I put into their hands a rough model in plaster of Paris, of the ground on which Edinburgh stands— marked as it is by so many peculiarities. This afterwards aided them (at least some) in understanding better than they would otherwise have done the stirring Tales of a Grandfather, by Sir Walter Scott, which filled up our evening reading hour for some months.

This is but a study of four months' standing, yet in that incredibly short time has he acquired as much as many children will take a year or two to master. In short, he loves, and is devotedly attached to anything he is engaged in, with the solitary exception of *reading with the finger.* *That* to him, as well as to the *great majority,* is a complete "bore." He *can* do as well as any one, but as he himself says, "it amounts to nothing; besides, *what* book are we to have? Of small type I can scarce tell one letter from another, and the other is *such* a size, that very few books can be expected." He read as well a year ago as he does now—his fingers are hardening with his work. The account this boy gave of himself to me lately was that, "he knew nothing beyond his mother's door— that even hearing the newspaper set him asleep, as he had not a single idea to what they related." The globular form of the earth puzzled him as well as all the rest, sadly. He could not comprehend (and scarcely would believe) that people stood with their heads down at the Antipodes, at which I had fixed a pin, and another at London, to make him understand me. "Now," said he, "sure you are making game, for two gentlemen who had been at Van Dieman's Land, were at my mother's lately, and I'm sure they did not say a word about standing with their heads down!"

Another youngster must not be forgotten. Music alone is all *his* forte—and in that he excels. Passionately fond of it, he never tires, and, while he has in reality pursued it for several years, yet the instruction he has received,— the study of thorough bass by means of the board and pins before-mentioned—improvement in fingering and execution during the eighteen months he has been in the school, has, as it were, completed him; and he has just entered upon his first engagement as an organist, at

Acomb, near York. This boy (for he is only past fifteen) has acquired in the space of time just mentioned, no less than sixteen or *eighteen* pieces of sacred music. I don't mean mere tunes, but choruses, and such like. "The Hallelujah," "The Dettingen Te Deum," "The glory of the Lord," "Comfort ye," "Every Valley," "Coronation Anthem," and "Overture to the Caliph of Bagdad," and other pieces of equally high standing, besides many Psalm and Hymn tunes, any of which he will acquire by their being sung or played over to him three or four times. Now, supposing this youth had had all these, and much more after the fashion of "music in relief for the blind," what benefit would he have derived? None whatever— no, not to the amount of a single bar—it would have proved quite a barrier to his progress had he been put to such drudgery. All he has acquired is by being read to by the teacher, or played over, as it were, sentence by sentence. Unlike the subject of the preceding notice, he progresses in nothing else—at least, only to a trifling degree.

We have some anomalies also. A girl, whom I alluded to before, presents something very extraordinary in her mental conformation. Slow, sleepy, dull, and inactive in the extreme, so much so as to render even knitting almost a hopeless task ; she possesses an excellent memory, but anything like explanation she cannot give. Yet, at times, her observations, as in some instances already given, possess point, and indicate a mind that *can* work. Again, while she has the whole of the multiplication table " at her finger's end," she can make no use of it! I spent five minutes (watch in hand) waiting until she could tell me what remained after taking 2 from 41, and ere she could add 4 to the 39, five minutes more elapsed ! The simplest question possible—3 oz. at 2d., 2 lb. at 7s., or any such are to her almost insurmountable difficulties—all kinds of answers are given. She is totally blind—is one of seven children who have only a widowed mother to support them—but owes much to the kindness of a lady in her neighbourhood. She seems never to have been accustomed to any kind of work, her whole hand is quite rigid from want of exercise. To me, she appears an example of what an asylum *might* have done for her, had she been placed there *at an early age.* At home, however anxious a parent may be, the blind have little chance, while on the other hand, in an institution adapted to their wants in all its machinery, they are far more likely to be rendered useful members of society. Nearly the same facts are true of a lad of sixteen here ; only he has a better judgment than most, it having, apparently, been assiduously cultivated by his (now deceased) mother. With a wonderful memory, stored with Psalms and Hymns, he can do nothing at arithmetic, reading, geography, and such like studies. Basket-making also was a failure, but he has succeeded better at rope mats.

There is also a chubby-cheeked rosy boy, of nine years of age, who is the oldest of *four* under a like privation. One of them, a little girl, was unhappily burnt to death very lately. Both parents have their sight, as well as their two eldest children. Will it be considered as unworthy of notice that this woman stated to me, that while *enceinte* of this boy, she made acquaintance with a blind woman who became, for many months, her inseparable companion ? Although only nine years of age, he has advanced so rapidly in basket-making, and that only in the course of a few months, as far to excel another pupil of thirteen years of age, who has been fifteen months at it. He is equally quick at arithmetic, committing to memory, &c., and is sportive as the day is long. His little brother is only five years of age, and a prettier little curly-headed fellow is not to be seen. If spared, he promises to become an enthusiastic musician, as no sooner does he enter the room than he wends his way to the piano. He has got a fife at home which he handles a little already. Few things would give me greater pleasure than to see them " endowed " into an institution. I must not omit to mention that their mother has done much for them, not only by drilling them herself, but sending them to school as early as possible. For this alone, they are much indebted to her. Both these children are instances of how necessary it is that institutions for the blind should admit pupils as soon as they display good, promising capacity, instead of putting them off until a certain age has been attained.

I here conclude these observations. My sole motive in undertaking this little work has been the wish to lay before those interested in the blind, or in institutions for their benefit, all the information which I have acquired by ten years' constant and close intercourse with them. I have candidly pointed out whatever I consider likely to retard or limit the usefulness of such institutions. I have considered the various plans now afloat for the intellectual improvement of their inmates ; and in doing so I have felt myself compelled to differ, so far as the *indigent* blind are concerned, from those persons now so actively engaged in promoting " Printing for the blind "—but I repeat that, while I do so, I sincerely respect the motive which has called forth those exertions ; so far as that has been the zealous wish to rescue those of our fellow-creatures labouring under so heavy a privation, from the listless apathy and hopeless despair to which they were too, too long consigned, from the unfounded idea that their hapless lot admitted of neither help nor alleviation.

Finally, let me hope that no one will be so uncharitable

as to criticise this humble work in the light of a literary composition;—should any feel disposed to do so, let them recollect in extenuation of its many faults, the *motive* which called it forth, and also, that, in the course of a life devoted to unremitting industry, the writer has found little time for the studies connected with literary attainments.

LONDON: PRINTED BY WILLIAM CLOWES AND SONS, LIMITED,
STAMFORD STREET AND CHARING CROSS.

THE ESTABLISHMENTS

FOR

THE BLIND

IN ENGLAND

A Report

TO

THE MINISTER OF THE INTERIOR AND OF FOREIGN AFFAIRS

BY

THE ABBÉ C. CARTON

DIRECTOR OF THE DEAF, DUMB, AND BLIND INSTITUTE OF BRUGES

"Even he, whose hapless eyes no ray
Admit from beauty's cheering day;
Yet, though he cannot see the light,
He feels it warm, and knows it bright."

TURLAGH CAROLAN, *Irish blind poet.*

BRUGES

IMPRIMERIE DE VANDECASTEELE-WERBROUCK

RUE DES DOMINICAINS

1838

LONDON

SAMPSON LOW, MARSTON, AND COMPANY

LIMITED

St. Dunstan's House

FETTER LANE, FLEET STREET, E.C.

1895

THE ESTABLISHMENTS

FOR

THE BLIND

IN ENGLAND

A Report

TO

THE MINISTER OF THE INTERIOR AND OF FOREIGN AFFAIRS

BY

THE ABBÉ C. CARTON

DIRECTOR OF THE DEAF, DUMB, AND BLIND INSTITUTE OF BRUGES

"Even he, whose hapless eyes no ray
Admit from beauty's cheering day;
Yet, though he cannot see the light,
He feels it warm, and knows it bright."

TURLAGH CAROLAN, *Irish blind poet.*

BRUGES

IMPRIMERIE DE VANDECASTEELE-WERBROUCK
RUE DES DOMINICAINS
1838

LONDON

SAMPSON LOW, MARSTON, AND COMPANY
LIMITED
St. Dunstan's House
FETTER LANE, FLEET STREET, E.C.
1895

LONDON :
PRINTED BY WILLIAM CLOWES AND SONS, LIMITED,
STAMFORD STREET AND CHARING CROSS.

CONTENTS.

CHAPTER I.

CHAPTER II.

CHAPTER III.

CHAPTER IV.

4

THE ESTABLISHMENTS

FOR

THE BLIND IN ENGLAND.

CHAPTER I.

OF THE NATURE OF ESTABLISHMENTS FOR THE BLIND.

STATISTICAL researches prove that the immense majority of the
blind belong to that class of society which has to get its living
by labour. This fact is certain, and should exercise a great
influence on the nature of an establishment to be formed for
these unfortunate creatures. Another fact, no less certain, is
that deprivation of sight does not make the blind unhappy.
Their great unhappiness is caused by having to depend upon
others for the primary needs of life, and by not knowing how to
make their existence useful. The world has no less delight for
them than for us, provided they can be usefully employed ; and,
if we were not so cruel as to remind them every moment of their
misfortune by useless expressions of sympathy and compassion,
they would not feel it. All blind people would reply almost in
the same words as he of Puiseaux : " I should like just as much
to have long arms as to have eyes. It seems to me that my
hands would teach me better what passes in the moon than your
eyes ; and, besides, eyes sooner cease from seeing than hands from
touching. So it is quite as well worth while to perfect in me the
organ which I have as to give me that which is wanting." They

do not ask society for enjoyment; they ask only for work and independence. Thus it was that the name of Blind Workers (*Aveugles travailleurs*) first gained from the public in France expressions of such lively interest; and it was the hope that the produce of their labours would suffice to cover the advances made which induced philanthropic society to pay the considerable expenses incurred in their favour from 1784 to 1790. Unluckily, experience soon sadly undeceived those who had founded too much hope on experiments, doubtless praiseworthy, but ill-calculated to attain their object. Little by little the means of the establishment became so reduced, that as early as 1791 it could no longer subsist on its own resources. The pupils lacked the most necessary requirements of existence. The interest they had inspired consequently became weakened. People had flocked enthusiastically to the public exhibitions of the blind people. They had applauded when they saw them—braving, as it were, the decrees of nature—reading, writing, cyphering, and speaking of arts and sciences. But they were looking, after all, for something more real, namely, that society would be relieved of a burden; and only that which is real is lasting even in France. The sole objection made to M. Haüy's institution—and he himself tells us so (chap. ii., " Essay on the Blind ")—relates to this point : " Had you the idea," he was asked, " when teaching your pupils all branches of education, of peopling the republic of letters with savants and professors, or of showing them how to find the means of subsistence ? " " People have done us the justice," replies M. Haüy, " to admit that we have accomplished the first object of our institution by offering an amusement to well-to-do blind pupils ; but, however, we do not claim that the most skilful of our pupils can ever be put in competition, in any way, with the most ordinary artist who can see. But we recommend them to public benevolence " (*ibid.*). After this disheartening response the establishment fell into total oblivion, and would long since have ceased to exist if the Government had not granted it annual subsidies, which sufficed for the entire maintenance, and without work, of three times as many blind as the Paris Institute contains.

Mr. Howe, director of the Boston Institution for the Blind,* visited the Paris establishment about 1830, and found it still in about the same state. "One in twenty," says he, "could scarcely get a living after eight years' apprenticeship, and even then not by practising one of the handicrafts learnt in the institution. He could only do so when chance or interest obtained for him a place as organist, or when he succeeded in obtaining some special post such as pianoforte tuner, which could only be in a large town."

M. Dufau, professor at the Paris Institute for the Blind, proposes in his essay a new organisation of these establishments, but, unfortunately, it suffers too much from the views with which this sort of establishment has hitherto been regarded in France.

There would be a higher institution at Paris, and secondary institutions in the departments. The limit of age of admission would be fourteen years, and the duration of residence in the institution four years. This time would suffice to go through the whole curriculum of primary instruction. Music would be taught there, especially with the object of finding out pupils who showed a real vocation for that art, and the complete instruction of whom would be one of the principal aims of the higher institution. Manual labour would also form part of the occupations of the children in the secondary institutions; but rather in order to initiate them into a number of processes which should make them more handy than to give them a real apprenticeship. Those pupils who, in the course of four years, had passed through the entire curriculum of instruction, and manifested a great natural taste either for science, letters or music, after having passed an examination proving their capacity, would be sent to the higher

---

* Dr. Howe, of the Perkins Institution and Massachusetts Asylum for the Blind at Boston, Mass., of whom and of the Institution itself an interesting account was given by Charles Dickens in "American Notes." Dr. Howe was the great benefactor and friend of Laura Bridgman, the poor blind deaf and dumb girl, and of him Dickens says: "There are not many persons, I hope and believe, who, after reading these passages, can ever hear that name with indifference."

institution at Paris, where manual labour would be excluded. The others would be sent back to their relatives or friends with a little knowledge, which is all very well, but without any means of subsistence, and more unhappy than before, because they would have tasted the pleasures of a studious life during those four years of youth which usually decide the habits of a whole life, and then would become a burden to their relatives, or perhaps would be obliged to beg for a living. These four years passed in the secondary institutions, instead of having contributed to their happiness, would thus only have served to increase their requirements, and to render the impossibility of satisfying them all the more painful. They will feel convinced they have the power of doing something really useful ; that they differ less from those surrounding them than they had imagined ; and that with some care and a little attention they could equal them in some respects, and always at least come near them. There they would have been the object of public attention, and felt that they possessed a place in society, however humble it might be, and that the barrier separating them from it might be passed. There they would have drunk (in Mr. Howe's words) at the fountain of knowledge so much as to have a thirst they would be unable to quench : they would have lived there long enough to make poverty and penury doubly painful ; and their minds would have been sufficiently cultivated to make even their instruction a source of misery. To send them away after those four years passed in a school would only be forming them for a hospital or a workhouse. The result is not worth the trouble.

The object aimed at then—above all in France—is to give these unfortunate beings an intellectual education, instead of trying to make them capable of getting their living by manual labour, so that they may become independent. It is science rather than a handicraft—it is the agreeable rather than the useful that is kept in view. The state of blindness, a celebrated French teacher said to me one day, takes away the physical rather than the moral powers. Therefore their beneficent teachers ought, above all, to try to develop the hearts and minds of the blind.

In England a different principle has guided those who have established institutions for the blind : this was to instruct them in manual labour—to make artisans of them, but not by any means to make savants of them. The principle of the economy of public charity was admitted, which teaches us that, since the poor blind are dependent upon society, it is better to procure them the means of gaining their living themselves than to provide for their wants by granting them a life annuity, and to attain this object schools were formed. The results are most satisfactory : a great number of the blind have succeeded in making themselves a position and in keeping their families by their industry.

At first this principle was applied too rigorously—every intellectual instruction being excluded—and in one of the first establishments in England the utility of teaching to read by means of letters in relief seems still to be doubted. Scotland modified these two too-exclusive principles, and combined them in such wise as to give the blind sufficient instruction to occupy them and raise their spirits, but taking care, nevertheless, not to employ in that way the time needed to make them skilful at a handicraft. This, as we see, was to bring them once more near to the position of those who have their sight, and worked, therefore, most efficaciously for their happiness. Public examinations have demonstrated the possibility of such a combination ; besides which their replies to questions have testified to the aptitude of the blind for the various branches of primary instruction and to the success of the philanthropic undertaking; while, on the other hand, the annual reports on the financial position of the homes have proved that this instruction does not in any way injure the material prosperity of the home ; but, on the contrary, that the instruction which they have received had assisted in inspiring them with the taste for work by the noble wish to be useful, or, at least, not to remain a burden on their fellow-citizens.

The instruction varies again in each of these homes and institutions as much in Scotland as in England, and the degree to which it is carried differs materially between one school and another, but nowhere is it given at the loss of time required for work. An hour, or an hour and a half, are given to it, and matters are so arranged as to make it a real recreation. We might have expected from the practical intellect of the English what they have done ; and Scotland—while modifying, by its enlightened zeal for the propagation of primary instruction amongst this unfortunate class, whatever was too material in the English ideas—may boast of having solved the problem of this instruction by mixing the useful with the agreeable, as M. Haüy says.

One very important question, however, remains for discussion. People are quite agreed in England as to the nature of the education to be given to the blind, and everywhere it is first of all industrial, but they vary materially as to the employment of the blind after their instruction.

There are institutions which I shall call *schools* (*écoles*). In them children receive during a certain fixed number of years all the care their condition demands, and they pass the apprenticeship to a trade suited to their strength and to the degree of ability they have shown ; but from whence they are sent away most of them with a gratuity of 50 to 100 francs (say, £2 to £4 sterling), destined to furnish them with the means to carry on the trade they have been taught, or perhaps with an assortment of all the tools necessary in the handicraft they have learnt.

The other institutions are rather homes (*asyles*). Their object is not solely to train their pupils to some handicraft during a certain period, and then to replace them by others, but to employ them after being educated in the home itself, should they desire it, or deserve it by their good conduct.

I have seen both systems, and I am now about to show their respective advantages.

The *schools* are founded with the idea that the blind are capable of doing when isolated what they can produce when working together, or at least that the difference is not considerable, and that the sending away those who have learnt a trade renders possible the admission of other blind pupils, and consequently extends the beneficial influence of the institution. This is the system which was first followed, and it is still in vigour in some establishments in England and in Ireland, but is now beginning to be generally abandoned, since the results obtained by those institutions in Scotland, where they are all homes (*asyles*). As a matter of fact, the system of *homes* (*système asylaire*) must be restricted to a more limited number of pupils than can be admitted into a school, and its beneficent work does not seem capable of being so extended as that of a school, and must necessarily shut out a crowd of unfortunates who would have received an education if all the establishments of the kind were schools ; but this is only apparent, or rather only temporary, and really ends by procuring the education of a greater number. Let us notice, first of all, that the mass of blind workers in a home change oftener than we suppose ; in one way or another, either by death or otherwise, from one-tenth to one-seventh leave the home every year,* which number is consequently renewed every ten, or at latest every fourteen years ; the succession of pupils in the schools is then at most only double relatively to that at the homes.

Notice further that this rapid succession of pupils subjects the institution to considerable losses, for they have scarcely acquired sufficient skill to give hope of their being useful by their labour than they leave the workshop, to give place to those who by their ignorance and awkwardness will in their turn occasion losses to the

---

* Subjoined are the admissions and departures of pupils in the home at Glasgow, where the changes are still more frequent.

From March 28, 1828, until	Pupils admitted.	Have left the Home or been sent away.	Number of Pupils deceased.	Total.
1829	38	7	3	10
1830	47	9	4	13
1831	57	10	5	15
1832	62	15	5	20
1833	70	19	5	24
1834	78	24	6	30
1835	86	24	7	31
1836	97	27	10	37
1837	105	29	12	41

house. The inequality of production which is unavoidable in a
school necessarily prevents being able to do business with
regularity. Then the markets fail, and this entails other losses ;
while a home, producing regularly every year almost the same
quantity, and being in a position to supply precisely the same
customers, because its staff is always nearly the same, is more
certain of finding where to dispose of its produce. The sales of
the blind schools of Paris, London, Liverpool, and Bristol compared with those of the Edinburgh and Glasgow homes will put
this point beyond a doubt.

SCHOOLS.

Place.	Year.	Number of Pupils.	Produce of Sales.	Produce of Sales.
			Francs.	Pounds Sterling.
Paris	1816	82	355	..
,, ...	1817	89	848·95	..
,, ...	1818	92	993	..
,, ...	1819	93	905	..
London . . .	1832	112	..	1,345
,, . . .	1836	112	..	1,469
Liverpool . . .	1835	105	..	1,839
,, . . .	1836	108	..	1,818
Bristol. . . .	1833	33	..	906
,, ...	1834	33	..	992
,, ...	1835	40	..	1,019
,, ...	1836	43	..	1,138

HOMES.

Place.	Year.	Number of Pupils.	Produce of Sales.
	Average from		Pounds Sterling.
Edinburgh	1822 to 1832	80	3,200
Glasgow	1828	22	231
,, ...	1829	28	642
,, ...	1830	34	665
,, ...	1831	42	887
,, ...	1832	42	1,101
,, ...	1833	45	1,189
,, ...	1834	48	1,303
,, ...	1835	55	1,953
,, ...	1836	60	2,514
,, ...	1837	64	2,472

The sales of the homes with the like number of pupils thus exceed by more than one-half the sales of the schools ; and the profits differ in consequence. Yet more ; the expenses of the school at London amount yearly to four thousand pounds sterling and those of Liverpool to three thousand pounds, while they are only about one thousand pounds in the Edinburgh and Glasgow homes with an almost equal number of pupils.

Recapitulating the calculations I have made, we find that the profits of the sales are at least double in the homes, and that the expenses are three times less than in those establishments which are simply schools ; so that if the succession of pupils be more rapid in the schools, and if the instruction may consequently be extended to a larger number of persons, this advantage is only apparent ; for it is really easier to form two homes than to establish one school. But I must say, and I say it with profound conviction, that we can in no wise impute it to the directors of these establishments that the profits are less and the expenses heavier. The disadvantages are the forced consequences of the system itself. But it is not less surely proved that, in regard to the interior economy of the house, a home is preferable to an institution which is simply a school.

But let us go on—let us follow the pupils out of the establishment after receiving their education and working isolated.

A blind person imbibes courage when in the company of other blind people ; but, as he is naturally prone to low spirits, he soon loses his courage if isolated, and this all the more quickly because at every moment he is forced to admit the superiority of those who can see, and because he no longer inspires in others that interest which is caused by a number of the blind assembled together. It has often happened that blind persons, hoping to succeed in providing for themselves, have voluntarily quitted the homes in Scotland, and have settled in towns which seemed to offer the means for disposing of the produce of their labour. A noble ambition inspired them ; others have tried the same thing after having been expelled for misconduct. All had been several years in the establishment, and were mostly good workmen.

After a few years', often only a few months', trial they themselves have realised the impossibility of continuing alone the struggle with workmen who could see, and have asked to be re-admitted. These facts are not rare. In the Annual Report for 1833 of the Institute for the Blind at Dublin the same remark is made. " We have seen with sorrow," the trustees say, " that pupils who had acquired great skill in one or more trades, and had left the establishment with a good character and had received in wages a pretty considerable sum, have not succeeded in their undertaking on returning to their native place, owing to want of support and encouragement which they so much deserved ; and that their funds having gradually become exhausted, they have been forced to return to Dublin and increase the already excessive mass of poverty."

At a meeting held in Manchester, during March 1834, relative to the erection of an institution for the blind, which is just about to be opened, the committee appointed to make the necessary inquiries assures us that also at Liverpool the need has long been felt of a home for the blind, who cannot provide for their needs with the wages they earn outside the establishment ; and that the result of all the information they have obtained is that the Manchester institution ought to be a home (*asyle*).

I am convinced by the unanimous testimony of all the superintendents of establishments for the blind in England that advantages worthy of the undertaking are only possible in a home (*asyle*) ; therefore all efforts should tend to attain this object.

But, even supposing that the blind person in his isolation can produce as much as in a home, it is not everything to be able to produce ; it is necessary to be able to sell.

A public institution which is always before the public has a power of attraction which the isolated blind man does not possess. People are proud of having a blind asylum, they look upon it as a national glory, and so they like to contribute to its reputation, and all the more because the influential men who are at its head can attract their acquaintance by assuring them that the primary materials used are always of the best quality, and that the prices are no higher than elsewhere. This again would only be possible in an asylum, which by means of its capital can procure for cash and at the lowest prices the best primary material, which ordinary workmen cannot do; and that which the workmen who have their sight gain by their greater skill they lose by the high price they must pay for their material. Thus competition becomes possible when the blind work in a body, and never when they are isolated.

In an institution where the blind pupils do not stay after receiving their education only those trades can be taught which do not demand a large capital, nor a number of workers, nor expensive machinery. Each trade must be an individual labour, whereas in an asylum the use of steam-engines and the division of labour for the making of a single production might be introduced with immense advantage.

It has been proved that more than one-quarter, if not one-third, of the blind have become so at an advanced age. Military ophthalmia alone caused 960 out of 4,117 cases of blindness in Belgium in 1835. For this numerous class, too old for acquiring the skill needed for a handicraft, a trade easily learnt and productive from the beginning is wanted. In an asylum you can make use of the strength of such unfortunate beings and employ them profitably, whereas in a school they would never be able to gain their bread. Thus the principal occupation in the Edinburgh asylum is the making of horsehair mattresses. The manipulation of the horsehair before it is twisted occupies those who have the least aptitude for a handicraft; the use of a steam-engine renders this work easier and more productive; others twist the horsehair. Many are employed in weaving the wool for the mattress. This occupation, if it were isolated, would scarcely bring in as much as a blind man could earn by doing anything else; but, in this asylum, the consumption is certain and the highest price is given. The girls sew the coverings, and the most adroit blind people fill the mattresses. This division of labour brings in wages which no trade could procure, and usefully employs the dullest blind inmate from the first day of entering the asylum.

Now let us speak of a rather numerous class of the blind hitherto but little thought of by those who have contributed to found schools, and which deserves all our attention. I wish to speak of men who have become blind after marriage. There are few cases more deserving of our sympathy. Having become blind at a time of life when all habits are formed, what can be done for them in a school ? But in an asylum work can be found for them suited to their taste and ability, and the hours of labour can be alternated with the time they wish to pass every day with their family. Thus it is that at Édinburgh there are twenty married men in the asylum, who have families they support by the fruit of their labour ; and at Glasgow the number is still more considerable.

Education in establishments for the blind ought then, before all, to be industrial, and all our care ought to tend to the making useful citizens of them, instead of wishing to fashion them into savants. Learned people are sufficiently numerous in the class which can see, so that we may dispense with seeking for them in the class to which this quality would be quite useless, if not a source of unhappiness. Besides, why wish to obtain more instruction for them when they are blind than would be given them if they possessed all their senses ? I could understand it if science made them happy, or if it helped them to get a living ; but that is not so. It has been proposed to make schoolmasters of them ; but whatever has been said or written on the subject, there is not only an insurmountable prejudice which declines to admit the blind as teachers of ordinary children, but there are very good reasons which will always prevent them. In fact, it is not simply a question of instructing the young, of teaching to read and write, but of giving an education ; and for this supervision at every moment is necessary, and of this they are incapable.

A profession, but not science, that is the object of their education. Amongst the means of more surely attaining this end, and of exercising the most influence on the happiness of the blind, an asylum is in all respects superior to a school, and is alone capable of procuring lasting good.

CHAPTER II.

Origin and Organisation of Establishments for the Blind in England.

Statistics of the blind have not yet been officially made in England. However, some private statements put us in a position to know their approximate number. The directors of the blind school at York have communicated the results of their researches on that county. A form was sent containing necessary questions on the age, the causes of blindness, &c. Nearly 700 replies were received ; the population of the parishes in the county of York which sent them was, in 1831, 862,533 ; corrected for 1836, 940,926.

The forms received give the number of the blind   840
> Below 50 years of age   326
> Below 25 years of age   143
> From 10 to 20 years of age . . .   58
> From 10 to 16 years of age . . .   40
> Below 10 years of age   49

In applying this result to all the population of the county, we find the numbers following :—

Population of the county of York in 1831, 1,374,296 ; corrected (in round numbers) for 1836, 1,500,000.

> Blind people in the county . . .   1,339
> Below 50 years of age   520
> Below 25 years of age   223
> From 10 to 20 years of age . . .   92
> From 10 to 16 years of age . . .   64
> Below 10 years of age   78

B

It is to be supposed that this number is below the real number ; but while admitting this, and extending it to all England, we find that there are, in a population of 15,000,000, 13,390 blind persons ; but if we include Scotland and Ireland, that is, a population of 25,000,000, we find 22,316 blind persons ; and the number of those capable of receiving instruction, only counting those aged from 10 to 25 years, is 2,296.

But the number of the blind appears to be still more considerable in England, and may be estimated at 1 in 1,000, or 25,000. Mr. Anderson estimates it at 1 in 890, or 28,000.

Supposing that a quarter of this number are incapable of receiving instruction because of their age or of illness, and that one-fourth are below 10 years of age, there still remain 14,000.

We deduct from this number 3,000 blind belonging to the upper or middle classes, and who do not need the aid of asylums. There remain 11,000 blind capable of instruction, and who have a right to claim from society the means of existence. The establishments throughout the United Kingdom contained in 1836–37 the number of pupils as follows :—

London		122
Liverpool		108
Edinburgh		82
Glasgow		60
Bristol		43
Norwich	(about)	40
Dublin		39
York		19
Belfast	(about)	10
Molyneux (Dublin)		30
	Total	553

Thus there are more than 10,000 blind who, in England, do not receive any instruction, and most of whom are a burden on society. For experience has demonstrated that, with few exceptions, a blind person left to himself is scarcely in a position to gain a living. In England, however, institutions for the blind are more numerous and better organised than in most other countries. There, too, those institutions have been established earlier than anywhere else, excepting France, which has the honour of having erected the first establishment of the kind ; but that at Liverpool is almost contemporary with it.

It was in 1791 that a humble citizen—Pudsey Dawson, Esq., who died in 1816—founded, with the aid of subscribers, a school for the instruction of the blind poor in manual labour, church music and organ playing. The establishment has hitherto been liberally supported by subscriptions, donations, and legacies ; and, as time went on, has gained such importance, owing to the number of its pupils, that it is sincerely to be regretted its directors have not raised it to the high standard of progress attained by the other institutions for the blind everywhere in England. It seems that some persons attached to the school know that a system of printing in relief has been invented for the use of the blind, and that they may be taught to read and write ; but hitherto the intellectual instruction of the pupils has not been deemed of importance ; they only learn some trade.

The principal employments are :—

	£	s.	d.
Rope-making : the sale of ropes in 1836 amounted to	754	11	10½
Basket-making gives work to a great number of hands: the home sold in 1836 baskets producing the sum of	368	18	8
Ordinary rope-matting, mats made of old tarred rope : rough rope mats and carpets were made and sold in 1836 for the sum of	502	11	10
There are also shoemakers there ; the girls knit slippers and some of them sew : the total sales of the year 1836 amounted to	1818	18	0¾

The machines there are very good. Masters who can see are regularly employed to teach these various trades. Notwithstanding the large output, the establishment does not profit by its productions. As I have already stated, the pupils leave the home at the moment they begin to be able to make themselves useful, and the masters' wages absorb the rest.

The staff of the establishment consists of the following officials :—

	£	s.	d.
Superintendent and his wife . . .	283	10	0
Supervisor of the wardrobe . . .	21	0	0
Master weaver	70	5	0
„ rope-maker	58	5	0
„ basket-maker	70	5	0 ·
„ shoe-maker	70	5	0
„ of music	90	10	0
„ „ singing	70	0	0
Domestic servants	59	6	7
Collector of subscriptions . . .	20	5	10
Chaplain	500	0	0
Total . . .	1313	12	5

The number of pupils received into this institution since its foundation until 1836 is 984, and there were 108 there on the 1st January, 1837. In 1836, 31 new pupils were admitted, and 28 quitted the establishment. Of these 11 were basket-makers, 4 shoe-makers, 2 rope-makers, 2 seamstresses, and 2 mat-makers. On leaving 3 received four guineas, and 4 three guineas. Of this number 9 worked well, 6 had only succeeded tolerably, 8 others had made no progress, and the rest very little. The blind there are classified as totally blind and partially blind, so much so, however, that what sight they have is of no practical use to them.

Statistics compiled at Liverpool.	Totally.	Partially.	Total.
Blind from birth	50	28	78
„ „ small-pox	170	42	212
„ „ inflammation of the eyes .	188	120	308
„ „ cataract	37	78	115
„ „ exterior causes . . .	56	28	84
„ „ a defect in the optic nerve .	63	46	109
„ „ an imperfect organisation .	3	9	12
Have lost their sight at sea	8	1	9
„ „ gradually . . .	4	0	4
„ „ in consequence of fevers . . .	9	2	11
„ „ from meales . .	5	3	8
„ „ „ hooping-cough	1	0	1
„ „ „ convulsions .	2	3	5
As the result of unknown or imperfectly described causes.	15	13	28
* Totals	611	373	984

The income of this home is rather large :—

	£	s.	d.
Parishes or friends of pupils paid for their maintenance in 1836	516	13	4
Various debtors have paid	37	13	8
Productions of the home sold for . . .	1767	18	11
Various legacies have realised	1032	10	0
Donations and subscriptions	1184	6	0
Interest of sums invested	81	11	2

* Below are corresponding statistics for Glasgow until 1837:—

STATISTICS COMPILED AT GLASGOW UP TO 1837.

Blind from birth	12
„ „ inflammation of the eyes	27
„ „ small-pox	17
„ „ amaurosis	6
„ „ cataract	5
„ „ accident	11
From scarlatina, typhoid and nervous fever	3
„ the obscuration of the transparent cornea, from measles	2
„ unknown causes.	14
Total.	97

		£	s.	d.
Received for clothes supplied to pupils.	.	249	0	6
Received for the sale of hymn books	. .	9	16	0
Found in (alms) boxes		55	12	3
In the Treasurer's hands since last Report		65	1	1
ditto this year	. .	613	18	5
Profits of the Chapel, with last year's bonus		2334	0	4

Total Revenues of the Home . £7948 1 8
or nearly 200,000 francs ; and the expenses for this same year
amounted to £5232 3s. 10d.—that is, at the most 130,000 francs.

The buildings are situated in one of the most beautiful parts
of the town, and have been constructed for the purpose they were
intended to serve. They are roomy and well ventilated.

The second establishment constructed for the blind was the
one at Edinburgh. The celebrated Dr. Blacklock, who long resided in that city, had often wished to erect an institution for
the education of persons who, like himself, had been deprived
of sight.

He imparted this idea to his friend Mr. David Miller, a teacher
in Edinburgh, and who had been blind from his birth. Mr.
Miller was a striking example of the influence which a judicious
education may exercise if early begun. After Dr. Blacklock's
death Mr. Miller consulted with the Rev. Dr. David Johnston, of
North Leith, whose actively benevolent character he had the
opportunity of appreciating. The worthy Dr. Johnston speedily
resolved to realise his friend's philanthropic idea. The project
was then brought before the public with a view to enlist its
interest in the undertaking. Mr. Miller also wrote to M. Haüy
for information, and received a very polite letter from him, together
with a copy of his " Essay on the Education of the Blind."

Immediately afterwards a meeting of some friends was held
under the auspices of Sir William Forbes, Bart., and it was
resolved to erect an asylum so soon as funds would permit, and
on the 20th December, 1792, they amounted to nearly £700.
They met again, and Mr. Johnston was appointed secretary. The

home was opened on the 23rd September, 1793, and nine blind persons were admitted.

Mr. Miller continued to attend to the blind, and rendered great assistance to the budding institution. He applied himself specially to teaching the girls various manual occupations ; but he did not live to see the separate establishment for girls, which the present secretary, Mr. Robert Johnston, has founded.

Dr. Henry Moyes, a blind man and a professor, gave at that time lessons in philosophy and natural history, and announced a public meeting in behalf of the blind, which attracted a crowd of the most prominent inhabitants of the city. This considerably increased the funds already at the disposal of the governing body, and permitted the purchase of premises in 1806. Another building in the same street was bought in 1822.

The chief object of the founders of the institution was to teach the blind a trade, so that they might, if possible, maintain themselves by their own industry.

At first the house was an asylum, and those who gave fifteen pounds sterling on entering had a right to all the advantages and privileges of the establishment for life ; but insufficient funds not permitting the continued admittance of new pupils, the original scheme had to be modified. Under what is termed the new system, there was added to the asylum a school for young blind persons, who only remained for a fixed term of years, whose board is defrayed by their parishes or friends. After three years' apprenticeship these pupils receive all that they earn, which, while diminishing the burden on their benefactors, is a great encouragement to these unfortunates themselves, and creates in them the wish to make themselves completely independent by their labour.

Dr. Johnston, who chiefly directed the asylum until his death, and the other members of the council, carefully supervised the industrial education of the pupils. They in no wise neglected their moral and intellectual instruction. Ever since the home was opened religious instruction had constantly occupied the directors' attention, and was the object of all their solicitude.

During the year 1820 the scheme of education began to be extended to other branches of useful knowledge. It is especially to the exertions of Mr. Robert Johnston, the present secretary, that the institution owes the brilliant position it now occupies. Since the death of his uncle, Dr. Johnston, he has never ceased to watch over the interests of the blind pupils with an indefatigable zeal, contriving whatever could enlighten their intellect and increase their happiness. Therefore he looks upon them as his children rather than as persons dependent on public charity.

A house had been founded separately at Sciennes (?) for lodging and boarding young blind persons ; but pecuniary considerations forced the governing body to abandon it in 1832. However at the time of my visit to this establishment the project had been once more adopted, and preparations for the admission of 16 pupils were already far advanced. It should be remarked, in order to understand the preceding statements, that the blind are not lodged in the asylum. Most of them reside in the vicinity of the establishment ; a great number are married and have families, and the benefits of the asylum are thus extended to more than 250 persons, women and children.

In the month of October the blind are accustomed to purchase their supplies of potatoes and coals for the whole winter. It is the blind themselves who bargain for these purchases, and do so with all the prudence of those who can see. When the bargain is concluded, it is referred to the secretary, who guarantees payment. This arrangement insures their getting the best articles at the lowest prices. Then every one applies for what his household needs out of the total quantity thus purchased. From the month of October the blind pay weekly to a treasurer, whom they have chosen from amongst themselves, the small sum of sixpence or a shilling, according to what they have received. These small sums are deposited in a savings bank until they amount to ten pounds sterling, when the treasurer pays them into the hands of the secretary, who gives him a receipt. This is, as we see, to imbue them with habits of forethought, and to form their minds by caring for their bodies. Nothing should be neglected in the education of the blind which may assist in giving them ideas of order. For instance, the day for paying wages has been changed, and wages have for some years been paid only on Monday evening, and the change has prevented several abuses.

The hours of labour for the blind from the 15th March till the 15th October begin at 6 o'clock in the morning ; during the other months of the year they begin at 8 o'clock. A time of not more than half an hour is allowed for prayer every morning and evening. On Saturday afternoons and Monday mornings religious instruction is given. All the blind are obliged to be present at these exercises, and absence without sufficient cause, or improper behaviour during this time, if not amended, involves dismissal. They are allowed one hour for going to breakfast and one hour for going to dinner ; in winter they have to bring their breakfast instead of going to their abode for it.

Any one coming too late undergoes a punishment proportioned to the time and to the number of repetitions of the offence. If any one be idle or pass his time in talking, if he spoil or destroy his materials, his wages are reduced, and if he do not amend he is expelled.

Their moral conduct is carefully looked after, and faults are severely reprimanded or punished by expulsion. Those who are ill, if they obtain a doctor's certificate, continue to receive their ordinary wages the first week—that is, if their illness be not caused by their own fault ; but if their illness continue, they receive only half their usual wages unless the secretary decide otherwise. The blind employed at the asylum are not allowed to work at the same trade at home. On this point the management insists ; and it is necessary to prevent the theft of primary materials.

Without claiming the right of preventing those from marrying who have that intention, the directors insist on the blind consulting them before entering into that state, and they are always ready to give the best advice in a matter of such importance. The blind are enjoined to be at their homes after nine o'clock at night, and the least appearance of drunkenness is severely punished. The directors recompense those who at the year's end have the largest amount in the savings-bank, and every one is obliged to have a small sum at least there. The selection of the dwellings for those pupils who are not married is made by the directors.

These rules are read to the blind four times yearly, so that no one can plead ignorance of them.

What I have said refers principally to the men's establishment. Some observations on the girls' establishment will be of interest. They are trained on the same liberal principles as the men. All the girls are lodged in the house, excepting two or three, whose parents reside in the city.

The moral and intellectual condition of the girls is nearly the same as that of the men. When conversing, they are gay and happy, and polite and obedient to each other. They pass the hours of recreation in converse, or in initiating one another into some of those acquirements which so powerfully contribute to elevate the mind and to develop the understanding. Several of the girls execute with taste the most complicated pieces of music.

The business of the asylum is directed by a committee chosen by the patrons and subscribers, and which consists of a chairman, four residents, a treasurer, a secretary, four auditors, two clerks, an accountant, and twelve ordinary directors. But the soul of the whole institution is the secretary, the worthy Mr. Johnston. It is to him I owe most of the notions I have acquired of the economy of an asylum, and I am happy to be able to express here all my gratitude to him.

Another institution was established in 1793 at Bristol, under the title " Bristol Asylum, or Industrial School for the Blind." Its object is not to employ the blind after being educated, but to teach them the means of getting a living by work. This establishment is also due to public charity, so powerful in England, and its beneficent influence has been extended since its foundation to more than two hundred unfortunate creatures. Blind persons from all the counties of England are received there.

In consequence of the receipt of two legacies in 1829 and 1830, it was resolved to build a new home. The land was bought for £1850 sterling, and a magnificent Gothic building was erected there for the accommodation of 70 boarders, with work-rooms for 100 persons. This edifice cost no less than £10,000 sterling, or more than 400,000 francs.

The number of pupils has of necessity been limited for want of room ; but there is every hope that the number will be increased. The subjoined table shows the position of this home in different years.

Years.	No. of Pupils	Income.			Sales.			Expenses of Management and Maintenance.			Observations.
		£	s.	d.	£	s.	d.	£	s.	d.	
1797	..	513	6	7½	154	6	7	387	15	11	
1802	..	1266	19	9	438	19	6	611	19	7	
1808	..	2526	3	4	1044	2	10	1998	16	8	
1810	..	2472	0	4	1088	11	11	2145	3	10	
1811	..	2662	13	8	1039	7	3	1917	14	8	
1812	..	2408	14	4	948	14	7	2085	12	8	
1821	20	2168	17	2	904	6	5	1730	10	10	
1822	21	2383	12	1	765	4	9	1594	6	11	
1823	23	2091	9	8	762	9	10	1806	19	6	Disbursements for
1824	22	2187	8	4	924	1	3	1763	14	0	the new building
1826	25	2006	17	2	975	19	2	1782	15	4	during the years
1827	28	1961	3	7	999	0	5	1899	8	3	1834 to 1836.
1833	33	11772	14	2	906	12	6	1977	6	10	Years. £ s. d.
1834	39	10525	3	3	992	11	2	1841	14	7	1834..1999 3 6
1835	40	10164	14	4	1019	7	3	2202	8	0	1835..5205 0 5
1836	43	9041	7	4	1138	1	8	1971	13	10	1836..6662 1 2

The parishes or private individuals who place blind persons in the asylum pay three shillings per week for the boys, and two shillings a week for the girls, and supply their clothes ; but after five years' apprenticeship they are entitled to all they earn. The asylum places the boys out to board with respectable families in the neighbourhood, and pays nine shillings per week for their food. Pupils under nine and above thirty years of age are not received. The ordinary course of education is seven years, but a great number leave the institution before the completion of this term. The teaching of reading by means of relief type on the Glasgow system has been introduced. Music is taught there ; many pupils learn to play the organ, and all are practised twice a week in sacred singing. Basket-making is the principal occupation of the pupils, and the productions of the establishment in this work surpass everything of the kind I have ever seen made by the blind.

The School for the Indigent Blind at London was founded in 1799 by Messrs. Ware, Bosanquet, Boddington, and Houlston. The object proposed was to teach the pupils a trade, so that they might gain a subsistence wholly or in part. In 1800 there were only fifteen pupils, and the Institution attracted very little public attention. But liberal subscriptions and legacies for more than a million and a half of francs (say £60,000) permitted an extension of the beneficent objects of the home. At present there are 122 blind in the Institution, sixty of whom are men and sixty-two women, and it is expected that the number may gradually be increased to one hundred of each sex. Pupils under twelve and over thirty years of age are not admitted, and those from twelve to eighteen years are preferred. During the time of their being educated, the pupils are lodged, fed, and clothed in the home. They are kept there until they have acquired sufficient skill at a handicraft, which is generally from four to five years, but necessarily depends on the capacity of the pupil. Then they leave the establishment with a portion of their wages, and a complete assortment of the instruments necessary for the trade they have learnt. Since its foundation, 252 blind have been admitted there, and several have left the home very thankful for the instruction they have received, and able to contribute a notable part towards their keep. Some of them who could gain a livelihood by their work have been retained in the home to assist in its business ; and, in consequence of a magnificent legacy of 250,000 francs (say £10,000), left by Mr. Tillard, some others who would not have been able to get a living are fed and lodged for an indefinite time, and are called the Tillard class ; so that this institution begins to partake by degrees of the nature of an asylum.

We owe to the institution at London an excellent idea, and one which will evidently diminish the inconveniences of the schools.

The pupils who have left this establishment are permitted to send there what they produce, and they are paid according to a tariff. Already in 1832 goods to the value of £237 had been received, and in 1836 to the value of £378 14s. 9d. ; and it may be safely predicted that these purchases will continue to increase from year to year.

A splendid building is just now being erected for this school. At the time of my visit it was nearly finished. It is also one of the richest foundations in England. It has a revenue of no less than 300,000 fr. (say £12,000) per annum, and funded property to the amount of one million and a half francs (say £60,000). Various trades are taught there. I shall speak more in detail of them in the next chapter, but some appear to me better calculated to show what a blind person can succeed in doing by sheer patience and care than to give them the means of providing for their necessities by work. There are several blind shoemakers in the home.

The sales in general amounted during 1832 to £1345, and in 1836 to £1469 14s. 1d., and the ordinary expenses to £5,568 4s. 8d.

Some of the blind learn vocal music, and some of the girls sing very well. One amongst them entrances you with her singing so long as you do not look at her ; but the impression is lost when you perceive that this lovely voice comes from so ugly a face. Music is taught as a profession to be utilised, and it is hoped to train organists there.

All the instruction is confined to reading, and the books used are those printed at Glasgow ; the pupils, however, prefer those printed at Edinburgh. But so little importance is attached to the teaching of reading that there are scarcely two pupils who read satisfactorily.

The blind belonging to the higher classes of society have often been the first benefactors of their poorer companions in misfortune. In this way the school at Norwich was started. Mr. Tawell, himself a blind man, first called the attention of his fellow-citizens to this class, still abandoned to a state of idleness.

He therefore proposed to give a large house with a garden of three acres, provided means could be found to organise it. A meeting of citizens was held on the 17th January, 1805, and it was stated that a sum of £1000 would be required to cover the expenses of its first establishment, and a further sum of £700 yearly to maintain it, and this was obtained from public liberality. The house is a school for the young blind, and a hospital for the aged. The latter must have attained their fifty-fifth year before they can be received. The former are not admitted under twelve years of age. For some time they were admitted from the age of ten, but this has been altered to the age originally fixed. Ordinary poor persons pay nothing for their admission, and stay in the establishment ; but if the blind are chargeable to their parishes, three shillings per week is charged. The young are retained until they have learned a trade ; but never longer than three years. The establishment was originally intended only for the blind of the city of Norwich ; but afterwards all those of the county of Norfolk were admitted ; and, in 1819, it was opened to the blind of the whole kingdom in order to be able to accept the donation of five hundred guineas which Mr. Henshaw, of Oldham, offered on that condition. The directors publish reports every year in the city newspapers, but they very rarely print them separately, so that it is difficult to obtain correct ideas as to its condition and progress. According to a report published in 1833, the house has admitted since its opening 153 young and 48 old blind persons. Of this number 77 have left the school in order to work on their own account ; 12 could not be taught ; 4 left the house without permission ; 13 have been expelled for irregularity in their conduct, and 16 have left voluntarily ; 45 died, and 36 still remained in the establishment in 1833.

In 1837 there were 50 pupils in the Norwich Institution for the Blind ; 35 young and 15 old. The aged blind are not obliged to work, for they are looked upon as being in a hospital ; which, it seems to me, must very much contribute to make their life a hard one.

The expenses of the house from its beginning have nearly always balanced the income. They were in round numbers :—

In	1805	1806	1807	1808	1809	1810	1811
£	1767	1843	869	1135	730	1483	1406

In	1812	1813	1814	1815	1816	1817	1818
£	1259	1189	998	967	1217	1251	928

In 1818 articles made by the thirty-three pupils the house then contained were sold for £230 11s. 1d., and these were not sold dearer here than anywhere else. The principal occupation both of the boys and of the girls is basket-making. Besides this, the girls knit and do other trifling work. The wages are from two shillings and sixpence to five shillings per week. Compared with what is paid in other institutions, this salary would appear low ; but the report of 1819 states that labour is less remunerated at Norwich than in other towns of the kingdom, that materials are dearer there, and the price of productions lower. The pupils are taught psalmody ; they sing in parts, and many of the blind play musical instruments and practise every evening. Books printed at Glasgow were introduced in 1837 : a dozen pupils then applied themselves to reading. Intellectual education was little cared for ; but the present governing body seems actuated by good sense, and it is to be hoped that in a little while other improvements may be introduced. The Norwich home (*asyle*) is the only one in England I did not visit on the journey I made in 1837 to study this branch of teaching ; but the information with which the superintendent of the home has kindly favoured me has enabled me to publish this note on the institution, which is the only one formed on this plan in England.

The home (*asyle*) at Glasgow also owes its origin to the beneficence of a rich man who had become blind. The late Mr. John Leitch, a Glasgow merchant, left £5000 to found an Institute for the Blind, which was to be annexed to the Royal Infirmary; but it was considered that the benevolent intention of the donor would be more fully realised by establishing it separately. Parliament granted the necessary authorisation, and the superb building, which at present serves as a school for the youthful blind and as an asylum for the aged, was erected on a beautiful site. At first this institution did not receive general approval, and was for some time even an object of satire and ridicule. Happily Mr. Alston, the treasurer and father of this asylum, had the courage to despise these attacks, and raised the home to such a degree of prosperity that the most envious were forced to applaud.

On the 1st January, 1838, the house contained sixty-four blind. Children are received from the age of ten to sixteen. After school hours they are shown how to make nets for covering fruit trees, to sew sacks, and such other easy work as seems to suit them, until their education is finished and they have acquired such efficiency as to begin an apprenticeship to some special craft. The period is three years. £6 6s. is paid yearly for boarding the young blind. Clothes must be supplied by their relatives. Whoever gives, either himself or conjointly with others, the sum of £50, will have the privilege of placing two children in the asylum on paying only £3 3s. for each, or can have one admitted without payment. Corporations and parishes can have the same privilege on paying the sum of £100.

Blind girls above eighteen years of age are admitted into the establishment as daily boarders. They come at ten o'clock and remain until after evening prayers. They dine in the asylum and receive their wages weekly. The rate of wages varies. Those who wind worsted receive one shilling and fivepence per week. Twopence-halfpenny per spindleful is given to those who wind the yarn for weaving sacks.

Every blind person capable of work and residing in Glasgow or the neighbourhood, either in his own abode or with his friends, can be admitted into the asylum.

Those who, on admittance, do not know any of the trades

followed in the home have the alternative of paying two to five shillings for their apprenticeship, or of working for three months without receiving any salary.

At first only three shillings and sixpence are allowed as recompense for the work done by the blind, and this wage is increased according to what they produce until their apprenticeship is finished. Then a fixed sum is allowed them every week, but a certain quantity of work must be produced, which is carefully marked. At the end of each month a return is made of what they have produced, and if they have worked more than is required of them, the overplus is paid to them ; and, as a recompense for their industry, an extra shilling per week above their ordinary and extraordinary salary is given them. But if they have not finished their task, nor produced the quantity of work required, or if it be badly done, they keep the salary received every week, but are refused the shilling given to the others as an encouragement.

We can easily imagine the result of this measure and the influence it must exercise. A very marked improvement in the quality and the quantity of the work produced has been immediately shown. This is what the adults are able to earn in the Glasgow Asylum.

					s.	*d.*
Basket makers, per week	.	.	.		11	0
Rope makers	,,	.	.	.	8	0
Weavers	,,	.	.	.	8	0
Mat makers	,,	.	.	.	11	0
Mattress makers	,,	.	.	.	9	0

In 1835 the extraordinary salary and the recompenses granted each week amounted to £68 15s. 2d.

A kind of savings-bank and mutual guarantee society has been founded by the exertions of the treasurer. Every man on receiving extraordinary wages and recompenses pays in one shilling and every woman sixpence. The sum produced by these monthly receipts, increased by ten pounds produced by the sale of a pamphlet published by Mr. Alston, is lodged in the bank, and remains there in reserve until an accident happens which gives the right of being compensated or aided by the common fund. However, the treasurer alone has the right of drawing upon it.

Every week, too, the blind also deposit a small sum to pay the rent of their house.

The benefit of this happy system of economy in the Asylum is extended outside the house to a large number of persons who have their sight. In 1836 one hundred and twenty persons profited by it; and in this way the blind, while gaining for themselves an honourable position in society, have the additional happiness of being able to think that they are making others happy.

Contrary to the custom in all other institutions, this asylum does not solicit annual subscriptions, but it is supported by its income, by legacies and donations. All that is demanded of public favour is the purchase of the articles made there, and the prices of which are not higher than those charged by other dealers. In this way (the directors say in their report for 1838) "our fellow-citizens may favour this establishment without making the slightest sacrifice."

The institution at York was opened on the 6th October, 1835, and owes its origin to one of the noblest conceptions that has ever been realised to honour the memory of a fellow-citizen.

William Wilberforce had represented the county of York during six successive Parliaments, a period of twenty-eight years, and had devoted himself to his country until the day of his death. A meeting of the most prominent men of the county was held on the 3rd October, 1833, to devise the means of worthily honouring his memory, and the following resolutions were adopted :—That Mr. Wilberforce had merited the veneration of his constituents : that a monument be erected to hand down to posterity the remembrance of a character so worthy of imitation by those engaged in public life. But, while the meeting approved the erection of a column at Hull, his native town, it was of opinion that it was expedient to erect a monument in which all the districts of this great county might take an interest, and that the nature of this monument should depend on the amount of the subscriptions which might be received.

At a subsequent meeting it was ascertained that public opinion was in favour of a school for the instruction of the indigent blind and for the training of them to habits of industry; and from the 10th February, 1834, the central committee announced that the subscriptions responded to the promises made, and the construction was decided on. The house has, from the beginning, taken first rank in this kind of institutions owing to the care and zeal of R. W. Taylor, who was appointed its superintendent. Mr. Taylor is a famous mathematician, a member of the Royal Society of London, and honorary member of the Society of Arts of Edinburgh, &c. Since 1820 he had already undertaken the education of a rich blind man, and had since printed in Paris type small books for his pupil's use. Subsequently, when the Edinburgh Society of Arts received most important communications in answer to the question, What is the best alphabet for the use of the blind? Mr. Taylor, whose knowledge was already highly appreciated, was chosen to give his opinion, which he did in a most interesting report. This was approved of and published by the Society. In 1837 the British Association for the Advancement of Science again selected him for the same subject. I speak of it more at length in the fifth chapter. Mr. Taylor is not a savant only, but he is also one of the most ingenious men I ever met. This is proved by the machines which he has invented or perfected for the use of the blind. In May, 1838, the home under his direction contained twenty-nine blind, thirteen of whom were girls. Pupils are admitted from the age of ten to sixteen years. At a meeting of the directors of the home, held in March 1838, it was decided to admit children from the age of nine years. Here, as in almost all other institutions of this kind, education and lodging are gratuitous; but remuneration is demanded for board and clothes, &c. At first the board was four shillings per week, which was afterwards altered to three shillings and sixpence. Music is taught to those having a taste for it and on paying an increased rate for board, unless the pupil be poor and have a very decided liking for the art. All the pupils learn arithmetic, reading, geography, &c. The trades are those which have been introduced elsewhere. One of the pupils at the end of an apprenticeship of eighteen months was in a position to earn eleven shillings per week as a basket-maker. The sales from the commencement of the institution until March 1837, amounted to £48 10s. 1d. The income, including donations and subscriptions, amounted to £9002 2s., and the expenditure to £3209 16s. 6d. I publish at the end of this account the general regulations of this institution.

Another institution was opened in May 1838, at Manchester. Mr. Thomas Henshaw left a legacy of £20,000 in 1810 exclusively for the maintenance of an asylum for the blind, and on condition the land should be bought and the house built by others. The inhabitants of Manchester subscribed nearly £10,000, and in 1837 I saw the building, which was almost finished. It is situated next to the Deaf and Dumb Institution. The chapel separates the two establishments and connects them so as to make one grand and splendid structure in the Gothic style, of which the English are at present so fond.

In 1837 Mr. David H. Wilson published in a Newcastle paper an interesting letter, wherein he showed the possibility and the necessity of founding an asylum for the unfortunate blind. His voice has found an echo, and an establishment has been opened there this year.

A large sum has been left for the erection of a charitable institution for the blind at Aberdeen, and Mr. Alston in one of his publications accuses the curators, and with reason, of negligence for delaying to comply with the wishes of the donor. A lady left, in 1837, a sum of £5,000 to establish a similar house at Dundee. But the largest legacy ever left for such an institution is that of the late Mr. Day, of London, who bequeathed £100,000 (or more than two millions and a half of francs) for the foundation of an educational home for the blind, which will be situated in the capital. There is another small school for the instruction of the blind in London, but the number of pupils is not large. I have not seen it.

In 1835 the late Mrs. Walker formed a school for giving a preliminary education to blind children destined to enter an asylum, and to show how easy it is to establish this sort of house even in the smallest towns. The ordinary number of pupils is eight; sixteen have already received their education there. Children pay three shillings per quarter. The mistress is blind. The expenses of the house are defrayed by Mr. Walker's son and some subscriptions. Reading, writing, arithmetic, and geography are taught there. The children learn to read in a few days; several have been able to leave the school after a few weeks' instruction, being capable of reading with facility.

In August 1837, Mrs. Greig published the prospectus of an institute she intends erecting at Edinburgh for the education of blind children belonging to the upper classes of society. Mrs. Greig herself has a blind child. She has visited nearly all the blind institutions of Great Britain, France, and America, and will adopt the best methods. The first professors of Edinburgh will assist in teaching the various branches of education.

The pupils will learn reading, writing, grammar, arithmetic, bookkeeping, algebra, geometry, geography, history, philosophy, languages, and music, according to their age and capacity.

About the year 1830, Mr. Thomas Lucas opened a small school for the young blind, where he taught reading by his stenographic system of relief-printing, which I mention in the fifth chapter. The class is not large, and the success is ordinary. One of the pupils, after a year's practice, could only with difficulty read one line which I gave him in St. John's Gospel, published by Mr. Lucas, and only succeeded after making frequent mistakes.

Such is the present state of the establishments for the blind in England and Scotland. The incomes of several of these institutions are immense, and the expenses very heavy.

I have calculated what a pupil costs yearly in most of these institutions, and have found that, without computing the primary materials which he uses in his trade, but including the wages which he receives, and all the expenses of housekeeping, supervision, &c., a blind pupil

					£	s.	d.
in 1835 cost at Glasgow	about	fr. 725	.	29	0	0
„ 1834 „ „ Edinburgh	„	fr. 733	.	29	6	5
„ 1836 „ „ London	„	fr. 1000	.	40	0	0
„ 1836 „ „ Liverpool	„	fr. 1105	.	44	0	0½
„ 1836 „ „ Bristol	„	fr. 1138	.	45	10	5
„ 1836 „ „ York	„	fr. 1512	.	60	9	7

I should mention, with regard to this last institution, that the expenses have necessarily been heavier than anywhere else, because of its recent commencement and the small number of pupils. The wise organisation and the talent of the superintendent lead us to hope with good reason that in a short time it will take the lead of the blind establishments in England.

It will be noticed that the economy with which the institutions of Scotland are conducted compared with that of England proves once more the advantage of the asylums over the schools.

However, whatever they may be, whether schools or asylums, the institutions for the blind in England deserve to be taken as a model for establishments to be formed in other countries, and their origin as well as their management do much honour to the country. An inexhaustible philanthropy and lavish subscriptions have permitted of palaces being built for these institutions. But people have had the good feeling not to make lords of this class of unfortunate beings, excepting as regards personal cleanliness, for which the greatest care is taken, and which is not usual in the class to which they belong. The rank of all is shown by their appearance. Their work is unremitting and well regulated; their clothes are very common and their food wholesome and plentiful, but such as they would always be able to get if their education were successful, and if they should not depart from those orderly and economical habits with which it is continually sought to inspire them.

The blind are very subject to depression and consequently prone to presumption. At some blind institutions there are notices requesting the visitors to abstain from all useless expressions of astonishment at what they see, and of pity for that great number of beings deprived of sight in whose presence they find themselves.

INSTITUTIONS FOR THE BLIND OPEN OR ON THE POINT OF BEING OPENED.

Names of Towns.	Date of their Foundation.	By whom founded.	Nature of the Institution.	Number of Pupils in 1837.	Age of Admission.	Duration of Course of Instruction.	Branches of Education taught.	Amount charged for Board.	Lodged in the house or not.	Years.	Amount of Sales during the	Income of the Establishment.
											£ s. d.	£ s. d.
Liverpool	1791	Mr. Pudsey Dawson and Mr.	Industrial School	208	12 years of age	Not fixed	Music	Not fixed	Lodged	1836	1818 18 0	5601 14 0½
Edinburgh	1793	Mr. Pavil Johnston and Mr. Miller	School and Home (*Asyle*)	81	Not fixed	,,	Music, Reading, Arithmetic, Geography	3s. 6d. per week	Infants and Girls lodged	1834	2758 4 1	3165 2 1
Bristol	1793	Mr. David Johnston and Mr. Miller	Industrial School	48	From 9 to 30	7 years	Music, Reading	3s. Boys; 2s. Girls	Girls lodged	1836	1138 1 8	See p. 39.
London	1799	Messrs. Ware, Boisanquet, Waddington & Houlston	School	122	12 to 30	4 to 5 years	,,	Not fixed	Lodged	1836	1469 14 1	11,968 1 6¼
Norwich	1805	Mr. Tawell gave the house and garden	School, Hospital	50	Young, 12.	3 years	,,	3s. per week	,,	1819	230 11 1	1439 4 3
Glasgow	1828	Mr. Leitch bequeathed £3000	School, Home (*Asyle*)	64	Aged, 55 10 to 16. Men any age	,,	Music, Reading, Geography, Arithmetic, Astronomy	£6 6s. per ann.	Infants are lodged	1837	2472 1 0	989 16 4
York	1835	In memory of Mr. Wilberforce	School	29	From 9 to 16	Not fixed	Reading, Writing, Music, Geography, Algebra	3s. 6d. per week	Lodged	1836	48 10 1	9002 2 0
Manchester	1838	Mr. Thos. Henshaw left a legacy of £20,000	Home (*Asyle*)	29	,,	,,	,,	,,	,,			
Newcastle	,,	A large sum has been left for a Home (*Asyle*)	,,	29	,,	,,	,,	,,	,,			
Aberdeen	,,		,,	29	,,	,,	,,	,,	,,			
Dundee	,,	A lady left a sum of £5,000	,,	—	,,	,,	,,	,,	,,			
London	1835	Mr. Day left £100,000	,,	8	From the most tender age	,,	Reading, Writing, Arithmetic, and Geography	3s. ½ per quarter	Not lodged			
Edinburgh		Mrs. Walker	Preparatory School	8	From the most tender age	,,	Reading, Writing, Grammar, Arithmetic, Book-keeping, Algebra, Geometry, Geography, History, Languages, Music	From 50 to 100 guineas yearly	Lodged			
Edinburgh	1837	Mrs. Greig	School for the rich class	8								
Bristol	1830	Mr. Thomas M. Lucas	Reading School	5	Very young	—	Reading and Writing.	—	Not lodged			

There is also a small Industrial School for the Blind in London, which I have not seen

CHAPTER III.

OF INDUSTRIAL EDUCATION.

WE ought to expect less from a blind person than from one who possesses all his senses; but owing to an injurious and widely spread prejudice, we exact more. Interest is diminished so soon as we find them only in the same rank with those who can see. They ought, it seems, to surpass the latter; just as if blindness were an advantage. Most of the institutions have come more or less under the fatal influence of these demands of the public. For, in order to satisfy them, one is bound to make some of the blind pupils do something extraordinary; and, while trying to show to what a degree of skill a small number may attain, the mass are neglected. The desire was to excite the visitors' surprise and admiration, and these attempts almost always succeeded, either owing to the patience of the masters or the special aptitude of the pupils. The real value of such displays is of little importance. It was desired to astonish, and astonishment has been produced, and that is the only fruit obtained. But we ought not to content ourselves with that. It is far less a question of knowing what some blind pupil favoured by his master and by nature can succeed in doing, as of knowing what we ought to teach him in order that he may employ his time most usefully.

On the choice of trades the future of the institution and the happiness of the pupils depend, and this choice itself depends in a great measure on the nature of the establishment which we form for the blind.

Let us recall the classification I have made of the institutions into schools where the blind are received for a time, but which they leave after their apprenticeship; and asylums or homes (*asyles*), where the blind after having learnt a trade work together as long as they wish.

It is self-evident that a school can hardly introduce into its course of trades those which demand a large capital or expensive machinery, nor those requiring the co-operation of several persons. Destined to work alone after leaving school, the blind cannot and ought not to learn any trade which cannot be carried on by one person with little capital and simple machinery. This is not the case in an asylum, where sufficient capital and the presence of a certain number of blind who are well taught and trained by long use allow the manufacture of objects needing the employment of several persons and the supervision of some one who can see. There is another consideration which should influence the choice. It is not enough to find out what we can produce ; we must see if we are able to sell it. It is necessary to study localities and the markets they offer.

As the asylum at Edinburgh was the first into which a complete and really useful system was introduced, I shall begin the account of the condition of the industry of the blind with that institution.

Nearly one-third of the pupils there are employed in making mattresses of all sorts—of horse-hair, of wool, of a kind of sea-weed (*Zostera marina*), and straw.

The horse-hair undergoes at the hands of the blind all the preparation needed before being used. It is bought as it is taken from the horse. The fine and the white hairs are put on one side by workers who have their sight in order to be spun and woven or knitted into gloves for friction. But the blind card it before winding it. It is then boiled so as to extract all foreign bodies, and it is dried in an oven and used for filling mattresses.

Several of these manipulations require little skill or intelligence. The aged blind may be employed at it from the time of their admission and earn a modest salary. The making of these mattresses renders the introduction of weaving possible as a practical resource for the blind. The produce is used in the house, and thus the highest price is obtained. The quantity of wool woven annually in the Edinburgh asylum is from 1250 to

1550 yards, and the blind earn at that from five to seven shillings per week.

The manufacture of mattresses also gives useful occupation to the girls, for they sew the cases. The blind are able to sew : experience proves that, but only the commonest work. It is profitable at Edinburgh, but would not be so except for the mattress making.

This branch of industry is the principal and most lucrative in the asylum, and ranks very high in public opinion ; for all the materials used are of the best quality, and nothing is sold under current prices.

The woollen, seaweed, and straw mattresses are not quite the best things the blind can make, but they sell. The horse-hair mattresses, however, sell the best. Again, it is to facilitate the sale that they make feather beds at Edinburgh. In their manufacture only workers who can see are employed. The directors would gladly relinquish several of these manufactures, but the utility, the requirements of their trade demand keeping them on. For we must sell in order to manufacture, and we must complete an article and be in a position to supply everything belonging to it in order to sell it.

It is impossible to calculate precisely what this labour brings in to each of the blind ; but we are assured that they earn from twelve to sixteen shillings weekly.

The sale of mattresses at Edinburgh during the year 1836 is as follows :—

	£	s.	d.
Horse-hair mattresses . . .	736	3	0
Palliasses	147	11	5
Woollen mattresses . . .	59	9	7
Cotton mattresses . . .	52	6	2
Seaweed mattresses . . .	37	12	6
Feather beds	289	6	5
Total . .	£1,322	9	1

In 1837 only two workmen were employed at Glasgow, and the sales produced £153 5s.

One industry completely suited to the Glasgow asylum is sack-making. A peculiar kind of canvas is woven in the house by the pupils. The girls sew the sacks, and the least skilful amongst the blind print on them the names of the buyers. This manufacture was only begun in 1832, and subjoined will be seen what progress has been made in so short a time. The sales have amounted to as under :—

1832	1833	1834	1835	1836	1837
£ s. d. 77 5 3	£ s. d.	£ s. d. 256 0 10	£ s. d. 744 14 8	£ s. d. 1136 12 1	£ s. d. 1134 18 8

It has become the principal occupation at the institution, for twelve men out of twenty are employed at this trade. The salary is eight shillings per week.

Basket-making has been successfully introduced into all the institutions in England. The blind are most skilful at this trade. Indeed, it is the only trade followed at Bristol, because it is the best suited for those who must work for their own profit after their apprenticeship. To the kindness of the superintendent of the Edinburgh asylum I am indebted for the following memorandum of what the blind basket-makers have earned during the year 1836. This is not a memorandum of wages they have received, but of what they have gained, the wages being calculated on what the Edinburgh basket-makers who have their sight receive :—

				£	s.	d.
A	48 weeks' work	} have been long in the Asylum {		15	14	6
B	50 „ „			15	7	7
C	50 „ „	} have been 5 years in the Asylum {		10	8	0
D	43 „ „			9	16	11
E	48 „ „			9	12	8
F	49* „ „	. . . . . .		7	10	6

* Has been nearly six years in the house; but he was nearly forty years old when he entered it.

					£	s.	d.
G	49 weeks' work, 4 years in the Asylum	.	.	6	11	6
H	50 „ „ 3½ years „ „	.	.	5	17	6
J	26 „ „ half-year „ „	.	.	1	8	5

At Glasgow, the basket-makers receive up to eleven shillings per week.

The following statement of the salary of the pupils at the Bristol Industrial School evidences the importance of this branch of the work for which the blind are suited :—

STATEMENT OF SALARY OF MALE PUPILS AT BRISTOL SCHOOL DURING THREE WEEKS OF THE MONTH OF OCTOBER, 1837.

Pupil's No.	OBSERVATIONS.	Oct. 7. s. d.	Oct. 14. s. d.	Oct. 21. s. d.
1	Aged 21 years	10 5	11 4	11 10
2	„ 17 „	9 9	10 4	13 2
3	„ 17 „	8 11	8 11	8 1
4	For 7 years in the house	11 1	10 0	10 5
5	„ 6 „ „	2 11	5 0	5 9
6	„ 6 „ „	7 11	7 5	7 11
7	„ 6 „ „	6 4	6 11	7 1
8	„ 11 „ „	10 6	7 7	11 7
9	Aged 42 years	4 11	4 7	4 8
10	For 10 years in the house.. ..	12 4	10 7	11 2
11	Aged 23 years	11 4	10 0	10 7
12	For 9 years in the house	8 8	8 0	8 0
13	„ 5 „ „	4 0	4 10	5 0
14	Is incapable of any instruction ..	—	—	—
15	For 4 years in the house	5 6	5 1	5 6
16	„ 3 „ „	5 1	5 6	5 0
17	„ 6 „ „	8 2	9 3	8 1
18	„ 2 „ „	6 5	5 11	5 2
19	„ 3 „ „	9 10	8 7	8 3
20	„ 3 „ „	5 9	5 2	2 9
21	„ 1½ „ „	5 3	5 0	6 2
22	„ 1½ „ „	3 11	4 2	5 7
23	„ 1½ „ „	0 6	1 2	1 0
24	„ 1½ „ „	7 5	6 0	6 1
25	„ 1 „ „	3 5	3 3	2 8
26	„ 11 months „	1 1	0 11	0 7
27	„ 6 „ „	1 2	0 10	0 10
28	„ 7 „ „	4 9	4 5	3 10
29	„ 7 „ „	1 2	0 7	0 10
30	„ 7 „ „	0 6	0 6	0 3
31	„ 5 „ „	1 3	0 11	1 1

STATEMENT OF WAGES PAID TO BLIND GIRLS AT BRISTOL SCHOOL DURING THREE WEEKS OF THE MONTH OF OCTOBER.

Pupil's No.	OBSERVATIONS.	Oct. 7.	Oct. 14.	Oct. 21.
		s. d.	s. d.	s. d.
1	For 12 years in the institution ..	5 0	3 4	2 0
2	Sickly	4 6	4 0	4 0
3	Absent	—	—	
4	For 6 years in the house	4 0	2 2	2 2
5	,, 3 ,, ,, ...	5 0	1 10	2 6
6	,, 2½ ,, ,, ...	2 0	2 3	2 0
7	,, 1¾ ,, ,, ...	1 9	1 6	1 9
8	,, 1½ ,, ,, ...	1 9	1 6	1 6
9	,, 1½ ,, ,, ...	1 0	1 0	1 0
10	,, 6 months ,, ...	1 0	1 0	1 0
11	,, 6 ,, ,, ...	1 0	1 0	1 0
12	,, 5 ,, ,, ...	0 5	0 5	0 5
13	,, 5 ,, ,, ...	1 6	1 6	1 6
14	,, 5 ,, ,, ...	—	0 2	—
15	,, 5 ,, ,, ...	1 0	1 0	0 6

STATEMENT OF TWO WEEKS' WAGES PAID TO BASKET MAKERS AT THE SCHOOL IN LONDON.

Pupil's No.	Value of the Materials used during the Two Weeks.		PROFIT.	
	1st Week.	2nd Week.	1st Week.	2nd Week.
	s. d.	s. d.	s. d.	s. d.
1	5 3	5 3	11 0	10 6
2	0 11	0 11	1 7	1 7
3	1 11	2 2	5 10	4 4
4	1 4	3 0	2 8	6 0
5	9 4	5 0	18 8	10 0
6	1 10	2 0	3 8	4 0
7	—	—	—	—
8	4 8	3 8	9 4	10 4
9	2 8	2 0	5 4	4 0
10	0 4	0 2	0 8	0 5
11	2 0	2 0	4 6	4 6
12	0 2	0 2	0 6	0 5
13	—	—	—	—
14	3 4	4 4	6 8	8 8
15	0 6	0 5	1 0	0 9
16	0 4	0 3	0 8	0 7
17	1 1	0 11	2 3	2 0
18	2 0	2 0	4 0	4 0

STATEMENT OF TWO WEEKS' WAGES PAID TO BASKET MAKERS
AT THE SCHOOL IN LONDON—*continued.*

Pupil's No.	Value of the Material used during the Two Weeks.		PROFIT.	
	1st Week.	2nd Week.	1st Week.	2nd Week.
	s. d.	*s. d.*	*s. d.*	*s. d.*
19	2 6	2 4	5 0	—
20	1 10	2 0	3 8	—
21	1 2	2 0	2 4	—
22	—	2 0	—	—
23	—	0 5	—	0 9
24	—	0 5	—	—
25	1 2	1 2	2 4	2 4
26	1 2	3 8	2 4	10 5
27	1 8	—	3 4	—
28	1 10	2 0	0 8	5 6
29	—	—	—	—

Experience has shown that the commonest articles in basket-making are those which the blind make with the most profit. Some superintendents, however, have told me that curious small articles which are well-made sell the best and bring in the most profit. The reason of this appears to me quite clear. These articles are ticketed at a very high price; and the visitor, impressed by what he has seen executed, and in order to show his generosity, wishes to buy such an object as a souvenir of his visit, and does not haggle about the price. Thus these little pieces of work are sold and bring in much, while the ordinary articles, the baskets in common use, are not sold because they are charged above current prices. A worse way of promoting the interests of the establishment could not be devised. True it is that at first its productions are disposed of at a higher price, but this generosity speedily cools. People do not trade in order to lose, and a business man who can procure the article at a lower price elsewhere will not go on paying more to assist an institution. Commerce is selfish. People would much prefer to give away in charity what they have earned than to gain nothing when buying. A spirit of sacrifice in business must not be expected.

The most useful productions next to baskets are mats. This article is very varied. They make mats of rope simply weaved, and rugs to be placed next doors and in passages. Old tarred ropes are used for making these. I have never seen anywhere mats made of rushes. That is a variety to introduce into our establishments. But in the English institutions they manufacture carpets of wool and of aloe leaves, which sell well. It is estimated that this manufacture may give a wage of from ten to fourteen shillings per week ; and, if the produce could be disposed of, it would be the most useful, the easiest, and the most productive occupation.

This article has realised in

	£	s.	d.
1836 at Edinburgh	163	4	5
1837 at Glasgow	162	5	2

Rope-making has been very advantageously introduced into several institutions, and it is only the want of a covered rope-walk for working in in winter and bad weather which prevents its being introduced almost everywhere. Mr. W. Taylor, superintendent of the blind school at York, has just remedied this inconvenience by inventing a very simple machine for twisting the strands even in a small room. In nearly all the institutions of England the blind are employed in twisting the cords for sash windows. This industry is peculiar to that country ; for windows which open by moving up and down are common there. But in modifying this trade (in Belgium) the blind could twist those girdles the priests wear for securing the alb when saying mass. They could also make very pretty bell-pulls and horse-whips. At Glasgow ten children and six men are employed in making ropes ; and, in 1837, the amount of sales was £438 9s. 11d.

The making of straps for beds and other purposes is a branch of rope-making, and this sort of work can be advantageously introduced into our institutions, especially since Mr. Taylor has invented a very simple instrument for making them. It is, therefore, at York that this manufacture is most perfect.

The blind are able to make boots. Several pupils learn this trade at the institution in London. There may be reasons for training a blind person to this trade, but it cannot be a means for gaining a living. It is true that the boots made can be disposed of at an asylum ; for, if they are not elegant, at least they are strong, and that is the most essential quality for the blind. But in London, for instance, it is admitted there is a loss ; nevertheless some pupils are employed at it. In 1835 at Liverpool shoes made by the blind were sold to the amount of £93 14s. 7½d. ; but the materials and the keep of the master bootmaker amounted to £128 1s. 2½d. ; so that there was a loss of £34 6s. 7d. In 1836 the sales amounted to £83 9s. 3d., and the expenses to £144 14s. 9d., thus showing a loss of £61 5s. 6d. This result is very unsatisfactory.

Spinning and knitting are useful and productive employments, but suited rather to the young blind, and girls, than to those who have strength to apply themselves to other trades.

The girls have tolerably varied occupations ; but it is more difficult to find lucrative work for them than for men. Besides, everything they can produce is sold elsewhere cheaper or better than they can produce it. They make different sorts of fringes ; and, if all they are able to produce could be sold, this manufacture would be still more useful.

Sewing is another rather general employment. The girls are able to hem linen and mend clothes. They learn pretty easily to thread their needles, and to sew with regularity ; but they, necessarily, work less quickly than those who can see, and can never enter into competition with them. If a blind woman enter the married state, sewing may be very useful to her. In an asylum it may gain a living, but never anywhere else.

In general, there, as in other countries, the blind girls make small articles of fancy work, which are sold in an establishment which is visited, and which excites general interest, but they would not be sold if they were made by isolated persons In London the girls make very pretty reticules of dyed silk. At

D

other places, they make little carpets (*tapis*) for lamps, and woollen shawls, which are the admiration of all who see them.

The blind are able to use the spinning-wheel. I have often seen a blind woman spinning with dexterity, lose her thread, find it again, and produce a yarn as neat as a person who had her sight. In London, women spin hemp. They afterwards double their thread, and use it for making cords to window-sashes.

Such are the principal trades I have seen introduced into the establishments for the blind in England. Almost everywhere the blind work nine hours daily after reaching a certain age. If they are employed after those hours, they are paid separately per hour.

CHAPTER IV.

OF INTELLECTUAL EDUCATION.

THOSE who can see use the same language as the blind; but words are the expression of an impression received by the senses, and a great number of words receive their value through ocular impressions. Consequently, the blind cannot always attribute to a word the same value we do; because they do not know Nature as we see it. If they make use of the same words, those words therefore are signs for other ideas. They express themselves as we do, and think differently; and if they attach ideas to some words, those words are necessarily more impregnated with their own experience than with our traditions. The remark has been made already by M. Dufau.

" I had often noticed with surprise," says he, "among the blind a sort of difficulty in expressing themselves, if not accurately and clearly, at least circumstantially, fully, and with copiousness of expression. After having in vain sought the reason from them, it occurred to me," he goes on to say, "to seek for it in the language itself. On closely examining our languages, I then recognised that almost all the words forming them are made according to impressions conveyed through the eye; and that it is not merely figuratively that we call speech a picture of the mind, but that it is really an enduring painting offered to our eyes."

M. Dufau's remark is just, but it is too general. Most words, on the contrary (and this has been remarked by M. Zeune), are founded on touch and motion. Such are the words comprise, express, penetrate, investigate, &c. Even when a word relates to the sense of sight, there exists almost always, if not always, another word expressing very nearly the same idea, and which is suited to another sense. For instance, we say : This truth is *clear*, *evident*. But we also have the expression : This truth is *palpable*.

Whatever their number may be, it is indisputable that many such words exist which have no meaning for the blind until they have been translated, so to say, into words which fall into the sphere of senses they enjoy. The intellectual education of the blind should therefore require a course of terminology. Other children understand language like us ; words have for them the same meaning as for ourselves. We can make use of this intellectual instrument without previous study, and put ourselves in communication with the disciple by its means. But before being able to use it with the blind, we must be sure that they understand it as we do. It is true that the blind make this translation themselves as far as they can, and often very happily. "When I find myself in a vast plain," said a blind man, raising his hand to his ear, and stretching out his arm with an expressive gesture, "it seems to me that I am *out of hearing*." This is a translation into the blind language of our *out of sight*. Another blind man, who found his way unassisted through the most crowded streets with the greatest ease, said that too loud a noise completely bewildered him, and he explained this by saying that he was obliged *to listen to himself walking*. "I understand," says M. Dufau, who relates this anecdote, "that being no longer able to hear, because of the noise, he was *dazzled*." But instead of waiting until a blind man has found for himself some happy synonym which makes him understand one of our expressions, this synonym ought to be shown to him practically beforehand. We ought to agree first of all on the expressions before using them as conventional signs. Otherwise the master will find himself stopped in his explanations, and will never be able to satisfy himself that he has given correct notions and plain ideas.

This instruction would be peculiarly facilitated by the education of their senses. By exercising their taste, smell, touch, and hearing, those senses would acquire an accuracy they have not. This is what M. Dufau calls a course of tactility, and it is practised in Germany and America with great success. By increasing the power of those organs the nature of a multitude of objects would be better understood by the blind, and the terms of comparison between what we see in them and what they are able to discover about them would be rendered easier.

Nothing of the kind has been introduced into the institutions in England. Praiseworthy attempts are made in the institution at York and in Scotland to render the education of the blind less material, but much remains to be done. In England one is generally satisfied to teach the blind what is immediately applicable, what is really necessary. In fact, a primary instruction is what is deemed useful to make intelligent artisans and not savants of them, and this is much more advantageous to the blind themselves. If there are exceptions to this rule, they are only to be found in the higher ranks of society. Mr. Littledale, a blind man and a pupil of Mr. Taylor, has become a remarkable man owing to his acquirements. He has a large fortune, which he employs in promoting the sciences and the happiness of his brethren in misfortune, and, in order to be better able to do so, he has chosen his residence next to the Blind Institution at York.

As I have already stated, there are institutions which admit the young blind and give them an intellectual education before initiating them into manual occupations. Other institutions there are which give no instruction and only employ the blind in manual labour from their admission. The system of the Edinburgh Asylum seems to me preferable to all the others. Young pupils are admitted there, and they receive instruction which occupies most of their time. The aged blind are not altogether neglected. At the suggestion of the worthy secretary, Mr. Johnston, the directors pay some one who has his sight to read to them every evening for an hour or two. The home subscribes to a reading library which contains nearly twelve thousand volumes. The blind themselves select the books, which are generally serious or historical works. This reading of an evening has given them a desire to have more. So they have of their own accord determined only to take twenty minutes to their breakfast and their dinner, and to utilise the time remaining before work in listening to the reading of some interesting book.

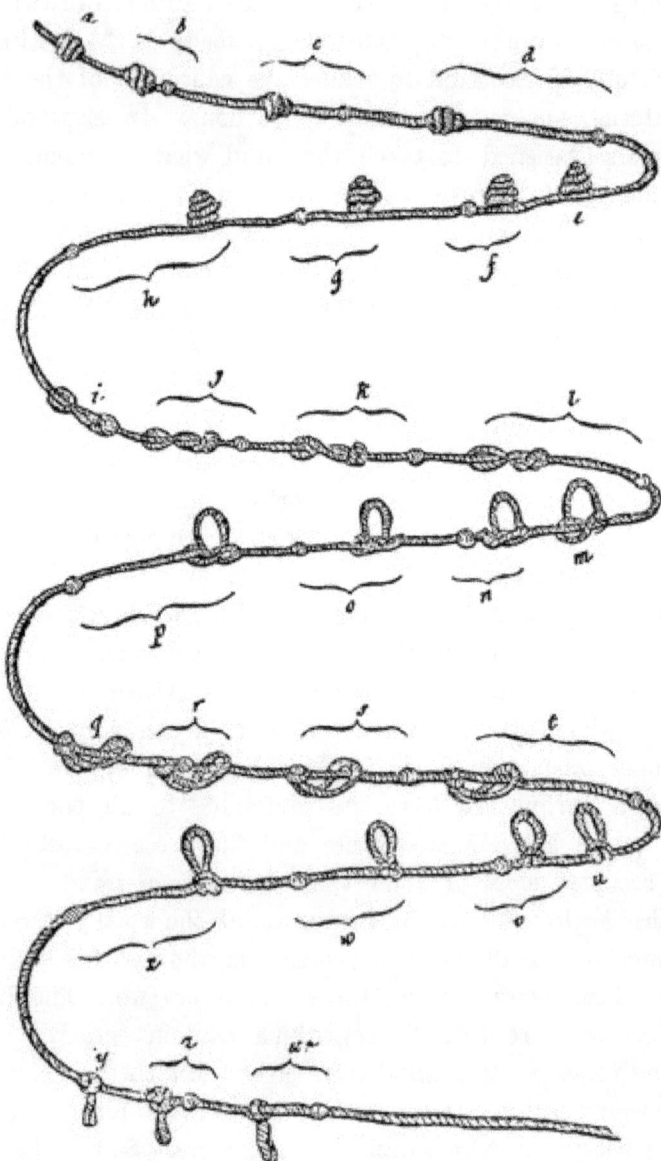

THE KNOT ALPHABET.

They even have a newspaper twice a week, and political questions are discussed there as warmly as in any other meeting in Scotland. In this way the blind, while they are resting, pass agreeable and useful hours, and thus their conversation is generally more interesting than we hear from people of their station.

Hitherto the reading of books in relief has not been taught at Edinburgh ; but the pupils are taught to spell from memory, and this is no doubt advantageous for teaching them afterwards to read the books in relief if desired. Before the printing in relief had begun, David Macbeath and Robert Milne, two blind men belonging to the Edinburgh Asylum, invented a kind of writing in knots, which is no longer of any use, but is, nevertheless, very ingenious. Seven different knots, which, by means of an additional knot, form seven classes of signs, express the whole alphabet. To avoid a description, which must necessarily be obscure, of this curious attempt of the blind to procure a means of communication, I have had it engraved.

There is only one institution in England of any importance in which writing is taught in the sense we attach to this word. The machine used is very simple. The pupil writes with a pencil or an iron stylus and blackened paper. The hand is guided by threads stretched to show the width of the lines. If the letter has a projection above or below the line, the pencil or stylus makes the thread yield and prevents the blind person from tracing too large letters and losing the line, for the thread goes back to its place.

The blind person cannot read the letters he has written in this way. In order to remedy this inconvenience, Mr. T. Lucas makes the pupils write on sheets of lead as thin as paper. The letters are impressed on the reverse side of it by means of a stylus. Leaden books would form a curious variety in bibliography, but unfortunately there are none. Mr. Lucas has succeeded in having some words written on these leaden sheets in order to prove that this kind of writing is possible, which no one doubted, but for practical purposes it is utterly useless.

WRITING MACHINE.

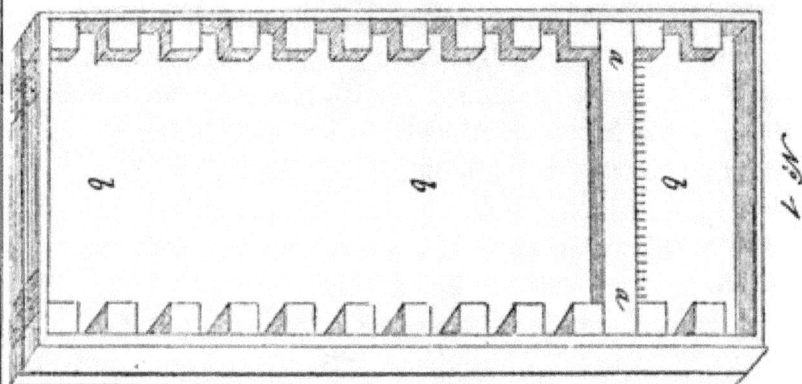

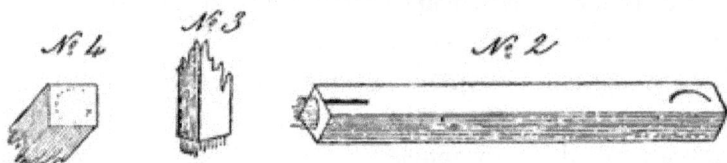

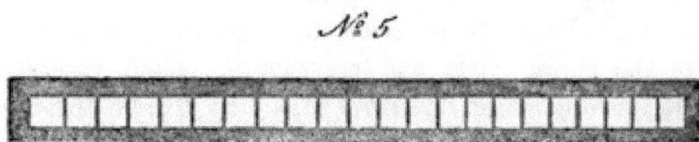

SPECIMEN OF WRITING.

JOHN ST CLAIR

In 1827 Mr. G. Gibson, of Birmingham, himself blind, invented an assortment of types, by means of which a blind person is able to write or rather to print his thoughts, to re-read them and communicate with those who are absent. His apparatus consists of a number of wooden cubes having at one end the form of the letters represented in relief by pins' points projecting about one-tenth of an inch, and the outlines of the same letter roughly cut at the other end. This enables the blind to distinguish the letter which has to be used without danger of being hurt.

The pointed letter is the printed character reversed. The engraved plan of this machine gives a tolerably correct idea of it. No. 1 shows the plan of the instrument, or rather of the frame. The paper is placed on *b b b*. The rule marked *a a* is moveable, and serves to guide the hand in placing the cubes, and the points on it are to fit into the small groove traced along the lower side of these cubes. By means of this point the necessity is avoided of always having two letters placed on the paper at the same time. The index-finger will only have to mark the point which has already received its letter. The only inconvenience of this way of proceeding is that all the cubes must be made the same size; but this inconvenience is largely compensated.

A similar writing is used in the Establishment for the Blind at Berlin. The diagram next page shows the letters and signs employed. It seems that the process has already been long known in this institution. I do not, however, know for certain that Mr. Gibson's invention is later than that of Berlin, and it is really of little consequence.

Mr. John St. Clair has invented a still more simple instrument for his own use (see No. 5 opposite). Square openings in a metal ruler serve to guide the hand in tracing with a pencil or stylus the form of the letters, which are nearly the size of capitals, as may be seen in the accompanying specimen of this writing.

Lastly, Mr. Gall, of Edinburgh, has invented a very ingenious little instrument which he calls a typhlograph, and by means of which the blind are able to write as well as those who can see.

ALPHABET
DE
BERLIN

ABCDEFGHI
KLMNOPQRS
TUVWXYZ,;
.,/!:;*-...+()
,123456789O

It consists of a board on which the paper is put ; (2) a slide with two branches (see the engraving next page, No. 1) ; and (3) a guide for the stylus or the pencil, No. 2. This guide is a small piece of copper, narrower than the space between the two branches of the slide and placed crosswise on a small piece of wood, which allows of raising or lowering it to form the various projections of the letters. At one end of this small piece of copper is an oblong opening with a small stop at one side. By raising and lowering the guide, letters may be traced in the hole that is in it without lifting the stylus or the pencil (see specimen No. 4).

The blind are very fond of arithmetic. Mental calculation is carried to great perfection by some blind persons. Several pupils, especially in the institutions of Germany, are able to solve the most complicated mathematical problems without any assistance from signs and more quickly than savants. This, however, is not sufficiently general to enable us entirely to dispense with notes. Mr. Saunderson, a blind man but Professor of Mathematics at Cambridge University, was the first who conceived the idea of an arithmetical board. Dr. Moyes, another blind man, proposed one which appeared to be more perfect ; but all have been forgotten since David Macbeath's invention of which I have spoken. This blind man deserves to be known. He was a dwarf of four feet six inches, but was not deformed. When thirty years of age, he was like a child of ten or twelve. Notwithstanding his misfortune, Macbeath had attained such a degree of culture as made him distinguished. He was received into the asylum at Edinburgh in 1809, and there he soon attained to the position of professor to his fellow blind pupils ; and which he continued to occupy until his sudden death in 1834. The board for teaching arithmetic which he invented is a frame pierced by several rows of square holes. The figures are marked on it by two square leaden pegs differently marked at their extremities. Each peg can be placed in four different positions. One of the characters indicates the odd numbers, 1, 3, 7, 9 ; and the other the even numbers, 2, 4, 6, 8. The second peg marks 5 or 0 according to its position. These two characters suffice for

TYPHLOGRAPHY.

N.º 1

N.º 2.

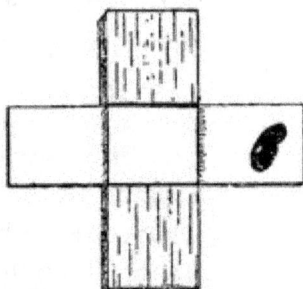

N.º 3.

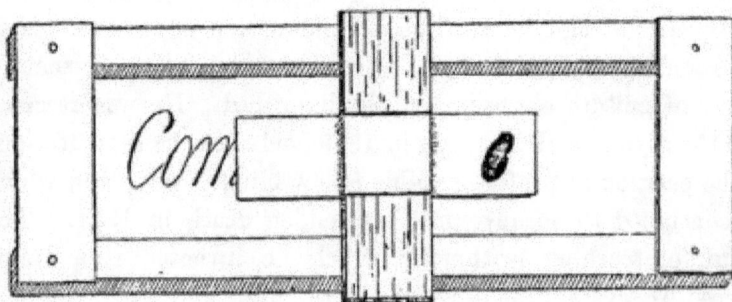

N.º 4

Commandment

all arithmetical operations, and render them easier than if the blind were obliged to use ten special marks. One of Macbeath's pupils, named William Long and teacher of the young blind at Glasgow, had the happiness of perfecting the board which his master had invented by making the square holes into pentagons. One single peg diversely placed now suffices for calculating, and

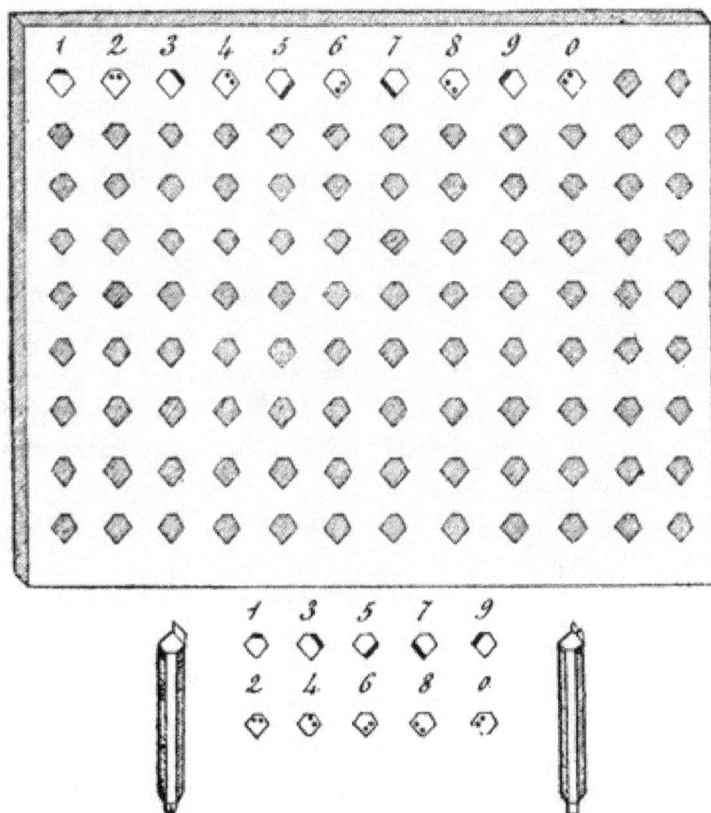

CALCULATING BOARD FOR THE USE OF THE BLIND.

the blind learner no longer loses his time in searching for his notes. I have had this board engraved, and it is so simple that the manner of using it can be understood on the first inspection.

As it is useful to be able to write or mark the different algebraical signs, Mr. W. Taylor, whom we are sure to meet when any improvement remains to be introduced, proposed the characters I have had engraved. The numbers 1, 3, 5, 7, and 2, 4, 6, 8, are noted as in Macbeath's board by the different positions of the two projections of the peg No. 1. The numbers 9 and 0, as well as the signs + (*plus*) and − (*minus*) and the letters W, X, Y, Z, are marked by the different positions of the two ends of the peg No. 2. He has preferred the square hole, the sides of which are more easily distinguishable than if they were pentagons. Besides, the pentagons would not have reduced the number of pegs, two of them being absolutely necessary. There is a groove between each range of holes. It is not deep, and is narrow, and is made to receive an oblong four-cornered piece of card for separating the sums. The example No. 5 contains an algebraical operation which will illustrate the use of this board.

Various other modes of calculating have been proposed, all offering more or less advantages. Mr. Gall has invented one requiring neither board nor pegs. All the numbers are represented by means of one or two pins diversely placed on a cushion or a mat, as may be seen in No. 4 of the engraving on p. 64. In case of necessity one's coat would suffice, and a blind person can in this way make calculations wherever he may be.

The terrestrial globes in use at the institutions in Edinburgh and Glasgow have no peculiar features, and the geographical maps are ordinary maps to which thin cords have been affixed, marking the boundaries of countries, the courses of rivers, and in which pins' heads or nails have been put to show the situation of towns. Mr. Gall has presented to the Edinburgh Society of Arts maps printed in relief, and has even received the silver medal for his invention. The earth is raised a little above the sea, and the boundaries of kingdoms are marked by a line of dots. The names of countries as well as of capital cities are written in black and by hand. Mr. Taylor has published a very neat map of England and Wales. It is made by means of a strong pressure brought to bear upon a sheet of paper placed on a copper plate engraved in cavities; dots marks the capitals. These maps are far from being as perfect as those made in America. One small map of Western Flanders of my own invention has gained the approbation of all the teachers in England. This map is only an experiment, on a space smaller than an octavo sheet; it gives the names of eleven towns, the name of the province, of the bordering districts, &c., and the position of the principal parishes of the province; the canals are distinguished from the rivers. I shall add the population to the names of the towns in the maps which I am going to make by the same process.

I saw at Glasgow a representation in relief of the comparative length of the principal rivers, and of the height of the principal mountains and the most remarkable buildings of the world compared with the height of the house they live in.

The science of astronomy is not entirely alien to the blind. After an approximate idea has been given them of the height of some terrestrial creations, they are made to understand what an insignificant portion our earth occupies in the general system of creation; and the life (*mouvement*) of the heavens and the position and comparative size of the planets are explained to them by a planetary instrument. Very little time, however, is lost in explaining to them these beautiful objects scientifically; and, in general, all these articles and machines are considered, even in the institutes, rather as being curious than useful.

An elementary knowledge of geometry is more useful. As the blind only know the relations of geometrical quantities by touch, this knowledge must necessarily be very limited, incomplete, and inaccurate. Mr. W. Taylor therefore believed himself well justified in publishing the figures of Euclid's elements as far as the 48th proposition. The relief is produced on the paper by a strong pressure upon a plate engraved in cavities. Mr. Howe has since published the figures of Euclid's elements, and there is another edition published at the institution in Paris.

Music is taught in several establishments as an useful profession. Various pupils have already succeeded in obtaining advantageous positions as organists. The art is learnt by principles, and the method of teaching differs in no respect from that for persons who can see.

M. Haüy at first combined the musical characters fit to

MR. W. TAYLOR'S (OF YORK) ARITHMETICAL BOARD.

N.º 1.

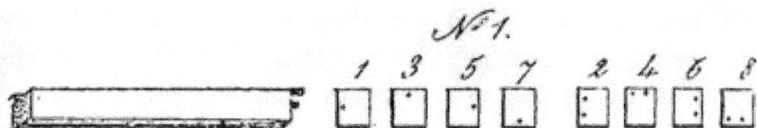

N.º 2.

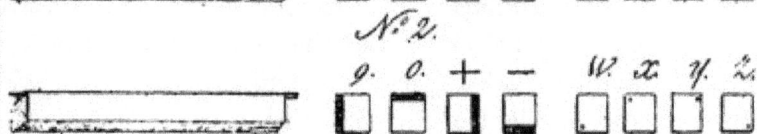

N.º 3.

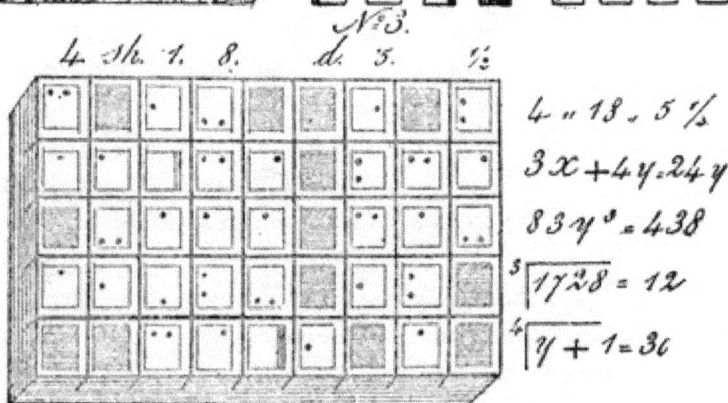

$$4 \, " \, 13 \, . \, 5 \, \tfrac{1}{2}$$

$$3x + 4y . 24 y$$

$$83 y^3 = 438$$

$$\sqrt[3]{1728} = 12$$

$$\sqrt[4]{y + 1} = 36$$

N.º 4.

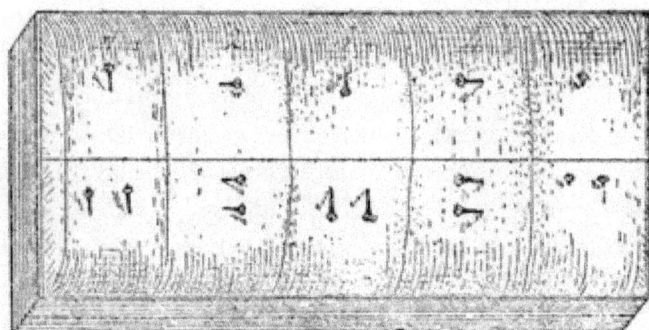

represent on paper and in relief all possible features of the art, and succeeded in making musicians. Mr. Tansure proposes in his Musical Grammar to use a not very complicated machine, the plan of which may be seen in the article " Blind " of the Encyclo-pædia Britannica. The board is three feet long and nine inches wide. The spaces are marked in relief, as they are traced on paper for those who see, by flat lines. The necessary lines above or below the ordinary spaces are shown by rounded lines. Holes pierced between and upon these lines receive musical notes of the ordinary form, or arbitrary notes as is the practice elsewhere. Mr. Cheese has considerably improved this board for writing music by substituting, for the ordinary or other notes of lead or wood, which would necessarily occupy much space, a pin, with or without a head, the end of which is diversely turned. In this way he has succeeded in giving thirty-two different forms to a pin, twelve of which however suffice for his teaching.

Mr. Gall, of Edinburgh, finds the great advantage of writing music by numbers. The gamut is represented by 1, 2, 3, 4, 5, 6, 7 for the twelve octaves ; so that the first note in each tone is expressed by 1, that is the clef which modifies all. If the notes descend below or ascend above the octave, they are marked by a comma turned upward or downward according to the nature of the notes requiring this sign. A colon marks the notes which ought to be pointed. The parenthesis) marks the flat and the parenthesis (marks the sharp. A space left between the notes marks the time.

The value of the notes is shown as under :—

Semibreve	1 . —	2 . —	3 . —	4 . —	&c.
Minim	1 —	2 —	3 —	4 —	&c.
Crotchet	1 ...	2 ...	3 ...	4 ...	&c.
Quaver	1 ..	2 ..	3 ..	4 ..	&c.
Semiquaver	1 .	2 .	3 .	4 .	&c.
Demi-semiquaver	1	2	3	4	&c.

In this way music written with letters in dots or impressed would take up little space.

E

Even pins would suffice for the writing ; and if a cord were stretched upon a cushion, the notes of the gamut being written on the cord, those of the other octaves could be written above or below the line as required.

The desire of procuring for the blind the means of writing music has led to seeking other methods. Don Isern, a nobleman of Catalonia, received in 1827 a silver medal from the London Society of Arts for the invention of a machine which does not appear to me to satisfy the conditions such an instrument ought to possess ; for the blind cannot read what has been written by this machine.

Whatever process may be invented, music readable for the blind will only be readable while they are singing. The hands being occupied in all other kinds of musical execution, the parts must be entrusted to the memory, and the memory of the blind is astonishing in this respect.

The method most used for teaching them pieces of music is to read to them the musical phrases by sol-fa-ing them. As soon as the first two or three bars are impressed on their memory, the reading is proceeded with, and in a short time the most complicated pieces are learnt and executed.

In England it is not thought proper to teach the blind any other instruments than the organ or piano, for fear of making them itinerant musicians, and exposing them to degradation by frequenting meetings of low people.

A short course of natural history would no doubt be of great use to the blind, and would have the advantage of pleasing them. Most persons born blind have no idea of the commonest animals. One of my pupils, eleven years old, had never touched a hen. Great was his delight when I gave him one to touch for the first time. Museums of stuffed animals have been formed in some institutes of Germany with the intention of making the animal kingdom known to the blind. But, apart from the fact that such collections cost sums of money seldom at the disposal of these institutions, and of which they could make much better use, they would only be of service while the blind are in the establishments.

So it would be useful to improve upon Mr. Gall's essay in relief-printing, and print in relief the forms of some animals with explanatory text. The outlines of the specimens published by Mr. Gall are not sufficiently defined.

Such is the plan of intellectual instruction for the blind in the institutions of England. It is yet far from the degree of perfection which will no doubt be reached in a few years; but it already undoubtedly contains the germ of all that is useful and necessary; and if prudence prescribes to directors a wise hesitation in adopting new systems, they have generally a sincere desire to accept every improvement, the reality of which has been proved by experience.

CHAPTER V.

Of Printing in Relief.

For the blind reading is not only a means of instruction—it is also an employment. To employ the blind is to divert them and to make them relatively happy. It is not likely that we shall ever succeed in printing for the use of the blind in such a way as to enable them to read as quickly as those who can see. The eye sees at once a group of letters which the finger can only pick out one by one. The difficulty then is with the reader, and not in the book ; and doubtless art will never replace that of which nature or misfortune has deprived the blind.

But I do not know if, in the case given, the powerlessness of art be not an advantage. Reading employs a blind person agreeably, and, as it is slow, a single book may occupy him a long time. It is right that it should be so ; for the number of books printed in relief will always be necessarily limited. The book trade will not speculate in this kind of printing on a large scale, because the number of blind readers being very few in comparison with others, the price would be too high for this generally poor class.

The slowness of reading amongst the blind arises too from the difficulty of recognising the shape of each individual letter ; and this difficulty sometimes makes reading repulsive and quite impossible. Therefore the selection of an alphabet is sufficiently important to deserve a searching discussion.

The discovery of printing in relief, moreover, is one which everybody is astonished at not having made the first. A sheet of printed paper forcibly pressed in the printing machine and showing the letters in relief ought to suffice to give the idea to every printer. The glory of this discovery belongs to France. M. Valentin Haüy tried it the first and succeeded. He successively used types of different sizes, and finally adopted one which

Specimen

d'impression en

relief de l'insti-

tut de Paris

ABCDEFGHIK

LMNOPQRSTUV

WXYZ

abcdefghijklmno

pqrstuvwxyz

1234567890

Jm'primé a bruges

SPECIMEN OF RELIEF-PRINTING OF THE PARIS INSTITUTION.
(Printed at Bruges.)

seemed to keep the proper medium amongst those the blind are able to touch, according to the degree of delicacy of touch which nature has given them, or which age and labour have left them. These letters are pleasing to the eye and differ very little from the ordinary form, as may be seen from the accompanying specimen (see preceding page). No important change has been made since M. Haüy's alphabet ; but long experience has already produced the conviction that the alphabet does not fulfil what was expected from it, and the blind did not preserve the delicacy of touch necessary for continuing to read the Paris printing. But the books had been printed in quantity and in different languages ; for it had been expected that this institution, having been the first and the model on which others were formed, would also become the chief depôt from which all printed productions for the use of the blind would be taken. This expectation was not realised. The great expenses incurred cooled the zeal of those who had taken an interest in this industry, and rendered all subsequent attempts to improve that kind of printing impossible.

At first the letters had the parallipedal form of ordinary printing. The blind set up [the type] in a case sheathed with a copper bottom and pierced by several rows of little holes. For printing in relief a wooden press was used like those employed for pressing out oil, pressing cloth, &c. ; but however little was the height of the plate, the tablet which ought to produce pressure on the paper was not equally pressed by the screw, and the sides were found to have received less pressure than the middle. This it was which originated the cylinder press made in 1784 by M. Beaucher, a locksmith and engineer. This press was very like that used by copper-plate printers. A lever moved the cylinder, which, rolling on the plate, exercised a successive pressure and produced a bad impression, because the paper was displaced by the rolling of the cylinder.

M. Clousier, printer to the king, thought that a perpendicular pressure on a whole sheet at once would be preferable to successive pressures. He used his ordinary presses for printing in relief and was perfectly successful, according to M. Guillié's avowal,* who, however, again introduced, about 1820, the cylindrical press in use until now in the Paris Institution.

The type at present in use is in the form of a hammer. The letter which has to be printed in relief rests on a transverse part, the object of which is to stop the letters which are placed on the composing stick or case leaded in wood. Such is the state of the art in France. Satisfied with the glory of this discovery, they do not seem to care to improve upon it in the least, and since its invention it has remained almost stationary.

Some experiments were made in Austria which were not unsuccessful, but it is in England and America that the art has progressed, principally owing to the disinterestedness of Mr. Gall, of Edinburgh, to the zeal of Mr. Howe, director of the Boston Institution, of Mr. Alston, treasurer of that at Glasgow, and to several other philanthropists. In order to unite and direct all these hitherto isolated efforts, the Edinburgh Royal Society of Arts in 1832 conceived the happy idea of proposing, as a subject for one of its annual prizes, the suggestion of a better alphabet for the use of the blind. The competitors were required to state what should be the shape and height of the letters or characters, and how many of them ought to be used to form a general alphabet for the use of the blind of Great Britain and Ireland, and, in the second place, the best and least expensive method of printing in relief with characters or letters in such a way as to allow of their being easily and rightly ascertained by the touch.

Every suggestion was to be accompanied by a specimen in relief.

The Society's appeal was heard. Six competitors sent in alphabets, and the examining committee decided, after consulting competent judges, that the system of signs invented by Mr. Hay, which I shall explain presently, merited the preference in all respects to that of Paris and Mr. Gall's, of Edinburgh; and, consequently, that Mr. Hay's system was worthy of the Society's encouragement and support, and the more so because he had already incurred great expense.

---

* Essay on the Education of the Blind. By M. Guillié. 3rd edition. 1820. Page 158.

The committee, however, remarked that, while recommending Mr. Hay's alphabet, it in no wise intended to propose it as an alphabet for the blind to be adopted definitely without further investigation. The matter seemed to it one of too great importance. It recommended that the attempts be continued and correspondence opened with all the institutions for the blind in order to obtain uniformity.

Following the views of its committee, the Society judged it expedient to obtain further information, and once more offered its gold medal of the value of twenty guineas for the best essay on the subject.

Fifteen other alphabets were received from different schools in England, some of them accompanied by physiological and philological remarks of the greatest interest, and which I was able to examine during my stay in Edinburgh.

Twelve of these alphabets consisted of very arbitrary characters ; the other three were simply modifications of Roman and Italian characters. The first question to be decided was : If an arbitrary alphabet was to be adopted, or if a common alphabet with modifications would be sufficient ? I shall give the arguments in favour of each opinion, and, in order to complete the discussion, I shall state at the same time all that has hitherto been attempted in this matter.

Amongst nearly all civilised nations words are composed of letters. But letters are not absolutely necessary, as the Chinese language proves, in which all words are represented by arbitrary signs. In our languages also, although we have letters, several words are quite arbitrary signs, and are, indeed, pronounced quite otherwise than they are written. For instance, the English words *bought*, *taught*, and *rough* are pronounced baut, taut, rof (*sic*, ? *ruff*), &c. So it is in the French language and in most of our languages. We pity the Chinese who have to commit to memory twenty thousand characters before they can hope to attain to any dignity in the empire, but the European languages often present as many difficulties. At least, the Chinese signs for words never vary, whereas our letters change their sound

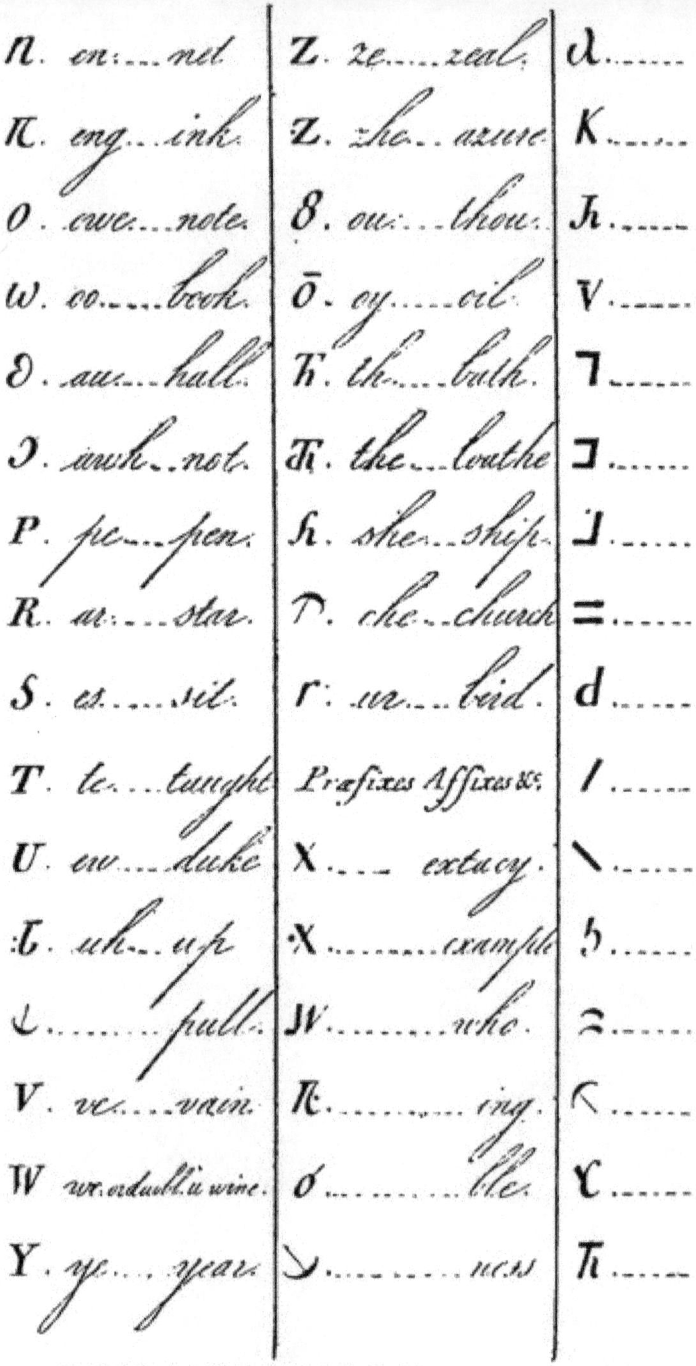

N. en....net	Z. ze....zeal	ᶑ.........
K. eng....ink	Z. zhe....azure	K.........
O. owe....note	θ. ou....thou	Jⱴ.........
W. oo....book	ō. oy....oil	V.........
Ə. au....hall	Tҕ. th....bath	˥.........
Ɔ. awh....not	Ꮷ. the....loathe	˩.........
P. pe....pen	ʃ. she....ship	˩.........
R. ar....star	ʈ. che....church	=.........
S. es....sil	ꭇ. ur....bird	d.........
T. te....taught	Prefixes Affixes &c.	/.........
U. ew....duke	X.... extacy	\.........
ʊ. uh....up	·X......... example	�.........
ꞁ......... pull	W......... who	ᴈ.........
V. ve....vain	K......... ing	ᴋ.........
W. wr or dubl'u wine	ꝺ......... ble	Ⅽ.........
Y. ye....year	Ꙃ......... ness	K.........

NEW YORK SONOGRAPHIC ALPHABET.

every instant. Thoroughly to realise these difficulties, let us suppose an Englishman wishes to pronounce the word *pharmacy*, which he meets with for the first time, and let us see how many chances he has of making a mistake. This curious calculation was made by the director of the institute at New York.

The letters *ph* separated or joined may be pronounced in 4 different ways, the letter *a* is pronounced in 8 ways, the three first letters therefore may be pronounced in 32 ways ; the letter *r* has two sounds, which doubles the different sounds ; each of these 64 ways of pronouncing the first four letters therefore admits of two more variations, or 128 ; *a* is pronounced in 8 ways. On multiplying 128 by 8 we have 1024. In the English language the letter *c* has five sounds : 1024 multiplied by 5 make 5120. The letter *y* is pronounced in 3 ways, from which it follows that a child, after having learnt the exact pronunciation of each of the letters forming the word *pharmacy*, has 15,360 chances of making a mistake. In this manner we may be assured that our system of writing sounds is quite calculated to embarrass him who wishes to learn it. But it is a case decided, and those who see and understand must put up with these difficulties, or cannot hope to enter into communication with society or to profit by the experience to be found in books. But it is not the same for the blind. Books ought to be printed exclusively for their use ; and (says the director of the New York Institute) it matters little whether or no they who see can read these books, provided that the blind understand them perfectly. These reasons have induced him to propose a way of writing the sounds of the language, which will obviate to a certain extent the inconveniences he has mentioned. We know, says he, exactly how to express with our characters the word *beau, belle,* by the letters *bo* and *bel* ; but we have more simple or elementary sounds than letters. So he has formed his alphabet of forty-one characters whose sounds never change, and which represent all the elementary sounds of words. Thus a person who knew these signs could spell almost all the words in a language after a few hours' practice. Besides, by printing with these characters the number of volumes would be considerably reduced, the more so because he proposes abridged signs for a certain number of prefixes and affixes. I give the alphabet as the author has proposed it, applied only to the English language, because I am of opinion, for the reasons stated, that it is far from possessing the conditions demanded for obtaining the result we ought to expect.

Another still more ingenious process was invented by M. Barbier. The blind only understand sounds, and the difference between written and spoken language must hinder them much in learning to read. He therefore considered that a system of notation, which should faithfully represent the vocal sounds, would greatly simplify the matter. As they cannot read our writing nor our ordinary books, and as books for their use must be printed in relief, why (asks M. Barbier) not choose characters easily recognised by the touch, and at the same time in harmony with the words ? So he has substituted the orthography of sound for grammatical orthography. The dot only enters as an element into M. Barbier's system. At first the author had divided all the sounds, vowels, and consonants, into horizontal ranks of six characters each.

1st line	a	i	o	u	é	è
2nd line	an	in	on	un	eu	ou
3rd line	be	de	gue	je	ve	ze
4th line	pe	te	que	che	fe	se
5th line	le	me	ne	re	gn	l *liquid*
6th line	oi	oin	ien	ste	x	ment

The consonants are articulated as if they were followed by an *e* mute ; but this letter is not written.

Each letter was represented by two perpendicular rows of dots. The first row showed the number of the horizontal line ; the second showed the place this sound occupied on the line.

In this manner :—

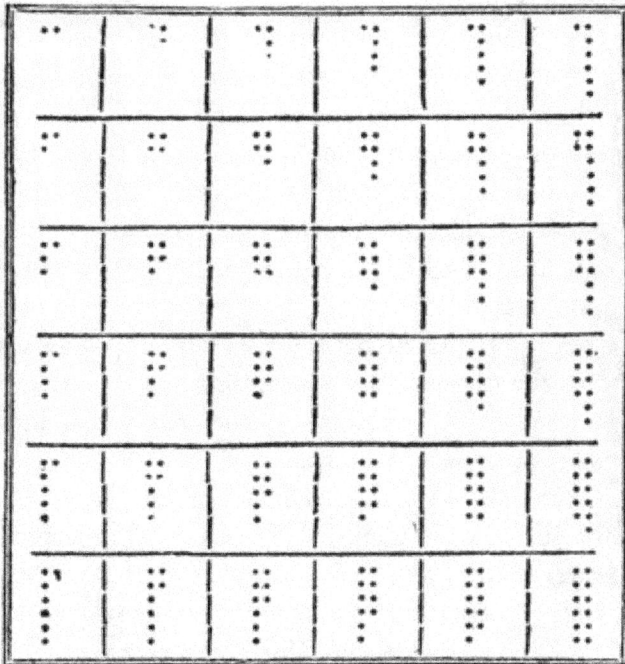

The only instrument is a rule in the centre of which are drawn six parallel lines sunken into the wood ; on this is placed the paper, which is held by a kind of clasp, or on which was placed a small flat copper rule pierced with squares.

As abbreviated writing M. Barbier's system was more ingenious than rapid. Its author, therefore, soon thought fit to introduce considerable alterations, and he found means to represent all the sounds and articulations by *three* dots placed in different positions. This is how he proceeds to obtain a result which at first seems so surprising. He first of all divides his *pronouncing alphabet* (vowels and consonants) into five horizontal rows instead of six, as he had first done.

Each series is represented by a special mark formed of two dots. For instance, the first, which is composed of vowels, is represented by two dots placed perpendicularly (:) ; the second, composed of nasal vowels, is represented by two dots placed obliquely (∴) ; the third, which is composed of a first line of consonants, is denoted by two dots placed horizontally (..), &c. Thus, as may be seen, we have the means of representing the series ; but each series is composed of six letters. The author fixes the rank of the letter which is wished to be put in the series by means of a third dot combined with the second. For instance, *o* is the third of the series. I begin then by showing the series by means of two dots (:), and I shall show the rank of the letter by means of a third dot, which shall be combined with the lower dot of the figure I have just drawn so as to present the two horizontal dots which belong to the third series (∴) ; the series and the rank are found in the manner shown, and the letter *o* clearly marked. The pupil need only know exactly the order in which the letters in the alphabetical table are ranged.

In this form M. Barbier's ingenious system has obtained the approval of the Paris Academy of Sciences. Three reports made in the years 1820, 1823, and 1830, at the foot of which are placed names which alone are a sufficient guarantee—those of Cuvier, Lacépède, Ampère, and Molard—authenticate this high approbation. They explain, too, M. Barbier's ulterior object, which is to give the blind books which they themselves have printed. This relief-printing neither requires a case nor moveable type, and would be always composed in a simple and uniform type. In order to obtain this result M. Barbier has had little quadrats (*cadratins*) cast, which have at one end a cross stroke and at the other a straight stroke. The first sign may take four positions according as the convexity is turned downwards, to the right or to the left. The second sign may have two positions, a horizontal and a vertical. On combining these two quadrats we are able to show, agreeably to the system I have just explained, by the one the horizontal rank and by the other the rank of the letter in the series. The process, as we see, requires little skill, and could easily be learnt by all blind persons.

Sonographic writing has drawbacks, as M. Louis Braille, tutor at the Paris Institution and himself blind, has partly anticipated by adapting to each of his letters a suitable sign formed of a certain number of dots arbitrarily placed.

Below are the ten primitive signs.

$$\cdot \mid : \mid \cdot\cdot \mid \cdot: \mid \cdot\cdot \mid \cdot\cdot \mid :: \mid :\cdot \mid \cdot\cdot \mid \cdot\cdot$$

The first four series (as shown in the engraving of M. Braille's alphabet, p. 79) are formed by adding another dot to these dots, either to the left or to the right, or perhaps two dots. The machine used in this system only contains three grooves instead of six.

M. Braille has at the same time shown how to print music by means of dots.

The notes C, D, F, G, A, B are represented by the following signs :—

$$\cdot\cdot \mid \cdot\cdot \mid \cdot: \mid :: \mid :\cdot \mid \cdot\cdot \mid \cdot\cdot$$

We can place these notes in seven different octaves, which are easily distinguished from each other. Here is C with seven octaves beginning with C counter-bass :

$$\cdot\cdot \mid \cdot\cdot \mid \cdot\cdot \mid \cdot\cdot \mid \cdot\cdot \mid \cdot\cdot \mid \cdot\cdot$$

Consequently the F of the clef of that name, in the process used by persons who can see, will be represented by $\cdot \ \cdot \ \cdot$; the C of the clef of that name by $.\ \cdot\ :$; the G of the clef of that name by $.\ :\ .$

If there be several consecutive notes belonging to the same octave, it suffices to write the indicator sign of the octave before the first of these notes.

The natural, the flat, and the accidental sharps are respectively marked by the signs ˙ . , : . , ˙ : , placed before the note ; the double sharps and the double flats are shown by the sign of the sharp and flat repeated.

The semibreve is shown by the two dots of the third series placed below the note ; the minim by the dot of the second series ; the crotchet by the dot of the fourth series ; the quaver is recognised by the white or blank space below the note.

EXAMPLE :

C semibreve	:	C minim	:
C crotchet	: ˙	C quaver	˙ :

The semiquaver, the demi-semiquaver, the quadruplet, and the quintuplet are respectively indicated as the semibreve, the minim, the crotchet, and the quaver. This double use of the same sign need not cause any mistake, for the simple inspection of the bar dissipates any confusion. However, in case of difficulty, . : ˙ may be put before the first four values, and . : : before the others.

The dotted value is shown by a dot placed after the note ; when the note is double dotted, two dots are placed. The triplets are marked by : placed before a series of notes ; a blank space marks the end of the bar ; : ˙ is the pause ; : . the half-pause. The rest is marked : . ; the half-rest is marked by : : to show that several notes must be struck in accord ; if there are two, . ˙ is put between them ; . : is put before three notes in accord ; and . : before four notes.

The Gospel according to St. John and a little reading book have been published at Bristol on the plan proposed by Mr. T. M. Lucas. The relief-printing is fine, but the characters are ˌstenographic : consequently a mass of abbreviations, which render reading more or less uncertain. He uses only three primitive signs : a line, a curve, and a dot.

He gives the line four different positions : perpendicular, horizontal, oblique, and vertical. The curve also allows of four positions, according as it is turned to the right, to the left,

M. BRAILLE'S DOT ALPHABET.

1st Series.

a b c ∂ e ſ g h i j

2nd Series.

k l m n o p q r s t

3rd Series.

u v x y z ç é ā è ŭ

ıeu   oin

4th Series.

â ê î ô û ë ï ü œ w

an in on un eu ou oi ch gn ill

n

Punctuation and other signs.

? ¡ : . ? ! (((* ×

V ※

upwards or downwards; each of the four positions of the line receives four additional characters by means of a dot, which makes twenty signs; each of the positions of the curve undergoes two changes by means of this dot. Which gives us thirty-two characters, then a dot, a circle, and two lesser curves turned to the right and the left. The elements could not be more simple; and, if an arbitrary alphabet could be or ought to be adopted, I prefer Mr. Lucas's. The author shows the two advantages his system offers in a little pamphlet entitled "Instructions for Teaching the Blind to Read."

Everyone knows, says he, that we can read less quickly by means of our fingers than with our eyes; because the fingers touch less at one time than the eyes can at once perceive. Therefore, the more words are simplified and abridged without being less distinct, the nearer we approach to the advantages of sight; since, by that means, laborious spelling is changed all at once into easy reading. Add to this, again, that the simplicity of the form, while making reading more rapid, renders it at the same time more sure. The second advantage of a stenographic character is that it may be applied to all alphabetical languages. We should only have to calculate the respective proportion in which use is made of each letter to adapt to that one which occurs most often the sign which occupies the least space. In the English language the letter e is used one hundred and twenty times for once that we use the letter z.

I have heard two of his pupils read a chapter of the Gospel according to St. John. One of the best pupils occupied three minutes twenty-nine seconds in reading the first thirteen verses of the twelfth and seventeenth chapters of the Gospel. I have heard other pupils read these same verses printed with Mr. Gall's characters in still less time. One of Mr. Lucas's pupils, who had attended the school during one year at least, could only read with great difficulty a line I pointed out to him in the middle of a chapter, and often made mistakes when a single sign denoted a whole word, as is often required by Mr. Lucas's system. Each isolated letter, for instance, stands for at least three words. There are even characters representing as many as seven words, so that a mistake is only too easy, and would suffice to cause the abandonment of this process.

The letter r sounds as if it were preceded by an a ; j and k as if there were an a after those letters ; j, l, m, n, s and x as if they were preceded by an e ; and b, c, d, g, p, t, and v, as if they were followed by an e.

The beginning of St. John's Gospel is thus written :—

t gospel b st jon, chap 1.

in t bgini ws t wrd a t w ws w g, a t w ws g, t sam ws n t bgini w g. l things wr mad b him, a w o hm ws nt a thing mad tht ws mad. in hm ws life a t l ws t lit f mn.

The words have very often to be understood by the context of the sentence, and it is possible to make such a sentence by means of his characters that the author of the process himself would be unable to unravel it.

Mr. Hay, a blind man in Edinburgh, contrived another alphabet. It is his work which suggested to the Society of Arts the idea of proposing the competition which it afterwards opened.

Mr. Hay, whose alphabet at first pleased the Society much, had calculated that books for the use of the blind printed with his alphabet would be reduced to a third of the size required by Mr. Gall's system, who himself had proved the fact that his books contained on a given space much more matter than those printed at Paris. He put 509 characters where there were but 408 letters in the French books, although his letters were much larger and consequently more easily recognised by the touch.

Mr. Mungo Ponton, Writer to the Signet, another competitor, was also of opinion that an arbitrary character is the only kind that can be serviceable to the blind. The blind alphabet, he says, ought to be easy to learn, easily impressed on the memory, and quickly read by the finger. It appears to me generally admitted, he adds, that the character used by those who can see, such as it is, does not supply these conditions, and that to adopt it in order to spare the friends of the blind the difficulty of learning

F

another is to sacrifice the interest of the blind to the indolence of those who enjoy their sight.

I do not believe, he continues, that it is possible to invent a collection of signs which the blind can easily read and print themselves, and which would preserve a sufficient resemblance to common characters for the friends of the blind to be able to read it easily and without a key. But, if a key be required, they would just as readily acquire an altogether arbitrary alphabet as if this alphabet preserved a vague likeness to the Roman character. Therefore, he adds, I believe that, in the choice of an alphabet for the blind, it is necessary to try to ascertain which is the form required by the sense of touch rather than to try to preserve some resemblance to known characters.

Mr. John Lothian, one of the competitors, who had sent in an arbitrary character, also explained his motives. The letter, he says, which perhaps seems very simple to the sight, may be very difficult to identify by the touch. The simplicity of a character is altogether relative. Therefore, I have abandoned without the least hesitation all idea of giving my characters sufficient resemblance to our alphabets for them to be easily identified on the first inspection. When forming an alphabet for the blind, we ought to prefer that which suits the blind rather than that which they who see would desire.

The adoption of the Roman character, says the Rev. Edward Craig, would doubtless offer some advantages; it would associate them more immediately with society, and would assure them of an assistance in their writing and reading from all sides which they will not otherwise meet with. But this is almost impossible; the difference between the Roman letters is not sufficiently palpable, they are too compound, and to use them in printing they ought to be very large, and their size would add very much to the expense.

I give an engraving containing sixteen arbitrary alphabets which were sent to the Society. Those who had invented them claimed that these characters possessed a greater characteristic difference, that they are more easily read by the touch, and that they take

D E F G H I J K L M N O P Q R S

PROPOSED ALPHABETS FOR THE BLIND, UNDER CONSIDERATION OF THE SOCIETY OF ARTS FOR SCOTLAND.
(Printed for the Society's Transactions, 1836.)

up less space than the ordinary alphabet. But I have no doubt, judging by what is before our eyes, that no one will be of this opinion. On the contrary, a very superficial examination will convince all those who will take the trouble, that the general form of our printed letters offers more variety than these arbitrary alphabets. It has also been asserted that by giving different positions to one character, the number of forms are reduced, and that these characters are consequently more easily fixed in the memory. But, in reality, each new position of a sign is a new form, or at least something new to be impressed on the memory. In this respect, the advantage of a new character is not very striking.

This was the opinion of Mr. W. Taylor, to whom the Society of Arts had forwarded all the communications it had received; and which he has stated in his very sensible and impartial report which the Society has decided to print in full. The prize was therefore awarded to the characters of Mr. Fry, of London. Mr. Fry's letters are those which have been adopted by Mr. Alston, of Glasgow, who has made their surface a trifle less flat.

In fact, if a character known to those who have their eyesight be used in relief-printing for the blind, these unfortunate creatures are brought nearer to other men than if they made use of another character unknown to those about them. Whatever may be said, it is troublesome to learn a new alphabet in order to teach it to children; and this difficulty will deter many persons who would otherwise apply themselves to it. To decrease the difficulty which those who can see would have in learning an alphabet for the blind is really to work in the interest of the blind.

The largest number of blind is found amongst the poor, and the greatest misfortune of the blind consists in their isolation. All our efforts should tend towards bringing them near to ourselves, and to make their education as like our own as possible, and to begin this education as quickly as may be, and not to think that a special institution is needed for teaching them to read. If the characters in their books are those which we teach to other children, ordinary schools will be able to admit from their infancy these unfortunate beings, who have been hitherto kept afar off under a false pretext ; and their misfortune will lie less heavily upon them, their intellect will be developed, and the advantage they will derive from their stay in special establishments will be in harmony with what they will have learnt before entering them.

Young blind people are very subject to low spirits because they are shut out from the occupations and games of other children ; always confined to the house, trained rather than guided, overwhelmed with careful but too often mistaken attentions, they are prevented from acquiring that confidence in themselves they ought to have ; and, for fear of a fall or a slight hurt, their relatives do not let them know the place where they live and the objects surrounding them, which would be so great an advantage to them. If the young blind went to school with other children, they would take part in their games and would be strengthened by the exercise. They would be obliged to rely more on themselves ; for from natural indifference the children who had their sight would often leave them to themselves, or would be satisfied to direct them by words, which would be still better. But choosing the ordinary character would render all this possible, and the teaching of the blind would thus become as simple as that of others.

Reading is very useful for the blind ; it occupies and instructs him ; but writing is still more useful, and a want more often felt. To communicate with others by writing it is necessary that he use a character known by those with whom he wishes to correspond. To give them one alphabet for reading and another for writing is to double their difficulties.

The question has been debated for some years, but is now decided. France, Germany, Switzerland, England and America have adopted the ordinary character. A single attempt of some importance has been made with arbitrary characters, and that is the printing of St. John's Gospel and of a small reading book with stenographic signs by Mr. Lucas, of Bristol. But no institution has adopted or will adopt it, for the conviction of the advantages of the ordinary alphabet are too strongly rooted in the mind of directors of these institutions (see Addenda).

But after this there remains another question to debate, the solution of which is less advanced than the former. It is to decide if the capital Roman characters, A, B, C, D, E, F, &c., ought to be adopted, or the small letters, a, b, c, d, e, f, &c., modified in such a way, however, as to preserve their known form.

The Edinburgh Society of Arts had decided in favour of the

A B C D E F G H I J K L M
N O P Q R S T U V W X
Y Z , ; : . ! ? - &

1 2 3 4 5 6 7 8 9 0

A B C D E F G H I I K L M N
O P Q R S T U V W X Y Z
, . ; : ! ? ' - & + ÷

1 2 3 4 5 6 7 8 9 0

GLASGOW ALPHABETS.

capital letters. Mr. Taylor's reports had very much contributed to this decision. This opinion had many more supporters than the other at the time of my journey, and books printed according to this system were introduced into more establishments than the books with the small letters modified.

Two men are still divided in opinion. Mr. Alston, of Glasgow, uses capital letters like the sample given above. As he is active and generous, his visits, his entreaties, and the low price at which he has offered his books to the directors of institutes, have decided them to try the system in most establishments.

Mr. Gall, of Edinburgh, uses the small letters, but modified and made angular. Mr. Gall argues the matter. Each of these letters has been the object of long and serious study. He challenges a trial, but he waits ; and, without wishing to hasten it too much, he resolutely hopes for the success of his ideas and the definite adoption of his printed books.

I have had the advantage of prolonged discussions with Mr. Gall on the form of the letters to be adopted. It is more than ten years since he undertook this printing, and he has not ceased improving it. No doubt it is still far from the perfection it will attain if he continue his efforts ; but the improvements adopted bear witness to the purity of his intentions and to the sincere desire which animates him of making what is really the best, for my remarks have induced him to modify again the forms of several letters.

I now give my readers a specimen of Mr. Gall's first attempts. There is many a letter which at first and on the first inspection cannot be recognised, and that is to be regretted. Mr. Gall has been unjust to himself in changing the form too much, and this has militated against the adoption of the system. Originally his alphabet was placed in the list of arbitrary characters, and it partly deserved this classification ; by making it more like the ordinary characters, it would lose none of the advantages it has at present, and would be infinitely more pleasing to the eye.

The beauty of the letters, although it cannot be appreciated except by those who have their sight, deserves our consideration. The first condition to observe in the formation of an alphabet is to render the letters as beautiful as possible, while preserving the qualities which make them easily distinguishable by the touch.

Letters are all the more tangible the more they differ from each other by their general form ; and this form in the capitals is very varied for the eye, which sees the inside strokes of the

EDINBURGH ANGULAR ALPHABETS.

letters ; but these letters are too uniform for the touch, which only perceives the outlines. Let us judge of this by the two lines which follow, and in which I have tried to show what part of a capital letter the finger can touch.

HNM KXZERBDOCCSUPFVYTIWJALQ

ⁿ letters too degraded to read clearly

When all the letters have the same height, their tangibility is necessarily less than if they had projections above or below the line. Thus the letters used by Mr. Gall, even if the interior be filled up, will preserve by their upper projections characteristic marks which capital letters do not possess.

I will try to make this understood by the line of letters which follows, and which shows very nearly what a blind person can feel of such a line.

a b c d e f g h i j k l m n
o p q r s t u v w x y z

I admit that the forms are more distinctly preserved in some of the characters than they would be for a blind person ; but we shall still be able to have an approximate idea of them. It suffices to point this out.

On the other hand, the adoption of the small letters is of advantage to the blind. This type is used in France, Germany, America, and England. Only one printing establishment makes use of capital letters, and that is Glasgow.* There is so little difference between the letters adopted in these different countries that every blind person who has learnt to read books printed at Edinburgh can after an hour's practice read books printed in

---

* I have heard that the Institute for the Blind at Philadelphia has also recently adopted capital letters.

SPECIMEN OF ALPHABETS.

N 1

a b c d e f g h i j k l m

n o p q r s t u v w x y z &

N 2

a b c d e f g h i j k l m

n o p q r s t u v w x y z

N 3

a b c d e f g h i j k l m

n o p q r s t u v w x y z

other countries. In this way different books can be usefully exchanged and libraries for the blind can be enriched.

The use of small letters does not prevent the use also of capitals as initials. On the contrary, this use will make books for the blind neater and more distinct. Besides, the knowledge of capital letters is useful on many occasions: for instance, in reading inscriptions, &c.

I have spoken already of the advantage there is in adopting the ordinary letters, because of its usefulness to the blind in enabling them to learn more easily the forms of the letters they have to trace upon paper; but the form of the small letters is nearly always that of written letters. This advantage has suggested to me the idea of proposing the alphabets engraved on the preceding page. See No. 3.

Alphabet No. 1 was that on which I had at first fixed. It was only a modification of the one finally adopted by Mr. Gall, and a copy of which will be seen engraved on p. 97.

This alphabet preserves exactly the ordinary form of letters, only, in order to make them more tangible, some accessory features have been removed from the letters.

a has become a **b** is open b

c is less round C, so as not to be taken for O, &c.

I had got thus far in drawing up my report when I had the honour of receiving a visit from Mr. Taylor, the man most skilled of any in England in all relating to the education of the blind. It was Mr. Taylor who decided the Edinburgh Society of Arts to award a gold medal to the capital letters of Dr. Fry, of London. It was he, too, who was recently commissioned by the British Association for the Advancement of Science to make the report on the art of printing for the blind which that Society has included in its memoirs, and in which it concludes in favour of capital letters. I had a conference with him last November on the choice of an alphabet, and I explained all the advantages of the small letters. After a searching study of this matter, he informed me that he had decidedly changed his opinion ; and that, in spite of all he had written, the evidence of the advantages connected with the system I extolled had forced him to acknowledge and accept the truth, and I make this known with his consent. This important conquest gives me a well-founded hope that we shall arrive at an uniform character in all countries in time, and sooner than I had before dared to hope. Mr. Taylor's conclusion has, besides, confirmed me in my opinion ; and, now that I know it, it is with yet more confidence I propose to adopt small letters for relief-printing in Belgium.

Mr. Taylor has not only adopted this alphabet, but he has introduced a real improvement which I shall explain.

The alphabet used for printing in relief in the Institute for the Blind at Paris occupies three spaces, as may be seen from the following diagram :—

The American alphabet (imitated from the Edinburgh one), and the one I propose, No. 1, only occupy two spaces.

In order to economise space no letter descends below the line, and the letters are nevertheless twice as tangible. To obtain this result, those letters the lower strokes of which descended have been raised, and their bases are placed on the level of those without projections ; as we see in No. 2, in the letters g, j, p, q, y, &c.

This displacement of the letters gives them characteristic points which prevent us from mistaking their name and value ; but the eye, not being accustomed to this, rather dislikes them ; and use has even been made of the Roman capital G in the American alphabet.

Mr. Taylor therefore proposes to reduce the upper projections a little, and to give the letters strokes descending below the line. These lower and upper strokes, while assisting to distinguish the letters, would, however, be so short that the characters would only occupy one-sixth of the space of the Glasgow characters No. 2. See the engraved alphabet No. 2.

This loss is too well balanced by the advantage the letters gain with regard to tangibility for me to hesitate one moment in believing that the adoption of these characters would be useful.

After choosing the alphabet, we have to find out what size the letters ought to be. If a person having his eyesight, who had learnt to read with his eyes, tries to do so by the touch, the progress he makes is so slow and so wearisome that he would be tempted to condemn reading books in relief as an Utopia. The conclusion he drew from his experience would, however, be erroneous, and a little reflection will show this. After the education the eye has received, it is capable of observing objects with an astonishing celerity and accuracy. But it did not always have this power.

At first the eye is a very sterile organ. Its primary object is colour, and that is all it is in a condition to distinguish as a sense. All the information we receive at present by means of this organ as to the shape, size, and distance of objects is information which originally was only communicated by the touch. We have always noticed that such and such changes of colours and shadows correspond to certain changes of form. This experience is so invariable that, at last, the eye concludes instantaneously from the colour as to the form. This education of the eye was already made even before we had begun to reason; and we had become so skilful at discerning distances and forms at a glance, before we were in a condition to know whence we had this power, that we have attributed to the eye what came to us by the touch. The eye having supplanted the touch so well, this latter sense has been neglected, and we have no idea of the extent it would be able to obtain. If we wish to form a correct idea of the power of this sense, we must put ourselves as far as we can in the position of the blind. They must be our guides, and here they will not be blind guides.

Experience ought to precede reasoning, but it is well known that the loss of one sense turns out of advantage to the others. That is, because we cultivate all the more those which are left. The loss of sight gives a delicacy to the touch, of which we, who are not accustomed to receive information by the touch, are unable to form a just idea. The touch replaces the sight to a surprising extent by practice and exercise, especially if we begin to exercise it early.

The wonderful rapidity with which we read is the result of long practice. The discerning and combining of letters is made slowly at first, and it is only by degrees that we succeed in reading with rapidity. Therefore, we must never compare the eye which has received its education with the touch which has not received any, but we ought rather to conclude from the power which our eye has acquired how much the touch may be able to acquire if it be properly trained. Analogy must lead us to this. So it is not necessary that the letters be too big, firstly, so as not to increase the bulk of the books, and so that the finger may more quickly distinguish the shape; for the larger the surface the letter fills, the more time the finger requires to find it out. But it would be a very dangerous error to believe that characters may be reduced to just what a blind person can feel. We ought to create in him the desire, the inclination, the thirst for reading, and we shall never succeed in so doing if reading be an effort. We ought to encourage them to read, and that is not to be done by showing the blind how very small are the characters which they cannot easily read, but by showing them that they can easily read the books which have been printed for them.

All the senses are modified by exercise, and are capable of acquiring a wonderful degree of susceptibility. That which the senses cannot do at first becomes easy after repeated attempts.

The nicety of perception which a sense has is exactly in relation with the habit it has of receiving those perceptions. Use improves. The size of the character proposed in No. 2 is that which a pupil can read distinctly, and which a man whose fingers are hardened by labour may continue to read. There is only a board wanted at the side of this character to print the alphabet in larger letters for the use of beginners, so that they may be able to note the characteristic points of the letters. The increasing delicacy of touch will necessitate, perhaps, or will permit, a reduction in the size of the characters; but the one I propose will provisionally answer the requirements of the moment.

Each letter has been studied separately, and this has been necessary in order to find the best means of rendering it most distinct by making the least alteration in its common form.

a is distinguished from **O** because the upper stroke is not curved as in the **a** of the ordinary alphabet. **b** is open, so as not to be mistaken for **h**. **C** is only a semicircle, so as to be distinguished from **e** and **O**. The lower stroke of **f** is a characteristic point, the better to distinguish this letter from **J** and **t**. **g** has an exterior outline, by which this letter is isolated from every other form. **j** instead of descending beneath the lower line, will be better placed upon the line **J**. For, in the former position, the upper part resembles **i**, and the lower part is like **f**, while, if placed on the line, **J** can only

be mistaken for $\mathbf{l}$, and is distinguished from it by the base $\mathbf{J}$.
The upper stroke to the right of $\mathbf{k}$, instead of being on the
level of the upper line, would be better projected above that line
$\mathbf{K}$, because this projection will distinguish $\mathbf{k}$ from $\mathbf{b}$ by
more characteristic points. $\mathbf{S}$ ought to have its lower semicircle larger than the other, for otherwise it might be mistaken
for $\mathbf{e}$, $\mathbf{o}$, &c.

The lower or upper projections and the forms are not the only
points by which a letter may be characterised and rendered easily
distinguishable by a blind man ; but the respective size of the
letters greatly contributes to prevent confusion. Therefore
$\mathbf{m}$ will be made wide; and $\mathbf{n}$ narrow $\mathbf{n}$. The same applies
to $\mathbf{V}$ and $\mathbf{W}$.

The relief may be too high, and that is the fault with which
most of the books printed for the blind may be charged.

The tangibility of a letter is not in proportion to the height of
the relief. However little this relief may be raised, from the
moment that is a clear projection above the plane surface of the
paper, the blind person can read what is printed. I have a pupil
born deaf, dumb, and blind. I have accustomed her to a relief
six times less elevated than the relief of the Paris books, and she
reads it with extreme facility. Another observation in support
of this : Mr. Gall has assured me that the blind read a book
which has been used more quickly than one just out of the press.

A relief which is too high not only impedes celerity in reading,
but materially increases the size of the books and necessitates the
use of cylindrical presses. These presses have the disadvantage
of wearing out the type more quickly than does a perpendicular
pressure : for all the pressure of the cylinder when in motion is
made successively on only one part of the type, instead of, as with
the other presses, bearing upon all the letters at once.

Lastly, Mr. Gall, of Edinburgh, has invented dotted letters, which may be seen in the next page. The letters are formed by a succession of dots, and these dots, raised and supported as if by a series of arches, resist the pressure they must bear during reading better than any other relief. A dotted line is more tangible than a plain line, consequently this kind of printing would no doubt be suitable for blind persons whose hands have been hardened by labour. Mr. Taylor has assured me that he has nowhere seen the blind read more rapidly than at Berlin, and the letters used there are dotted. As the aged blind could not possibly continue reading the Paris printing, it has been deemed advisable to print books for their use with dotted letters. This again seems to prove favourable to Mr. Gall. Besides, the books would cost much less printed in this way, as the workmanship would be much easier. I admit, however, that, in spite of my conviction, I have not succeeded in convincing persons who are interested in this kind of printing of the utility of dotted letters, as I have been able to convince them of the advantages of small letters. They generally fear that the roughness of this printing may be injurious to the delicacy of touch of the young blind. No doubt all opinions might be conciliated by using the two types, plain and dotted, the one for the young blind and the other for those who are more aged. Experience alone will be able to decide.

A B C D E F G H I J
K L M N O P Q R
S T U V W X Y Z

a b c d e f g h i j k
l m n o p q r s t u v
w x y z . ; . &

a b c d e f g h i j k l m n o
p q r s t u v w x y z . ; .
1 2 3 4 5 6 7 8 9

A B C D E F G H I J K L M N
O P R S T U V W X Z

a b c d e f g h i j k l m n o
p q r s t u v w x y z . ; . ? &
1 2 3 4 5 6 7 8 9 0

EDINBURGH DOT ALPHABETS.

G

ADDENDA.

Page 19, line 9.

The Rev. Mr. Dennet began to teach a small number of blind, but only imperfectly succeeded, and was about to abandon the undertaking, when, owing to Mr. Dawson's zeal, a subscription having been made, a house could be bought. Dawson drew up the rules and organised the institution.

Page 80, line 10.

Mr. J. H. Frere has just proposed another arbitrary alphabet. It is made according to Mr. Lucas's plan. Subscriptions were raised immediately, and a great part of the New Testament has already been printed. The friend who communicates this news (August 2, 1838) does not say where this new experiment is made. The characters are stenographic.

GENERAL RULES

OF THE SCHOOL FOR THE BLIND AT YORK.

1. The object of the institution is to put the pupils in a position to gain their living, at the same time caring for their moral and religious education.

2. The pupils will attend the churches which their relatives shall direct; or, if they are adults, those they shall choose for themselves.

3. Only those trades are taught which the blind can follow with advantage; but everything which is profitable to their intellectual development may be taught.

ELECTIONS OF PUPILS.

4. Persons who have subscribed £1 per annum and those who have made a donation of £10, or those who having made a donation of £5 will subscribe 10s. yearly, have a right to vote in the election of a pupil; those who contribute double will have the right to two votes, and so on.

5. A legacy of at least £50 will authorise the first executor under a will to give one vote in the election of each pupil for life.

6. Before the elections the Committee will fix the number of pupils to be elected, will examine the claims of the candidates, and publish the list of those who are eligible.

7. The Committee must place on this list children from ten to fifteen years of age in preference to those who may be older or who shall not yet have attained that age.

8. Those who may have preserved a more perfect sight than to

distinguish darkness from light, or those who would be incapable of learning a trade from weakness of intellect, will not be elected.

9. Those who may be subject to a contagious disease and who may not have had the small-pox or who have not been vaccinated will not be admitted.

10. Every pupil elected, before he can be received into the institution, must find a person who will make himself responsible by a written engagement for payment of the board required by the rules, and who will engage to take back the pupil when discharged from the institution.

11. The elections are held twice a year.

12. Voting may be by proxy.

13. The Committee will fix the sum to be paid by the pupil for his board and clothing.

14. The children of well-to-do parents may be admitted to receive their education on favourable terms.

15. Subscribers can only vote when their subscription is paid.

16. Annual subscriptions are payable in the month of January.

GOVERNORS.

17. Those who shall have made a donation of at least £20 and subscribers of £2 per annum, or those who after having made a donation of £10 shall have subscribed at least £1 per annum, shall be governors of the institution, and shall manage its affairs.

18. The governors shall meet the first Thursday in the month of May, and the first Thursday in October, at one o'clock in the afternoon; and they shall be summoned by five of their number. Seven governors make a quorum.

COMMITTEE.

19. The governors shall choose yearly a directing committee which shall consist of fifteen members, chosen among the sub-

scribers, of a president, two vice-presidents, the secretary, and of the treasurer of the institution, and of the secretaries and treasurers of the local committees. Three members at least of the fifteen shall vacate their posts annually, and shall be replaced at the annual meeting in the spring.

20. The Committee shall meet regularly on the second Thursday of every month ; and extraordinarily when it shall be called together one day in advance. At these extraordinary meetings no resolutions can be taken as to the medical men or the money to be invested. Three members suffice to form a quorum.

21. The Committee will take the necessary measures for the education and supervision of the pupils. The Committee will ask the superintendent for an annual report of the state of the school, and will visit it from time to time. The Committee will manage the affairs of the establishment in the interval between the governors' meetings, it can invest money or change its investments, but it shall not be able to sell or buy funded properties except when so authorised by the governors.

22. The members of the Committee cannot be purveyors to the institution nor have an interest in any contract relating to it.

23. The doctors, the teachers, and the servants are chosen by the Committee.

24. The superintendent and the master will be elected at a special meeting of the Committee ; all the members having had fifteen days' preliminary notice of it.

SUPERINTENDENT.

25. The superintendent-general will watch over the conduct of the pupils, the teachers, and the domestics. He will regulate the system of education, under the supervision of the Committee, and will present a report on the state of the school every month.

VISITORS.

26. Two members of the Committee will be nominated to visit the school monthly. They will write their remarks in a book, which the Committee will examine at each monthly meeting.

27. Two ladies will be engaged to visit the girls, and to record their remarks in a similar book.

MASTER.

28. The housekeeping of the Home is entrusted to a master under the supervision of the Committee. He will give instruction to the pupils under the direction of the superintendent ; some branches, however, will have a special professor. He will receive the subscriptions and the pupils' board. He will sell the articles manufactured in the institution. He will keep the accounts of the home and present a monthly statement of them to the Committee. He will deposit his monies in the bank, and never reserve more than twenty pounds sterling in cash.

MISTRESS.

29. The mistress will assist the master in the management of the home and will specially supervise the girls. She will look after the cleanliness of the house and the pupils. In the master's absence the mistress is entrusted with the general management.

PUPILS.

30. The boys and the girls are always separated, at least when the master and mistress are not present.

OF GOING OUT OF THE INSTITUTION.

31. The pupils shall not leave the enclosure of the institution without permission.

32. Pupils who may have members of their family residing at York may go out between two and seven o'clock on the first Saturday of each month.

33. Pupils may take a holiday if they wish to do so at Christmas for a fortnight and in July for a month.

ORDER OF THE DAY.

34. The pupils rise at six from the Annunciation until Michaelmas Day. The other months of the year they rise at seven o'clock.

35. The pupils retire to rest during all the year at half-past eight o'clock in the evening.

36. For breakfast at eight o'clock in the morning the children receive a pint of milk, or milk soup alternately, with bread.

37. For dinner they receive at one o'clock daily meat and potatoes, with puddings or tarts.

38. Their supper at half-past six o'clock daily consists of a pint of milk, or milk soup alternately, and bread.

39. There is playtime from noon until one o'clock and from five until half-past six o'clock. During the summer, if the weather be fine, recreation is allowed from five till eight o'clock. There is no work on Saturday afternoon.

TIME OF PRAYER AND RELIGIOUS INSTRUCTION.

40. In the morning half-an-hour after getting up the pupils shall meet together to hear reading and for prayer. The same is done in the evening at eight o'clock.

41. This article regulates the order for Sunday.

HOURS OF WORK.

The pupils will work from nine till noon and from two o'clock until five, unless the master teaches them during this time.

All the pupils will learn church singing. Those only whom the superintendent shall judge have a particular taste for music will receive special lessons in the art.

The pupils who may show a special gift for any art will be principally exercised in its practice.

TIME OF GENERAL INSTRUCTION.

The pupils will alternately receive lessons in arithmetic, reading, writing, &c., from ten o'clock until noon daily excepting Saturdays and Sundays. During the summer the time not passed in prayer will be occupied during the morning in the instruction of the pupils. During the winter evenings, if the weather will not allow of going out, they will be read to.

Questions to be answered before the Admission of Pupils.

1. What is the name of the applicant for admission ?
2. What is his age ?
3. What is his native place ?
4. What is his present place of abode ?
5. What are his pecuniary means ?
6. Does he receive assistance from the parish or elsewhere ? What is the amount of such assistance ?
7. Where does his family reside ?
8. What are they ?
9. How long has he been blind ?
10. Has he been employed in any work ?
11. Has he received any religious instruction ?
12. What is his conduct ? Has he a character for truth and honesty ?

The answers to these questions must be made by the minister of the parish.

1. Is the applicant quite blind, or does he possess such a degree of sight as to permit his distinguishing light from darkness ?
2. What appears to have been the cause of his blindness ?
3. Is he intelligent and healthy enough to learn a trade ?
4. Has he had the small-pox or has he been vaccinated ?
5. Is he not affected by a dangerous disease ?

A doctor must reply to the preceding questions.

1. By what subscriber is he recommended ?
2. Who is the person in or near York who will render himself responsible for the payment of the board, and who will receive him on his leaving the school ?

The replies to these questions must be made by him who recommends the blind applicant.

CATALOGUE OF BOOKS

Written in England on the Blind and their Education.

PHILOSOPHICAL TRANSACTIONS. 1729, 1774, 1778.
ENCYCLOPÆDIA BRITANNICA. Edinburgh, 1783.
> The article "Blind" is remarkable. It is the work of TH. BLACK-
> LOCK, a blind Doctor of Divinity.

GENTLEMAN'S MAGAZINE. 1808.
> Pp. 40 and 41. A Deaf, Dumb, and Blind Woman.

INSTRUCTION OF THE DEAF AND DUMB. By JOSEPH
WATSON, LL.D. London, 1809.
> Contains, pp. 64 and 65, a letter by Astley Cooper on James
> Mitchell, who was deaf, dumb, and blind.

WARDROP, JAMES. HISTORY OF JAMES MITCHELL, a boy born
blind and deaf, with an account of the operation performed, &c.
London, 1813. 4to.

ACCOUNT OF THE SCHOOL FOR THE INDIGENT BLIND.
1814.

EDINBURGH TRANSACTIONS. 1814.
> On James Mitchell.

ENCYCLOPÆDIA BRITANNICA. 1817. Art. "Blind."
SCRAP BOOK, a selection of interesting and authentic anecdotes.
Dublin, 1825. 12mo.
> Contains a report on a deaf, dumb, and blind girl.

TRANSACTIONS OF THE SOCIETY FOR THE ENCOURAGE-
MENT OF ARTS, ETC. London, 1827.
> Speaks of a machine for writing, invented by Don Isern.

APPEAL ON BEHALF OF THE INDIGENT AND INDUS-
TRIOUS BLIND. Edinburgh, 1829.
> This appeal states the object of the institution and its history.

PURSUIT OF KNOWLEDGE UNDER DIFFICULTIES. Illustrated by anecdotes. London: Charles Knight, Pall Mall. 1831.
2 vols.
> The first volume contains the lives of several blind persons, who, in
> spite of their misfortune, attained a deserved celebrity.

A HISTORICAL SKETCH OF THE ORIGIN AND PROGRESS
OF LITERATURE FOR THE BLIND. By JAMES GALL.
Edinburgh: James Gall. 1834.

H

BIOGRAPHY OF THE BLIND. By James Wilson. 3rd edition. Birmingham, 1835.

This is a work by a blind author about blind people who have made themselves famous.

ANECDOTES AND ANNALS OF THE DEAF AND DUMB. By Charles Edw. Herbert Orpen, M.D. 2nd edition. London, 1836.

The 2nd Part contains three chapters treating of the blind. The 5th draws a parallel between the deaf and dumb and the blind. He thinks that their education is almost impossible, and says that there is not an instance of such a being being able to acquire the knowledge of language. The 7th speaks of means of communication between the deaf and dumb and the blind.

PENNY CYCLOPÆDIA. Art. "Blind."

This article is written by Mr. Charles Baker, director of the Deaf and Dumb Institute at Doncaster.

STATEMENTS OF THE EDUCATION AND EMPLOYMENT ADOPTED AT THE ASYLUM FOR THE BLIND. By John Alston, Esq. Glasgow, 1836.

AN ACCOUNT OF THE RECENT DISCOVERIES WHICH HAVE BEEN MADE FOR FACILITATING THE EDUCA-TION OF THE BLIND. By James Gall. Edinburgh, 1837.

INSTRUCTIONS FOR TEACHING THE BLIND TO READ. By T. M. Lucas. Bristol.

REPORT BY A COMMITTEE OF THE SOCIETY OF ARTS IN SCOTLAND ON THE BEST ALPHABET AND METHOD OF PRINTING FOR THE USE OF THE BLIND, 1837.

This report is very interesting.

TO THE DIRECTORS OF THE INSTITUTIONS FOR THE BLIND IN GREAT BRITAIN AND IRELAND. By John Alston, Esq.

OBSERVATIONS ON THE EMPLOYMENT, EDUCATION, AND HABITS OF THE BLIND. By Th. Anderson. London, 1837.

THE ATHENÆUM. London. Saturday, September 30, 1837.

On printing in relief.

NARRATIVE OF THE PROGRESS OF PRINTING FOR THE BLIND AT THE GLASGOW INSTITUTION. By John Alston, Esq., Treasurer. 1838.

BRITISH ASSOCIATION FOR THE ADVANCEMENT OF SCIENCE. London, 1838.

This number contains Mr. W. Taylor's report on "Printing in Relief."

THE SCOTTISH CHRISTIAN HERALD. May 5, 1838.

This number publishes an article by Mr. Charles Baker, "The Origin and Progress of the Art of Printing for the Blind." 1838.

MUSICAL GRAMMAR. By MR. TANSURE.
REID'S INQUIRY INTO THE HUMAN MIND.
This work has appeared in many editions.

THE DEAF AND DUMB AND BLIND SCOTTISH BEGGAR.
Edinburgh.

BOOKS PRINTED IN ENGLAND FOR THE BLIND.

YORK.

THE DIAGRAMS OF EUCLID'S ELEMENTS OF GEOMETRY
IN AN EMBOSSED OR TANGIBLE FORM FOR THE USE
OF BLIND PERSONS. By the REV. W. TAYLOR. York,
1828. 8vo.

CARTE D'ANGLETERRE ET DU PAYS DE GALLES (Map of
England and Wales).

SELECTION OF PSALM TUNES AND CHANTS, IN RAISED
CHARACTERS, FOR THE USE OF THE BLIND. By the
REV. W. TAYLOR. York, 1836. Oblong 4to.

A SHORT HISTORY OF ELIJAH THE PROPHET, AND OF
NAAMAN THE SYRIAN. York.

THE HISTORY OF JOSEPH. York.

> These two little books were printed by Mr. Littledale, a rich blind
> man, for the use of his brethren in misfortune of the Institute at York.
> See page 53 of this Report.

EDINBURGH.

THE GOSPEL OF ST. JOHN, PRINTED ON LARGEST TYPE
FOR THE BLIND. 4to. 6s.

THE EPISTLE TO THE EPHESIANS. Printed on largest type for
the Blind. 1s. 6d.

THE EPISTLE TO THE PHILIPPIANS. Ditto. 1s. 6d.

THE GOSPEL BY ST. LUKE, on fretted type. 4to.

THE ACTS OF THE APOSTLES, on fretted type. 4to.

FIRST OUTLINE OF CHRISTIAN DOCTRINE. 2d.

SECOND OUTLINE OF CHRISTIAN DOCTRINE. 6d.

SCRIPTURE STATEMENTS. 8d.

ABRIDGEMENT OF OLD TESTAMENT HISTORY. 1s.

THE FIRST CLASS-BOOK FOR TEACHING TO READ, printed
for the Blind.

PLAIN WORDS FOR THOSE WHO READ BUT LITTLE. 4to.
6d.

POOR JOSEPH. 4to. 6d.
THE SINNER'S HELP. 4to. 6d.
DO YOU WANT A FRIEND? 4to. 6d.
YE MUST BE BORN AGAIN. 4to. 6d.
THE WAY TO HEAVEN. 6d.
MAPS OF ENGLAND.
,,   EDINBURGH.
,,   WESTERN HEMISPHERE.
,,   EASTERN HEMISPHERE.

BRISTOL.

THE GOSPEL BY ST. JOHN.
A LITTLE READING BOOK (Un petit livre de lecture).

GLASGOW.

FIRST BOOK OF LESSONS   6d.   Large type.
SECOND BOOK OF LESSONS. 2s.   Large type.
LESSONS ON RELIGION AND PRAYER. 1s. 6d.
LESSONS ON NATURAL RELIGION. 1s. 6d.
THE BOOK OF RUTH. 1s.
THE EPISTLE OF JAMES. 1s.
THE EPISTLE TO THE EPHESIANS. 1s. 6d.   Large type.
THE FOUR GOSPELS : MATTHEW AND LUKE. 5s. 6d. each.
                    JOHN. 4s. 6d.
                    MARK. 4s.
THE ACTS OF THE APOSTLES. 5s. 6d.
THE EPISTLE TO THE ROMANS.
THE FIRST AND SECOND EPISTLE TO THE CORINTHIANS.
THE EPISTLE TO THE GALATIANS.
MUSICAL CATECHISM, with tunes for the use of the Blind.   In
      the press.
BOOK OF PROVERBS.   In the press.
FABLES AND PROVERBS.
A few copies of the NEW TESTAMENT will shortly be finished, on
      fine paper, neatly bound for £2 2s.

LONDON: PRINTED BY WM. CLOWES AND SONS, LIMITED, STAMFORD STREET
AND CHARING CROSS.

[REPRINT, 1894.]

STATEMENTS

OF THE

EDUCATION, EMPLOYMENTS,

AND

INTERNAL ARRANGEMENTS,

ADOPTED AT THE

ASYLUM FOR THE BLIND,
GLASGOW.

WITH A SHORT ACCOUNT OF ITS FOUNDER, AND GENERAL
OBSERVATIONS APPLICABLE TO SIMILAR
INSTITUTIONS.

WITH LITHOGRAPHIC ILLUSTRATIONS.

SEVENTH EDITION, TO WHICH HAS BEEN ADDED AN
APPENDIX.

MARCH, MDCCCXLII.

The Profits arising from the Sale of this Publication go towards the Funds.

SOLD AT THE ASYLUM FOR THE BLIND,
AND BY
JOHN SMITH & SON, BOOKSELLERS,
70, ST. VINCENT STREET, GLASGOW:
JOHN JOHNSTON, EDINBURGH; J. ROBERTSON & CO., DUBLIN;
W. M'COMBE, BELFAST;
GALT & ANDERSON, MANCHESTER; AND
SMITH, ELDER & CO., LONDON.
Price Two Shillings.

LONDON:
SAMPSON LOW, MARSTON & COMPANY,
LIMITED,
ST. DUNSTAN'S HOUSE, FETTER LANE, FLEET STREET, E.C.
1894.

IT IS AN INCUMBENT DUTY TO ENLIGHTEN THE MINDS, OF THE BLIND, THOUGH WE CANNOT OPEN THEIR EYES WE CAN TEACH THEIR HANDS TO SERVE THE PURPOSES OF EYES, AND BY MEANS OF THE POWER OF TOUCH, WE POUR IN THE LIGHT OF IN-FORMATION ON THE EYES OF THEIR UNDER-STANDING ON A SYSTEM KNOWN TO ALL.

[REPRINT, 1894.]

STATEMENTS

OF THE

EDUCATION, EMPLOYMENTS,

AND

INTERNAL ARRANGEMENTS,

ADOPTED AT THE

ASYLUM FOR THE BLIND,

GLASGOW.

WITH A SHORT ACCOUNT OF ITS FOUNDER, AND GENERAL
OBSERVATIONS APPLICABLE TO SIMILAR
INSTITUTIONS.

WITH LITHOGRAPHIC ILLUSTRATIONS.

SEVENTH EDITION, TO WHICH HAS BEEN ADDED AN

APPENDIX.

MARCH, MDCCCXLII.

The Profits arising from the Sale of this Publication go towards the Funds.

SOLD AT THE ASYLUM FOR THE BLIND,
AND BY
JOHN SMITH & SON, BOOKSELLERS,
70, St. Vincent Street, Glasgow:
JOHN JOHNSTON, EDINBURGH; J. ROBERTSON & CO., DUBLIN;
W. M'COMBE, BELFAST;
GALT & ANDERSON, MANCHESTER; AND
SMITH, ELDER & CO., LONDON.
Price Two Shillings.

LONDON:
SAMPSON LOW, MARSTON & COMPANY,
LIMITED,
St. Dunstan's House, Fetter Lane, Fleet Street, E.C.
1894.

LONDON:
PRINTED BY WILLIAM CLOWES AND SONS, Limited,
STAMFORD STREET AND CHARING CROSS.

PREFACE TO THIS REPRINT.

THE truly wise gladly add to their store of information, by observing the success, or failure, of others; especially by noticing the causes which led to it : this reprint is therefore issued, with the desire that the experience recorded sixty years ago may be found useful.

It is not generally known that much careful attention has been given to the education and training of the Blind in this country for more than one hundred years, and that many books and papers have been written on the subject. As long ago as November, 1774, there was a paper in the "Edinburgh Magazine and Review," and in the year 1793 a translation of the Essay by Haüy, dedicated to the King of France, was printed in London. In the year 1801 Dr. Lettsom published his "Hints," with an account of the School for the Blind at Liverpool. In 1819 an illustrated translation of the Essay of Guillié was issued by a London publisher ; and in the year 1837 James Gall, of Edinburgh, published his book, "The Education of the Blind," with illustrations.

Before forming an opinion respecting results, the amount of capital employed, in addition to skill and labour, should always be taken into account. And it should be remembered that want of permanent success in some cases arose from want of funds; while other schemes have become popular owing to the large amount of money expended upon them, the patronage of influential persons, and the publicity given to them by "the Press."

It is well known that Blind children can be trained to do almost anything; but comparatively few of the Blind are children. It is therefore after school age that help is most needed; and when any plan for helping the Blind is under consideration, the wants of adults should receive very careful attention.

NOVEMBER, 1894.

TO THE DIRECTORS OF THE GLASGOW ASYLUM FOR THE BLIND.

GENTLEMEN,

Having had numerous applications for statements of the manner in which our Asylum is managed; and finding it impossible to give a proper view of its system in the short compass of a letter, I have endeavoured in this new Edition, succinctly, to draw up the following account of the Education and employment it affords, and of its Internal Arrangements, including all the improvements to the present time. Should this attempt merit your approbation, and prove in any way beneficial to similar Institutions, the labour will be more than compensated to,

GENTLEMEN,

Your most obedient Servant,

JOHN ALSTON.

GLASGOW, 22nd March, 1842.

TABLE OF ILLUSTRATIONS.

APPENDIX.

EDUCATION OF THE BLIND.

PRELIMINARY REMARKS.

IT seems strange that in the mind of any one there should exist a doubt respecting the expediency of educating the Blind, or that it should be supposed enough has been done for them, when their bodily wants have been supplied.

They are rational and immortal beings, and capable of all the enjoyments which others feel from the cultivation of their moral and intellectual powers. It therefore becomes not only a reasonable but incumbent duty, to employ every means for cultivating the moral and intellectual faculties of the unfortunates deprived of sight, and storing their minds with general knowledge.

Should it be objected that they are incapable of receiving instruction through the same means by which it is communicated to others, the objection only proves the necessity of endeavouring to devise such methods of conveying instruction as may be best suited to their particular circumstances.

The ear has been happily called the vestibule of the soul, and in the annals of the Blind, those who have become illustrious by their mental acquirements confirm the remark ; for they show that few intellectual studies are inaccessible to them. It has always been observed, and has received a kind of universal assent among those who have associated much with them, that in certain branches of study they have a facility which others rarely possess. But in order to assist them, it is necessary that the other senses should supply the want of the eye. If, for instance, we wish

B

to teach them the art of reading, letters must be prepared palpable to their touch. If we wish to communicate to them a knowledge of the surface of the earth, globes and maps must be prepared, with the divisions, &c., &c., in relief. Knowledge obtained in this way must, of course, be acquired much more slowly than that acquired by sight; but this very circumstance should excite to more vigorous efforts for the removal, as far as possible, of every obstacle that retards its progress.

The invention of characters in relief was amongst the earliest measures adopted for the instruction of the Blind; and it is worthy of remark, that the letters chosen were of the Illyrian or Sclavonian alphabet modified. This alphabet was preferred on account of the square form of the letters, which it was thought would be more obvious to the touch than the Roman character; but it was soon abandoned, the square or angular form of the letters not having afforded the advantages that were expected from it.

Moveable letters were next tried, which were placed in small tablets of wood, and made to slide in grooves; and moveable leaden characters were afterwards cast for the use of the Blind at Paris, but the work was attended with difficulties and expenses which the inventor was not prepared to meet.

Large pin cushions were also brought into use for the Blind, on which characters were formed with inverted needles. Various other attempts were made in wood and metal, till the time of M. Hauie, of Paris, in 1784, who invented the art of printing in relief for the use of the Blind.

No successful efforts were subsequently made to improve the method of printing, and it is but of a very recent period that any other means were generally adopted for their improvement, except by oral instruction.

The inefficiency of a method of communication so disproportioned to the end in view, and in which the pupil was rendered totally dependent on the instructor, by being debarred from acquiring any portion of his education by his own exertions, suggested the propriety of attempting to form a system of notation as a substitute for reading, which should, in some measure, supply the desideratum, and enable the scholar to co-operate with the teacher.

Various were the methods that were adopted, and amongst the rest, the ingenious system of writing on twine ; but this was found to be by far too intricate ever to be generally useful, and was superseded by the invention of printing with arbitrary characters in relief, sometime ago revived in this country by Mr. James Gall, of Edinburgh, and Mr. Lucas, of Bristol ; but this plan also involved many serious difficulties both to the Blind reader and their teacher.*

I had long been convinced that arbitrary characters, however ingeniously constructed, threw unnecessary obstacles in the way of the Blind, and that an assimilation of the alphabet of the Blind to that of the seeing, would, from its great simplicity, not only be free from all objections, but that, in the case of those who, having lost their sight after they were familiar with the Roman alphabet, it would be attended with manifest and peculiar advantages,† while its similarity to the common printing would enable Blind children, at a distance from any institution, to attend an ordinary school without giving more trouble or

---

* See Specimen of the Alphabets prepared for the Blind.

† The Glasgow Institution affords an interesting illustration of this at the present time. There is a young woman in the Asylum, who, after being educated in the Institution for the Deaf and Dumb, lost her sight, and thus became totally deaf, dumb, and blind. Having left the Deaf and Dumb Institution previously to the latter calamity befalling her, she remained for a considerable time with her relations in a state of utter helplessness, incapable of any rational intercourse with the external world, and sunk in the deepest despondency. She was accidentally discovered by her former benefactors, and placed in the Glasgow Asylum for the Blind, the inmates of which have been taught to communicate with the Deaf and Dumb; and she may be seen daily receiving instructions from one of the more advanced Blind children tracing by the touch the shapes of the relieved Roman characters, which she still remembers (and greatly prefers to the angular character, which she also understands to some extent), and then indicating them by spelling the words on the fingers of her blind companions. The restoration of this interesting individual to intercourse with the rational world is a source of exquisite pleasure to herself, and of gratification to all connected with her.

inconvenience to the teacher than any of his other pupils, having this farther advantage—being common to the seeing and the Blind, the former cannot only judge of the correctness of the latter's reading, but are qualified to assist them in the process wherever they are, at any period of their life.

In my first experiments, I adopted the Capital letters of the Roman alphabet, merely depriving them of the small stroke, at the extremities, as suggested by the late Dr. Fry, of London, to the Society of Arts, in Edinburgh, when one of the competitors for their Gold Medal for the best alphabet for the Blind. But it was found that letters cut after that model were too broad to be easily deciphered by the sense of touch. Having therefore made numerous improvements on the size and sharpness of the type, and to obviate the sameness of some of the letters by adding the hair-strokes as will be seen in A. R. and N., &c., &c. I brought out several elementary books as my first specimen of printing for the Blind, in January, 1837, from two founts of types, with which I have now finished the New Testament (the whole Scriptures were completed in Dec., 1840), with the Scotch metrical version of the psalms and paraphrases, and English Grammar, also other elementary books, including Musical Catechism, with Tunes, &c., &c. The whole of my experiments were submitted, in detail, to the Blind themselves, and to my being guided by their judgment I attribute much of whatever success has followed my exertions.

The advantages of a literature for the Blind, so simple, practicable, and so easily taught, are obvious to every one. Deprived of the delights of vision, the Blind are naturally inquisitive, and thrown more than others upon their mental resources for enjoyment, they will thereby soon become convinced of the benefits of this mode of instruction : it will afford them profitable and pleasurable occupation in their solitary hours.

It is therefore an incumbent duty to enlighten their minds by unfolding to their touch the pages of that blessed volume, the principles of which afford the best security for their happiness here, and the surest foundation for their hopes of eternity. Thus, though we cannot open the eyes of the Blind, we teach their

DIFFERENT ALPHABETS

Mr. ALSTON.

A B C D E F G H I J K L M N O P Q R S T U V W X Y Z .

1 2 3 4 5 6 7 8 9 0   . : ; _ ! ?

Mr. JAMES GALL

◁ ⊃ ⊂ ⊏ ⋔ φ ᕲ ⊢ I J K I M ∧ ◇ Я 𝖸 ⊢ ∪ ∨ W X Y Z .

Mr. T.M. LUCAS.

hands to serve the purposes of eyes—by means of the power of touch, we pour in the light of information on the eyes of their understanding. To the outward eye, the page of nature is still a blank ; but we thus illuminate the inner man, not with the light of science only, but with the far more glorious light shed abroad by the Sun of Righteousness, who brought life and immortality to light by the Gospel ; they having these advantages over the seeing, that, in the darkest hour of the night they can finger over the pages of their Bibles, and hold communion with their God.

> " Our hands can read, our finger trace,
> The page of truth and love;
> And thus we joyfully embrace
> The message from above.
>
> " Then let us willingly record
> His praise, who maketh known
> To our benighted hearts His word,
> And seals it as His own."

After I had successfully introduced types adapted to the Blind, it was apprehended, that from the expense attending this mode of printing, it might be limited in its operations. But at the annual examination of the inmates of this Asylum, on the 25th of October, 1836, I presented to a numerous and respectable assembly the first specimens of printing from the Roman alphabet for the use of the Blind : and being satisfied that the demand for the Blind must, for a long period, be necessarily so limited as to hold out no adequate inducement to a publisher, I stated, that my object was, if possible, to raise a fund distinct from that of the Institution, to be devoted exclusively to the printing of Books for the Blind, and to their diffusion, at a cheap rate, throughout the country. With this view I made my first appeal to the ladies of Glasgow and its neighbourhood, who are ever eager to respond to the call of benevolence ; and I am proud to acknowledge, that, to their generous exertions, I owe the origin of the Printing Fund, which has already enabled me to provide a Press and two founts of Types. My next application for assistance was made to the different Institutions for the Blind and other benevolent Societies : and I am happy to say, that their aid and co-operation have been cheerfully granted. These Institutions receive copies of the books at nett cost, so as to enable them to supply the poor at a moderate charge, or gratuitously, as they may see proper ; all profits go to the Printing Fund.

The printing for the Blind being in relief, it is obvious that these books must always be considerably larger than those for the seeing, and that any attempt to reduce them to ordinary dimensions must be followed by a corresponding sacrifice of their adaptation to the touch of the reader. I am satisfied, from experience, as well as from the opinion of those with whom I have corresponded, and who have given much of their attention to the subject, that it would be injurious to reduce the size of the letters below that of our type of Great Primer, on which the New Testament is printed.

It has been asked by many, what has to become of those advanced in life and engaged in trades, whose sense of touch cannot be so acute as that of the young ? My answer is, that just as seeing people, when advanced in life, require glasses to aid their sight, so must the Blind have a larger type to suit their sense of touch. To meet this, I have adopted the large Double Pica type, on which the elementary books are printed, and the difficulty referred to has been completely obviated.

The invention of such letters forms a new era in the history of literature, and no limits can be set to the benefits which future generations may derive from it.

Perhaps the best statement of the progress of the pupils, and the advantages derived by them froms this Institution, may be obtained from the Report of the last Public Examination, as it appeared in the *Scottish Guardian* newspaper, Glasgow, 10th May, 1838.

PUBLIC EXAMINATION.

Extracted from the " Scottish Guardian" of May 10, 1838.

PRINTING FOR THE BLIND.

THE Tenth Annual Examination of the inmates of the Asylum for the Blind took place on Monday afternoon, in the Trades' Hall, in presence of a vast assembly of ladies and gentlemen. The ·Lord Provost presided, and amongst the Directors and friends of the Institution present were, the Very Rev. Principal Macfarlan, the Rev. Dr. M'Leod, Rev. Mr. Gibson, of College Church, Rev. J. B. M'Craa, of Dublin, Bailie Campbell, Bailie Bain, Mungo Nutter Campbell, Esq., of Ballimore, William Leckie Ewing, Esq., William Smith, Esq., of Carbeth-Guthrie, John Smith, Esq., of Crutherland, Henry Knox, Esq., William Buchanan, Esq., James Bogle, jun., Esq., John Thomas Alston, Esq., of Liverpool, Bailie Martin, of Greenock, and several other gentlemen from a distance. The meeting was opened with prayer by Principal Macfarlan.

Mr. Alston, of Rosemount, the Honorary Treasurer, and the ardent and persevering friend of the Blind, conducted the examination with the assistance of the teachers. Before proceeding to the business of the day, Mr. Alston stated that on the 25th October, 1836, when he had last the pleasure of appearing before a similarly numerous and respectable audience, he submitted some specimens of printing for the Blind, and appealed to them for the support necessary to carry forward his undertaking, when he pledged himself that he would enable the Blind to read as well as those who have the use of their sight. The present meeting had been expressly called for the purpose of affording them an opportunity of judging whether that object had been attained. There were sixty-five Blind persons before the assembly, and he bespoke indulgence for them in the progress of the examination.

Having formerly described minutely the routine of these agreeable meetings, we do not deem it necessary on this occasion to enter at large into the proceedings. The exercises were commenced with an anthem. The junior class was next examined in orthography and the Shorter Catechism. Then the same class gave specimens of their reading in the elementary books printed at the Institution Press, which evidently afforded lively satisfaction to the meeting. Mr. Orme, who prepared the beautiful music-book which Mr. Alston has printed for the Blind, afterwards examined several of the children in musical notation, and his pupils showed a readiness and exactness which really did great credit to him and to themselves. What rendered their proficiency more remarkable, was the fact that the book they were so familiar with had not been above four weeks out of the press. After being exercised for some time on the tune "Kilmarnock," the whole of the inmates united in singing that beautiful and popular piece in a very effective manner. Mr. Alston requested permission, on account of the limited time, to withdraw from the programme the exercises in geography, arithmetic, and grammar, the company being sufficiently acquainted with the attainments of the children in these branches of their education, and he pledging himself that they were at least not falling behind their former proficiency. The first multiplication table printed for the Blind was here produced. The more advanced class next came forward with their New Testaments lately completed, and read whatever passages the Lord Provost desired, with a degree of fluency and accuracy which surprised and delighted all who witnessed it. There was no doubt about the completeness of the triumph over difficulties that once seemed insurmountable—there could be none ; but to add to the other proofs, Mr. Alston broke up the seal of a parcel, and produced printed copies of Locke's opinion of the Bible, which had been thrown off from the Institution Press, and retained under seal in order that they might be submitted to the Blind for the first time at the meeting. This was accordingly done—the children were put upon their mettle for the honour of being allowed to read it ; and a girl having rapidly fingered the words, and announced she was ready, read it to the audience with perfect ease.

The next exercise was one of a peculiarly interesting character. A young woman, deaf, dumb, and Blind, read a portion of the New Testament, and afterwards wrote in presence of the meeting the subject she had read. Her manuscript was read by Principal Macfarlan, amidst the approbation of the meeting. Mr. Alston expressed himself in terms of characteristic benevolence in regard to this interesting individual, remarking that had his labours been productive of no other effect than to restore her to intercourse with society, and communion with God and her Bible, he would consider all the expense, as well as his own labours, more than compensated. (Cheers.) As an instance of the ease with which any Blind child may be taught to read by his friends or teacher in ordinary circumstances, Mr. Alston brought forward a boy belonging to the Town's Hospital of Paisley, who, according to the statement of Mr. Brown, the teacher in that institution, did not know a letter four months ago ; and the meeting had an opportunity of hearing him read with the utmost facility and correctness. Many other proofs could be given the same as this.

Mr. Alston having finished the examination, left it to the audience to decide whether he had implemented his engagement with his supporters. (Applause.) They had witnessed the examination of the pupils—they had heard a boy reading who had been taught at a common school, and if they wished farther proof of the success of the system, he would refer them to the testimony given in other quarters on the subject. In an advertisement in the London papers last month respecting the School for the Indigent Blind, St. George's Fields, there was an announcement that, " in addition to the usual instruction the pupils are now taught to read by means of printing in raised or embossed letters, according to the plan of Mr. Alston of Glasgow." At the seventh meeting of the British Association for the Advancement of Science at Liverpool in September, 1837, the report given in on the best mode for teaching the Blind, gives a decided preference to this system of Mr. Alston ; * and at a Public examination of the Yorkshire School for the Blind, in York, on Thursday, the 11th January, the Rev. Mr. Taylor, superintendent of the school, explained the means employed for teaching the Blind to read, and gave decided preference to the alphabet furnished by Mr. Alston, which was adopted in the Yorkshire School. The same system was now in active and successful operation in Norwich Institution. A gentleman who had visited the Glasgow Institution, wrote him respecting a young girl, whom his daughter is instructing, as follows :—"You will be glad to learn that the poor Blind woman at Leeds has, under the instructions of my daughter, made great proficiency. She can read the large type well and pretty well the small type." They have sent for new books. (Loud cheering.) In a letter dated Jan. 18 from the Institution Philadelphia, there is intelligence so gratifying that he could not withhold it. There were fifty pupils in the Institution. One of the late vice-presidents, Mr. Birch, had bequeathed an income nearly equal to their utmost wants. The object of their present letter was to inform Mr. Alston that they had lately established a printing-press. The letter goes on to state with respect to the printing :— "Understanding that you adopt the same characters, it appears to our Board of Management that both Institutions will gain by an interchange of volumes," &c. Mr. Alston stated that he had made a shipment, the first of the kind ever made from this country, of 150 volumes, ten full copies of the New Testament, and fifty single copies of the Gospels, besides multiplication tables and other books. He had also a most gratifying letter from the Bristol Asylum or School of Industry. In a letter to

---

* "In December last the Society of Arts for Scotland presented Mr. John Alston the Silver Medal of the Society, bearing the following inscription :—' To John Alston, Esq., of Rose Mount, Hon. Mem. Soc. Arts, and Honorary Treasurer to the Asylum for the Blind at Glasgow, awarded 26th December, 1838, for his Tables, with wood-cut illustrations, and his Musical Catechism, with Tunes, printed in relief, and exhibited to the Society on the 16th and 30th May, 1838; and for his zealous, energetic, and benevolent exertions for the Education of the Blind.' And subsequently two Honorary Medals were voted to Mr. Alston for his continued exertions in behalf of the Blind."

Mr. Alston, the writer says :—" One of the pupils sends her best thanks to you for your exertions, and says she esteems the books she has got more than all the world, and if she were possessed of ten thousand pounds, she would freely give it in such a cause." The same pupil writes from Providence Cottage, Bristol, that she had derived great benefit from hearing the Scriptures in the Bristol Asylum, and adds—" but never did I anticipate the arrival of this glorious day when I should peruse the sacred pages for myself ;" and she proceeds, " I doubt not that the Holy Spirit will explain and apply unto the hearts of many of my fellow-sufferers, and hundreds will have cause to bless God through time and eternity for your benevolent exertions." (This individual was above 40 years of age when she acquired the art of reading ; she has now perused the Scriptures.) Mr. Alston again submitted that he had given sufficient proof of the success of his plan. (Great applause.) He had only one other request to make, and in the presence of the ladies, who had done him such essential service in the furtherance of the cause, he had no apprehensions that it would not be complied with. He was anxious that the Psalms should be added to the New Testament— and the Blind were anxious too—and he was desirous to be enabled to meet the expense of this undertaking, which would not be great. The Trustees had done him the honour to assign him the premium of £8 from Coulter's mortification for inventions, which he had dedicated to the fund for printing the Psalms. The importance of this addition to the works already completed, warranted him in hoping that the public would extend the assistance they had already afforded him. (Cheers.)

The Lord Provost said he was sure there could be but one feeling, that of gratification, arising from the examination they had witnessed this day. It had been a most interesting exhibition, although mingled somewhat with melancholy at seeing so many of our fellow-creatures deprived of one of the greatest blessings— the use of their eyes. But it was gratifying to have seen that by the exertions of one benevolent individual they had been in a great measure enabled to extend their enjoyment of life. They had been enabled to read for themselves, as had been most satisfactorily proved by what we had witnessed to-day, the Scriptures of truth ; and he was sure he spoke the sense of this meeting when he proposed their thanks to Mr. Alston for his exertions in behalf of these individuals. (Cheers.) May he be long spared to continue his exertions in their behalf. (Cheers.)

Principal Macfarlan, having been requested by the Lord Provost to address the meeting, said, since his Lordship had done him the honour of calling upon him, and as he had been pretty closely connected with the progress of this Institution since its commencement, he held it to be his duty to say a very few words explanatory of the principles on which they had endeavoured to proceed ; the details they had already seen. Their object certainly is in the first place to afford to all within the walls of the Institution, old as well as young, the elements of knowledge, and especially that most important of all knowledge, an acquaintance with the Gospel of Christ. This they had for a length of time attempted to do by oral instruction and various other expedients ; but at last they had succeeded, by the blessing of God, in making the young read the Scriptures, as they had this day seen and heard. They likewise endeavoured to furnish them with the elements of general knowledge ; and on former occasions the meeting must have remarked their proficiency in geography, arithmetic, and grammar. They had also endeavoured to teach them in the school of industry various employments, by which they are enabled to earn the means of subsistence by their own exertions, instead of becoming a burden on society. They had added music and many other subsidiary branches of education to their instruction ; and although the former might appear at first sight unnecessary, it enabled them to pass soothingly many, many a weary hour ; to pass in innocent recreation those hours when labour must be intermitted, and when the absence of such occupations would leave them in a more melancholy condition than can well be conceived. It was on the Continent, he thought, that the idea was first struck out of teaching the Blind to read by embossed letters. A great many ingenious plans had been invented for this purpose ; but it at last occurred to their Treasurer to adopt the simple Roman capital alphabet, with some modifications ; and it was found by experiment to be as easily learned and discriminated by their touch as any other set of letters, and to have the peculiar advantage of being equally adapted to ordinary schools, and of being similar to the letters which the Blind may have learned to read before losing their sight. He would refer to two instances in illustration of this. There was the boy from Paisley, whose master had stated that he had become familiar with the books within the last four months ; here was a proof that by the use of these characters any schoolmaster with a moderate share of patience and perseverance may teach a Blind person to read with perfect accuracy. The other case is that of the young woman who labours under the singular complicated deprivation of being deaf, dumb, and Blind. She lost her hearing and became dumb when only four years old. She lost her sight when more advanced in life ; and the loss preyed on her temper, her health, and spirits ; but, by the mercy of God, she was brought here to this Institution, and into contact and intercourse with the Blind, who have learned to communicate with her ; and, by her own declaration, her life has been converted from melancholy and languor into the greatest enjoyment. There was no medium by which she could have communicated with others, had she not before losing her sight been accustomed to read ; but she found the characters familiar to her recollection, and, as has been seen, she reads without difficulty. It would not be considered pedantic and ultra-professional in him to remark, that this was not only a singular blessing, but they had witnessed a most important philosophical experiment. Dugald Stewart and Sir James Mackintosh, men whose names were high in scientific reputation, had regarded it as impossible to convey knowledge to those who are born deaf, dumb, and Blind ; but here is an experiment which shows that study and perseverance may suggest the means of conquering what at first sight might appear an impossibility. (Great applause.)

The Rev. Principal having pronounced a benediction, the

meeting broke up, evidently much pleased with what they had seen and heard. From the important educational improvements introduced into the Asylum since the last public examination, the proceedings were peculiarly gratifying and rendered this the most interesting meeting of the kind ever held in Scotland. The instrumental band diversified the exercises by performing a number of musical pieces in a very creditable style.

Having thus proved before so many competent witnesses the entire fitness of the system of reading in which the Blind are instructed, and having now had two years' experience of it in our Asylum, I may be permitted to say, that with these facilities, it is surely incumbent on all who take an interest in the Blind, to adopt the means thus placed at their disposal for their moral, and religious, and intellectual education.

This system of printing, and indeed the idea of educating the Blind by any kind of typography, are alike new, and there may still be differences of opinion respecting its adaptation to adults. But there can be but one opinion with regard to its fitness for the young, an opinion founded on experience, that if the same attention is given to the instruction of the Blind in reading that is bestowed on the seeing, the progress of the former will scarcely, if at all, be inferior to that of the latter; for as they are not liable to be distracted by external objects, their attention is wholly engrossed with the work they have to do.

If it is of importance to educate the seeing in early life, it is of much more importance to put the young Blind under proper moral training; for the neglect of the early education of the indigent Blind has led to the wandering, mendicant habits of thousands, who, had a little early care and attention been bestowed upon them, would have become useful both to themselves and to society. The surest method of suppressing public begging by the Blind, is to train them when young to habits of industry, by which they can provide for themselves.

The mode of instructing them is the following :—After the pupils have acquired a knowledge of the shape of each letter of the alphabet, they are taught orthography; they next proceed to

the study of etymology; the derivation of words and their relation to each other are particularly explained. After they have
attained this, words of two and three letters may be submitted to
their touch. They should then be made to feel the words with
two or three of their fingers, placing a finger on each of the
letters; by this means they will be able to decipher two or three
letters at once, which by practice will give a dexterity and fluency
to their reading; their finger nails to be kept short to prevent
them from injuring the surface of the letters. By this system of
tuition, the memory and the understanding, as well as the sense
of touch, become the channels through which instruction is conveyed. The Blind have in general retentive memories, those best
grounded in the knowledge of grammar make the most expert
scholars.

At present there are above thirty individuals, whose ages vary
from ten to thirty-two years, who can read, and the attainments
of some of them would bear a comparison with those who have
their sight of the same age and time under tuition.*

I may here notice a question that has been often put, and is
considerably agitated at present, viz. :—How long will the Blind
take to learn to read? and do they read with fluency?

I have known some young persons learn in a few days; others
take a much longer time. The same differences obtain in schools
for the seeing. But I am led to think that were the experiment
made upon an equal number of the Blind and of the seeing, from
the same age and class of society, with the same attention on
the part of the teacher, the Blind would lose nothing by the
comparison.

As to reading with fluency, we have several who read as freely
as the seeing; but my wish has always been to get them not so

---

* I may mention, till we had full occupation for a teacher, for some time
we got a person two hours a day, making the hours to suit his time, which
answered both our purposes. Now we are enabled, besides the classes for the
young, to have a class for the adults, who, being in advanced life, without
having acquired the art of reading, meet in the evenings thrice a week, when
appropriate books for their improvement are read to them.

much to read quickly, as to understand what they do read ; and this I hold to be the main object. Where there is a desire to learn, I have never known our teacher experience much difficulty in making fluent and intelligent readers.

In evidence that this is also the case in other Institutions for the Blind, I may mention the following facts :—I have visited the Institutions in England, most of them three times. On my first visit, in May, 1837, with a view of introducing this system, there were not ten persons who knew letters ; now there are some hundreds who can read our books most distinctly, from the child of eight to adults of upwards of sixty. So generally has it come into practice, that of late the young are instructed before they come to our Institution, either by their parents or at the common schools, which is now nothing uncommon.

But there is another advantage not to be overlooked. That is on the Sabbath days ; when they are prevented from attending church by unfavourable weather, they read the Bible and other books now provided for them, the same as the seeing ; and in the evenings, instead of being congregated together, and instructed orally by their teacher, as was the practice before the introduction of this system of printing. Now each pupil has his book and lesson assigned them ; the whole retire to their apartments, and peruse the lessons. At the hour fixed, they assemble in the school-room or chapel, and repeat what they had learned. To the seeing, nothing can be more delightful than to contrast the advantages they now possess, and their former situation. As books are expensive, we give a volume to one of the Blind, viz. Genesis, when that is read through, then we give the next volume and so on ; by this means the whole can be reading the different portions of the Bible without interfering with one another.

The importance of furnishing this interesting class of our fellow-creatures with the means of moral and intellectual improvement, appears in a striking light, when we consider the proportion generally.

We have unfortunately no statistics of their number in this country ; but in the kingdom of Belgium, Government statistics of the Blind were made in 1835, the result of which was that there were 4117 blind in a population of 4,154,922—establishing the ratio of 1 to 1009. Of this great number 960 were Blind from the effects of ophthalmia.

It is worthy of observation, the same Government, with a benevolent liberality deserving to be imitated by others, have enacted that every indigent Blind and dumb person, belonging to the country, shall be educated at the expense of the State.

In the Prussian dominions, in 1834, there were 9575 for 13,509,927, being 1 to 1410.

From a careful investigation, by Mr. Zeum, of Berlin, it appears that the number of persons affected with blindness is less in the temperate latitudes, and increases either as we advance to the Line or to the Pole. In the one case the reflection of the rays of a burning sun producing the same effects on the eye-sight as those from a snow-covered plain on the other. The ratios of these remarkable observations are thus given in round numbers by Mr. Zeum :

From 20 to 30 Deg. Lat., 1 Blind to each 100 Inhabitants.

30 to 40	,,	1	,,	300	,,
40 to 50	,,	1	,,	800	,,
50 to 60	,,	1	,,	1400	,,
60 to 70	,,	1	,,	1000	,,

Great Britain being situated between 50 and 60 degrees of latitude, and the population is allowed to be fully 25,000,000, then we have a population of Blind persons nearly 18,000.

Having thus ascertained what may be the probable amount of the number of the Blind in this country, let us next examine what has been done for their amelioration. The following are the Institutions for the Blind in this country, with the numbers each contained, according to their last Reports :—

London Institution contains	...	...	...	...	...	130
Liverpool	,,	...	...	...	...	108
Edinburgh	,,	...	...	...	...	80
Glasgow	,,	...	...	...	...	80
Bristol	,,	...	...	...	...	60

Exeter Institution contains	...	...	...	...	...	10
Norwich ,,	...	...	...	...	...	50
Dublin, Richmond ,,	...	...	...	...	...	39
Do. Molyneaux ,,	...	...	...	...	...	30
York ,,	...	...	...	...	...	30
Belfast ,,	...	...	...	...	...	11
Manchester ,,	...	...	...	...	...	30
Newcastle ,,	...	...	...	...	...	20
						668

Thus, in a Blind population of nearly 18,000, there are only 600—at most, not 700—in all the Institutions in this country where any provision is made for their instruction in mechanical arts, and for their moral and intellectual training. Before the introduction of the mode of printing in the Roman letters in relief, in January 1837, there were only very few who knew letters, and the greatest proportion of these were in the Glasgow Institution. Fortunately this is no longer the case; for in London, Edinburgh, Bristol, Norwich, York, and Newcastle, there are many who will bear a comparison in their attainments with persons of the same age, who have all their faculties.

It is earnestly to be hoped that the success which has attended the introduction of this system into these Institutions will induce others to adopt the same; so that, all acting upon the same mode of printing and teaching, it may be the more effectual for the general benefit of the Blind, and may carry into practical operation what we aim at, their moral and religious interest.

EDUCATION.

RELIGIOUS INSTRUCTION.

THE teacher regularly instructs the children in the principles of religion, and is diligent in communicating information to those under his charge, adapted to their capacities, taking notice of the

different events therein recorded; illustrating them as regards
nations, as well as individuals, and setting before his pupils the
inestimable superiority of virtue and religion over immorality and
vice.

The very Rev. Principal Macfarlan has paid great attention,
since the opening of the Asylum, to the spiritual interest of the
inmates, by attending on them every Saturday, when the questions
put by him, and the answers received, generally prove to his
satisfaction the intelligence and diligence of the teacher as well
as that of his pupils.

Family worship is performed morning and evening, the teacher
or one of the Blind reading out the line in the singing of the
Psalm; reading a chapter in the morning, sometimes by one of
the Blind, and another in the evening. The teacher, who acts as
the chaplain, offers up the prayer, which concludes the exercises
for the day.

SABBATH-DAY EXERCISES.

On the Sabbath, after breakfast, and before the inmates
prepare for church, they are assembled in the school-room, when
one of the Blind reads a chapter, and each boy and girl repeats a
Psalm or hymn. Afterwards they are attended to church—the
boys by the Superintendent, and the girls by the Matron. Those
farthest advanced in their education take the Psalm-book with
them to church, and find out the Psalm with most of the seeing.
In the evening, each has his book.

It is most encouraging to perceive with what ease the pupils
acquire the task assigned them. They will repeat six, eight, and
twelve verses with great correctness. At the hour fixed, they all
assemble in the school-room before the teacher, and repeat the
task which they have learned; afterwards they read a chapter,
and closes the exercises with prayers. At eight o'clock they
retire to bed; each is taught a prayer, and enjoined to repeat
it every morning and evening.

READING ON STRING.

PLATE I.

The string alphabet is formed by so knotting a cord that the protuberances made upon it may be qualified by their shape, size, and situation, for signifying the elements of language. The letters of this alphabet are distributed into seven classes, which are distinguished by certain knots or other marks ; each class comprehends four letters, except the last, which comprehends but two. The first, or A class, is distinguished by a large round knot ; the second, or E class, by a knot projecting from the line ; the third, or I class, by the series of links vulgarly called the "drummer's-plait" ; the fourth, or M class, by a simple noose ; the fifth, or Q class, by a noose with a line drawn through it ; the sixth, or U class, by a noose with a net-knot cast on it ; and the seventh, or Y class, by a twisted noose. The first letter of each class is denoted by the simple characteristic of its respective class ; the second by the characteristic, and a common knot close to it ; the third by the characteristic, and a common knot half an inch from it ; and the fourth by the characteristic, and a common knot an inch from it. Thus A is simply a large round knot ; B is a large round knot, with a common knot close to it ; C is a large round knot, with a common knot half an inch from it ; and D is a large round knot, with a common knot an inch from it, and so on. The alphabet above described is found by experience to answer completely the purpose for which it was invented. In this alphabet, the greater part of the Gospel of Mark, and the 119th Psalm, and other passages of Scripture, and historical works have been executed. The string is wound round a horizontal revolving frame, and passes from the reader as he proceeds.*

---

* On each side of the string alphabet in the plate, the names of two gentlemen, as they would appear on knotted twine, may be easily deciphered by referring to the alphabet.

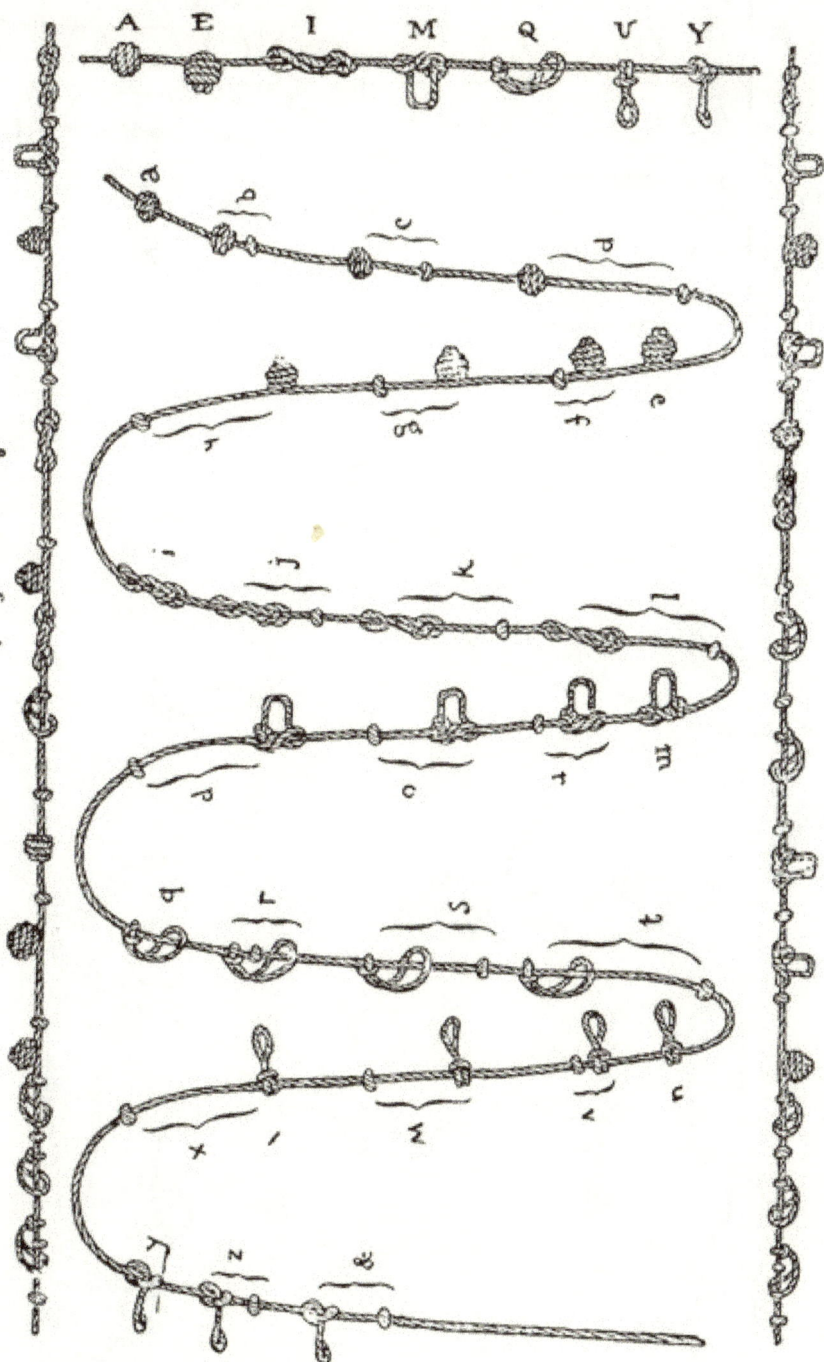

Specimens of String Writing.

Fig 1

Example in Multiplication

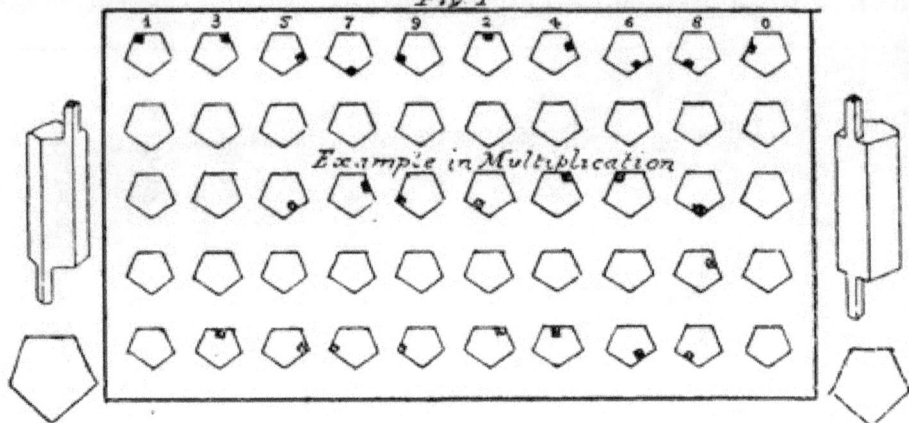

THE TERRESTRIAL GLOBE.

Fig II

ARITHMETIC.

PLATE 2, FIG. I.

The arithmetic board has been so improved at the Glasgow Asylum, that the 10 numerals are represented by one characteristic pin (while in similar Institutions two are used), according as it is placed. It is simply a pentagon, with a projection at one end on an angle, and at the other end on a side. Being placed in the board, with the corner projection to the left hand-upper corner of the hole, it represents 1 ; proceeding to the right-hand upper corner, it is 3 ; the next corner in succession is 5 ; the next 7, and the last 9. In like manner the side projection, by being turned to the sides of the hole progressively, 2, 4, 6, 8, 0. The size of the pentagon, and a drawing of the pin, showing tho projections on the side and angle, are given along with the board. In the drawing of the arithmetic board, an example in multiplication is represented, which may be deciphered by reference to the figures above. The original invention of this board was the united work of Dr. Moyes and Dr. Sanderson.

GEOGRAPHY.

PLATE 2, FIG. II.

The terrestial globe, which is made of oak, measures about nine and a half feet in circumference, and weighs 147 lbs. The weight of the brass meridian is 57 lbs., and of the wooden horizon and supports 48 lbs., making in all 2½ cwt. Notwithstanding its great weight, the whole is so nicely constructed as to render it easy, comparatively speaking, to give the poles any elevation which may be required with regard to the horizon. The water is made smooth, and the land is distinguished from it by being slightly elevated, and its surface rendered rough by a coating of fine sand, painted in oil of various colours, in order to distinguish to the eye the political divisions. These divisions are also surrounded by a slight prominence, for the purpose of enabling those for whom the globe is more particularly intended to grope their way. Rivers are denoted by smooth and slightly raised sinuous lines, traversing the rough land in their proper directions; mountains by a series of elevations indicating the position of the range; and towns by a small brass knob. The equator is divided into 360°. The point where the first meridian crosses it is marked by a round knob. A different mark is placed at every 100, and the intermediate degrees are also distinguished in an appropriate manner. An hour circle is fixed at the North Pole; and an Analemma, of an ingenious construction, showing the sun's declination, stretches equally on each side of the equator. In short, this globe has all the usual appendages of such pieces of apparatus, only so modified as to enable the Blind to solve geographical problems, and *feel* their way upon it, with as much precision as those who have eyes and can *see* their way upon globes of the usual construction.

Maps of Great Britain, Europe, Palestine, and all the divisions are laid out by cords to divide separate kingdoms and districts, and the names of the places printed in relief, is pasted on alongside of the printed names; by this means the map answers both the seeing and the Blind, and the seeing know whether they are right or not. In addition to the maps in relief, and the terrestrial globe by which the Blind are enabled to acquire with facility an intimate knowledge of the relative situation and magnitude of the principal features of our earth, whether physical or political, the following models have been added to their teaching apparatus, and are well adapted to accomplish the end for which they were intended :—

PLATE 3, FIG. I,

contains, on a rectangular board, a representation in relief of the comparative lengths of the principal rivers in the world, reckoning from the Forth and Cylde up to the mighty Amazon. From the knotted cords appended below the mouth of each river the Blind are enabled to read the names of the rivers, the places of their rise and termination, and their lengths in miles. The principal towns on the rivers are denoted by small brass knobs. Upon the same board a method is adopted for enabling the Blind to acquire by the sense of touch a correct idea of the relative bulk of the

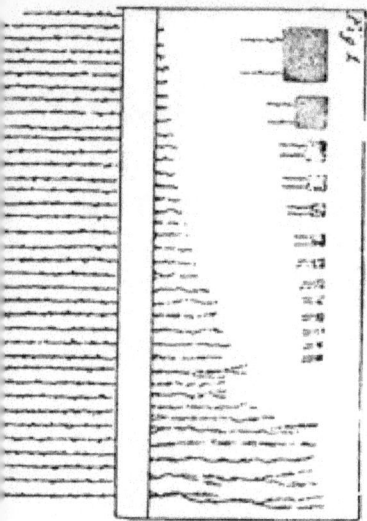

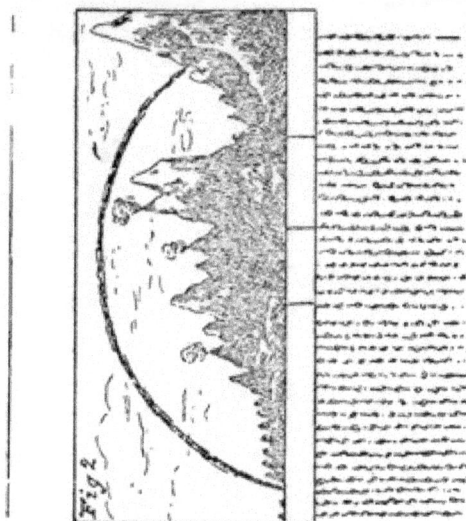

SOLAR SYSTEM,

Showing the comparative magnitude of the Planets, and their relative distance
from the Sun.

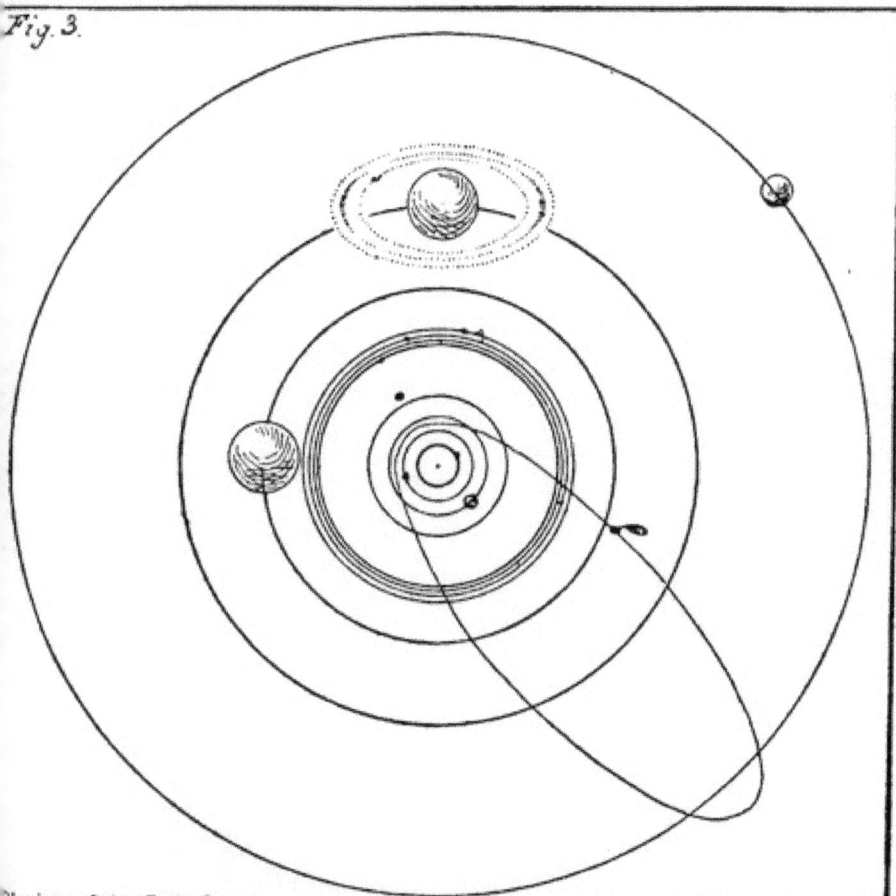

Designed by D. Anderson.

Presented by J. Alston Esq.

different political divisions of the earth. The countries are represented by elevated squares, the comparative areas of which correspond with those of the countries ; and their numerical areas, as well as their respective populations, are also expressed upon knotted cords.

is another rectangular board, containing in relief a representation of the comparative heights of the principal mountains in the four quarters of the earth, ascending gradually from elevations with which the inmates of the Asylum are familiar (such as Gad's Hill), to the loftiest peak known, viz. Dhawalagiri, ort he White Mountain, one of the Himmaleh range, which is at least five miles above the level of the sea. In this model of the elevations upon our globe, and the level of the sea can be distinctly felt : the line of perpetual snow or congelation on the equator is rendered sensible by the mountains being rougher from that line upwards by means of a coating of sand ; a tangible rainbow is represented, bestriding the mountains, and Gay Lussac's balloon can be felt soaring in the air at the height of 22,990 feet above the level of the sea, being the highest altitude of balloons. The names of the mountains, the parts of the world in which they are situated, and their elevation in feet, can all be ascertained by consulting the knotted strings which are attached to a suitable part of the board.

ASTRONOMY.

PLATE 3, FIG. III.

Having by such means elevated their minds to a somewhat adequate idea of the grand features of our globe, they are next directed to the relation in which it stands to the other parts of the system, of which it forms but an insignificant portion. This is effected by a delineation of the solar system upon a board six feet square. A ball in the centre of the board denotes the situation of the sun, and around that ball are represented in relief, by means of cords, the orbits of the different planets at their proportional distances from the sun. On each side of these orbits is fixed a ball. These balls exhibit the relative magnitude of the primary planets, the great terrestrial globe of the Institution being assumed as the size of the sun. This is judicious, as all the pupils are quite familiar with its bulk. In this scheme of the solar system, the eccentric, elliptic orbit of a comet is represented.

GEOMETRY.

There is a species of what may be termed ocular geometry, with which all except the Blind are more or less conversant, and which is of vast importance in the ordinary affairs of life. As a knowledge of the relations of geometrical quantities is by the Blind derived solely through the sense of touch, the field of their investigation must necessarily be very limited, and their ideas equally circumscribed. To remove this grand desideratum as much as possible, and at the same time to habituate them to close and connected reasoning, it was deemed proper to introduce them to the elements of Euclid through the medium of diagrams upon strong paper, the lines and letters standing out in relief from the surface. This is accomplished by simply fixing a thick thread upon the paper by means of glue, with split peas at the angles to represent the letters. The split peas are thus arranged :

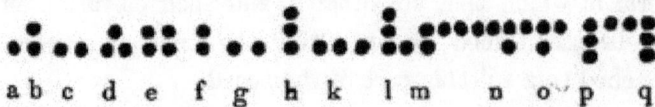

a b c d e f g h k l m n o p q

The following is the Diagram of the 5th Prop. of Book 1st :—

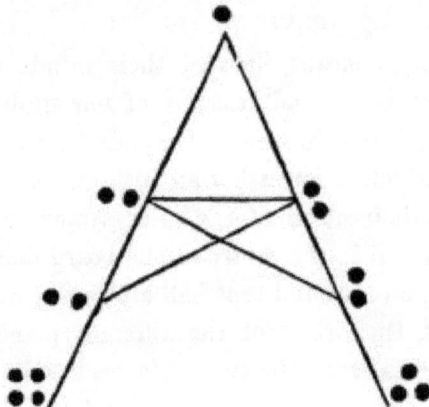

ESTABLISHMENT AND EMPLOYMENT.

MALE DEPARTMENT.

THE SUPERINTENDENT.

THE Superintendent, who resides in a house attached to the Asylum, takes charge of the male department, together with the general management of the work. He gives orders for the different articles for the manufactures ; makes the sales ; keeps an account of the work done by the workmen, from which a statement of their earnings is made ; pays their wages every Saturday ; and gives his assistance generally, wherever it is required. From the very correct manner in which the account books are kept, the cost price of all the articles manufactured is exactly known, as well as the profit or loss on each department. From the great increase of the inmates, workmen who see are appointed to take charge of the weaving, basket, and twine-spinning departments : their wages are charged on each of these departments. The two who act as porters, when not out with messages, are employed about the establishment ; their wages are charged on the manufacturing.

WORK BY THE MALE ADULTS.

The male adults are employed in the weaving of sacking cloth, making baskets of various kinds, spinning twine, making and repairing mattresses, making door mats, hearth rugs, door and table rugs, with fringed rugs for parlour doors.

The wages are regulated in these departments by the amount of work performed. They are allowed the same rate that other workmen have for the same kinds of work. It being ascertained that a man can make 7s. or 8s. per week, he receives that as his weekly wages. At the end of every four weeks a statement of his earnings is made up from the work-book, and whatever he has earned over that sum is paid him ; and as a reward to industry, he receives 1s. per week of premium. Having now enabled these men to earn 9s. or 10s. weekly, the premium is only given to new beginners for the first year ; but, if the weekly amount be not kept up, or the work be badly done, there is no premium allowed.

Ever since this regulation has been adopted a marked improvement has taken place both in the quantity and quality of the work produced. At the monthly settlement, the over-earnings which some of them have had to receive have amounted to 6s., 10s., and even 12s. It is the practice also in this Institution that as soon as a person has acquired a proficiency in one trade he is instructed in another ; so that if there be over-stock from the one occupation he can betake himself to the other. It is therefore not uncommon that the same person is at different times employed in two or three departments.

The delight exhibited by the Blind workmen and families when they return with the fruits of their labour may be easily conceived. A spirit of industry is not only excited and kept up (very different indeed from their former habits), but an opportunity afforded of enjoying all those blessings resulting from the endearing relations of home, which they never could enjoy were they (as is the case in some Institutions) maintained within the establishment.

On the 19th December, 1839, I gave into the funds of the Institution, from the sale of the Statements of Education of the Blind, £40, together with all the books remaining on hand, with a request, that as we had no provision for the Blind by our charter, when any of them were unwell, that the Directors would allow a sum annually for that purpose. In consequence of this, it was recommended to the General Meeting that the sum of £10 annually should be given, agreeable to my request, which was confirmed.

Thereafter a Society was formed, with regulations for their government ;—all Blind inmates receiving wages pay into the fund every four weeks, on the day that the over-earnings is paid, each male 6d., and each female 3d. When confined to bed and unable to work, each male receives 6s. per week, and each female

Fig. I.

Net Making.

Fig. II.

Winding.

Fig. III.

Sewing.

Fig. IV.

Knitting.

Fig. V.

Sack Printing.

Fig. VI.

Flax Dressing.

Fig. VII.

Mattress Making.

Fig. VIII.

Weaving.

Fig. IX.

Basket Making.

Fig. X.

4s. If confined for three months, the aliment is reduced ; the male to 4s., and the female 3s. On the death of any member or their wives, the sum of £3 is allowed to the survivor for funeral charges ; and if a child, £1. As yet the funds have been sufficient for all demands ; but if at any time there should be a deficiency, the participators are so convinced of the advantages of the Society, that if it should at any time fall short, they cheerfully agreed to add to their monthly contributions. The Superintendent keeps the accounts, makes up the statements of the funds yearly, in December, when they make choice of one of their number to act as preses, with a committee, to visit those that are confined and unable to work.

BOYS.

Boys from ten to sixteen years of age reside in the establishment ; and during the time they are not attending their classes (sufficient time for recreation being allowed), they are employed in making nets for wall-trees, sewing sacks, and such work as they are found capable of doing, till their education is finished, and they have acquired strength sufficient to be put to regular trades in the Asylum, it being the great object of this Institution to give the pupil a regular education, and afterwards to instruct him in a trade so as to enable him to earn his bread by his own industry, both of which, with very few exceptions, have been fully attained.

FEMALE DEPARTMENT.

MATRON.

The Matron is allowed an assistant ; both reside in the house, and have the charge of the domestic arrangements of the Institution, superintending the education of the female department, providing the articles necessary for the different branches of female work, provisions for the house, and other matters connected therewith. They also conduct the sales of the female work, and every day pay over the amount of cash to the Superintendent.

WORK BY THE FEMALE ADULTS.

Females are admitted into the Institution above 18 years of age as day-workers. They come in at 10 o'clock and remain till the worship is over in the evening. They are employed in sewing, knitting, netting, spinning, and winding of pirns for the weavers. They dine in the Asylum, and are allowed regular weekly wages.

Their apartments are separated from those of the males, and no intercourse whatever is permitted. At worship they sit in a part of the chapel by themselves. It is found advantageous to have an elderly woman who has sight to take charge and work along with them, as they are in apartments separate from the children ; and those who have not relatives in Glasgow reside with this person, the rent of whose house is paid by the Directors, and who is responsible for their conduct when absent from the Asylum. A like arrangement is made for the adult males.

GIRLS.

The girls, like the boys, reside in the Asylum ; assist in the household work, and, in addition to their general education, they are instructed in knitting silk purses, stockings, and caps. From the neat manner in which these are executed they command a ready sale.

GENERAL OBSERVATIONS.

The implements employed for the different kinds of work that are carried on by the inmates of the Glasgow Asylum are of the strongest materials, as those who use them labour under difficulties that other workmen have not to contend with, and thereby the machines are more liable to be broken. The raw materials for manufactures are all of the best kind, otherwise the work could not be so well executed. In spinning twine, not only is it necessary to have a person who has sight to superintend the spinners, and ball the twine and prepare the flax, but the wheel-boys, who are seeing, should be active in assisting. In the weaving and other departments of labour pursued it is necessary to have, in an Institution of this kind, persons who have sight, of good acquirements in various kinds of work, and of considerable ingenuity ; but their number must be regulated by the number of the inmates.

With respect to the kinds of work most suitable for such an Institution, circumstances of locality and experience alone can determine ; but in general, the making of sacking cloth, making baskets, spinning twine, making mattresses and door mats are those which can be taught to advantage.

The result of these different branches carried on in our Asylum for the year 1841, is as follows. The amount of the cost of the materials is always included in the amount of sales :—

	SALES.
	£ s. d.
Baskets, including the foreman, employs men and boys—27	698 17 1
Twine spinning (six wheels) employs 9 men and boys, 6 seeing wheel boys, 1 foreman, 1 flax dresser—17...	716 18 3
Door mats (making). These are wrought in the loom, employs 1...	188 11 6
Mattress making employs only 1 man and occasionally another, with one woman to assist in sewing ...	128 5 9

This, owing to the high price of hair and other materials, shows a large amount of sale, while few are employed; a mattress may cost from £3 to £4, and only a few shillings of the work done by the blind.

Weaving of sacks employs 22 weavers, with 9 women to wind the pirns, besides gives employment to 14 others, in sewing the sacks, belonging to families of those employed about the Institution, and 1 foreman —in all 45 ... ... £1,790 15 6

Deduct sacks on hand at last balance ... 374 6 0

      1,419 9 6

This shows the exact amount of industry. In this department, when experienced workmen leave the Institution to work at home on their own account, their places are supplied by young persons that have finished their education. When this is the case in any branch the amount of sale will vary.

I consider weaving the most advantageous, as giving the greatest amount of employment at the least expense, which is the great object aimed at in all Institutions ; and in general these goods, from the superior quality of the yarn, last longer than other ordinary sacks of the same description. Attention to the quality of the yarn, with salvage of a stout quality, very much assists the weaver, and always commands a sale.

The females can be instructed in many useful branches of industry, such as knitting, spinning, netting, &c., as well as household work ; in proof of which, it may be stated that several of the girls, after having acquired the usual branches of education taught, have been engaged as domestic servants in the Asylum, and perform their work to the satisfaction of the Matron. Other young women have made such progress as to be able to take charge and assist in the education of others.

To several of the boys, who were admitted into this Institution, their training has been of the most important benefit. After going through the usual course of education in reading, English grammar, arithmetic, music, and geography, and being of sufficient strength, they were put to regular trades. During the time the boys reside in the house, to encourage them to habits of industry, they receive 2d. per shilling on all they make ; and after they leave the house and are working as out-workmen, many of them earn from 8s. to 10s. per week. This is noticed to exhibit the great advantage of admitting the young to such Institutions early, they thereby acquire a proficiency in their trade that those who are further advanced in years can never attain to.

Several of the Blind men are employed in calling on the customers of the Asylum, in Glasgow and suburbs, to deliver and solicit orders. It is common for adults, who reside in the distant parts of the city, to come to their employment without a guide, and no accident has happened to any of them in going or returning.

In farther proof of their capability of walking without an assistant, a young boy of fourteen years of age, whose parents resided six miles from Glasgow, was in the habit of visiting them. He was accustomed to leave the establishment without an attendant, traverse the whole length of the city, finding his way through the Calton, Bridgeton, along Rutherglen bridge, through that town, and to his father's house. This he did with as much correctness as if he had been in the full possession of vision.

The advantages, however, arising from an Institution of this kind accrue not only to its inmates, but to the community at large. There are, at this date, in the Asylum, eighty individuals enjoying comforts they could have not otherwise obtained; nineteen of them are married, heads of large families; and thus, besides being comfortable themselves, all those connected with them participate in the benefits.

John Leitch, Esq., of this city, was the benevolent founder of the Blind Asylum. He himself had suffered under a partial infirmity of sight, and bequeathed the sum of £5000 towards opening and maintaining the Institution.

Much as has already been done, a great deal more is capable of being done; and many persons have contributed, and many, it is trusted, will still do so—imbued with the spirit that actuated the founder—by legacies and donations. It still requires additional support, that it may extend its accommodation to many destitute persons deprived of sight, and yet unprovided for in this district of Scotland.

Hitherto this Institution differs from all others of the same kind known to its managers. It solicits no annual subscriptions, but depends for its support entirely upon contributions and legacies of the pious and benevolent. The patronage of the public, also, does much on its behalf by purchasing its manufactures.

A hundred and fifty-four Blind persons have been admitted into the Asylum since it was opened in January, 1828, who have been educated and employed in the manner already described.

By the constitution of the Asylum a contributor of £10 is constituted a member for life; and a donation of £50 from an individual, or £100 from a parish, entitles either to recommend a child to the Asylum. Contributors of £10 and upwards, uniting to the amount of £50, have the like power to recommend.

The table annexed exhibits the progress of the industry of the inmates and the amount of proceeds since its commencement. When experienced workmen leave the establishment they are replaced by younger ones ; the change in different kinds of work may also make a difference in the amount ; and thus it may happen that there may be more labour and exertion on the part of the inmates, while the amount of sales may not be so large. The price of the materials as well as the wages are all included in the amount of sales.

The different articles are made of the best materials, and sold at the same prices with others in the regular trade.

TOTAL NUMBER OF BLIND PERSONS

Admitted into the Asylum for the Blind since the commencement, together with the causes of their blindness, so far as is known.

Blind from their Birth	... ...	24
In consequence of Inflammation	... ...	43
,, ,,	Scarlet Fever	1
,, ,,	Small Pox	24
,, ,,	Typhus Fever	1
,, ,,	Nervous Fever	1
,. ,,	Opacity of the Cornea	1
,, ,,	Vitriol thrown into the eyes	1
,, ,,	Amaurosis	10
,, ,,	Cataract...	8
,, ,,	Cataract, also Deaf and Dumb	1
,, ,,	Accident...	18
,, ,,	Vomiting of Blood	1
,, ,,	Measles...	1
,, ,,	Apoplexy	1
From causes not known	... ...	18
		154

ABSTRACT STATEMENT

OF THE MANUFACTURING DEPARTMENT, AND WAGES.

						£	s.	d.
Manufacture Sales for 1828			...	...	...	213	10	7
,,	,,	1829	...	...	...	642	14	0
,,	,,	1830	...	...	...	665	16	11
,,	,,	1831	...	...	...	887	11	5
,,	,,	1832	...	...	...	1,101	9	7
			Carried forward		£3,511	2	6

						£	s.	d.
		Brought forward				3,511	2	6
Manufacture Sales for	1833	...	...	...		1,189	17	6
„	„	1834	...	...	...	1,303	0	1
„	„	1835	...	...	...	1,953	16	3
„	„	1836	...	•••	...	2,514	15	2
„	„	1837	...	...	...	2,472	1	0
„	„	1838	...	...	...	2,846	11	3
„	„	1839	...	...	...	3,207	7	10
„	„	1840	...	...	...	3,408	11	11
„	„	1841	...	...	...	3,625	4	0
		Total	...			£26,032	7	6

WAGES PAID BLIND PEOPLE, ETC.

							£	s.	d.
Wages paid for	1828	...	...	...	...		127	19	0
„	„	1829	...	...	...	...	274	11	7
„	„	1830	...	...	...	...	351	8	7
„	„	1831	...	...	...	...	405	10	2
„	„	1832	...	...	...	...	428	4	9
„	„	1833	...	...	...	...	503	6	11
„	„	1834	...	...	...	...	547	14	10
„	„	1835	...	...	...	...	621	2	7
„	„	1836	...	...	...	...	807	13	3
„	„	1837	...	...	...	...	832	16	1
„	„	1838	...	...	...	...	865	0	11
„	„	1839	...	...	...	...	964	13	9
„	„	1840	...	...	...	...	1,024	4	3
„	„	1841	...	...	...	...	1,079	11	5
		Total	...	...		...£8,833	18	1

34

TO

THE LORD PROVOST, CHAIRMAN, AND DIRECTORS

OF THE GLASGOW ASYLUM FOR THE BLIND.

My Lord and Gentlemen,—Permit me shortly to lay before you a statement of the Printing Fund, which is kept apart from the other funds of the Institution.

In my humble endeavours to have books printed in raised Roman letters for the use of the Blind generally, and in particular for the children attending our own Institution, and being satisfied that for a long time the demand must be limited, and the returns from that source necessarily small, I made my first appeal for aid to the ladies of Glasgow and neighbourhood in October, 1836, and I am proud to acknowledge that to their generous exertions I owe the origin of the Printing Fund.

My next application for assistance was made to the different Institutions for the Blind and other benevolent Societies, and I am happy to say that their aid and co-operation have been cheerfully granted. These Institutions have got books at nett cost, so as to enable them to supply the poor at a moderate charge or gratuitously, as the case may be ; and all the Institutions in England and Scotland, with a single exception, are now teaching their children on this system. All the profits arising from the sale of books are applied to the Printing Fund.

With this assistance I was enabled to purchase a printing press, with two founts of types, and all the implements necessary for carrying on the printing in one of the apartments of the Institution. After considerable difficulty and exertion, I brought out several elementary books in January 1837, and in March 1838, I completed the New Testament in four volumes. I then brought out a Musical Catechism, with tunes adapted to the touch of the

Blind; and in like manner Æsop's Fables, with wood-cuts, all which are much prized by them.

Another desirable object remained to be accomplished, and that was to print the metrical version of the Psalms as used in Scotland, so as to enable the Blind to unite in public and private in singing the praises of God. Notwithstanding the kindness of many friends in purchasing books, my fund was by this time sunk in the publications on hand; and in order to attain my new object I issued a circular from the Institution Press, making known my difficulty to a number of benevolent individuals, who responded with alacrity to my application, and whose generosity, which I acknowledge with gratitude, enabled me to print the Psalms and Paraphrases in two volumes. In June, 1839, I made application to Her Majesty's Government to assist me in completing the printing of the Bible—of which see Appendix.

To those advanced in life who labour under the difficulties of a decayed sense of touch—to encourage them—premiums are given when they acquire the art of reading; and it will be further gratifying to our generous donors to know that their kindness enables us to supply all the children in the Institution with books free of expense. These volumes are now habitually read by all the children in the Institution, and those farther advanced are permitted, as a mark of distinction, to take their Psalm-books to church.

The liberality of our friends has also enabled me to procure a new fount of types, cut in a superior style, with which I have completed the printing of the Bible.

To a generous and an enlightened public I am under many obligations for the assistance they have at all times cheerfully given to my humble but earnest endeavours to render the Institution and the printing scheme available to the end for which they were intended. And I am also deeply indebted, my Lord and Gentlemen, to your indulgence and encouragement in prosecuting the great object I have had in view, of enabling every Blind child in the country to read the inestimable truths contained in the Word of God.

That this important object may be speedily and satisfactorily achieved, must be your sincere desire, as I assure you it is that of,

My Lord and Gentlemen,

Your very obedient Servant,

JOHN ALSTON.

GLASGOW, 21st *March*, 1842.

ABSTRACT STATEMENT

OF PRINTING FOR USE OF THE BLIND.

There have been Published—

	Copies.
First Lesson Book	400
Second „ „	400
Church of England Catechism	600
„ „ Liturgy	600
Church of Scotland Catechism	150
History of the Bible	150
Second Edition, enlarged...	200
Selections from Eminent Authors	300
„ „ „ with Music ...	500
English Grammar...	300
Remarks on the Bible	400
Multiplication Tables	300
Fables, with wood-cuts	400
Lesson on Prayer	250
„ Natural Religion	450
Musical Catechism, with tunes	800
Ephesians and Galatians, double pica	100
Ruth and James	100
Psalms and Paraphrases, in 2 vols.	300

Carried forward 6,700

	Copies.
Brought forward	6,700
The Whole Bible, in 15 vols.	3,300
The New Testament, in 4 vols.	100
St. Matthew's Gospel	400
St. Mark's ,, ...	150
St. Luke's ,, ...	150
St. John's ,, ...	150
The Acts	250
Acts, with the other portion of the Epistles ...	150
Psalms in the Metrical Version, used by the Church of England	210
Introduction to the Sciences	200
Tod's Lectures, 3 vols. (200 each)	600
Description of London	200
Description of Birds, with wood-cuts	650
Outlines of Natural History, with wood-cuts ...	250
Map of England, Wales	
Total	13,460

APPENDIX.

No. I.

LETTER

From the very Reverend Principal Macfarlan.

COLLEGE, GLASGOW,
22nd March, 1842.

MY DEAR SIR,

I HAVE repeatedly had occasion to bear testimony to the religious knowledge, generally speaking, of the inmates of the Glasgow Asylum for the Blind. Their aptitude to learn, their willingness to receive instruction, and the information which most of them have attained on the sacred truths of the Gospel, place them, in my opinion, at least on a level with those of the same age who have enjoyed the blessings of sight and the ordinary advantages of education. It gives me now very sincere satisfaction to add, that they have received an inestimable benefit from the introduction of learning to read, in the Roman letters, and in embossed characters, as an ordinary exercise in the Institution. The enlarged acquaintance with the Scripture which many of them has thus been enabled to attain, the facility which this attainment gives to their progress in biblical and all useful knowledge, and the occupation, equally interesting and improving, which it provides for their hours of intermission from labour, especially on the Lord's day, are advantages which it is not possible to appreciate too highly, and which have not failed to produce marked and progressive improvement on their mental enjoyments and intellectual character. Trusting that a steady perseverance in this excellent system will continue to be attended with results still more favourable, in proportion as it is better understood, and brought to bear on a greater variety of subjects,

I am, my dear Sir,

Yours very sincerely,

D. MACFARLAN.

JOHN ALSTON, ESQ., &c. &c.

LETTER

Addressed to the Right Honourable Lord John Russell.

GLASGOW,

19th June, 1839.

MY LORD,

ON the 8th Nov. 1837, I took the liberty of transmitting to your Lordship, for presentation to Her Majesty, the Gospel of St. Luke, in raised Roman letters, as specimen of printing which I had brought forward for the use of the Blind. On the 13th your Lordship was pleased to let me know that you had forwarded the Book to its destination, and, on the 26th Dec., I was favoured by the information from Mr. Glover that Her Majesty had most graciously received my humble present.

Since that time I have continued this mode of printing for the Blind. I have finished the whole of the New Testament, and published many other books, as may be seen from a catalogue at the end of a Pamphlet herewith sent. In the same Pamphlet there is a letter addressed by me to the Directors of our Blind Asylum, along with a state of the funds belonging to the printing establishment, stating that I have received pecuniary aid from several Institutions for the Blind, as well as from other benevolent Societies in the United Kingdom,—encouraged by the favour of these Strangers, and by the liberal aid of the benevolent in my native city and neighbourhood, I have ventured on an attempt to print the Old Testament, and I now humbly beg leave to forward to you as an offering for the acceptance of Her Majesty the first part containing the Book of Genesis, and along with it the Liturgy of the Church of England in the same character.

The Old Testament will contain 15 volumes, the same as the one sent— and 250 will cost, for paper and printing alone, about £1,000 in expense. Before engaging farther in such an undertaking I visited all the Institutions for the Blind in England and Scotland, viz., Liverpool, Manchester, Exeter, London, Norwich, York, Newcastle, and Edinburgh, and they all, with the exception of Liverpool, agreed to take some copies according to their circumstances of the whole books as they were brought out from the press. All these Institutions, except Liverpool, make daily use of the books already printed, and they are found to answer their purpose completely, and receive all the books at nett cost. My object in making these statements to your Lordship is, that I may humbly but earnestly solicit your Lordship, that you may be pleased to recommend to Her Majesty, to vouchsafe some grant from the Royal Bounty in aid of this good work. I am not begging for the Institution in our city, the liberal munificence of my fellow-citizens have amply provided for all its wants, and have enabled me to improve the condition of the inmates to the full satisfaction of every benevolent mind. The printing here has now become, as appears from the above statement, a national office, as it affords the means by which the Blind in the United Kingdom, amounting as is generally calculated at nearly 18,000 of Her Majesty's subjects, besides others in all parts where the English language is used, may of themselves have access to the sacred treasures contained in the Scriptures, and may read the Bible as easily as those whose sight is entire. The advantage of such a privilege to persons whose bereavements have always and in all places excited the tenderest sympathy need not be here dwelt upon, a favourable view of it will be amply secured by the innate affectionate feelings of the royal breast.

My Lord, I beg most respectfully to refer you to my highly respected friend and townsman, James Oswald, Esq., late member for Glasgow, and with much respect,

I have the honour to be,

My Lord,

Your Lordship's

Most obedient Servant,

JOHN ALSTON.

To the Rt. Hon. Lord John Russell.

REPLY

To the foregoing Letter addressed to Lord John Russell.

TREASURY CHAMBERS,

11*th Sept.*, 1839.

SIR,

THE Lords Commissioners of Her Majesty's Treasury having received a communication from the Secretary of State for the Home Department, upon the subject of the steps taken by you, connected with the Printing of the Bible in raised Type for the use of the Blind throughout the Kingdom, their Lordships have commanded me to express to you their great approbation of your philanthropic exertions for so meritorious an object, and they have been pleased to direct that an Issue of Four Hundred Pounds be made to you from Royal Bounty, for the purpose of assisting you in the prosecution of the work.

I am, Sir,

Your most obedient Servant,

J. G. PENNINGTON.

JOHN ALSTON, ESQ., Glasgow.

E

GLASGOW, *9th March*, 1841.

To Her Most Gracious Majesty the Queen.

MADAM,

IN June 1839 I had the honour, through the Right Honourable Lord John Russell, to present for your Majesty's acceptance the first Volume of the Bible, printed in Raised Roman Letters for the use of the Blind, and to express a hope that your Majesty would be pleased to aid me in printing the whole Bible for their use. That application was forwarded by the Right Honourable Lord John Russell to the Lords of your Majesty's Treasury, when it met with a cordial reception. It is now my most pleasant duty to present to the Royal Library a complete Copy of the entire Bible, the first that has been printed for the use of the Blind. A blank has thus been filled up in Christian Literature by which the whole Word of God is put into the hands of a class who are supposed to amount to about 20,000 of your Majesty's subjects, and to whom the Holy Scriptures have hitherto been a sealed book. I have also printed other books for the Blind to the extent of 11,000 Volumes; specimens of the first Book of the Sciences is sent along with the Bible for the inspection of your Majesty.

It may be gratifying to your Majesty to know that when I visited all the Institutions for the Blind in May 1837, there were not ten Blind in England who knew letters, and that now there are several hundreds who can read these books.

When your Most Gracious Majesty's illustrious Grandsire was pleased to express a wish that every individual in the British Dominions might be able to read the Bible, his benevolent desire cannot be supposed to have at that time contemplated the Blind, and it may be pleasing to your Majesty now to be informed that it now has been realised in a manner equally unexpected and gratifying to a class of your Majesty's subjects so numerous and so interesting as the Blind.

Will your Majesty also be graciously pleased to permit me to present to your Majesty specimens of Knitting by the female Blind at the Glasgow Institution, where they are acquiring habits of industry and economy which will enable them to maintain themselves in future, instead of being burdens as heretofore on their friends or the community.

I am,

Your Most Gracious Majesty's

Most humble and most obedient Servant and Subject,

JOHN ALSTON.

Lord Normanby's Reply to the Letter addressed to Her Majesty the Queen.

WHITEHALL,

17th April, 1841.

SIR,

I HAVE had the honour to submit to Her Majesty the Copy of the Holy Bible prepared by you for the use of the Blind, together with your smaller Works upon Science and the articles manufactured by the Blind in the Asylum at Glasgow.

Of these latter Her Majesty was pleased to admire the neatness of their manufacture and the perfection which had been attained in this branch of handy-work.

But Her Majesty has commanded me especially to convey to you Her sense of the great benefit conferred by you upon that portion of Her subjects whom it has pleased the Almighty so severely to visit, by placing within their attainment the knowledge of those sacred truths from which they can derive their best consolation under their affliction in this world and their sacred hope in that which is to come.

Her Majesty is pleased to accept the volumes which you have transmitted, and to express Her hope that so charitable an undertaking may be amply blessed.

I have the honour to be, Sir,

Your most obedient Servant,

NORMANBY.

To JOHN ALSTON, ESQ., Glasgow.

Extract from the " Polytechnic Journal."

ON ALPHABETS FOR THE BLIND.

FROM MR. GALL'S LITERATURE FOR THE BLIND.

" Those who interest themselves in behalf of the blind are frequently led into error by attaching the idea of 'community' to that heavy affliction. The reason of this is that the blind are only seen by the public when they are congregated together in their schools and asylums, for the purposes of labour and instruction. But no idea can be more fallacious or more distant from the truth. The blind, in at least twenty-nine cases out of every thirty, are to be found insulated and alone, concealed from the public eye, and thinly scattered among the seeing population in separate, and often in distant localities. Separate schools for their use, accordingly, while thus divided will always be impossible ; and they must, therefore, in almost every instance, depend either upon the local teachers of their district or upon their parents or friends for assistance to learn. A known alphabet gives the blind at all times the full benefit of these local conveniences ; while an arbitrary or unknown character would render them almost useless, because few would be found willing to learn to read such a character themselves, merely for the sake of teaching it to an individual," p. 36.

" From the very circumstance of the blind being scattered widely over the country, from their being insulated and alone, unable to procure well-qualified teachers, it becomes necessary that the character employed in their books should be of the most common kind, such as every one can read, even such as a little child is first taught to read, from some real or supposed simplicity. No other character can penetrate into the lonely habitations of the blind, nothing but what is equally plain to the gentle and the simple, to the educated and uneducated person, can meet the exigency of their case."

MR. LUCAS'S SYSTEM.

" The late Mr. Lucas, of Bristol, invented a stenographic character for the blind, which has met with a certain amount of encouragement. Directions accompany it which explain the system of abbreviations for prefixes and affixes, the signs, and tables of words and contractions, and which develop the doctrine of signs on which the characters are founded. The following extract from the ' Penny Cyclopædia,' Article BLIND, is stated by Mr. Lucas to contain a fair exposition of his principles :—

" The alphabet is composed of thirteen simple characters, and thirteen formed from the roots of these with a crotchet-head to each. There are ten double letters from the same roots, distinguished also by the crotchet head ; these also represent the nine figures and the cypher, whether used as numerals or ordinals ; in all, thirty-six characters are employed. The advantages attending the use of stenographic characters seem to be in the saving of types, paper, and labour, thus materially diminishing the cost of books for the blind. The disadvantages attending the system we are speaking of appear to consist chiefly in the confusion which the learner must feel in having but one character employed in various offices, as in the double letters, numerals, and ordinals, and in the necessity that every person should be a stenographist who communicates with the blind by writing. These difficulties are not very great for persons to overcome who have never been accustomed to a written language.

" The manner in which the characters of Mr. Lucas are employed may be seen in the following commencement of St. John's Gospel, only that we give the extract in Roman letters instead of using stenographic characters :—

t gospel b st jon, chap. 1.

in t bgini ws t wrd a t w ws w g, a t w ws g.   t sam ws n t bgini w g.   l thins wr mad b him, a wo hm ws nt a thin mad tht ws mad.   in him ws lif a t l ws t lit f mn.

" It will be observed that the repetition of numerous letters is avoided ; particles are represented in most instances by their initial letter, and when a word, having been once mentioned, recurs immediately, it is represented by its initial letter also.

" We cannot but think that the general adoption of a stenographic system would tend to dissociate the blind from the seeing population, and from correspondence with their friends. An undoubted defect in Lucas's system is the confusion which must arise from having letters and figures represented by the same sign. Thus, the characters which form the word FAT also form 304 ; and the passage, FAT BULLS OF BASAN, might be read 304 BULLS OF BASAN. POOR PEOPLE might be read 6,991 PEOPLE.

" Pages 25 to 28 of Lucas's 'Book of Instructions' are occupied with lists of words to be committed to memory. We find that one stenographic sign may represent a number of words which possess no similarity and have no relationship to each other. The sign for A may represent, and, any, after ; G, good, God, against ; P, up, upon, patience, put ; Q, queen, question, quiet ; X, except, example, exercise ; ll may represent I, one, once, first, altogether ; ss, 2, two, twice, second, synopsis ; and so on with other words. Thus a child must be guided by the sense of the passage he is reading, a stretch of mental exertion which it is unreasonable to look for in a child. These obstacles render a stenographic system harassing, and nothing but a strong determination on the part of the reader can overcome them. When they are all overcome we may readily allow that the reading may be swifter than in the case of long-hand, but then arises the question, where shall the blind find stenographic teachers ? "

MR. FRERE'S SYSTEM.

" We ought not to omit all mention of a second stenographic system, which threatens to be extensively carried forward : the author and inventor of it is Mr. J. H. Frere, who resides in or near the metropolis. We possess specimens

of all the books that have been printed for the blind; those of America,
Glasgow, Edinburgh, Bristol, are well and beautifully executed; but those
we have seen of Frere's are, we are sorry to say, positively discreditable.
The system is professedly founded on Gurney's short-hand, as Lucas's is on
Byrom's. If we could transfer to our pages the directions for learners, or
'Memoria Technica,' which accompany the books of Frere, we should be sure
to amuse our readers."

MR. ALSTON'S ALPHABET.

" We have now to speak of Mr. Alston's labours in the cause of relief-
printing, and as this gentleman has done more than all others in perfecting
the art, with that active benevolence which is his great characteristic, it will
be our duty to make most honourable mention of him. It is owing to his
exertions that the thousands of volumes now in circulation throughout the
country have been brought out, and made available to the needs of the solitary blind. It is his practical knowledge which has given such permanence
to the art that it can never again be lost nor even fall into disuse.

" Mr. Alston's labours were commenced during the competition for the medal
offered by the Society of Arts, and they were consequent on the request of
the Edinburgh committee made to him, as well as to the directors of other
institutions for the blind, that he would turn his attention to the subject, and
state his opinion to the Society. Though as thoroughly qualified for the
race to be run as any of the competitors by the daily occupation of several
hours snatched from his extensive commercial interests, and devoted to the
affairs of the Glasgow Asylum, it had not occurred to him that he could be
of any service in this particular department of usefulness till the circumstance of the above-named communication from the Society of Arts. From
the trials previously made among pupils of the Glasgow Asylum, he was
convinced that arbitrary characters, however ingeniously contrived, threw
unnecessary obstacles in the way of instructing the blind, and that the
closest assimilation the characters for the blind could be made to bear to the
commonest of the known alphabets, would be the most desirable consummation
should it be found, on trial, that such an alphabet could be made so tangible
as to allow the blind to read it with tolerable rapidity.

" With these views, when the forms of all the competing alphabets were submitted to him, he was struck with the simplicity of form which Dr. Fry's
alphabet presented, and immediately conceived the idea of making such
alterations in it as to render it suitable for his object.   Dr. Fry's alphabet is
the SANS-SERIF, of type-founders,—plain Roman capitals, merely deprived of
the small strokes at their extremities.   Mr. Alston was aware that all the
seeing who had had the commonest education would read this at once, and
consequently anyone might become a teacher of reading to the blind; that
it would be attended with a manifest and peculiar advantage in the case of
those who became blind after they were familiar with the Roman alphabet
that a blind child with a book of this character might become a pupil in an
ordinary school, without any greater inconvenience to the teacher than the

seeing pupils ; and his reasoning was confirmed by the knowledge, that in some of the German schools for the blind the Roman character had been adopted with success.

"In his experiments with the pupils at Glasgow he found that Dr. Fry's characters were too broad and obtuse to the touch, that their extent of raised surface added to their bluntness, and delayed the finger in deciphering their form. This disadvantage was at once evident and the remedy was quickly applied. The faces of the letters were rendered thin and sharp, so as to present a wedge shape, from the surface of the paper to the surface of the letters. The advantage of this change was manifest : the children read the letters with much greater ease and satisfaction. He next had the letters considerably reduced in size, found that they were then fully adequate to his purpose, and then began to consider how he should turn his experiments to account for the good of the blind. The expense of a fount of types seemed formidable, and he did not feel warranted to resort to the funds of the Institution for so extraordinary an outlay. An appeal was made to the ladies of Glasgow for assistance, and to their generous exertions the Printing Fund of the Glasgow Asylum owes its origin.

"The success which attended Mr. Alston's efforts was a new assurance to the Society of Arts that they were right in regarding the stenographic, the arbitrary, and the angular modifications of the Roman alphabets unfavourably."

STATEMENT OF THE SOCIETY OF ARTS.

"Upon the whole—looking to the terms of the Society's advertisement, and the other circumstances above referred to—the committee beg to state that, in their opinion, the late Dr. Fry's communication is entitled to 'the Society's Gold Medal, value twenty sovereigns,' being the prize offered 'for the best communication on a method of printing for the blind,' &c. In suggesting further premiums to some of the other candidates, whose labours have apparently been greater, and whose general observations may seem even more interesting than those of the late Dr. Fry, it may be proper to mention that the principal prize should be divided, but that these honorary premiums should be provided for, separately, out of some other fund." They then proceed to point out some modifications which they think are required to be introduced into Dr. Fry's alphabet, in order to make it the most practical set of characters for the use of the blind.

EXTRACT FROM THE PROCEEDINGS OF THE BRITISH ASSOCIATION.

"The Rev. Mr. Taylor, of York, made a report on the different Modes of Printing for the Blind, prepared at the request of the Association. He mentioned several methods which had hitherto been adopted for this purpose. Haüy, in 1784, first invented the art of printing in relief, and in 1831 or 1832

Mr. Gall, of Edinburgh, introduced a triangular alphabet. At Boston the art
has been carried to great perfection, several books have been printed in
modified ITALICS, with good and sharp impressions. The cost of a copy of
the New Testament there was £2 10s. Other methods had been recommended,
including arbitrary characters, contractions, fretted type, and a modification
of the capitals of the Roman alphabet. Mr. Taylor, however, was strongly in
favour of that adopted by Mr. Alston, of Glasgow,—viz., the adoption of the
Roman capitals deprived of the small strokes at their extremities, and cut with
very sharp and thin faces. He objected to the use of what printers call the
'lower case' letters; and in reference to the result of certain examinations
of the pupils in their proficiency in particular systems, he observed that the
test of the merits of those systems was not the proficiency of the cleverest
pupils, but of the bulk of them, and its adaptation to those who, as the vast
majority of the blind must, would have the sensibility of their fingers
impaired by labour. Several specimens of the different kinds of printing were
handed round. Arbitrary characters he considered decidedly objectionable, as
cutting off, in a great degree, the means of communication between the blind
and others. For instance, at school, if the common type be used, the blind
could learn with other children, and get assistance from them. He was
opposed to the use of contractions, and to printing on both sides of the page,
as, in his opinion, they tended to create confusion."—ATHENÆUM, No. 518.

FIFTEENTH REPORT

BY THE DIRECTORS OF THE ASYLUM FOR THE BLIND.

GLASGOW, 17th JANUARY, MDCCCXLII.

At a General Meeting of the qualified contributors to the Glasgow Asylum for the Blind, held within the Black Bull Inn of Glasgow, upon the 17th day of January, 1842, at Three o'clock Afternoon,

JOHN SMITH, LL.D., Esq., of Crutherland, in the Chair,

The following Report was presented from the Directors from last year :—

I. PUPILS.

The number admitted since the opening of the Asylum, in 1828, 154
Of these there have left the house 57
And there have died 17
— 74

Number at present in the Establishment . . 80

There have been nine admissions—one died, and eight left the House during the year; the number of Pupils, therefore, is the same as the former year.

II. EMPLOYMENT.

This Table will show how the Inmates are employed.

	Twine.	Baskets.	Mattresses.	Mats.	Rugs.	Weaving.	Knitting and Netting.	Spinning and Winding.	Total.
Men	5	13	1	1	1	18	—	—	43
Boys	9	4	—	1	—	4	2	—	16
Women	—	—	—	—	—	—	—	9	9
Girls...............	—	—	—	—	—	—	21	—	21
Porters	—	—	—	—	—	—	—	—	2
	14	17	1	2	1	22	23	9	91

Thus the Manufactory consists of eighty blind people, and eleven not blind, viz., five men, five wheel boys, and a woman.

III. SALES.

Twine...	...	£698 17 1
Baskets	...	716 18 3
Mattresses	...	78 19 0
Baked Hair ...	...	49 6 9
Door Mats ...	...	138 11 6
Door and Hearth Rugs	...	6 9 8
Female Work	...	127 2 0
Sacks...	...	1790 15 6
Friction Mitts	...	8 11 9
Nets ...	...	9 12 6
Total sales for the year	...	£3625 4 0
Total sales for last year	...	3408 11 11
Excess in favour of this year...	...	£216 12 1

IV. ARTICLES ON HAND

Articles Manufactured at the end of the year	...	...	£460 1 10
To which there fall to be added—			
Value of Raw Materials on hand	...	£689 11 3	
Debts due to the Asylum	...	954 17 4	
			1644 8 7
Amount of Manufacturing Capital ...	...	...	£2104 10 5

V. EXTENT OF PRODUCTION.

Amount of sales during the year	...	£3625 4 0
Value of Articles Manufactured on hand ...	...	460 1 10
		£4085 5 10
Deduct Value of Articles on hand at the beginning of the year ...	...	463 16 3
Value of articles wrought up during the year	...	£3621 9 7
Value of articles wrought up during last year	...	3407 1 3
Increase this year	...	£214 8 4

VI. REVENUE.

Our Revenue is either Ordinary or Extraordinary.

ORDINARY.

Ground Annual of St. Mungo's Cemetery	...	£150	0	0
Interest on Capital	...	96	2	0
Amount of Board from Pupils	...	137	1	5
Manufacturing gain on work	...	1	13	6
		384	16	11

EXTRAORDINARY.

Donations	£43	14	6
Contributions	198	2	0
	241	16	6

Total Income for 1841	£626	13	5
Total Income for 1840	1251	6	5
Less this year	£624	13	0

VII. EXPENDITURE.

The Expenditure may be reduced to three heads. — 1. Household Expenses. 2. Salaries and Wages. 3. Charges on Manufacturing Establishment.

1. Ordinary Provisions...	£332	8	11		
Coals	33	5	0		
Candles and Soap	21	14	3		
Incidental Charges	94	15	8		
Stationery and Printing	40	8	0		
				522	11	10
2. Salaries			238	1	0
3. Tradesmen's Accounts	214	8	9		
Implements for Manufactory	34	5	10		
Furniture, &c.	21	3	6		
				269	18	1
Total Expenditure		£1030	10	11
Income during the year		626	13	5
Less this year...		£403	17	6

VIII. THE STOCK.

Amount of Stock, January, 1841	...	...	...	... £3711 14 7
Less income	... ...	...	...	... 403 17 6

£3307 17 0

Dr.   **BALANCE.**   **Cr.**

To Heritable Bond	£2500 0 0	By Cash due Printing Account...		£74 17 8
To Cash in hand	14 5 6	By do. do. Glasgow and Ship		
To Manufacturing Stock ...	2104 10 5	Bank Company		1231 0 0
		By do. do. Sundries		5 1 2
		By Stock		3307 17 1
	£4618 15 11			£4618 15 11

It is hoped that the above statements, which are given in the same form and order as formerly, will be satisfactory to this General Court, showing that the Institution still maintains its former prosperity.

It will be observed that the Extraordinary income has been less this year. Donations and contributions must vary in different years; and though a deficiency may happen, it is not from any want of regard on the part of the public for the prosperity of the Institution. It will be seen that the sales of this year exceed the sales of the former year by more than two hundred pounds, and that the extent of production exceeds that of the former year to nearly the same amount; but notwithstanding this excess, a very small sum, as the profit of the manufacturing department, is carried to the ordinary revenue, and the salary of the Superintendent, as formerly, is taken as a part of the ordinary expenditure. The reason of this falling off can easily be given, and will be considered as satisfactory—the price of the raw material in most of the articles manufactured is much higher, and yet the articles themselves, in their finished state, could bring no higher price, and it would, on many accounts, be altogether inexpedient to keep the goods on hand.

In the expenditure for this year the sum of above two hundred pounds is charged on the head of Tradesmen's Accounts. A considerable part of this outlay has been expended in making improvements in the Buildings of the Institution. Such alterations have been made in the interior, that accommodation is provided for one hundred ordinary inmates, as well as for a few parlour Boarders; while at the same time some alterations are introduced to give facility for the different manufacturing processes. By the removal of the partition between the Chapel and the School-room, a spacious Hall is formed. This has been finished with as much taste and elegance as a due regard to economy would allow; and it is hoped it will be found useful for various purposes; among others, for the Annual Examination of the Pupils, being more convenient than any other place remote from the Institution.

The education of the Pupils in Reading, Writing, Arithmetic, Geography, Grammar, Music, and other Branches, has been carried on during the year with the usual success. In proof of this we appeal to the occasional visits of strangers; and particularly to the Annual Examination which took place on the 17th December last, when a very numerous and highly respectable assembly of Ladies and Gentlemen expressed their entire satisfaction in no ordinary terms.

In reference to the Honorary Treasurer, John Alston, Esq., of Rosemount, the Directors candidly confess, and they are sure that this General Court, as well as the public at large, will cordially join in the acknowledgment, that the Institution is yearly under deeper obligations to him. But the gentleman himself is at present daily receiving reward full and ample in the estimation of a Christian philanthropist. He has in his own mind the conscious satisfaction that he is devoting his time and exertions, and that successfully too, to ameliorate the condition of his fellow-men in their forlorn state ; and at the same time wherever he goes, he finds that sympathy for this bereavement is so deeply rooted in our common nature, that every one owns for himself a share of the public debt of gratitude which is due to the zealous benefactor of the Blind.

The Matron, Miss Lamond, and the Superintendent, Mr. Matthew Semple, as well as the Teachers, have discharged their respective duties to our satisfaction, and we therefore take this opportunity of returning them our thanks.

Dr. David Gibson has, during the year, acted as Medical Attendant to the inmates; and we therefore respectfully tender to him our acknowledgments for his gratuitous and important services.

Principal Macfarlan, in addition to his duties as a Manager, has continued to discharge with kindness and assiduity his pastoral superintendence in the Asylum ; regarding the inmates as part of his parish and congregation.

To Andrew Buchanan, Esq., of Mount Vernon, we beg leave to tender our thanks for a donation of coals. The Glasgow Water Company continue to supply the Institution with water, for which we again return them our grateful acknowledgments.

Which Report having been read, and the accounts of John Alston, Esq., the Treasurer, examined, were unanimously approved of, and the thanks of the Meeting to the above Gentlemen were tendered accordingly.

The thanks of the Meeting were given to Dr. Corkindale, by whom the Report was prepared ; and on the motion of Matthew Fleming, Esq., seconded by John Gibson, Esq., the thanks of the meeting were given to Messrs. R. Freeland and J. Bogle, for their services as secretaries.

On the motion of Robert Freeland, Esq., seconded by Wm. Leckie Ewing, Esq., Robert Jamieson, Esq., was unanimously elected Secretary.

The following Gentlemen were then declared to be Directors for the present year :—

President :

THE HON. JAMES CAMPBELL, LORD PROVOST OF GLASGOW.

Honorary Vice-Presidents :

HENRY MONTEITH, Esq., of Carstairs.
ARCHIBALD STIRLING, Esq., of Keir.
JAMES EWING, Esq., LL.D., of Levenside.
JAMES OSWALD, Esq., of Auchincruive, M.P.

From the Directors of the Glasgow Royal Infirmary—ROBERT DALGLISH, Esq., JAMES SOMMERVILLE, Esq., PROFESSOR RAMSAY.

From the Town Council—WILLIAM WILSON, Esq.

From the College—THE VERY REV. PRINCIPAL MACFARLAN.
From the Merchants' House — WILLIAM GRAY, Esq., DEAN OF GUILD;
   ANDREW WINGATE, Esq.
From the Trades' House—GEORGE DICK, Esq., CONVENER; ROBERT HOOD, Esq.
From the Faculty of Physicians and Surgeons—JOHN GIBSON, Esq.
From the Ministers—THOMAS BROWN, D.D.

Elected by the Meeting.

John Alston, Esq.	William Campbell, Esq.
John Smith, Esq., LL.D.	Mathew Fleming, Esq.
James Bogle, jun., Esq.	William Leechman, Esq.
William Leckie Ewing, Esq.	James Hutchison, Esq.
Robert Freeland, Esq.	

The thanks of the Meeting, upon the motion of the Very Rev. Principal Macfarlan, were tendered to the Chairman.

John Alston, Esq., Treasurer.	Mr. William Finlay, Teacher.
Robt. Jamieson, Esq., Writer, Sec.	Mr. John Orme, Music Master.
Miss Catherine Lamond, Matron.	David Gibson, Esq., M.D., Surgeon.
Mr. Matthew Semple, Superintendent.	

The Males work ten hours per day; but when any particular articles are wanted, they are permitted to work twelve hours.

None of the Females who are not attending classes work more than seven hours in summer, and six in winter. Those attending classes work three hours each day, and none of them more than two hours at a time.

GLASGOW ASYLUM FOR THE BLIND.

ANNUAL EXAMINATION.

(From the *Scottish Guardian* of December 21st, 1841.)

THE twelfth annual examination of the inmates of this excellent Institution took place in their new hall in the Asylum, on Friday, December 17, in presence of a numerous and a select assemblage of ladies and gentlemen. The Lord Provost presided. Amongst the company were Lord Belhaven and Lady Belhaven, who came to town from Wishaw House expressly to be present, Sir Archibald Campbell, of Succoth, Lady Campbell and Miss Campbell, the Very Rev. Principal Macfarlan, the Rev. Dr. Hill, Professor of Divinity, the Rev. Dr. Fleming, Professor of Moral Philosophy, the Rev. Mr. Gray, Professor of Oriental Languages, the Rev. Dr. Muir, of St. James's, the Rev. Mr. Menzies, of Martyrs, the Rev. Mr. Smith, of Cathcart, John Smith, Esq., LL.D., Wm. Angus, Esq., LL.D., Rev. Mr. Almond, Mr. Leckie Ewing, Dr. Doyle, from Dublin, Mr. John Ker and party, from Greenock— in addition to strangers from Kilmarnock, Campbelton and other parts of the country.

A number of improvements have taken place in the Institution since the last occasion of this kind. The interior has been altered so as to accommodate a hundred inmates, besides a few parlour boarders; and increased facilities have been given by the improvements for carrying on the various kinds of manufacture. The partition that formerly separated the chapel from the school-room has been removed, and the whole thrown into one spacious hall of fifty-five feet in length The hall is tastefully fitted up, being painted oak colour. At the head of the room is the fine organ, on the right of which is suspended the admirable portrait of the Treasurer and father of the Institution, and on the left is placed a tablet inscribed with the name of the founder (the late Mr. Leech, of Kilmardinny), donations from the corporations, together with a list of legacies, including the Government grant for printing the Bible for the Blind at the Institution press.

After a sacred piece had been sung by the children, accompanied by a blind girl on the organ, Principal Macfarlan opened the meeting with prayer. The examination embraced the various branches of education pursued in the Asylum, such as reading, arithmetic, geography, grammar, &c., and the proficiency made by the children was highly satisfactory. In turning up passages in their books, especially in the Bible, and in the ease with which they read them, without more than a moment's previous warning, they exhibited a readiness and dexterity which could be surpassed by few blessed with the use of their eyes. Their rapid solution of questions in arithmetic and geography was equally surprising. The exercises were diversified by pieces of vocal music, accompanied on the organ, which had a very pleasing effect. The interesting woman who is deaf, dumb and blind, showed the method by which she communicates with her blind companions, all of whom can converse with her by means of the finger alphabet of the deaf and dumb; and she also exhibited specimens of her writing. In the course of the proceedings, Mr. Alston brought forward for the first time a very recent improvement which he has introduced into the educational department. It is a substitute for writing suited for the use of the blind; and cannot be better explained than by quoting the following description which has just appeared in Mr. Alston's supplementary statement to the Directors dated this month :—

" Although we apply the word WRITING to a method of teaching the blind to communicate with each other and their friends at a distance, it is not the writing which is used by the seeing. Numerous plans have been suggested for this purpose. In a work published in Vienna in 1818, by Mr. Klein, Director of the Institution for the Blind in that city, the author gives specimens of a mode of printing in the Roman character which resembles letters perforated through the paper with a pin point, and is read on the rough surface on the other side. I am not, however, aware how the details of the process are managed. A beautiful specimen of this writing was sent to me last year, from Paris, where the system is also introduced. In turning my attention to this improvement, with the view of attempting to render it useful here, I adopted a set of wooden instead of metal types, with the face of the letter formed of brass points ; but, as the delicacy of the finger might be impaired by touching the sharp metal points forming the face of the type, the letter is also impressed in relief on its side, and the type required is thus easily ascertained without injury to the fingers. A full set of types being completed, they are arranged in a drawer or case, sub-divided into compartments for the respective letters, each compartment being labelled in relief to guide the person using it to the letter he requires. In another drawer contained above in the same case, there are a series of grooves or lines exactly fitting the breadth of the types ; and in these grooves the words are arranged with suitable spaces. The whole being fixed in a very simple manner, the paper is put upon the types, and pressed down with the thumb, covered with a piece of leather, or, what answers the purpose better, a piece of soft elastic cork. The object being to produce a distinct impression on the upper side of the paper, this is accomplished with the utmost ease, simplicity and accuracy. The whole apparatus does not exceed twelve inches by nine, and from three to four in depth, and may be conveniently placed on the knee by the fireside, and employed either for amusement or correspondence. It can be purchased for fifteen shillings, and the types at 1s. 6d. per dozen. The impressions produced in this manner can be read as easily by the seeing as the blind."

A blind girl, with less than a week's practice, showed the working of this simple apparatus ; and most of the company were proud to possess themselves of specimens of so novel and useful a mode of communication.

Without dwelling on the details of an examination which gave the public renewed assurance of the progressive efficiency of the Institution, we may simply add, that the whole afforded unmixed delight to the numerous and respectable audience, who testified their satisfaction by the intense interest with which they watched each successive step of the business of the day. At the conclusion,

Lord Belhaven said—My Lord Provost, this being, I regret to say, only the first time I have visited this Institution, I hope to be permitted to express the gratification which I feel at the scenes we have witnessed this day. I am quite sure that I express the sentiments of every stranger present, when I say that a feeling of gratitude must exist in the minds of those whom I may be permitted to call the pupils of Mr. Alston, towards that excellent man ; and that the same feeling must be shared by every one present, and not only by all who are here, but by the inhabitants of this city, and the people of this great country. (Applause.) And I hope and trust, my Lord Provost, that Mr. Alston may long continue to follow out this great work, which, I believe, he has been the first person to introduce; and would say to him that we owe him a debt of gratitude which no language of ours can express, for his efforts in behalf of the blind; but he has that high consolation which can only belong to him who zealously, and honestly, and faithfully does his duty to his country and his God. (Applause.)

Being called upon by the Lord Provost,

Sir Archibald Campbell said—I had a strong inclination, my Lord Provost, before your Lordship did me the honour to call upon me—indeed, I could hardly refrain from expressing the very high gratification which I, in common, I am sure, with every person present this day, have felt at the wonderful exhibition we have witnessed since we met together. It is unnecessary for me to say that it is in a great measure to be attributed to the great exertions of the gentleman who takes charge of this Institution. We owe a debt of gratitude to him, and to those who act under him; and we should also give due praise to the persons themselves who have profited by the instructions they have received in this Institution. By means of the various branches of education to which their attention is turned, these young persons have been brought from darkness into light; and enabled to amuse themselves, and not only to amuse themselves, but to improve their minds with those useful works which tend so much to their benefit; and thereof we should not refrain from expressing our high sense of the value of such an Institution, and congratulating Mr. Alston and the Directors on the manner in which its affairs are managed and on the success which has followed their exertions in bringing these individuals into the advantageous situation in which they now stand. (Cheers.)

The LORD PROVOST said it was creditable to the city of Glasgow to have such an Institution, equally so that there had appeared on this occasion so respectable an assemblage as the present. It is a very flattering compliment, continued his Lordship, to be countenanced on such an occasion with the presence of Lord and Lady Belhaven and Sir Archibald and Lady Campbell. (Cheers.) But, in fact, on all occasions, we find our friends in the country, the nobility and gentry, crowding around us when the interests of benevolence require their countenance and aid. (Applause.) We must all have been very much pleased with the proofs of the efficiency of the Institution which we have received since we came together. Lady Belhaven has just shown me a letter from America pointing out a recent discovery in connection with the education of the blind; and one of which we were not previously aware; but Mr. Alston has proved to us that that discovery is already in full operation in the Glasgow Institution. (Applause.) His Lordship concluded by thanking Lord Belhaven, Lady Belhaven, Sir Archibald Campbell and Lady Campbell, for the honour they had done the Institution by their presence.

Principal Macfarlan concluded the proceedings by pronouncing the benediction.

The ladies afterwards went into the warehouse, and examined the beautiful specimens of manufacture which were there exhibited.

Lady Belhaven paid the most minute attention to the whole proceedings and remained for some time after the company dispersed, questioning the teachers and their pupils in the kindest manner.

F

No. IX.

The following Books are printed at the Glasgow Institution Press in raised, Roman letters, for the use of the Blind, by JOHN ALSTON, Honorary Treasurer, and on Sale at the Asylum; and Sold by JOHN SMITH & SON, Glasgow; SMITH. ELDER & Co., London; JOHN JOHNSTON, and at the Asylum for the Blind, Edinburgh; Wm. M·COMBE, Belfast; J. ROBERTSON & Co., Dublin; GALT & ANDERSON, Manchester, &c.

THE BIBLE, 15 VOLS., £8.

Vol. 1, Genesis, 10s.

Vol. 2, Exodus and Leviticus, 13s.

Vol. 3, Numbers, 9s.

Vol. 4, Deuteronomy, 7s. 6d.

Vol. 5, Joshua, Judges, and Ruth, 10s.

Vol. 6, Samuel, 11s.

Vol. 7, Kings, 11s.

Vol. 8, Chronicles, 11s.

Vol. 9, Job, Ezra, and Nehemiah, 9s.

Vol. 10, Psalms, 13s.

Vol. 11, Proverbs, Ecclesiastes, Song of Solomon, and Esther, 8s. 6d.

Vol. 12, Isaiah, 10s.

Vol. 13, Jeremiah and Lamentations, 11s.

Vol. 14, Ezekiel, 10s.

Vol. 15, Daniel, to the end, 11s.

These sold separately, or in whole, as may be wanted.

First Book of Lessons, 1s.

Second Book of Lessons, 2s.

The Epistles to the Ephesians and Galatians, 3s.

Selections of Æsop's Fables, with Wood-cuts, 2s.

Lessons on Religion and Prayer, 1s. 6d.

Lessons on Natural Religion, 2s.

The Four Gospels — Matthew and Luke, 5s. 6d. each.

John, 4s. 6d.

Mark, 4s.—bound separately.

The Acts of the Apostles, 5s. 6d.

Musical Catechism, with Tunes for the use of the Blind, 3s. 6d.

English Grammar, 5s.

The New Testament, bound, £2, in 4 vols

The Psalms and Paraphrases, in 2 vols, 16s.; neatly bound in cloth, 20s.

Psalms in the Metrical Version, used by the Church of England.

The Morning and Evening Service of the Church of England, 2s. 6d.

The History of the Bible, large 2s.

The Church of England Catechism, 1s.

Church of Scotland shorter Catechism, 2s. 6d.

Selections from Eminent Authors, 1s. 6d.

Selection of Sacred Poetry, with Tunes, 2s.

Introduction to the Sciences, with beautiful Maps, Solar System, &c., &c., 3s. 6d.

Todd's Lectures to Children, familiarly Illustrating Important Truth, in 3 vols., 2s. 6d. each.

Statements of Education, Employments, &c., &c., at the Glasgow Asylum, 2s.

Beautiful Map of England and Wales, Description of London, 3s.

Remarks on the Bible by an Old Author, 6d.

Description of Birds, with Wood-cuts, 6d.

Arithmetic Boards.

IN THE PRESS.

Outlines of Natural History, with Wood-cuts, 2s.

The following articles, manufactured by the Blind, of the best quality and charged on the lowest terms, are exhibited for sale at the Asylum, viz. :—

House Baskets of various kinds.	Hearth and Door Rugs.
Mill Baskets and Hampers, made to any pattern.	Table Rugs.
	Fringed Rugs for Parlour Doors.
Door Mats, do. do. do.	Articles of Needle-work, Reticules,
Twines, do. do. do.	Silk Purses, &c., &c.
Mattresses made and repaired.	Stockings and Pansoufles.
Hair Friction Gloves.	Small Nets, &c., &c.
Curled Hair for Upholsterers.	Sacks and Sacking.

*** Orders are received at the Asylum for any of the preceding Articles, of whatever size or quality required.

By the constitution of the Asylum, a Contributor of £10 is constituted a Member for Life; and a Donation of £50 from au Individual, or £100 from a Parish, entitles either to recommend a Child to the Asylum. Contributors of £10 and upwards, uniting to the amount of £50, have the like power to recommend. As there are no Annual Subscriptions, Donations and Legacies to any amount will be thankfully received.

☞ The Public are respectfully requested to visit the Institution.

No. XI.

The following letter, from a blind woman aged forty, who lost her sight when she was five years old, affords a most gratifying example of the facility with which the art of reading can be acquired by a person of mature years, besides deciding the question of the superiority of the raised Roman letters to the shorthand system. The letter was written by a boy of ten years of age to the dictation of the woman whose name it bears :—

PROVIDENCE COTTAGE, NEAR BRISTOL,

April 13, 1839.

"Sir,—I beg to inform you that I still feel a heart overflowing with gratitude to the divine source from whence every good and perfect gift proceeds, and who hath raised you up as an instrument in his hands benevolently to come forward and to communicate to us the means of reading that Word of God which never fails to preserve us from all error and to direct us to all truth. The attainment of such an exalted privilege a short time ago I could not entertain the slightest hope of ; but Jehovah has proved that he has all power in heaven and in earth, and that he can open rivers in high places and fountains in the desert; and, Sir, I present to you my heart-felt thanks for having favoured me with so large a portion of the Holy Scripture. To them I daily repair for strength, wisdom, and consolation ; nor am I disappointed, for I find in them all I want for life and death—for time and for eternity. And if, Sir, any class of the human race needs personal

access to the Scripture more than another, it is the Blind, for they are
frequently deprived, although in perfect health, of attending divine service
for the want of a guide. Here I speak feelingly, having known many such
mournful instances; and for such whose hearts are panting after the sanctuary,
to be able to read the Holy Scriptures and other Scriptural books would be of
the utmost importance, for it would convert their prison into a sanctuary,
and render their burthen comparatively light; and, Sir, I cannot forbear
expressing my decided approbation of your system, believing it to be most
conducive to the benefit of the Blind, and that for the following reason:—A
few months previous to the arrival of your alphabet at the Asylum in Bristol,
I was favoured with Mr. Lucas's alphabet, which I received with joy and
thankfulness; but, alas! after considerable attention, I remained unacquainted with its nature, nor was there any person among all my friends
able to give me the least information, and, being myself much debilitated by
weakness, I was totally incapable of attending their establishment, and
therefore was compelled to relinquish all hopes of success. But, Sir, as soon
as I was happily favoured with your alphabet, I in a short time became
acquainted with the letters, as the most inferior scholars and even children
were able to give me information; and, Sir, during the past summer, I sent
one of your spelling-books to a female residing in a country village, and
although born Blind and totally destitute of the formation of letters, she
became acquainted with several of the letters during the few moments the
bearer remained with her, and she hoped to succeed, depending upon the
instruction of one of her neighbours. Dear Sir, had I sent her a shorthand
spelling-book it would have been utterly useless unless I had sent to her a
shorthand teacher, which would have been a moral impossibility. Other
reasons I could state, but I hope, Sir, this will be sufficient to prove the
superiority of your system, and that our benevolent friends will come over
every mountain of prejudice, and help us by assisting you, Sir, in your noble
undertaking.

　　　　　　　" I remain, Sir,

　　　　　　　　　" Your humble but ever benefitted Servant,

　　　　　　　　　　　　　"ELIZABETH ALLPORT.

" JOHN ALSTON, ESQ.,
" *Hon. Treasurer to the Asylum for the Blind, Glasgow.*"

THE FOLLOWING QUESTIONS

are to be minutely answered in words at length, on behalf of every Person
applying to be admitted into the ASYLUM FOR THE BLIND at Glasgow; and
a Certificate of the facts of the Case, and of Moral Character, must be
added, upon personal knowledge, from a Clergyman, two respectable
Householders or Elders, and a Medical Practitioner:—

1. Where do the parents or friends reside? What is the name, age, parish,
present residence, and maintenance of the applicant?

2. Are the parents or friends, or the parish to which the applicant belongs,
ready to pay the sum required for instruction or Board?

3. Is the applicant of sufficient intellect to receive instruction? and willing to obey the Rules of the Institution made or to be made?

4. Is the applicant free from epileptic or other fits, and from any disorder which may be prejudicial to those already in the Asylum?

5. Has the applicant had the small-pox or the cow-pox?

6. Has the applicant ever wandered about as a beggar, or played on a musical instrument in the streets or ale-houses?

7. What is the nature of the blindness of the applicant? Is it partial or total? How long has the applicant been Blind?

No. XIII.

Articles of Clothing for Inmates of the Asylum for the Blind.

MALES.	FEMALES.
1 Sunday Suit, with Hat.	1 Cloak.
1 Suit for Week Days.	1 Sunday Gown.
3 Shirts.	2 Week Gowns.
1 Shirt for Sabbath.	2 Flannel Petticoats.
3 Pairs Stockings, Coloured.	2 Upper do.
2 Neckcloths, do.	1 Bed Gown.
2 Pocket Handkerchiefs, Coloured.	3 Shifts.
2 Night Caps, do.	3 Pairs Stockings, Coloured.
2 Pairs Shoes.	2 Neckerchiefs, do.
	2 Pocket Handkerchiefs, do.
	2 Pinafores.
	3 Night Caps.
	1 Pair Stays.
	1 Bonnet.
	1 Pocket.
	2 Pairs Shoes.

Each Boy and Girl to have a Chest to keep their Clothes in, which must be kept in good repair, and when worn out replaced by their friends. Every article to be plain and substantial.

REGULATIONS

FOR THE

GLASGOW ASYLUM FOR THE BLIND.

Head I.—Superintendence.

1. The Institution shall be under the charge of a Matron, a Chaplain, and a Superintendent, with such Servants as the number of Inmates may render necessary.

2. The Matron shall reside in the House, see it kept in proper order, provide Board for the Pupils who live in the Asylum, have the control of the Domestic Servants, superintend the work of the Female inmates, conduct them to Church on the Lord's-day, and attend to their behaviour there.

3. The Chaplain shall attend in the Asylum every morning and evening for half an hour, for the purpose of conducting Family Worship; and on Saturday to give the Pupils instruction in the principles of Religion.

4. The Superintendent shall reside at the Lodge, take charge of the whole premises, check every disorder or impropriety, procure such materials for work as shall be ordered by the Directors, and attend to the personal cleanliness of the Boys residing in the House. He must also conduct the Boys to Church, and attend to their behaviour on the Lord's-day.

5. Instructors shall be provided for the various branches which it may be found proper to teach; and Blind persons are to be preferred as such, in all the departments which they are capable of filling.

6. One of the Directors, in turn, is to visit the Asylum, and make a weekly report.

Head II.—School of Industry.

1. All Blind persons capable of working, who have a residence permanently or occasionally in Glasgow, or its immediate neighbourhood, so as to sleep and take their meals in their own or their relations' houses, and whose characters and circumstances shall be approved of by the Directors, may be admitted into this branch of the Institution.

2. Every person who has not previously learned some branch of industry practised in this Institution, shall, when so admitted, have the option of paying, at entrance, the sum of £2 5s., or of working three months without receiving wages. The wages are to be, at first, 3s. 6d. per week, and to be increased in proportion to their earnings.

3. All persons admitted into the School of Industry shall behave orderly and peaceably, observe the hours, and comply with the Regulations of the Asylum.

Head III.—School of General Instruction.

BOYS.

1. No Boy shall be admitted under ten, or above sixteen years of age.

2. Each Boy shall pay the sum of £6 6s. at his admission, and annually, during his abode in the House.

3. Each Boy will receive his Board, Washing, and Lodging, in the House ; his parents or friends being required to provide him with Clothing, according to the List annexed.

4. Besides Religious Instruction and Elementary Education, each Boy shall be taught such branches of Trade, carried on in the House, as may be suited to his capacity and inclination.

GIRLS.

1. Girls shall be admitted into the House appropriated for their reception, in the same manner as Boys, on paying £6 6s. for each year they remain in the Asylum.

2. Girls shall receive Board, Washing, and Lodging, at the same rate as the Boys ; and be instructed in the various branches of Female Industry, and in the Principles of Religion, and the Elements of General Knowledge.

Head IV.—Terms of Admission.

1. No person shall be admitted to work, nor any Boy or Girl received to reside in the Asylum, till the Directors be satisfied as to their health, character, and qualifications.

2. Each Contributor to the amount of £50, or upwards, shall, for each £50 subscribed, be entitled to have one Boy or Girl, recommended by him, received into the Asylum. Contributors of £10 and upwards, uniting to make up the sum of £50, shall have the same privilege.

3. Every Corporation, Parish, or Public Body, subscribing £100, or upwards, to the funds of this Institution, shall be entitled to have at all times in the House, for each £100 so subscribed, one inmate, in conformity with the limitations in the third head.

4. The period of education in the Asylum is to be three years ; but those young people who have conducted themselves properly during that time, may be continued in the House, at such a Board as the Directors shall judge equitable.

Head V.—General Rules.

1. Family Worship shall be performed every morning, from 1st March to 1st November, at Half-past Six, and from 1st November to 1st March, at Eight in the morning ; and every evening at Seven o'clock.

2. The Hours of Working shall be from Seven in the morning till Seven in the evening, an hour being allowed for Breakfast, and another for Dinner.

Hours for recreation shall also be allowed occasionally, according to the age and health of the scholars.

3. Every Individual admitted into the Asylum, whether merely during working hours, or as an inmate, shall be regular in keeping the hours of the House, and especially in attending on Family Worship.

4. Females who reside out of the House shall commence their work at Ten o'clock, and receive their Dinner with the inmates. For such as have no relations to reside with, the Directors have provided a house in the neighbourhood, and pay a woman to take charge of them.

5. The strictest attention must be paid to cleanliness, both in the persons of the inmates, and in every part of the House.

6. The inmates of the House, in turn, shall do as much of the work of the House as they are capable of performing.

7. No intercourse shall be permitted between the Male and Female branches of the Asylum; nor shall the boys and girls enter the buildings appropriated to each other's use, except when they are assembled for Family Worship or Religious Instruction.

8. Every instance of inattention to hours, improper language, disorderly conduct, indecency, or immorality, shall be reported to the Treasurer, who shall report the same to the Committee of Directors if necessary; and punished by admonition, forfeiture of earnings, or in cases of gross delinquency or repeated misconduct, expulsion from the Asylum.

LONDON : PRINTED BY WILLIAM CLOWES AND SONS, LIMITED, STAMFORD STREET AND CHARING CROSS.

BY

CHARLES BAKER

from "The English Cyclopædia" (1859)

Reprinted by permission of
MESSRS. BRADBURY, AGNEW & CO., LTD.

1. *CENSUS OF THE BLIND*
2. *EDUCATION OF THE BLIND*
3. *ALPHABETS OF THE BLIND*

LONDON
SAMPSON LOW, MARSTON & COMPANY
LIMITED
St. Dunstan's House
FETTER LANE, FLEET STREET, E.C.
1895

BY

CHARLES BAKER

from "The English Cyclopædia" (1859)

Reprinted by permission of
MESSRS. BRADBURY, AGNEW & CO., LTD.

1. *CENSUS OF THE BLIND*

2. *EDUCATION OF THE BLIND*

3. *ALPHABETS OF THE BLIND*

LONDON
SAMPSON LOW, MARSTON & COMPANY
LIMITED
St. Dunstan's House
FETTER LANE, FLEET STREET, E.C.
1895

LONDON:
PRINTED BY WILLIAM CLOWES AND SONS, Limited,
STAMFORD STREET AND CHARING CROSS.

CENSUS OF THE BLIND.

In Great Britain and the islands of the British seas (exclusive of Ireland), there were 21,487 totally blind persons at the time of the last census—11,273 males and 10,214 females. Previous to 1851, no account had been taken of the number of the blind in Great Britain and Ireland, so that there are no means of ascertaining whether their number is increasing or decreasing relatively to the population. The numbers above given furnish a proportion of 1 in 975 in Great Britain, 1 in 979 in England and Wales, 1 in 960 in Scotland, and 1 in 837 in the Channel Islands and the Isle of Man. These proportions vary in different parts of the kingdom ; in London the proportion is 1 in 1025, and it is nearly the same in the north midland, the south midland, the northern (including Yorkshire), and the south-eastern divisions of the kingdom ; the west midland division presents us with 1 in 906 ; the eastern, 1 in 888 ; Wales, 1 in 847 ; and the south-western, 1 in 758 ; while the north-western district shows only 1 in 1167 ; the southern counties of Scotland, 1 in 1065 ; and the northern counties, 1 in 823.

On comparing these results with those obtained in other countries, we find that in the flat champaigns of Belgium, Hanover, portions of Saxony, Prussia, and some other German states, and the plains of Lombardy and Denmark, the proportion is 1 in 950 ; in the more elevated portions of Saxony, Prussia, Wurtemburg, Nassau, the duchies of Altenburg and Hesse, and also part of Brunswick, 1 in 1340 ; in Alpine regions, and countries elevated from 2000 to 8000 feet above the sea-level, as in some of the Swiss cantons, Sardinia, &c., 1 in 1500 ; while in Norway, according to the returns made in 1845, the proportion was 1 in 482. Thus the level portions of Europe present nearly the same results as Britain, while there are certain discrepancies in the above numbers which cannot at present be accounted for.

It has been thought that blindness has been increased by many of the employments followed in populous manufacturing towns; but it is clear, from the census returns, that a much larger proportion of blind persons is found in agricultural than in manufacturing and mining counties. For example, in Wilts, Doret, Devon, Cornwall, and Somerset (south-western division), the average is 1 in 758; in Essex, Suffolk, and Norfolk, 1 in 888; and in the northern counties of Scotland, which include the Highlands, 1 in 823; while the highest proportion, namely, 1 in 665, is observed in Herefordshire. Contrasting these averages with the following manufacturing or mining counties, no unfavourable inference can be drawn as to the physical effects of manufactures on the sense of sight, in the West Riding of Yorkshire the blind are 1 in 1231; in Cheshire and Lancashire, 1 in 1167; in Durham, 1 in 1163; in Staffordshire, 1 in 1082. It should be remembered that the asylums and schools which have been established for the reception and instruction of those deprived of sight are located in the principal cities and towns. Where, however, the towns are large, the number of inmates of these establishments only slightly affect the proportion which the blind bear to the general population. In London the proportion is 1 in 1025; in Manchester, 1 in 1107; in Liverpool, 1 in 999; in Birmingham, 1 in 1181. Conclusions unfavourable to the rural districts should not, however, be deduced from a mere comparison of the proportion of the blind to the population of all ages. Blindness is a common infirmity of old age; and an examination of the ages of the blind shows that nearly one-half of the persons deprived of sight are above 60 years of age. It follows, therefore, that in those localities in which the largest numbers of old men and women are living, the largest proportion of the blind will be found. In the great seats of manufacturing industry the population generally is much younger than in most of the agricultural counties, where persons in large numbers, and especially females, are living, in circumstances favourable to

longevity, at very advanced ages. Thus, in counties presenting
the highest and lowest proportions of blind persons, the influence
of age is sufficiently apparent. The proportion of population in
Herefordshire aged 60 years and upwards is 10 per cent., while
the proportion of blind of the same age is 61 per cent. In Wilts,
Dorset, Devon, Cornwall, and Somerset the proportion aged 60
years and upwards on the whole population is 9 per cent. ; on the
blind it is 53 per cent. In Essex, Suffolk, and Norfolk only 8
per cent. of the whole population attain 60 years and upwards,
while of the blind in the same locality 50 per cent. attain this
age. In the northern counties of Scotland 9 per cent. of the
population reach the advanced age specified ; while of the blind
54 per cent. attain the age of 60 and upwards. These four
geographical divisions are those in which the highest proportion
of blind persons is found. The four divisions in which the lowest
proportions prevail present a very striking contrast with the
above. In the West Riding of Yorkshire the proportion per cent.
of the population aged 60 years and upwards is only 6, while the
proportion of the blind of the same age is 43 per cent. In
Cheshire and Lancashire the proportion on the whole population
is 5, that of the blind 31 per cent. In Durham the proportion
on the population is 6 per cent. ; on the blind, 52. In Staffordshire the proportion of the population is 6 per cent., and of the
blind, 42.

In the early ages of life the numbers of the blind are not large.
Of the 21,487 blind persons in Great Britain only 2929, or less
than 14 per cent., are under 20 years of age—a circumstance
tending to show that cases of blindness at birth are not common.
Between 20 and 60 years of age there are 8456 persons, or about
39 per cent. of the whole number, while 10,102 persons, or 47 per
cent., are at the advanced ages above 60. These facts point to
the conclusion that blindness, in many cases, may have arisen as
a natural infirmity attendant upon old age, and also show the
great longevity of the blind, notwithstanding the accidents to
which they are liable.

It is clearly shown in one of the tables comprised in the

Registrar-General's returns, that this affliction is not confined chiefly to particular classes and trades, but exists amongst all ranks and in a great variety of employments. None of the great branches of manufacturing industry seem to be peculiarly liable to it ; indeed, the small numbers returned against cotton, linen, silk, woollen cloth, iron, and earthenware are remarkable when the immense amount of labour employed in these manufactures is considered. Factory workers are, however, mostly young persons, and none would be employed in the midst of machinery with any defect of vision. Amongst the items which present the largest numbers in the classification of employments are (in Great Britain) : agricultural labourers, 907 ; labourers not otherwise described, 512 ; Chelsea pensioners and soldiers, 586 ; Greenwich pensioners, 70 ; farmers, 505 ; domestic servants (chiefly females), 438 ; weavers, 295 ; coal-miners, 195 ; copper- and lead-miners, 68 ; stone and limestone quarriers, 51. Of the class described as " annuitants," and " living on alms," there are 1062 ; and 2833 blind paupers are returned in workhouses without any statement as to previous occupation. Of the blind following employments presumed to have been acquired after loss of sight there are : musicians and teachers of music, 535 ; mat, sacking, and net-makers, 127, and knitters, 92. With respect to 2853 males and 5960 females no returns as to their actual or previous pursuits are made.

Of the persons returned as blind in Great Britain, 11,273 are males and 10,214 females. Accidents and diseases resulting in loss of sight are more likely to arise in the employments followed by males than in those of females. The proportions in England and Wales are 113 males to 100 females ; in Scotland the difference is slighter—a result probaby traceable to the preponderance of aged women in that country.

The Census Report of the Commissioners on " The Status of Disease " in Ireland is one of the most valuable documents ever published in this kingdom on the amount and distribution of disease. The inquiry was conducted with much intelligence, and with such precautions as are not usually manifested in matters of this nature. As a *first* contribution on the permanent maladies to which the inhabitants of a country are liable, its importance can scarcely be over-estimated, while it has opened a field for investigation which will hereafter prove a source of lasting benefit to science, and which cannot fail to be a means of directing attention to the afflicted classes whose position it exhibits.

According to the returns made to the Census Commission Office, there were 7587 persons (3588 males and 3999 females) totally deprived of sight resident in Ireland on the 30th March, 1851. Of this number, 1672 were in the civic and 4920 in the rural districts, the former localities including the different asylums and public institutions for the blind ; and 995 persons (373 males and 622 females) were in the various workhouses and auxiliary workhouses at the time specified.

Without an accurate medical examination and special inquiry into the circumstances of each case, it would not be possible to define or tabulate the diseases or accidents which produced the large amount of blindness ascertained. How many were born blind there are no means of knowing : congenital cataract, the most frequent cause of blindness from birth, is not very common ; loss of sight from purulent ophthalmia and ulceration of cornea is the most common ; and in some districts, particularly in the west of Ireland, internal inflammations of the eyes of a rheumatic character prevail to a great extent, and are a frequent cause of blindness.

The limited space we can devote to this subject prevents us from giving the important Tables included in the Report, from which we have drawn the above facts and observations. To that Report all who are interested in the state of the blind in Ireland may be referred. We give the heads of these Tables.

Table I. shows the number of blind in the civic and rural districts and the workhouses, together with the proportion of males to females, and proportion to the population in the several provinces, counties, cities, and towns in Ireland.

Table II. shows by ages and sexes the number and previous or present occupations of the blind.

Table III. shows by ages and sexes the state of education and marriage among the blind in workhouses and in the civic and rural districts.

Table IV. shows the number, distribution, means of support, date of erection, and other circumstances relating to the various asylums for the blind in Ireland.

Table V. (taken from the reports of St. Mark's Ophthalmic Hospital, Dublin, from 1844 to 1852) shows the varieties of diseases and accidents of the eye in 11,233 instances, together with the colour of the eye in 7354 cases.

(Compiled and extracted from the *Official Returns of the Census of Great Britain in* 1851, published under the authority of the Registrar-General ; and from *The Census of Ireland for* 1851,— *Report on the Status of Disease.*)

EDUCATION OF THE BLIND.

BLINDNESS perhaps meets with more general sympathy than any other calamity. Our most beautiful and correct perceptions are derived through the medium of sight ; the want therefore of such a medium is an evil for which no other possession can compensate. Hence it is that we at first consider the blind as an unfortunate race, whose conceptions must not only be confined to that narrow sphere in which they live and move, but, as far as a knowledge of external objects is concerned, must be limited to that imperfect acquaintance which is obtained by the sense of feeling. Looking, however, further into the subject, we find that the sense of hearing is constantly communicating knowledge to a blind person which helps him to analyse and compare ; from which he draws inferences, and arrives at conclusions more or less correct ; that constant experience enables him to modify any false impressions which he may have received ; that association, memory, and other powers of the mind are active ; that the senses of smell and taste are continually contributing some small additions to his stores of knowledge ; and that, by these united means, he may become well informed on subjects of ordinary discourse, though labouring under a disadvantage at first appearance insurmountable. The self-education of a child born blind commences as soon as that of one who sees, and if parents in such cases would give themselves trouble in its instruction, instead of looking upon their case as one of despair, they would be amply rewarded by the improvement, surpassing all expectation, which their child would make. They would find little difficulty in communicating to him the names, shapes, and many other particulars of objects ; and indeed language, with the exception of some classes of words denoting colour, or other qualities which can only be known by means of sight, might be as perfectly conveyed to him as to the

child possessing all its senses.   They would find that they could
give correct ideas of numbers to a large amount by means of
tangible objects, and of still larger numbers by analogy ; that
they could also give ideas of time, space, distance, so as to impress
him with correct notions of the earth, its size, inhabitants, productions, climates, the occupations, the pleasures, and the pains
of mankind.   All this is knowledge of a useful and pleasing kind,
and many parents would become highly interested in such a work.
They would soon find that they might proceed still farther, and
enable their blind child either to attain a certain degree of perfection in some mechanicl art, or by educating his higher faculties
train him to occupy a more intellectual and important station.

The parent who reasons and acts thus upon his child's calamity
will be supported and animated by the knowledge that he is
supplying by his own attention the defect of nature, and that he
is educating his child to fulfil important duties with the same
pleasure to himself that others have who possess a more perfect
organisation, and that he is providing a most efficient check to
listlessness and mental torpor.

The ear has been happily called " the vestibule of the soul," and
the annals of the blind who have become illustrious confirm the
remark, for they show that few intellectual studies are inaccessible
to them.   It has even been said, and has received a kind of
universal assent among those who have associated much with
them, that in certain branches of study they have a facility which
others rarely possess, The blind appear to have immense advantages
over the deaf ; their intercourse with the outward world, by
means of speech, is more direct, and consequently more rapid, and
their knowledge of passing events is equal to that of mankind
generally.   The deaf and dumb *see* indeed all that passes within
their immediate sphere, but owing to the circuitous mode of communication which they have to adopt they can know little beyond
it, and enter very partially into the spirit of passing events.   In
addition to this, finding that they do not always understand
perfectly, nor guess rightly, their temper becomes impatient, and
their countenance acquires an anxious or irritable expression,

which is sometimes mistaken for cleverness. We know of no deaf persons who have attained to any great degree of eminence, even under circumstances favourable to the development of their powers ; but with regard to the blind, they have enriched the arts, the sciences, and literature by their successful pursuits, and not unfrequently under circumstances of extraordinary difficulty. Viewing both these classes of men as devoid of education, dependent upon themselves for support, and for the enjoyment of life, the blind are *physically* greater objects of compassion than the deaf, because, without peculiar modes of education suited to their privation, they cannot obtain a livelihood ; but so far as happiness is dependent upon knowledge, and from this source some of the purest enjoyments arise, they are nearly on a level with ordinary men. Through the ear they can acquire knowledge of the highest order, and cannot remain long in any company of their fellow-men without becoming in some degree wiser. The case of the deaf is the reverse of this ; they are not *physically* so dependent as the blind : having the advantage of sight, they may apply themselves to and acquire the simpler imitative arts, and thus earn a subsistence, but *mentally* they are little above brutes ; they can know nothing of the things around them, they feel themselves depressed and degraded among men ; the language, the customs, the enjoyments of society, where these rise higher than what seems to exist among the more perfect animals, are to them unknown, and by them unregarded ; and it requires only a small amount of reflection to perceive that an uneducated deaf person is not morally responsible for his conduct.

These remarks, and the comparison with which we have opened this subject, are not designed to show that the blind are less in need of education than the deaf and dumb ; we are advocates for education in its fullest extent among all classes, but more particularly among persons who labour under impediments so distressing as those we have mentioned. Our advice would be to educate such persons as highly as possible, to improve especially those faculties which they appear to possess in a superior degree to mankind generally; but not to waste time and labour in endeavouring to instruct them in arts in which they can never attain to an equality with persons who possess the full enjoyment of their senses.

In this and in other countries, some attention has been paid to alleviate the sufferings and diminish the ignorance of the blind ; the hand of kindness has been extended to lead them into society, and the voice of sympathy has been heard by them in the midst of their darkness. Asylums in several parts of Great Britain have rescued a few from a life of listlessness and anxious care, who have been instructed in various arts with the view of wholly or partially relieving them from dependence on their friends, their parishes, or the temporary bounty of the benevolent. To all who are entrusted with the charge of the pauper blind, and especially to boards of guardians, the words of Dr. Lettsom, the benevolent advocate of the charities for the indigent blind, may be addressed : " He who enables a blind person, without any excess of labour, to earn his own livelihood, does him more real service than if he had pensioned him for life."

It is invariably found that persons who are deficient in one sense exercise those that are left to them more constantly, and for this reason more accurately, for the senses are improved or educated by exercise. The exquisite fineness of touch and smell in the blind, the quickness in the eye of the deaf, the accuracy with which a seaman discovers a distant vessel long before it is discernible to the unaccustomed eye of a landsman, and the acuteness of sight, hearing, and smelling in many savage tribes are all to be referred to the same cause, namely, the constant exercise of those organs. Those persons who are deprived of one or other of their senses will, to a great degree, supply the deficiency by the aid of those which they still retain. Hearing and touch are especially cultivated by the blind ; by the first they recognise speech, and the endless variations and modifications of sound ; by the second they become acquainted with the external form of objects. The chief art of the instructor of the blind therefore consists in supplying through an indirect medium those ideas of which his pupil cannot obtain a conception through the ordinary channels; and in doing this he will act wisely to ascertain what ideas on kindred subjects his pupil possesses, whether such are true or false, and by what process he became possessed of them; to become, in fact, the pupil of his pupil—to draw forth the stock of knowledge already attained, in order to form a ground-work on which to proceed with his future instructions.

The mode which would probably first occur to a teacher in the intellectual education of the blind would be lessons delivered orally, illustrated by such analogies as would enable them to follow their teacher, taken, if necessary, from objects appealing to their senses. At first they would advance by slow degrees in comparison with pupils who see, but this very slowness would be accompanied by a sureness which would amply repay the pains taken to make the lessons understood. It is a fault in ordinary schools that the first steps are taken too rapidly, and one advance too quickly follows upon a former. Such schools might derive a useful lesson from the methods used in the instruction of those who are deprived of one or other of their senses. From oral instruction, the transition to a palpable language is natural. Accordingly, we find that the invention of *characters in relief* was among the earliest measures taken for instructing the blind.

An ingenious *string alphabet* was contrived a few years ago by David Macbeath, a blind teacher in the Edinburgh School, in conjunction with Robert Milne, one of his blind companions. The following is their description of this invention : "The string alphabet is formed by so knotting a cord that the protuberances made upon it may be qualified by their shape, size, and situation for signifying the elements of language. The letters of this alphabet are distributed into seven classes, which are distinguished by certain knots or other marks; each class comprehends four letters, except the last, which comprehends but two. The first, or A class, is distinguished by a large round knot; the second, or E class, by a knot projecting from the line; the third, or I class, by the series of links vulgarly called 'the drummer's plait'; the fourth, or M class, by a simple noose; the fifth, or Q class, by a

noose with a line drawn through it; the sixth, or U class, by a
noose with a net-knot cast on it; and the seventh, or Y class,
by a twisted noose. The first letter of each class is denoted by
the simple characteristic of its respective class; the second by the
characteristic and a common knot close to it; the third by the
characteristic and a common knot half an inch from it; and the
fourth by the characteristic and a common knot an inch from it.
Thus, A is simply a large round knot; B is a large round knot
with a common knot close to it; C is a large round knot with a
common knot half an inch from it; and D is a large round knot
with a common knot an inch from it, and so on." The alphabet
above described is found by experience to answer completely the
purpose for which it was invented. In the Glasgow Asylum the
greater part of the Gospel according to St. Mark, the 119th Psalm,
and other passages of Scripture and history have been executed
in this alphabet. The knotted string is wound round a vertical
frame, which revolves and passes from the reader as he proceeds.

This alphabet reminds us of the *Quipos*, or knot-records of
Peru, in which the history of their country was recorded long
before the discovery of America by the Spaniards. Their *quipos*
were formed of the intestines of animals, and there is a similar
diversity in their symbols with that in the string-alphabet of
which we are speaking. An account of these *quipos* was published in London in 1827. They were purchased by Alexander
Strong for ten pounds from a person who bought them at Buenos
Ayres.

In further explanation of the string-alphabet the inventors say,
" It must readily occur to everyone that the employment of an
alphabet composed in the manner which has been explained will
ever be necessarily tedious; but it should be borne in mind that
there is no supposable system of tangible figures significant of
thought that is not more or less liable to the same objection.
The inventors are aware that among the different methods by
which people at a distance might be enabled to hold mutual
intercourse through the medium of a language addressed to the
touch, there are some that would doubtless be more expeditious

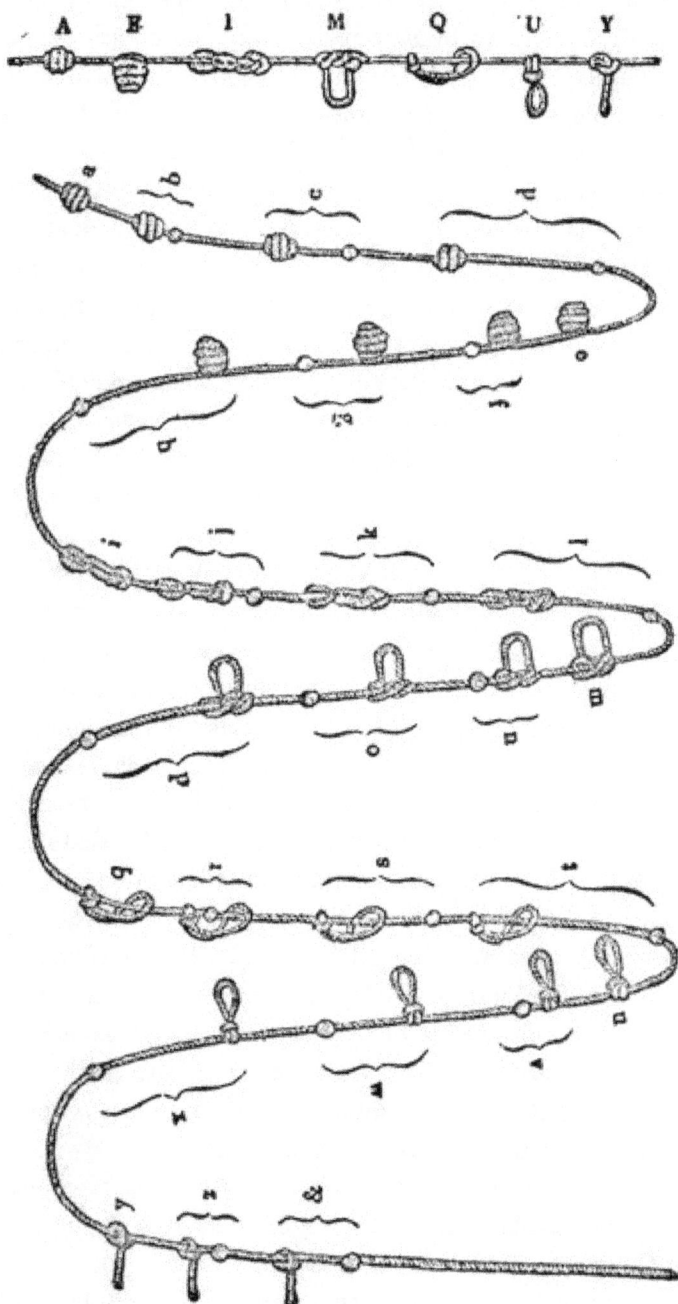

THE STRING ALPHABET.

than theirs ; but they flatter themselves that, when all the advantages and disadvantages of each particular method are duly considered, the plan which they have been led to adopt will appear, upon the whole, decidedly the best. There can scarcely be any system of tangible signs, which it would be less difficult either to learn or to remember, since a person of ordinary intellect may easily acquire a thorough knowledge of the string-alphabet in an hour and retain it for ever. Yet the inventors can assure their readers that it is impossible for the pen or the press to convey ideas with greater precision. Besides the highly important properties of simplicity and accuracy which their scheme unites, and in which it has not been surpassed, it possesses various minor, nor yet inconsiderable, advantages, in which it is presumed it cannot be equalled by anything of its kind. For example, its tactile representations of articulate sounds are easily portable—the materials of which they are constructed may always be procured at a trifling expense—and the apparatus necessary for their construction is extremely simple. In addition to the letters of the alphabet, there have been contrived arithmetical figures, which it is hoped will be of great utility, as the remembrance of numbers is often found peculiarly difficult. Palpable commas, semicolons, &c., have likewise been provided to be used when judged requisite. The inventors have only to add, that sensible of the happy results of the invention to themselves, and commiserating the fate of their fellow-prisoners of darkness, they most earnestly recommend to all intrusted with the education of persons deprived of sight carefully to instruct them in the principles of orthography, as the blind being in general unable to spell is the chief obstacle to their deriving, from the new mode of signifying thought, the much-wanted benefit which it is designed to extend to their melancholy circumstances."

We entirely agree in the views here taken of the string-alphabet ; as an auxiliary to the blind in the acquirement and application of language, and in the absence of a tangible writing on paper, we think no invention is superior to it, and we should be glad to have seen it in more common use among the blind in our recent inquiries at various institutions. The advice to instruct the blind carefully in spelling is important, for if this acquirement be not made they cannot communicate by language with their fellow-men otherwise than orally. To those blind persons who have lived together in institutions, and formed friendships which they wish to continue when separated by distance, the string-alphabet offers a mode of correspondence as perfect as our pen, one too which may be intrusted to ordinary persons to convey without any probability of the communication being deciphered.

David Macbeath, one of the inventors, was connected with the Edinburgh Asylum as pupil and teacher for twenty-five years. His inventions for teaching were numerous, and applicable to instruction in music, arithmetic, and mathematics. His string-alphabet was fully described in the *Edinburgh Philosophical Journal* some years ago. He conducted the public examinations of the Edinburgh pupils, where he never failed to excite the interest and attention of those present towards the objects of their solicitude.

In the infancy of the art of teaching the blind, *raised music* was invented, in order that they might be enabled to acquire their lessons independent of a master. This invention is at present little used, for the constant practice of those who pursue this branch of study is a continual exercise of the memory, and they are able to learn very long pieces by the ear alone. The reason assigned by Dr. Guillié for the disuse of embossed music is very satisfactory: "The scholar could not read with his fingers and perform at the same time." Thorough bass is, however, as readily studied by the blind as by the seeing by means of "Tansure's Musical Board," described in his "Musical Grammar." This board is three feet long, about eight or nine inches wide, and has two staves, with ledger lines above, between, and below. These are raised upon the surface of the board about one-sixteenth of an inch, the top of the stave lines being flat, while that of the ledger lines is round. It is pierced all over with little holes, so as to receive the pins which represent the notes. We may here mention the invention of Don Jaime Isern, the object of which

is to enable a blind composer to transfer his thoughts to paper
in the usual musical notation without the necessity of employing
an amanuensis.   For this invention the large silver medal of the
London Society for the Encouragement of Arts, Manufactures,
and Commerce was given to Don J. Isern in 1827.   There is a
full description of it, with illustrative engravings, in vol. xlv.
of the "Society's Transactions."   In the same volume there is
an interesting communication on the subject of types for the
blind by Mr. G. Gibson, of Birmingham.   This communication
is connected with various inventions which we have had the
pleasure of inspecting, and of which we shall give a short
account, referring our readers who desire to be made perfectly
acquainted with the invention to the work above mentioned.   Mr.
Gibson's aim has been to supply the blind with a mode of writing
and keeping their own accounts.   "A cube of wood, or of any
other convenient material, the size of which will depend on the
delicacy of touch in each blind person, is to have raised on one
side of it a letter, or figure, or stop, in the manner of a printer's
type.   On the opposite or lower side of the cube is a representation of the same character as is on the upper side, but formed of
needle-points inserted into the wood.   If, therefore, a piece of
paper be laid on a cushion, or surface of felt, and the type be
pressed down, the points will enter the paper, and form on the
under surface of it a raised or embossed representation, by the
projection of the burs where the points have penetrated, and this
embossed character may be distinguished, and consequently read
by the touch."   In its outward appearance, the whole apparatus
of Mr. Gibson forms a small piece of cabinet furniture.   When
the top is thrown open an even surface of cushion presents itself.
Upon this there is a flat piece of mahogany about an inch broad,
which can be moved from one notch to another, to any part of
the desk.   This is for the letters to lie against, like the composing-
stick of a printer.   The letters he uses are a composition of tin
and lead : the upper surface is elevated so that he can distinguish
the letter, and the under surface has inserted in it needle-points
of the shape of the letter on the upper surface.   In writing the

Lord's Prayer, after the paper is placed, he takes O out of its division, and puts it at the beginning of the line, then U, then R, gently pressing each letter down as he puts it next the preceding one. At the end of a word he inserts a small mahogany space, and proceeds till his performance is complete ; whether it be a copy of anything which he wishes to make, or an original piece of composition. It will be observed that, by putting two or more pieces of paper underneath his pointed types, copies will be multiplied. The letters are in small divisions, which occupy side-drawers in his printing cabinet. The use of this machine implies more knowledge than the uneducated blind possess, as they must know how to spell. However, it is a part of its object to teach spelling. For this communication to the London Society for the Encouragement of Arts, &c., Mr. Gibson was presented with the gold Vulcan medal of the Society. Another of Mr. Gibson's inventions may be here noticed. It forms a drawer of the cabinet above mentioned, and is intended for working the rules of arithmetic. This Mr. G. calls his slate. It is divided into rows by elevated slips of wood, along which the figures are to slide. Like the types they are formed of metal, but have no needle-points underneath. We have seen him perform examples in multiplication and other rules by this apparatus, which is simply and beautifully conceived. It is obvious that all the elementary operations may be performed by it, and that by the union of this and the writing apparatus, a blind person may write his own letters, and keep his own accounts. We have dwelt upon the subject of reading and writing for the blind, feeling that they are deserving of all the importance which can be attached to them. Lieutenant Holman, the blind traveller, used Wedgwood's apparatus for writing in the dark. A very ingenious instrument of this nature has been invented by the late Mr. Hughes, who was for many years the governor of the School for the Blind at Manchester. We return to the early methods pursued in this art.

Embossed maps and globes for teaching geography would naturally be suggested to those persons who were engaged in teaching reading to the blind by raised figures. M. Weissembourg, a blind

man of Mannheim, appears to have been the first person who made
relief-maps, up to which time the instruction given to the blind on
geography was merely oral.   Various methods for producing maps .
of this character are now employed.

Palpable methods have also been adopted for making the blind
acquainted with different branches of astronomical knowledge, and
in addition to raised maps of the heavens, various ingenious
instruments have been contrived to further their progress in the
science of astronomy.   The application of such apparatus to the
purposes of teaching has been attended with encouraging success.
We shall detail some of the methods pursued in teaching arithmetic when we speak of the Edinburgh Institution, where the
well-known invention of Dr. Saunderson has been so much
improved that, by its means, any operation may be readily
performed.   For a description of the original invention, which
was the united work of Dr. Moyes and Dr. Saunderson, we refer
to the article " Blind " in Rees's " Cyclopædia," or in the " Encyclopædia Britannica."   By the improvements which we shall
describe, it will be seen how greatly the simplicity of the contrivance has been increased.   Previous to these tangible methods of
teaching arithmetic the blind were instructed on this subject
orally, the process on their part being entirely mental.   A publication of late years, which is intended exclusively for the blind, is of
a higher character and aim than any that have preceded it, though
not one which will generally be considered as equal to many of
these mentioned, in point of utility.   The work to which we
allude is an elementary treatise on mathematics by the Rev. William
Taylor of York, called " The Diagrams of Euclid's Elements of
Geometry, arranged according to Simpson's edition in an embossed
or tangible form, for the use of blind persons who wish to enter
upon the study of that noble science," York, 1828.   As a means
of leading to the acquisition of a science for which some blind
persons have shown a predilection, this beautifully executed work
is of great value, and we hope that the blind generally who show
a superior aptitude for the exact sciences, even though instructed
in a degree at the public expense, will have all the advantages

which works like Mr. Taylor's, aided by good instructors, can confer. It is stated that some of the pupils of the London School for the Indigent Blind worked a few problems for Mr. Taylor, their examiner, at their examination last Christmas.

Institutions of a philanthropic tendency have frequently originated with members, individual or collective, of learned societies ; and such societies have lent their assistance and patronage to various efforts for advancing the condition of mankind, and removing the obstacles to improvement. The attempts of M. Haüy to systematise a plan for the education of the blind are the first which are deserving of special notice. His methods were submitted to the Academy of Sciences of Paris, where they received all the encouragement he looked for. The commissioners chosen to report upon the means which he proposed to employ suggested to the Academy not only to bestow its approbation upon M. Haüy, but also to invite him to publish his methods, and to assure him of their readiness to receive from him an account of his future progress. It appears that many of the plans recommended by Haüy in his " Essay on the Education of the Blind," were not so much his own inventions as adaptations of the ingenious contrivances of individuals of different ages, and in different countries, who had preceded him in this benevolent work. The celebrity of certain blind individuals, partly the result, perhaps, of painstaking teachers, and partly of their own highly gifted minds, had reached the ears of Haüy. By a happy exercise of benevolence and talent, aided by that enthusiasm without which the greatest labour is ineffectual, he formed the outline of a system of instruction, which required only time, and the modifications which discover themselves in every course of rational teaching, to be brought into successful operation. He wished to make the sense of touch do that for the blind which the Abbé de l'Epée had made the sense of sight do for the deaf and dumb. He wished to see the fingers of the blind employed in reading written language, and for this purpose he invented the noble art of printing in relief, which will hand down the name of Valentine Haüy with honour to posterity.

Haüy offered to instruct gratuitously the blind children who were under the care of the Philanthropic Society. He commenced his instructions in 1784, and taught his pupils reading, writing, arithmetic, geography, composing types, and printing. In 1786 public exercises were performed by the pupils at Versailles, in the presence of the king. These exercises excited much astonishment, and there seemed to be little doubt of the stability and success of the undertaking. Large funds were subscribed, and the school was filled with pupils ; but the commencement had been made on a scale too extensive for its regular maintenance, the warmth of popular feeling cooled, and as the institution was unsupported by Government, Haüy never enjoyed the fruits for which he toiled. His school was not, however, suffered to fall entirely ; it was taken up by the Constituent Assembly of the Revolution, and has since been supported at the expense of the Government. The establishment of which we are speaking is the School for the Young Blind, at Paris.

There are at Paris two celebrated institutions for the blind. The more ancient of these is the Hôpital Royale des Quinze Vingts, founded by St. Louis in 1260, for the reception of such of his soldiers as had lost their sight in the East. At its first establishment it consisted of *blind* and *seeing* persons, the latter being the conductors of the former. As its name indicates, it receives *fifteen score*, or three hundred blind persons. This noble asylum continues, as it was originally placed, under the government of the Grand Almoner of France. To obtain admission it is necessary that applicants be blind and indigent ; they are admitted from all parts of the kingdom, are lodged in the hospital, and receive twenty-four sous (about a shilling) a day for their food and clothing. No instruction is afforded to the inmates of the Quinze Vingts ; some of them, however, execute works, which, for their ingenuity, attract and deserve attention. The other Parisian establishment for the blind is the Institution Royale des Jeunes Aveugles, of which Haüy was the founder. It contains about a hundred young persons of both sexes, who are maintained and educated at the expense of the State for eight years. Paying pupils are also admitted. During the last quarter of a century the education of the blind has made great advances, as will be seen when the present state of the various establishments is compared with their actual condition, as described in the article BLIND of the " Penny Cyclopædia." The writer of that essay lamented that there was so much that appeared to him censurable, and that called for animadversion in the modes of education pursued in some of the schools for the blind. The article was, however, transmitted to three of these schools, previous to its publication, and it was allowed to be a correct statement of facts. A great change for the better has since taken place, not only in the schools referred to, but in others also ; new asylums have been established, and the attention of many experienced men has been directed to various branches of education, and especially to the provision of books in raised type, of which an account is given in the article ALPHABETS FOR THE BLIND.

The first British Asylum for the Blind was established at Liverpool, in the year 1791. This institution has hitherto been liberally supported. During the year 1858, its expenditure was 3000*l.*, its income about 3400*l.*, derived from goods disposed of (the work of its inmates), from the payments made on behalf of the pupils, from legacies, donations and subscriptions, from dividends, and the pew-rents of its chapel. The sums received for articles manufactured exceeded 900*l*, but the produce of these labours does not assist the funds of the establishment. The instruction of the blind in manual labour seems to be the primary object with the directors of the institution. The trades which are taught are those of basket-making, ropemaking, weaving, shoemaking, sewing, knitting, and plaiting sash-line. The most profitable of these arts is the ropemaking ; the locality of the institution contributes to the advantages derived from this trade. The sugar-houses require so vast a supply of cordage, that it can scarcely be furnished in a sufficient quantity. The next most profitable labour is the weaving of carpets, lobby-cloths, and bear-rugs. Masters possessing sight are regularly employed in teaching the various trades ; the reasons why the institution derives no pecuniary advantage from the extensive labours carried on are sufficiently obvious when the expense of experienced masters is considered, the waste of materials by the labourers who are chiefly learners, and their quitting the asylum when they can earn enough to maintain themselves.

The total number of persons who have been received into this asylum from its commencement to the publication of the report, January 1859, was 1429. Some very interesting details are given in the same document on the causes of the calamity under which the pupils labour, so far as could be ascertained by the officers of the institution.

LIVERPOOL INSTITUTION, TOTAL NUMBER RECEIVED, 1429.

			Totally.	Partially.	Total.
Blind from their birth			70	49	119
,,	,,	small pox	202	48	250
,,	,,	inflammation	278	177	455
,,	,,	cataract	56	93	149
,,	,,	external injury	99	47	146
,,	,,	defect in the optic nerve	76	64	140
,,	,,	amaurosis	25	15	40
,,	,,	imperfect organisation	6	14	20
Lost their sight at sea			8	1	9
,,	,,	by gradual decay	5	3	8
,,	,,	after fever	14	5	19
,,	,,	after measles	8	5	13
,,	,,	after convulsions	3	3	6
,,	,,	from causes not mentioned, or imperfectly described	28	27	55
			878	551	1429

From the reports of the Liverpool Asylum, as well as from others which we have seen, the blind seem to be pretty equally scattered in all parts of the kingdom. Of the 1429 persons who have been inmates of the Liverpool Asylum, 225 have belonged to Liverpool, 294 to other parishes in Lancashire, and 910 to distant parts of the kingdom. A large proportion of the income of the institution is derived from Liverpool and its vicinity.

The blind of that district have therefore a just priority of admission. There are 79 pupils in the Liverpool Asylum; 18 were admitted in 1858, and 21 left. Among those thus admitted, 8 are between fourteen and twenty, 4 are between twenty and thirty years old, 4 are upwards of thirty, and of 2 the ages are not specified. Most of those who have completed their education receive a gratuity of from two to five guineas when they quit the asylum, which sum is intended to assist them in procuring a few tools and materials for commencing the trades they may have been taught. This provision is both benevolent and wise; for there are numerous cases which come under the notice of the directors where poverty accompanies the deprivation of sight, and where, consequently, the instruction imparted would be of no practical benefit were not some means afforded of making it available to provide for their common necessities. The observances of religion appear to be regularly regarded: prayers are read in the chapel morning and evening, and the chaplain attends twice in each week to teach the catechism. The appointed hours for labour in the Liverpool Asylum are from six in the morning to six in the evening, one hour being allowed for breakfast and recreation, and another for dinner. Some of the pupils occupy a large portion of their time in the practice of music, singing, reading, &c. Frere's system of raised type is used, but the superintendent is not prepared to say which of the several series of books is most eligible for the blind. There are no fixed hours for acquiring the art of reading by touch, but instruction is given at such times as the teachers can spare from their other duties. Many of the inmates are middle-aged adults, whose object in entering the institution is expressly to acquire facility in some employment by which they can maintain themselves, and who leave as soon as they have succeeded in learning a trade, some of them only remaining under instruction from six to twelve months. This information has been supplied by the superintendent.

In the year 1792 an Asylum for the Blind was established in Edinburgh. The benevolent Dr. Blacklock, who resided in that city many years, had long anxiously wished that such an establishment should be formed for the education of those persons who, like himself, were deprived of sight. He mentioned his wishes to his friend Mr. David Miller, who was also blind, and was himself an eminent example of what might be effected under the influence of early and judicious instruction. In the year mentioned, it was determined by Mr. Miller and the Rev. Dr. David Johnston, of Leith, that an attempt should be made to provide an asylum, and means were taken to call public attention to the object. Mr. Miller communicated with the Abbé Haüy, and in many ways rendered important services during the infancy of the institution. The chief end in the formation of the contemplated asylum, next to imparting ordinary instruction (orally, it is presumed), and imbuing the minds of the objects with religious truth, was to place them under such superintendence as should train them in those trades in which the blind "are best fitted to excel" ; at the same time rewarding them for their labours according to their progress and proficiency. In later years the directors of the asylum have extended their views, devoting increased attention to the intellectual culture of the pupils; but still the main object appears to be that of training them to habits of manual labour. The economical character of the Edinburgh Asylum must be a striking feature to all who compare its expenditure, considering the amount of good it accomplishes, with that of similar institutions. We have frequently heard of the excellent management of the public charities of Edinburgh ; but in none is such management more visible than in this. In 1806 the directors formed a separate establishment for females, and since that time they have opened a school for the instruction of the young blind. It is by early training only that the blind, in common with others, can be brought under an effectual mental and moral discipline. By giving instruction to the young in the higher departments of knowledge, and by thus raising the intellectual character to the elevation of which it is capable, we are of opinion the directors will discover that the arts in which the blind are best fitted to excel are not the ordinary mechanical trades, to which, in our British institutions, and too generally abroad, all higher considerations have been sacrificed. Why are not their mental powers, which are unaffected by their physical calamity, cultivated? Such cultivation will qualify them for occupations in which they may succeed as well as those who possess the advantages of sight. The enlightened policy of the directors of the Edinburgh Institution has placed them in the first rank among the benefactors of the blind : their school for the young is a most interesting section of their establishment ; and it may be hoped that many of its pupils will be trained to higher occupations than those of basket-making, weaving, &c. We do not anticipate that all the blind can be exempted from manual labour, any more than that all other men are fitted for employments requiring a high degree of intellectual vigour, and acquirements which even the greater portion of mankind are unable or unwilling to make : but we do not hesitate to affirm that the blind have been systematically trained in arts in which they never can enter into competition with seeing persons ; and that they have not been sufficiently educated in that kind of knowledge in which they might have become at least as perfect as those who possess all their faculties. The former part of our proposition is allowed by the directors of the Edinburgh Asylum, who say that " when they (the blind) become as skilful workmen as their circumstances admit, they still labour under a disadvantage unknown to others." An argument which might with great propriety be used to enforce the advantage of mental cultivation in preference to manual dexterity, is the loss invariably attendant on the manufactures carried on at the asylums. It appears to us from our examination into the expenses of different establishments, that the more extensive the scale on which the manual arts are conducted, the greater the losses, from waste of materials, a succession of learners, &c. On the score of cheapness, therefore, it is desirable that such operations should be confined within as narrow limits as may seem prudent, and that intellectual education should be extended as widely as the talents and

qualifications of the pupils will allow. Instead of the accounts
of such institutions showing so great an amount of positive
losses, we should not only see this item reduced, but find the
pupils qualified for a sphere of usefulness superior to any which
they can ever reach by any attainable degree of dexterity in
manual occupations.

In the Edinburgh Asylum, the whole machinery seemed to be
of a high order ; the devoted attention of the different officers
is visible in the discipline and happiness of the inmates, and there
can be no doubt that the institution is effecting great good.
The young blind are instructed in reciting the Scriptures, in
spelling, in grammar, in vocal and instrumental music, in reading, by means of the sense of feeling ; in writing, arithmetic,
mathematics, history, geography, and astronomy. The means
by which instruction in these various branches is conveyed have
been mentioned ; in all institutions of this nature they must be
generally the same, varying perhaps in some of their details.
Several of the mechanical contrivances for conveying scientific
knowledge to the pupils are the inventions of Mr. Johnston, the
former secretary (nephew of Dr. Johnston, who was named as one
of the founders of the institution), in conjunction with Professor
Wallace, a gentleman who was deeply interested in all that
concerned the institution. An orrery, a cometarium, and raised
map of the heavens, all so constructed as to convey information
by the touch—while the reasoning powers are at the same time
addressed—are among the inventions of these gentlemen. The
map of the world is described as comprising "the eastern and
western hemispheres, represented on each side of a circular board.
The land is made rough, the seas, lakes, and rivers smooth.
Towns are represented by small pins. Mountains are ridged,
and boundaries simply raised. Degrees of latitude are marked
round the edge of the circle, of longitude along the equator,
which is raised above the surface of the earth. The orrery
represents the orbits of the planets by brass circles, and the
planets themselves are shown by spheres indicative of their
relative dimensions ; the spheres slide upon the brass orbits.

The ecliptic exhibits raised figures of the signs of the zodiac, the degrees of the circle, and the days of the month, all tangible, and adapted to the learner who has to depend upon touch for his impressions. The *arithmetic board* is 16 inches by 12, and contains 400 pentagonal holes, with a space of a quarter of an inch between each. The pin is simply a pentagon, with a projection at one end on an angle, and on the other end on the

THE ARITHMETIC BOARD.

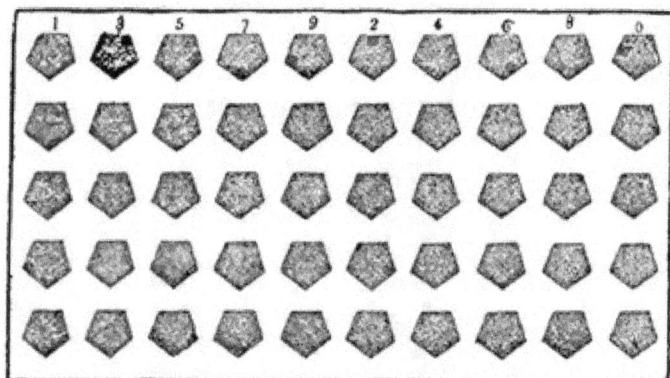

side. Being placed in the board, with a corner projection to the left upper corner of the board, it represents 1 ; proceeding to the right upper corner it is 3 ; the next corner in succession is 5 ; the next 7, and the last 9. In like manner the side projection, by being turned to the sides of the hole, progressively gives 2, 4, 6, 8, 0. The size of the pentagon, and a drawing of the pin, showing the projections on the side and angle, are given with the board above.

By the use of this board the pupils may be carried to any extent in arithmetical knowledge, and make their calculations with as much satisfaction as those who see. The last improvements in the Arithmetic Board were made by William Lang, at first an inmate of the Edinburgh Asylum, afterwards of that of Glasgow. Further to illustrate its use an example is given below of a sum in multiplication, which will be at once understood on comparing it with the board above ; this example shows $259 \times 4 = 1036$. The pentagons represent the pins with their projections as supposed to be in the holes of the Arithmetic Board.

MULTIPLICATION SUM.

We have the testimony of Dr. Guillié, that the blind study the exact sciences under great advantages, and with remarkable success ; but we cannot agree with the doctor that the blind, any more than *les clair-voyans*, have a natural disposition for mathematical studies. The eminent success of Saunderson, Moyes, Gough, and others, afford sufficient proof that blindness is no great impediment to such pursuits ; there may possibly be some advantages consequent on the degree of abstraction which appears necessarily to accompany blindness. On this supposition, however, we do not lay much stress, because we cannot admit that there is *naturally* any compensative principle by which men who labour under one defect or deprivation, are enabled to exercise the powers which are left to them with greater accuracy than others who have no such deficiency. If a seeing person would cultivate his sense of feeling to the same extent as the blind, his perceptions of touch would be as delicate as those of the blind man. It is not probable that so refined a cultivation will ever be tested by experience, as it would require a greater degree of philosophical curiosity than we ever witnessed or heard of, and be attended with a longer and more painful effort than we think any one would voluntarily undergo for the sake of making the experiment.

The Bristol Asylum for the Blind owed its origin to the benevolent exertions of two members of the Society of Friends, Messrs. Bath and Fox. It was opened in 1793, in a disused Baptist meeting-house. After attempting several of the trades, basket-making was commenced, and although other occupations are followed, fine and coarse baskets have been the staple manufacture of this asylum to the present time. In 1803 its funds were so greatly increased that the committee of management were enabled to spend 1800*l*. on the purchase of premises in Lower Magdalen Lane, and its operations were there carried on till its removal in 1838 to the present eligible situation at the top of Park Street, where a building was erected in the early English style, with a chapel in architecture of a later character, and became a prominent ornament to the city. This building provides workshops for one hundred pupils, and bedrooms for seventy. At a subsequent date, rooms were added for washing, baths, and shower-baths, and a more recent purchase of land in Tyndall's Park gives ample room for exercise and amusement. If the utility of the asylum may be deduced from the progressive increment of the sales the conclusion will be satisfactory, as in 1794, its second year, their amount was 18*l*. 8*s*. 6*d*., and in the year ending 1857 there was received "for baskets, table-mats, flower-stands, hearth-rugs, door-mats, and knitting, 1088*l*. 2*s*. 2*d*."

The distribution of time in mental occupation and manual labour is as follows:—The pupils rise at 6 a.m., and work or take exercise till breakfast at 8 o'clock; at half-past 8 prayers are read by the master; the school-room is then occupied from 9 to 6, the classes being changed every hour. By this arrangement each pupil receives two hours' instruction daily. One hour in the day is allotted to musical practice, two hours' instruction

being given to each pupil every week ; the remaining time till
6 o'clock is occupied in manual labour, and, as occasion offers,
the master or matron reads to the pupils while at work ; but
three days in the week they read collectively. On two evenings
the pupils assemble for practice with the music-master, and the
remaining evening they attend the chaplain for religious instruction.   Supper is served at half-past 7 ; immediately after
prayers are read by the matron, and the household retires to rest
about 10.

Instruction in the Bristol Asylum is conducted by a chaplain ;
by the master, who teaches reading, arithmetic, geography, and
history, and who has a blind assistant of either sex ; by a music-
master, with similar aid ; by a basket-maker for the men, who
has also two blind assistants ; and by a female basket-maker,
with one assistant possessed of sight and one who is blind.
Great advantage is thought to be obtained by this employment of
blind teachers, especially in the initiation of new pupils.   The
system of printing preferred in this asylum is that in the Roman
character, by the late Mr. Alston, of Glasgow. The books
published by that gentleman were introduced in 1837, and have
continued in daily use to the present time. A " Life of James
Watt," an " Elementary Geography," " Our Lord's Sermon on
the Mount," and a " First Reading Book," have been published
at this institution in Roman capitals and lower case.

The report of the chaplain on the scriptural instruction of the
pupils is very satisfactory. The report from which we quote
states that nine of the younger ones had received confirmation, five
of whom had become communicants. The master's report to the
committee on their secular instruction is equally satisfactory :
biography, history, arithmetic, grammar, and geography are the
subjects of his statement ; while the music-master considers the
progress of some and the proficiency of others in music and
singing as deserving commendation. All who are engaged in the
management speak of the pupils as intelligent and well-disposed,
and as manifesting a spirit of cheerful obedience. The welfare
and conduct of the former pupils are not overlooked in the report of

the committee : special instances are recorded of some of the advantages the asylum has conferred on individuals, and it is also stated that satisfactory accounts continue to be received from others, who, from the trades they learned and the industrial habits they acquired while at the asylum, are now earning a living in such a manner as not only to reflect credit upon themselves, but also on the institution. There are in the Bristol Asylum 66 pupils : males, 42 ; females, 24 ; upwards of 40 of them are under twenty years of age.

The School for the Indigent Blind in London was established in 1799 by four gentlemen of the metropolis,—Messrs. Ware, Bosanquet, Boddington, and Houlston. At first the pupils were few, and it did not attract any extraordinary share of public attention. About eleven years after its formation, the patronage of the public enabled the managers to take on lease a plot of freehold ground in St. George's Fields, opposite to the end of Great Surrey Street, where suitable buildings were erected, within which the institution is still carried on. An Act of Parliament was obtained in 1826, which invests the committee with all the rights and privileges of a corporation, and they then purchased the freehold of the ground on which the buildings had been erected. These buildings were found insufficient for the purposes of the establishment, and the committee purchased an adjoining plot of ground, upon which a new and enlarged building is erected. In 1800 there were only 15 persons in the asylum : the present number of inmates is 154 — 78 males and 76 females. The inmates are "clothed, boarded, lodged and instructed." The funds of the charity are ample. The receipts have seldom exceeded the expenditure. In addition to its annual subscriptions, donations and legacies, it possesses a funded capital amounting to above 80,000*l.*, besides other available property. The articles manufactured by the females are, for sale, fine and coarse thread, window sash-line and clothes-line, fine basket-work, ladies' work-bags, and other ornamental works in knitting and netting ; for consumption by the pupils, knitted stockings, household linen and body linen.

The occupations of the males are making shoes, hampers, wicker-baskets, cradles, rope-mats, fine mats, and rugs for hearths and carriages. These articles are sold at the institution, and it is said that the window sash-line is highly approved of by builders of the first eminence. The sale of articles manufactured during the year 1857 produced 815*l*.

An extraordinary change has taken place in the educational aspect of this establishment in the lapse of the last twenty-five years; its chief object at that time was instruction in manual labour; a few of the pupils were taught music, but the attempt to teach reading and writing had been abandoned from the unwillingness of the inmates to receive instruction. The recent reports contrast most favourably with those of former years. Not only are the pupils carefully instructed in the principles of the Christian religion, including the Holy Scriptures, and in vocal and instrumental music, but the following secular subjects are also well taught, namely, reading, writing from dictation, history, and geography; the emulating test of half-yearly examinations is also applied to this part of their education, and their inspectors in successive years (the Rev. J. D. Glennie and the Rev. W. Taylor) reported most favourably of the results. The former of these examiners says: "Both boys and girls are carefully and thoroughly instructed in the Holy Scriptures, Church Catechism, and Liturgy of our Church, and they have done justice to the instruction so received." In the boys' school, he was "much struck with the accuracy and rapidity with which the arithmetic, as far as Proportion and Practice, were performed." He congratulates the committee on the "efficient and satisfactory state of the school." The Rev. W. Taylor states that "the first and second classes read steadily and carefully on Alston's system, showing that they did not read from memory, but made out the words as they occurred. The lesson on English history given by the school-mistress was very satisfactory." The examiner of the boys' school, at Christmas last, reported favourably as to their proficiency in reading, religious knowledge, ciphering, embossed writing, English history, and geography; a small class also worked some problems in Euclid for him in very good style. The chaplain's classes, held on four days in the week for special religious instruction, comprise some not in daily attendance at the school, and exclude those who have not yet learned the Catechism.

The report states that "few of those who study music attain proficiency as readers or workers, and that great difficulty exists in procuring situations for blind organists. It is therefore most important that before making application for a pupil to receive musical instruction, his friends should well consider whether they have a fair chance for securing for that pupil employment as an organist or teacher of music. If a pupil becomes a good musician and is able to command employment, he may do well, but if from lack of talent, or other causes, he is unable to find employment as a musician, or to gain a living at a trade, he will probably become a burden to his friends."

During the year 1857, a novel and most important feature was introduced into the school, by the formation of a band of about forty instrumental performers, who are instructed in secular as well as sacred music. The band contains about an equal number of wind and stringed instruments, and during last year they gave a concert at the Hanover Square Rooms, which cleared upwards of 120*l.* for the charity, after all the heavy expenses were paid. The report states, "that though an attractive feature of the school, it is difficult to assign the band a higher office than that of supplying to the pupils a most pleasant and welcome recreation in their leisure hours."

One other feature in the operations of this school, derived from the example of a contemporary institution, demands especial notice from the writer of this article, with whom the idea originated, and by whom it has been carried out for many years at the institution with which he is connected, namely, an inquiry at certain intervals as to the after-life of the pupils. Such an inquiry can alone truly show the results of education; it is applicable to all schools, but more especially to those where children are boarded and educated for a series of years, and in whose future welfare, those who have directed their education, known their failings, and their better qualities, cannot but be interested. To all schools of poor-law unions it ought at once to be applied. The managers of the London School for the Blind have sent out since the year 1854 about 150 forms of inquiry respecting pupils who have left school, and are now at work in the country. The inquiries embrace the following points : their present mode of gaining a livelihood ; their average weekly earnings ; their power of reading ; their knowledge of music, and the use they make of it ; and their moral character. The result of these inquiries is very satisfactory ; about ten only have not been answered ; the pupils, with rare exceptions, possess good moral characters for steadiness, diligence, and Christian principle ; for the most part these returns are attested by the minister of the parish. Most of them retain, to a greater or less degree, their power of reading, though many of them are greatly in want of books. Few are able, even with the utmost exertion, to maintain themselves fully, but most of them are doing what they can, and only twelve receive parochial relief. Those able to do most towards their support are workers at baskets and mats, but the greatest difficulty prevails in finding employment for the musical pupils, many of whom, having been educated for musicians, are unfitted for work of any other kind, and spend most of their time in idleness. The importance of the industrial work taught in the school is thus clearly established.

The Hospital and School for the Indigent Blind of Norwich was originally established in the year 1805, first for that city, and subsequently (as the condition of receiving a donation) for the county of Norfolk also ; but its doors have been opened to other parts of the kingdom since the year 1819. The blind in the more elevated sphere of society appear not unfrequently to have been the first benefactors of their more indigent brethren. Mr. Tawell, a blind gentleman residing in Norwich, first called the attention of that city and its neighbourhood to the wants of the blind, and with a munificence commensurate with his zeal, he purchased " a large and commodious house, with an adjoining garden of three acres in extent," which he offered as the basis of the institution. The plan of the Norwich Asylum was to unite a school for the young with an hospital for the aged. It designed to admit the young pupils at the age of twelve years, and to keep them in the school till they should have attained a sufficient knowledge of some trade, as far as this could be accomplished within three years, but under no consideration to keep them longer than that time : some, however, have been kept longer. With respect to the aged, the rules express that none shall be admitted who have not attained the age of sixty-five. It appears from the account of the institution published up to the end of 1833, that from the establishment of the institution to that date, 153 pupils had been admitted and 48 aged persons : 77 had been discharged qualified to work for themselves ; 12 had proved incapable of instruction ; 4 had left the asylum without leave ; 13 had been discharged for irregularity, and 16 at their own request ; 43 had died, and 36 remained on the books. The expenses seem to have averaged about 1100*l.* per annum, and the income about equalled the expenditure. (We can give no more recent account of the Norwich school, as no answer has been received to our inquiries.)

The Asylum for the Blind at Glasgow is pre-eminently a manufacturing establishment, although much attention is also given to the religious and secular education of its inmates. It was founded by John Leitch, Esq., of Glasgow, who was himself partially blind ; he bequeathed 5000*l.* towards opening and maintaining the institution. Since the opening of the asylum in 1828, to the commencement of the present year (1859), 334 blind persons have been admitted ; of this number 103 are now in the establishment. The manufactures carried on are of sacks and sacking, twine, baskets, mats, mattresses, and knitting. The sales in 1858 produced 5960*l.*, which was about 870*l.* less than the previous year, and the value of the manufactured materials on hand was 2024*l.* The revenue is chiefly derived from the sales, and in this respect the Glasgow Asylum differs from every other in the kingdom. It solicits no annual subscriptions, but depends entirely for its support upon donations and legacies ; this source is precarious, and sometimes, as during the past year, a deficit occurs. By the system pursued in this asylum the blind are placed, as nearly as circumstances allow, on a level with other workmen. Many of the adults reside with their families in the city, and go to their labour at the asylum like other artisans. The superintendent purchases the raw materials for the manufactures, and keeps an account of the work each person performs, from which a statement of their earnings is made, and they are paid every Saturday. The male adults are allowed the same rate that other workmen have for the same kinds of work ; if a man can make five or six shillings a week, he receives that sum for his weekly wages. At the end of every four weeks a statement of his earnings is made up from the work-book, and whatever he has earned over that sum is paid to him, and also an additional shilling a week as a premium upon his industry. If the amount which he ought to earn be not earned, or the work be bad, no premium is allowed. At the monthly settlement some of them will have several shillings to receive in addition to their regular wages and premiums. Ever since the regulations regarding wages have been adopted, a marked improvement has taken place both in the quantity and quality of the work produced. The blind workmen and their families receive the fruits of their labour with much pleasure. A spirit of industry is excited and kept up very different to their former habits, and an opportunity is thus afforded them of enjoying the blessings of home, which could not be cultivated when they were maintained within the establishment. A few elderly females are placed upon the same system ; they work in the institution, but reside at their own homes. Females generally, above the age of eighteen years, are admitted as day-workers ; they dine at the asylum and receive regular weekly wages ; their apartments are separated from those of the males, and no intercourse is permitted. Boys and girls from ten to sixteen years of age reside in the house, and in addition to attendance on their classes, they are taught to perform light works suitable to their age, till old enough to be removed into the regular workshops. The girls and female adults are under the superintendence of a matron, who also has the management of the sales. Several of the blind men are employed in calling on the customers of the asylum to deliver goods and solicit orders. It is common for adults who reside in distant parts of the city to go to and from their employment without a guide, and no accident has ever happened to any of them. The usual branches of learning are taught to the young blind in the Glasgow Asylum ; the time devoted to school by both boys and girls is five hours a day on five days of the week, the chaplain being their teacher. The books used are printed in the Roman alphabet, which was arranged under the superintendence of John Alston, Esq., the former treasurer of the asylum ; these books are printed on the premises, and are so numerous as to form a library in raised type.

There are three Asylums for the Blind in Dublin. The oldest of them, Simpson's Hospital, was opened in 1781 ; it was founded and endowed by a merchant whose name it bears, who was himself subject to a disorder of the eyes, and was also a martyr to the gout. The design of the hospital is to provide an asylum for blind and gouty men, the preference being given to those of good moral character, who have formerly been in affluent circumstances. About fifty persons partake of the benefits of this charity. It was incorporated in 1799, and its income is about 3000*l*. per annum.

The Richmond National Institution for the Indigent Industrious Blind is supported by subscriptions and donations ; it was opened in 1809 ; the inmates, who are all indigent, are instructed in the trades ordinarily taught to the blind. At present the institution contains forty men and youths, who are lodged, maintained, and clothed there.

The Molineux Asylum is supported by subscriptions, by the profits of a chapel, and by charity sermons ; it is solely for the reception of females, who are admitted at all ages. Those above

fifty have here a permanent abode. The younger section of the
establishment are lodged, clothed, and fed ; and for a certain
number of years receive instruction in those employments by
which it is intended they shall earn their living. This asylum
was opened in 1815, in the mansion of Sir Charles Molineux,
Bart. This family has been among its most liberal benefactors.

In 1835, the Ulster Institution for the Deaf and Dumb,
established at Belfast in 1831, admitted blind pupils also. This
union of the two classes is a speciality in which this establishment does not stand quite alone. Between the two classes of
inmates there is nothing in common, so far as their education is
concerned ; different senses being addressed, the process of
instruction is essentially different, but when a medium of intercourse has been established between them by means of the
manual alphabet, their being associated together is not without
some points of interest.

On subjects of instruction the first place is given to religious
training, and as a result of this, some of the blind pupils have
become devoted and efficient city missionaries ; one of them
occupies an important position as one of the ministers at
Brooklyn, New York. The other common branches of an
English education also receive attention, and all who have voice
and ear practise vocal music. About six hours daily are devoted
to school, and two and a half hours to manual labour. A large
amount of the instruction conveyed is given orally, but the relief
books printed at Glasgow, and those produced at Bristol are used
by the pupils. Ninety-one deaf and dumb, and thirteen blind,
are now in this institution.

The Limerick Asylum for Blind Females was established in
1835, chiefly through the instrumentality of the Dean of
Waterford. It is capable of accommodating twenty inmates,
but the funds of the institution do not afford support to this
number.

The Yorkshire School for the Blind was instituted at York in
memory of the late William Wilberforce. Its design is not so
much to provide maintenance for the blind as to give them such

instruction as may help them to gain a livelihood for themselves, attention being at the same time paid to their moral and religious instruction ; their friends or parishes therefore contribute towards their support while they are in the institution. Those persons only are admissible who have lost their sight to such a degree as to be able at most only to distinguish light from darkness—those who have a capacity for instruction—those who are free from any dangerous or communicable disease—and those who have no vicious habits.

It is found from the recent reports of the Yorkshire school that less time is devoted to manual labour than in these asylums generally ; but it must be remembered that the inmates are young. Music is much cultivated, and affords satisfactory evidence of its utility. With the view of forming a correct opinion on this subject, inquiries were instituted in 1856, as to the condition of the pupils who had left school. It was found that eleven had obtained situations as organists, and were enabled to maintain themselves fully ; four others were engaged in teaching music and tuning instruments, and thus maintained themselves to a great extent. In addition to those who had left school, there were six male adults and one female still resident in the school, who were filling organists' situations. The results of these inquiries as to other industrial pursuits were less satisfactory, and the inference drawn was, that music was the only really remunerative pursuit for the blind, under the present arrangements of the Yorkshire school.

Another hint of considerable value may be drawn from the series of reports of the Yorkshire school. A year or two ago, a sergeant was engaged to drill the pupils, and it has been found of the most essential benefit to them. One of the pupils remarked, that he walked with much greater confidence since these exercises had been practised, and this feeling will be one of general experience ; it may therefore be commended to the attention of other establishments for the blind. The superintendent of the Yorkshire school is W. D. Littledale, Esq., who is himself blind, and whose whole heart seems to be given to the improvement of the school. The general branches of education are taught, and books in the Roman type are preferred. The Rev. W. Taylor, author of the "Tangible Euclid," formerly devoted to the interests of this school, has left York ; his attention, however, is still directed to the welfare of the blind. The number of pupils in the York school is sixty.

Henshaw's Blind Asylum, at Manchester, was opened for the admission of inmates in 1838. An endowment of 20,000*l.* was left in the year 1810 for the support of such an asylum, by the will of Thomas Henshaw, formerly of Oldham. Notwithstanding the large accumulations arising from this source, no part of Mr. Henshaw's bequest could be appropriated to the purchase of land for such asylum, nor for the erection of a suitable building ; and the sum of 10,000*l.* was subscribed by the inhabitants of Manchester for these objects. The building, together with one in exact correspondence for the education of the deaf and dumb, was erected at Old Trafford, and the approximation of the two charities was rendered closer by a subsequent agreement of the respective committees for the erection of a chapel in the space between the two buildings, thus connecting them as consistent parts of one uniform structure, in the English Academic style of architecture. The object of the asylum is not only to afford a home to the impotent and aged blind, but also " to maintain and afford such instruction to the indigent blind of both sexes capable of employment, as will enable them to provide, either wholly or in part, for their own subsistence, and to promote the employment of, or to employ, blind persons." The training of the inmates is therefore both intellectual and industrial, but it is not stated in the last report how the school instruction is carried on. It may be inferred that books in Roman type are used ; the late governor, Mr. Hughes, emphatically says, " I would discourage all systems of embossing which could not be read and taught by seeing persons." The articles manufactured are more various than in the generality of these asylums. The number of inmates in 1858 was seventy-five.

The Royal Victoria Asylum for the Blind, at Newcastle-upon-Tyne, was founded in the year 1838, to commemorate the coronation of Her Most Gracious Majesty the Queen ; its object, as expressed in its first regulation, "being to afford to the blind an elementary education and instruction in those branches of trade and manufacture which shall be found suited to their capacity," as well as to afford them spiritual instruction. During the existence of the asylum, 115 pupils have been received into it, of whom thirty-seven are now under its care, twenty-two of whom are males, and fifteen females. Pupils are received into it from the four northern counties of England. The works of the inmates are of the usual kinds ; the forenoon of each day is given to manual labour, the afternoon to music and general education. The relief books in Roman capitals are preferred.

The West of England Institution for the Blind was established at Exeter in 1839. It contains twenty-five inmates of the two sexes, all of whom are taught the usual branches of education, including music, and some to make baskets, mats, rugs, sash-line, &c. Sixty-two of its boarders and forty-one day pupils have quitted since its commencement. Its income is derived from the usual sources, namely, subscriptions, donations, board of pupils, and sale of work. Lucas's raised alphabet is used, and it is one of the regulations of the committee that "the system of teaching to read shall be that by means of the raised stenographic character."

An Institution for the Blind and Deaf and Dumb was formed at Bath about the year 1840. A considerable number of pupils of both these classes have been instructed under its care ; and at the date of the last report (1858) it contained fifty-one boarders, of whom twenty-eight were deaf and dumb, twenty blind, and three partially blind and deaf and dumb ; it also extends its benefits to day and Sunday scholars, of whom it numbers twelve deaf and dumb, and four blind. Miss Elwin, of Bath, has taken a benevolent oversight of this establishment, from its first commencement to its present mature condition. A "Home" for blind girls has also been formed, for those who, having passed the allotted period of five years' instruction, have no friends able to provide them with a suitable place of residence. The training which the blind children receive is both intellectual and industrial; the former comprehends reading on Lucas's system, arithmetic, geography, music and singing; the latter is confined to basket-making. The morning hours are devoted to labour; the afternoon to mental and religious instruction. In the "Home," the greater part of the day is spent in basket-making, which contributes in part to the support of the establishment, and the inmates are frequently read to while they are at work.

An asylum for the young blind was established in Brighton in 1841, the pupils not to be under six, nor exceeding twelve years of age. It is designed for the town of Brighton and the diocese of Chichester, with power to the committee to receive candidates from other localities. This school is under the management of Mr. Moon, one of the inventors of raised characters, to whose system attention has been directed in the article, ALPHABETS FOR THE BLIND. The school contains twenty-one pupils.

The Midland Institution for the Blind is situated at Nottingham, and comprehends the counties of Nottingham, Derby, Leicester, Lincoln, and Rutland. Its chief object is the education and training of the younger part of the blind community. The age of the inmates varies from nine to twenty-four. The usual intellectual and religious instruction is imparted, and the trades are much the same as those followed in other establishments; it is thought some new trades might be profitably commenced, and, among others, brush-making. No male pupils are allowed to commence work till they can read; but the female pupils, from the day of their admission, spend half the day in their workroom, to be instructed by the governess in sewing and knitting, and the other half in school. The teachers, except the governess, are all blind. Lucas's system of raised type is generally adopted, but some of the pupils can read Moon's and the Roman books. The schoolmaster, who is blind, reads books on six different systems, but gives the preference to that of Lucas. In arithmetic the pupils are considerably advanced, and can work and comprehend fractions and decimals; the arithmetical board and pegs differ from those used in the institutions of Scotland. The admission of day-pupils *free* on the recommendation of a governor is a good feature in this establishment, though it is not confined to it. Such pupils may remain as long as there is room for them ; and when they have acquired a trade, so as to make articles sufficiently well for sale, they are employed and paid journeymen's wages.

The General Institution for the Blind, at Edgbaston, near Birmingham, was commenced in 1846 by private benevolence, and adopted by the public in the following year. Its income is derived from the usual sources, namely, subscriptions, legacies, donations, payments on behalf of pupils, sale of work, &c. The present number of pupils is fifty-nine, and they are classified both for school and labour, so as to give all the advantages suitable for their age. The school teaching comprehends reading, spelling, arithmetic (peg and mental), geography with the aid of globes and maps, and object lessons. There are upwards of sixty maps, and one is used by every two pupils. These maps are made by friends of the superintendent, and have been much admired by the conductors of different institutions. In music the pupils practise from one to three hours a day, according to their progress and talent. Church music only is taught. Four of the pupils, from sixteen to eighteen years of age, have obtained situations as organists, at salaries varying from 20*l.* to 30*l.* a year. In reading by the touch, Moon's system is used. This institution has the advantage of an indefatigable treasurer, Thomas Goodman, Esq., whose exertions for this and other charities which have for their object the relief of human suffering, are beyond all praise.

The title of the next institution to be noticed would lead to the supposition that a new sphere of operations was to be brought under observation. It is called "The London Society for Teaching the Blind to Read." It is situated in Avenue Street, Regent's Park, and it has been in existence twenty years. The indications of its distinctiveness are few, and chiefly relate to its plan of admitting pupils, and its adhesion to Lucas's system of reading, in which it has published the whole of the Scriptures and many other works. The usual kinds of school instruction and of labour are taught to the pupils, of whom there were sixty in the institution in 1858. As an auxiliary in the cause of the blind, it must prove beneficial. According to its rules, it receives free boarders on the nomination of donors of 250*l.* in one sum, and by election of subscribers for three years; indigent boarders on payment of 15*l.* per annum; music being an extra charge of two guineas per annum. Male adults are not lodged in the house, and have to pay 2*s.* a week for lodgings in the neighbourhood. Day-pupils are admitted free on the recommendation of a subscriber.

The establishments of which some account has been given are not the only means carried on in these days for alleviating the condition of the blind, and increasing their means of happiness. Other appliances are also in action. Although blindness cannot be considered as the heaviest of human calamities, it is ône which claims the most immediate sympathy and prompts the universal desire for its relief. Societies have been established for teaching the adult blind to read, many of which are connected with Moon's system. Mr. Moon, himself blind, commenced his printing labours at Brighton more than ten years ago; his books are not only largely used in that place, but in many other provincial towns, which have been supplied with home teachers, and in which lending libraries have been established. One of these societies has been formed in London; from it have emanated two lending libraries of Moon's books; and its first report (1857) states that in eighteen months 236 blind pupils had, for longer or shorter periods, been under instruction; of these 117 had learned to read, of which number 53 were above 50 years of age, and 8 were from 70 to 75. It would be very ungracious to cast a shade of doubt on the statements put forth of the rapidity with which the art of reading was acquired by these aged persons through the medium of touch; yet there must be some fallacy, the facilities given by a previous knowledge of reading and spelling must have existed, for even aged persons with all their senses cannot learn to read *in three lessons!* If they could read and spell before they lost their sight, or if they had learned to read

on some other system previously, the wonder ceases to some
extent. The work is a good work, and requires nothing marvellous to sustain it. The London depository for the books on
Moon's system is at 25, King William Street, Trafalgar Square.

In Euston Road, near St. Pancras Church, a thoroughly
practical work is going forward for the amelioration of the
condition of the industrious blind. It is known as "The
Association for Promoting the General Welfare" of this class of
people. It has been in operation about five years ; it provides
means of industrial employment for those who have not been so
fortunate as to obtain admission, and consequently instruction,
in asylums ; it supplements the education of those who have had
this advantage ; it teaches trades to those who have learned none,
and finds a market for the work, thus enabling many of the
adults so taught to support their families ; it supplies regular
work to many at their own homes ; it finds workshops for others
within the precincts of its own humble establishment. At present
it affords employment to sixty-seven blind men and women, some
of whom have been withdrawn from begging and destitution,
and it has a list of upwards of ninety candidates, who desire to
be put into a similar mode of earning their bread, and who will
be gratified in their desire when the public favour to the
establishment demands more articles than the present workers
can supply. The town traveller and the porter of the establishment are both blind, yet they traverse crowded thoroughfares,
and walk long distances, self-dependent, or trusting on the good-
will of strangers for information and direction. Blind agents
are also employed in selling the goods manufactured in several
towns in different parts of the kingdom. This society is assisted
by subscriptions and donations, for from the waste of materials
and the slowness of the learners it cannot be self-supporting.
The foundress of this truly beneficent association is Miss Gilbert,
a daughter of the Bishop of Chichester, herself blind, and a
contributor of 2000*l*. to its endowment fund ; for more than a
year she worked the plan alone. Its control is now made over
to a committee of influential men, and it may be hoped that the

practical wisdom which devised its plans will be carried out with that ability which will ensure success commensurate with its object. The above account of this excellent charity is abridged from an article in " Household Words."

Charities for the blind also exist which grant annuities under certain conditions. The oldest of these is Hetherington's ; it was established in 1774. The other is the Blind Man's Friend, established by Mr. Day; in October, 1858, there were 2,500 applicants waiting for this charity.

It appears that voluntary benevolence, together with the provision made under the Poor Law Act, by which the blind may be maintained during education in the asylums established, will in the course of time provide for the training in industrial pursuits of all the blind who require such aid. Great has been the progress towards this end during the last twenty-five years. The intellectual training will doubtless keep pace with the industrial, now that the public are aware how much can be done. The increase of books is also certain, with so many competitors for public favour in the field. It has been already stated that the Scriptures are published in four distinct systems. Attention should now be directed to the publication of a good reading-book on secular knowledge, the subjects of which should be consecutive, progressive, and systematic. The republication of some existing school-book is more desirable than the preparation of an original work for many reasons ; but it should not be a miscellaneous collection of lessons without plan or arrangement on every variety of topic in succession, tending to bewilder and excite rather than to satisfy the mind. The moral tone of the inmates of the various schools is a subject of special mention in many of the accounts we have received ; yet it is thought some advantages would arise from a stricter classification, so as to prevent the young blind from mingling with the adults and the aged. In the workshop, the restraint which is necessary for the young is irksome to the older inmates, and the exercise of all their good principles is requisite to prevent the rising of a rebellious spirit. Separate establishments for children and adults, or an entire separation in the same building, seems desirable. At Norwich there is such a provision. The inmates of Henshaw's Asylum, at Manchester, are not restricted as to age, and are in for life ; but the old are not separated from the young, consequently they cannot have that quietude which age and infirmity require. In one or two of the establishments drill and gymnastics receive attention. These physical exercises are highly commended by Dr. Blacklock, as giving confidence, and they should be universally cultivated among the young blind. It is a question worthy of some consideration by the managers of our asylums, as to what extent blind teachers can be eligibly employed in the various departments. As far as the communication and transmission of ideas are concerned, the blind teacher may possess some advantages over the seeing one, yet circumstances arise in which the evils attendant on the want of sight counterbalance these advantages. In the *schoolroom* we find bad habits and positions of the body ; in the *workshop*, badly shaped articles and waste of materials ; in the *musical department*, wrong positions of the hands, and a bad system of fingering, with an awkward attitude and distortion of the countenance in singing. It cannot be expected that blind teachers should be aware of these things. An exact record of the after-life of all the pupils should be kept in every asylum for the blind. Such records are the result of the care and attention of teachers, and of the application and attainments of pupils, and the blind themselves should know that such an account of their future course will be recorded, and published for the satisfaction of those who generously support these establishments for their benefit.

The number of blind men who have become eminent is large ; for some account of them we must refer to the work of Dr. Guillié on the " Instruction of the Blind," to blind James Wilson's " Biography of the Blind," to the first volume of the " Pursuit of Knowledge under Difficulties," and to Dr. Kitto's " Lost Senses—Blindness ; " in these works we read of philosophers, mathematicians, divines, musicians, rhetoricians, lawyers, historians, poets, naturalists, road surveyors, mechanics, travellers, and even sculptors, who laboured under the infirmity of blindness.

The addition of deafness to blindness seems almost to shut out a human being from the external world. It is difficult to conceive how the mind of a deaf, dumb, and blind person can be occupied—much more difficult to say how it can be improved and educated. Yet there are many cases of this three-fold deprivation known, and there are always one or more such instances undergoing instruction in our blind or deaf and dumb institutions. The case of *James Mitchell*, the son of a Scotch clergyman, which was investigated by Dugald Stewart, Mr. Wardrop, and Dr. Spurzheim, is the best known ; *Julia Brace,* a pupil in the asylum for the deaf and dumb at Hartford, Connecticut, is another instance of the same kind ; *Victorine Morisseau*, a pupil in the Imperial Institution for the Deaf and Dumb of Paris, was another sufferer under this accumulated calamity ; *Laura Bridgeman,* a pupil of Dr. Howe, in the Boston Asylum for the Blind, is not only defective in these senses, but also in that of smell. She has had companions in the same affliction in *Oliver Caswell* and *Lucy Reed*. *Edward Meystre*, of Lausanne, is another case of the kind. He too has met with an instructor. Each of these instances is a history in itself of a mind sealed up, but unsealed by the indefatigable zeal and skill of their respective teachers. Space is not allowed us to go into the manifold processes which patience and enterprise invented for conquering the difficulties which interposed between these minds and the world without. The results are not merely satisfactory, they are marvellous.

The blind are not a moody or a discontented class—fun, frolic, and mischief are as inherent in them as in others. We extract a few anecdoctes from an interesting pamphlet published some years back by Mr. Anderson, who passed many years of his life as teacher and superintendent in the several asylums of Edinburgh, York, and Manchester, which show their vivacious habits.

" Romping, jumping, laughing, and screaming are as delightful to them as with boys and girls who see. The cross-bow, bow and arrow, trundling each other in a wheelbarrow, spinning tops, and to those who have a glimmer of light, called 'blinkers,' marbles, and a kind of cricket, all afford ample amusement, while there is no want of the usual boyish plotting and mischief. The girls also enjoy their playhours very much, and contrive to stand in as much need of the needle as their more favoured sisters of sight.

"A girl at York took up a book lying beside me, turned up her face towards the gaslight above my head, and playfully observed, as she whirled over the leaves, 'Dear me, sir, what bad gas this is; I can't see to read a word by it!' The same girl, standing near the fire, heard a companion trying to decipher some of the letters of the book in relief, 'Let me see,' said the latter, 'what's this—b i t, t e r; bit—what does that mean?' 'Sit a little nearer the light, my dear,' said her fireside companion; 'I know you don't see very well, Jane.' The tone of this indicated genuine playful mischief.

"A young man at the Edinburgh asylum, born blind, was at all times the essence of cheerfulness. He was one of our most correct 'messengers,' and a good collector of accounts, of which, from the amount of our annual sales, we had many. He, as well as several others, could easily take from four to eight of these at a time. Coming along the passage whistling—he was always whistling—he began to grope about for his hat, which, not finding on its usual peg, he cried to a companion, whose foot he heard not far off, 'Willie, come here, man, and look for my hat; ye see better than me.' The one was as blind as the other.

"It is a remarkable fact that the blind scarcely ever hurt themselves, either against furniture or in play. At Edinburgh they were constantly walking about the crowded streets. There were four or five 'messengers,' whose business it was to carry home all the goods sold—baskets, mattresses, rope-mats; and not only did they do this with the greatest exactness, but they were daily in the habit of going to all parts of the city, Leith, Portobello, and environs, to take measurements for bedding. I have many times had the dimensions of two, and even three beds brought to me—all on memory—with a precision not exceeded by the most expert workmen, including the exact allowance of so many inches to be cut out for the bed-posts.

" I had occasion one evening, at Edinburgh, to send out one of these blind men with a mattress. I gave him the bill with it, that he might receive payment. He returned with the account and the mattress too. ' I've brought baith back, ye see, sir,' said he. ' How so ? ' ' Indeed, sir, I didna like t'leave't yonder, else I'm sure we wad ne'er see the siller—there's no a stick of furnitur' within the door ! ' ' How do you come to know that ? ' ' Oh, sir, twa taps on the floor wi' my stick soon tell't me that ! ' Having to send the same man to Portobello, towards evening, I warned him (rather inadvertently !) that if he did not make haste it would get dark. ' My word, sir,' said he, laughing, ' I wish I had a shillin' for ilka time I've been in Portobello i' the dark.'

" As a body, the blind are the most habitually cheerful of mankind. How it comes to be so I cannot tell, and I have no wish to theorise. I cannot designate the blind, as is almost universally done, 'the unhappy,' 'melancholy,' 'pitiable,' and so on. I know nothing more erroneous, or more opposed to the feelings of by far the greater majority." So says Mr. Anderson in his " Observations on the Employment, Education, and Habits of the Blind," and he was a man of large experience among them.

ALPHABETS FOR THE BLIND.

The early instructors of the blind felt the irksomeness of oral instruction, and the dependent condition of their pupils. Without being aware what results might follow, they early made the first step towards tangible printing, by the invention of letters in relief, by which the alphabet might be taught—letters put together to form words, and these arranged in sentences. In the first attempt thus made, the letters chosen were those of the Illyrian or Sclavonian alphabet modified. [ALPHABET.] This alphabet was doubtless preferred on account of the square form of the letters, which it was thought would make them more obvious to the touch than ours. ("Essai sur l'Instruction des Aveugles," &c., par le Docteur Guillié, p. 134, 2nde edition.) The principle of square or angular letters was afterwards abandoned, as "not offering greater advantages than common characters." Moveable letters were next invented, which were placed on small tablets of wood, and were made to slide in grooves, on a similar plan to some of the toys which are used for the purpose of inducing children to learn their letters, spelling, &c. It was with similar letters that Usher, Archbishop of Armagh, was taught by his two aunts, who were both blind ; but this process was found defective for teaching blind persons. Moveable leaden characters were afterwards cast for the use of the blind, by Pierre Moreau, a notary of Paris ; but the work was attended with difficulties and expenses which he was not prepared to encounter. Large pin-cushions were also brought into use for the blind, on which the characters were figured with "inverted needles." The relief caused by the heads of pins would have been more eligible. Various other attempts were made in wood and metal till the time of Haüy, who invented the art of printing in relief for the blind, and thus devised a plan by

which the blind man might acquire knowledge, and derive amusement during his solitary hours independent of a teacher or an
attendant.   The invention of printing in relief is said to have
arisen from the sight and feeling of a proof of common printing
fresh from the press.

Previous to the time of M. Haüy no success had been obtained
in the art of printing for the blind, though it had been
attempted in a variety of ways, and by different persons.
Letters were engraved in wood, not cut in relief, but in the
ordinary manner of wood-cutting. The configurations of the
letters were found to be difficult to trace, possessing none of the
advantages which letters in relief afford. Haüy's was a bolder
invention than any other offered to the public. Not only has
it never been superseded, but from it have arisen all the
modern efforts to teach the blind reading by means of relief
characters.

Various attempts were made in our own country to produce
tangible alphabets, and embossed books for the blind.   An
impetus was given to them in 1832, in consequence of the
Society of Arts in Scotland offering their gold medal, value
twenty sovereigns, for the best alphabet and method of printing
for the use of the blind.   Twenty-one alphabets were submitted
to the committee appointed on this occasion, fourteen for competition and seven for non-competition.   Of all these, *four* only,
with or without modification, have survived, while two additional
systems have come into use.   All these will be presently examined.   The character which the French schools had adopted
was an upright script, widened, as was falsely thought, to
render it more obvious to the touch.   Two alphabets were also
employed, one of capitals and another of small letters.   To these
two errors in the outset may be attributed the failure of the
attempts in France to make the blind readers, and to furnish
them with books.   The wide and complicated forms of script
letters detained the finger in tracing their shape.   The
acquisition of fifty-two letters instead of a single alphabet
doubled the amount of time required to become familiar with

them, to say nothing of the complicated mental operations to be at the same time carried on by the readers. For two or three years previous to the wise and liberal offer of the Edinburgh Society of Arts, James Gall, of Edinburgh, was the sole labourer in the cause of printing for the blind. He adopted a modification of the Roman alphabet, in which he excluded curves and

GALL'S ALPHABET.

circles, and substituted straight lines and angles. He also abolished the capital letters, and thus reduced the number of characters to be acquired to twenty-six. He succeeded in producing beautiful and enduring workmanship on good paper. He printed several preparatory books which the blind read with ease ; and he offered to print the whole of the Gospel of St. John as soon as a sufficient number of subscribers should be obtained, at a guinea a copy. The immense cost of a single gospel acted as a great discouragement to his plans, and before he could remedy it other labourers were in the field, and his market was in the possession of other producers. Great merit is however due to Gall, and he must be looked upon as the forerunner of that success which has followed the labours of others. He had removed some difficulties. The works of the French were bulky and expensive ; by Gall's angular alphabet much economy in space was gained, and experience proved that it possessed merits of tangibility not to be found in the French alphabets.

The character which found the greatest favour with the committee appointed to award the gold medal of the society was the Roman letter of Dr. Fry, to which the prize was finally awarded. But the committee, before deciding, called in the aid of several experienced men to assist them in coming to a right judgment ; among others, the Rev. W. Taylor, a gentleman who had been practically engaged in inventions for and in the instruction of the blind for many years. He was an honorary member of their society, and at the time when his opinion was sought he was at the head of the recently established School for the Blind at York. Better aid the society could not have procured. To him all the alphabets and communications were submitted, and upon them. he made a very copious and able report. Mr. Taylor sets out with saying there does not appear to him "*sufficient* reason for departing from the *common Roman letter.*" He then mentions a few modifications which he would introduce in Dr. Fry's sans-serif Roman capital, and speaks decidedly against any merely arbitrary character. It is unnecessary to go into Mr. Taylor's report in all its details. The practical part of the subject was taken up by the late Mr. Alston, then the treasurer of the Asylum for the Blind in Glasgow ; he found the letters of Dr. Fry too broad in the relief, and increased their tangibility by having them made sharper ; some other slight alterations were also introduced by his skill and experience. The encouraging approval of his efforts by many of the schools for the blind, together with the pecuniary aid they and the various Bible Societies afforded by the purchase of his books, enabled him to print the entire Scriptures in the course of a few years, as well as some elementary books, and others of more general interest. The Society of Arts for Scotland did not leave his efforts unrewarded, but gratified him and encouraged him to persevere by presenting him with the silver medal of the society in 1838 for his Fables with wood-cut illustrations, printed in relief, and subsequently with three honorary medals for his continued exertions on behalf of the blind.

The decision of the committee of the Society of Arts in 1837 is worthy of being recorded. For five years the subject had been under consideration, and the aid of the most intelligent and practical teachers in the kingdom had been obtained. It appeared to that committee : " 1. That although an arbitrary character might possess in itself superior advantages in simplicity and tangibility, yet there would be great, and in many cases insuperable obstacles to the blind generally acquiring a knowledge of any character not familiar to those possessed of sight, and, consequently, such an alphabet would not be generally adopted throughout Europe and America. 2. That the same objection applies, although perhaps in a less degree, to Mr. Gall's angular modification of the Roman alphabet ; and while the want of capitals and the difficulty of tracing the lines are said to be also serious objections to the use of his character, it does not in other respects seem to offer sufficient reasons for its adoption in preference to the Roman alphabet slightly modified. 3. That, from being almost universally known both in Europe and America, and taking all other circumstances into consideration, the common Roman capital alphabet, as represented by the

ALSTON'S ALPHABET.

ABCDEFGHIJKLMNO.

PQRSTUVWXYZ&.

1234567890.;:._!?()

late Dr. Fry, * * * seems not only the best adapted for teaching the blind to read, but also as a medium of written correspondence. Hence there is every reason to believe that it would be sooner brought into general use than any of the other characters in competition—that books printed with it would be more in demand—and, consequently, that their expense would be greatly diminished." The committee guard themselves against the one or two inherent defects in Dr. Fry's alphabet by further stating, that in proposing his communication as best entitled to the society's premium, they "do not wish it to be understood that they consider his modification of the Roman alphabet as *now* in every respect the best adapted for teaching the blind, but only that it was superior to any of the others given in to the society for competition and remitted to the committee for consideration," and they then allude to the improvements on it since proposed and partly carried into effect by the Rev. Mr. Taylor, Mr. Anderson, of York, and Mr. Alston, of Glasgow.

One of the alphabets submitted for competition was of stenographic characters, the invention of Mr. T. M. Lucas, of Bristol. As this alphabet has many adherents, it claims respectful notice, premising that it was in use some years before the Society of Arts

LUCAS'S ALPHABET.

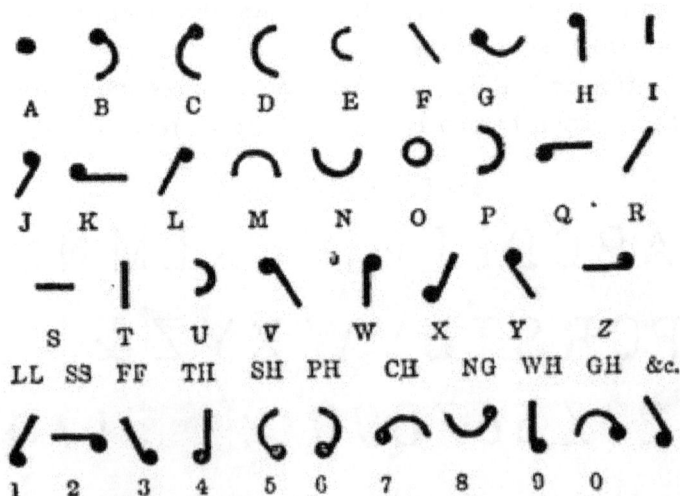

arrived at its decision, and that its claims were very ably advocated by the late Rev. Dr. Carpenter, LL.D., of Bristol, whose letter addressed to the society contains many valuable suggestions on printing for the blind. Mr. Lucas has himself stated that the " Penny Cyclopædia " contained a fair exposition of his principles, which we are glad to reproduce :—" The characters are employed for reading, writing, arithmetic and music, and they are so simple, that to any book for the blind not more than half the number of types are required that are necessary to print the same for those who are blessed with sight. Should the event prove as successful as is intimated in the above announcement, and so great a barrier to the improvement of the blind be removed, it will be desirable that the different institutions should unite their exertions and set apart a common fund to supply their pupils, as well as other blind persons, with so powerful an auxiliary to their progress in knowledge. The alphabet is composed of thirteen simple characters, and thirteen formed from the roots of these with a crotchet-head to each. There are ten double letters from the same roots, distinguished also by the crotchet-head ; these also represent the nine figures and the cypher, whether used as numerals or ordinals. In all thirty-six characters are employed. The advantages attending the use of stenographic characters seem to be in the saving of types, paper and labour, thus materially diminishing the cost of books for the blind. The disadvantages attending the system we are speaking of appear to consist chiefly in the confusion which the learner must feel in having but one character employed in several offices, as in the double letters, numerals and ordinals, and in the necessity that every person should be a stenographist who communicates with the blind by writing. These difficulties are not very great for persons to overcome who have never been accustomed to a written language.

" The manner in which the characters of Mr. Lucas are employed may be seen in the following commencement of St. John's Gospel, only that we give the extract in Roman letters instead of using the stenographic characters.

t gospl b st jon, chap : 1.

in t bgini ws t wrd a t w ws w g, a t w ws g. t sam ws n t bgini w g. l thins wr mad b hm, a wo hm ws nt athin mad tht ws mad. in hm ws lif a t l ws t lit f mn.

" It will be observed that the repetition of numerous letters is avoided ; particles are represented in most instances by their initial letter, and when a word, having been once mentioned, recurs immediately, or frequently, it is represented by its initial letter also."

An undoubted defect in Lucas's system is the confusion which must arise from having double letters and figures, whether cardinal or ordinal, represented by the same stenographic signs ; thus the signs for th, ch, and ll also represent 471. The contractions are very numerous, many words are expressed by a single character, and other words are contracted by the omission both of vowels and consonants. The value of full spelling is great, especially to the young blind ; those who have already learned to read while possessing sight would in time get over the difficulties the system presents.

The next system which came into use in point of time was Frere's, also stenographic, founded on Gurney's shorthand, as Lucas's was on Byrom's. This system is phonetic, and is formed on the " combination of elementary sounds." It professes to be composed of twenty-nine signs, to be extremely simple, and to have only four descriptions of signs, which represent thirty-two different sounds. Its distinctive principle, compared with Lucas's, is the phonetic one, the powers or vocal sounds of the letters rather than their name-sounds being taught, " each word being embossed according to its actual pronunciation, the names of the characters combined, or sounded together, give the word." The " Memoria Technica," which accompanies the lessons, is most burdensome, and the twelve rules in verse for supplying the omitted vowels could never be regarded by blind or other readers who had to commit them to memory in any light but as a distasteful task. We learn, however, that their employment is *optional*, though the system would be incomplete without them ! The twelfth of these rules is—

" Whene'er the proper rule don't yield you satisfaction,
    On trial you will find the word is a contraction."

"A fair knowledge of the system may be acquired *by those who have sight* in three or four hours." Two things are noteworthy in this agreeable announcement. 1. That a system of

stenographic reading can be acquired in three or four hours.
2. That stenographic systems require ordinary readers to learn
them before they can assist their blind brethren in the acquisition
of the art of reading.

The last system to be described is Moon's ; although it is not
stenographic in one sense, its characters have sufficiently the
appearance of stenography to be taken as such ; and again,
although it claims to be the common alphabet simplified, it is
certainly arbitrary enough for a first observer to recognise no
similarity between it and the forms to which he has been
accustomed. Mr. Moon, like Mr. Frere, is himself a blind man,
and he has laboured hard to establish a system which he believes
is destined to supersede all others. If all that he says in its
favour could be taken for granted, no further question could
arise as to the best alphabet for the blind. The judgment and
experience of those who have means and opportunities for
deciding, at least equal to Mr. Moon's, but whose zeal,
enthusiasm, and interest are not fettered by partial views, do not
bear out his statements.

"Moon's system is adapted to the cottage, *because anybody can
teach it.*" This statement is more than questionable. Anybody
of moderate intelligence can doubtless acquire it if they can
already read. The same may be said of Alston's books, and
herein consists their superiority—anyone who can read may at
once be a teacher of reading to the blind. "It is adapted to the
dull finger of the labourer, because it is *very plain to the touch.*"
This is no exclusive advantage in Moon's letters. "It is suited
to the aged, the sick, and the ignorant, because it is so *easy to be
understood.*" This is a benefit compared with Lucas's and
Frere's, but in this respect Alston's is certainly more deserving of
praise. "The words are spelt at full length," and "full spelling
is essential to accuracy." Granted, so are Alston's, which system
does not employ even the few contractions Moon introduces ; in
this respect Moon's books are superior to Frere's or Lucas's, but
inferior to Alston's. Moon's alphabet consists of "the *common
letters simplified*, and therefore is easily learnt and taught by all who

know their a b c." But, Alston's consists of the common letters
themselves. We have doubts about the easy recognition of the
transformed letters, though none as to the increased tactile power
of the new forms in comparison with the certainly more intricate
forms of the ordinary alphabet. "Six of the Roman letters are
retained *unaltered;* twelve others have parts left out so as to be
left open to the touch, and yet be easily remembered as half of a
well-known letter." Of these twelve none would be recognised
from any similarity they bear to the letter they represent; they
must therefore be regarded as arbitrary characters. "Five or six
new and very simple forms complete the alphabet." These are
arbitrary; so that this system of the "common letters simplified"
is in fact composed of six of the Roman letters unaltered and
eighteen arbitrary characters. Most certainly Moon's alphabet
does not possess the superiorities over others to which it lays
claim. That it is a *good* arbitrary character for the blind no one
who has paid the least attention to the subject can deny. The
question, however, has yet to be settled whether an arbitrary or
an alphabetical character is the best for the blind. And on this
point evidence must be adduced.

MOON'S ALPHABET.

We find the schools for the blind in London, Glasgow,
Newcastle, Manchester, and York use the books in Alston's
Roman characters; those of Bristol and Belfast also use these
books, and in addition some printed at Bristol with lower-case
letters as well as capitals. (Several of the parties competent to

form a judgment on the matter, advocate the use of capitals.) We find Lucas's stenographic system in use at Bath, where the defective orthography is considered objectionable for young readers; the Roman alphabet has also been used in some cases; while for adults generally Moon's system is considered the best. At the Nottingham school, Lucas's system is generally adopted; some of the pupils also read Moon's books, and also those in the Roman characters. The schoolmaster, who is blind, reads on six systems, but gives a decided preference to Lucas's. The pupils read quite as rapidly as is necessary, and as correctly as others of the same age with sight. The superintendent of this school says, "Lucas's books are less bulky than those in the Roman type and consequently cheaper." The statement received from Birmingham is similar to the above : "All the pupils read on Lucas's system, it is much liked by them, and preferred to any other ; the value of a full orthography is understood, but the bulk and expense are considered objectionable. The Roman type is not generally considered readable." (Whether Alston's or the American Roman type is here referred to is not stated.) The Exeter school furnishes the following information :—"Lucas's books are used here, and with but one or two exceptions, all have been able to read the Scriptures. Our pupils have tried several systems, all of which they could learn, but they find Lucas's the easier to read." "The London Society for Teaching the Blind to Read," situated in Avenue Road, Regent's Park, has become the headquarters of Lucas's system. This society has published the whole of the Bible, which is sold in separate books or portions, the Liturgy, and several elementary works. The system has been revised and improved under the superintendence of the Rev. J. W. Gowring. Mr. Moon's printing establishment is at Brighton, but it has agencies at work in London, Birmingham, Edinburgh, and many other places for the introduction of the books. Moon's system has been well received by the blind and extensively adopted ; it is used in the schools of Brighton and Edinburgh. The testimony of Thomas Campbell, in the name of the inmates of the asylum in the latter-mentioned city, speaks of Moon's books as superior to all others; his letter traces the efforts made in that asylum with respect to Gall's, Alston's, the American, and Lucas's systems, and his conclusions are entitled to consideration, for they are the results of experience strongly supported by facts which are adduced. He emphatically states "that Mr. Moon's system is not only the best ever devised, but that it is the only one capable of imparting lasting benefits to the working blind." In the various publications advocating the use of this system great stress is laid on its adaptability for the aged, the nervous, and the working blind—those generally in whom the sense of feeling is less than ordinarily acute. It is clear that as a system it can afford to stand on its own merits, and that its adherents need not depreciate other plans while they support its peculiar claims to public favour. This observation is made with reference to the disparaging remarks on other systems in Moon's "Blind Readers and their Books." Frere's publications are used in the Liverpool asylum; a society was also established at Blackheath some years ago for teaching the blind to read on Frere's system.

The price of these comparatively expensive books is a consideration which must not be lost sight of in any estimate of their respective claims on public notice. In another part of this article it is stated that a guinea was the sum proposed by Gall for a copy of the Gospel of St. John; this, however, was the fancy price of an article new in itself, and for which there was no known market. All this is changed, as will be seen by a comparison of the prices annexed. The Gospel of St. John is now charged 4*s*. in Lucas's stenographic character; 4*s*. 6*d*. in Alston's Roman capitals; 8*s*. in Moon's arbitrary character. The book of Genesis is 8*s*. in Lucas's; 10*s*. in Alston's; 21*s*. in Moon's. The New Testament is charged £1 16*s*. in Lucas's; £2 in Alston's; £4 17*s*. in Moon's. The Old Testament, £8 1*s*. 4*d*. in Lucas's; £7 15*s*. in Alston's; and £11 11*s*. in Moon's, without the books of Leviticus, Numbers, and 2 Chronicles; the addition of these will make the cost not less than £13 10*s*. This discrepancy in price is very great, and it is clear that Mr. Moon must reduce his prices to obtain that favour which he doubtless desires. How strange it is, however, that

Alston's Old Testament in Roman capitals, without signs or contractions, can be had for less money than Lucas's with the aid of
stenography and its very numerous contractions! Does stenography actually increase the bulk and expense of the books for
the blind? The American books are much lower in price than
any of the above; the letters are capitals and lower-case, but so
small that, in this country, they are considered unreadable by the
blind. We have four systems in England, the Scriptures in each,
besides many other books. And another character is projected.
Mr. Littledale, himself blind, and the present superintendent of
the school at York, proposes to bring out a " selected alphabet,"
made up of capitals and lower-case letters, readable by any seeing
instructor of a blind child; his strong impression being that the
Roman character ought not to be set aside for one less universally
known, and that no stenographic, or otherwise arbitrary alphabet
will meet the requirements of both children and adults for reading,
writing and accounts.

The writer of this article is not connected with any school for
the blind; he does not wish to appear as a partisan of any system
of typography for them; he has endeavoured to set forth the
excellences and the defects of existing systems of printing, and
to show the results as given by their respective advocates, while
his wish is to see the superiority of a single system established,
in order that the united efforts of all who are now engaged on
methods so diverse may be combined for the production of
good and cheap books for the blind. Enormous expenses have
been incurred, chiefly by the benevolent public, in the purchase
of the numerous founts of type, and in the establishment of
several printing offices, where one would have sufficed if
unanimity had prevailed. Each system has its adherents, but
little good has been accomplished compared with such results as
would have arisen from unity of purpose and willing co-operation. There cannot be a remunerating sale for the books produced
on all the different systems. Zeal and benevolence may commence
a good work of this nature, but it can only become an enduring
benefit on the commercial principle. When this principle cannot

be applied, zeal and benevolence will fail in providing heart-work and funds which must be so largely wasted. It may be a hard thing for men to sacrifice wishes long indulged and to forget objects for which they have lived and striven, but if the interests of the community, or of a class, require it, men of ardent and kindly feeling will not be backward in making such sacrifices. A conference should be held, partly composed of intelligent blind men, to ascertain whether it is possible to unite all parties in the prosecution of one system of printing, or whether all should persevere in a course which divides the friends of the blind and injures their cause. There are men living who have devoted years to the consideration of the question, and who would be glad to consider it by the lights of science and experience.

LONDON: PRINTED BY WM. CLOWES AND SONS, LTD., STAMFORD STREET AND CHARING CROSS.

Reprinted by permission of

MESSRS. CHAPMAN & HALL, LIMITED,

From "The National Review"

No. XIX.

JANUARY, 1860

LONDON

SAMPSON LOW, MARSTON & COMPANY
LIMITED
St. Dunstan's House
FETTER LANE, FLEET STREET, E.C

1895

Reprinted by permission of

MESSRS. CHAPMAN & HALL, LIMITED,

From "The National Review"

No. XIX.

JANUARY, 1860

LONDON

SAMPSON LOW, MARSTON & COMPANY
LIMITED

St. Dunstan's House

FETTER LANE, FLEET STREET, E.C.

1895

LONDON:
PRINTED BY WILLIAM CLOWES AND SONS, Limited,
STAMFORD STREET AND CHARING CROSS.

ART. IV.—THE BLIND.

*Des Aveugles: Considérations sur leur état physique, moral et
intellectuel, avec un exposé complet des moyens propres à
améliorer leur sort à l'aide de l'instruction et du travail.* Par
P. A. DUFAU, Directeur de l'Institution Nationale des
Aveugles de Paris. Ouvrage couronné par l'Académie Fran-
çaise. Seconde édition. Paris: Jules Renouard et Cie.,
1850.

Souvenirs d'une Aveugle-née, recueillis et écrits par elle-même.
Publiés par P. A. DUFAU. Paris: Renouard et Cie., 1851.

The Sense [of Vision] denied and lost. By THOMAS BULL, M.D.
Edited by the Rev. B. G. Johns, Chaplain of the Blind
School, St. George's Fields. London: Longman and Co.,
1859.

The Land of Silence and the Land of Darkness. By the Rev.
B. G. JOHNS. London: Longman and Co., 1857.

The Lost Senses. By JOHN KITTO, D.D., F.S.A. Series II.—
Blindness. London: Charles Knight and Co., 1845.

*Essai sur l'Instruction des Aveugles, ou exposé analytique des
procédés employés pour les instruire.* Par le DOCTEUR
GUILLIÉ. Seconde édition. Paris: imprimé par les Aveugles,
1819.

"IN the month of August, 1425, as we read in the *Journal de
Paris*, under the reigns of Charles V. and Charles VI., p. 104,
four blind men," says M. Dufau, "covered with armour and
armed with staves, were shut up in the lists at the Hotel
d'Armagnac with a pig of great size, which was to be the prize
of the man who should kill it. When the contest began, the

poor blind men, pursuing the pig and striking at random, gave
one another such rude blows, to the great delight of the lookers-
on, that they grew angry ; for when they were most confident
of hitting the pig, they hit one another ; and if they had not
been covered with armour, they would in truth have slain each
other."*

We are reminded by this story of Sydney Smith's remark
in criticising some philosophical speculations of the earlier
Greek schools, that common sense was not invented then.   In
the fifteenth century, natural human feeling seems scarcely to
have been invented.   But against the incident above related it
is only fair to put the foundation of the Hospice des Quinze
Vingts by St. Louis IX., in 1265, as an asylum for three hundred knights who had lost their eyesight in the crusades ; and
of a similar institution, dating also from the thirteenth century,
at Chartres.   We fear, however, that while the story told in
the *Journal de Paris* illustrates with only too much truth the
unthinking cruelty of a barbarous age, the establishments mentioned in the last sentence are to be attributed chiefly to the
personal benevolence of the saintly monarch.   Impulses good
and bad, of the noblest generosity and the intensest selfishness,
are not unfrequent in any nation at any time.   They are most
frequent, perhaps, among uncultivated people.   But the systematic and deliberate consideration, to which it is as a rule
and duty,

> "Never to blend our pleasure or our pride
> With sorrow of the meanest thing that feels,"

is of slow growth.   To whatever extent it can be said to exist
now among Christian communities, it is indisputably quite
modern.

Of the condition of the blind in the ancient world little is
known.   The fact that they form the subject of special and
benevolent legislation in the Jewish code—witness the precepts, "Thou shalt not put a stumbling-block in the way of

---

* *Des Aveugles,* p. xiii.

the blind, but shalt fear thy God," and "Cursed be he that maketh the blind to wander out of the way "—is no doubt due to the fact that throughout the East the blind form a very considerable proportion of the entire population. These injunctions are in contrast with the Jewish belief (possibly of later origin), that blindness was a divine judgment on, and a punishment of, sin. This belief is itself reversed in other Eastern countries, "where," as Mr. Johns remarks, "the blind are regarded in some sense as sacred persons under the special favour of Heaven. Not long since," he adds, "an intelligent friend of ours, a great traveller, who happens to be blind, in passing through Tetuan, an old Moorish city of Africa, was welcomed and fêted with peculiar honours, chiefly on account of his blindness."*

If we do not find among ancient heathen nations any systematic provision for the relief of the blind, as little do we find any trace of inhuman feelings directed towards them. Medical works leave no doubt, M. Dufau tells us, that the blind were numerous in Italy and in Roman Asia, though one of the most prolific causes of congenital blindness did not then exist. His statement, that institutions of public benevolence are foreign to the spirit of nations among whom slavery reigns, is substantially true.† The reason is, that the necessitous in such countries are principally slaves ; and that slaves, being private property, are naturally also a private charge, and not a public burden. We cannot, therefore, accept the non-existence of asylums and training-schools for the blind in Greece and Italy as an illustration of heathen indifference to suffering. M. Dufau's remarks on this subject contain a larger amount of conjecture than is consistent with sound historical judgment.

"Among the thousands of slaves," he says, "possessed by an opulent Roman, the child which was born blind sometimes no doubt became a kind of drudge (*souffre-douleur*), exposed to the caprices of

---

* *Lands of Silence and Darkness*, p. 98.

† It is not, however, entirely true, as the relief given to the ἀδύνατοι at Athens, and to the *alimentarii* at Rome, shows.

his master, and the barbarous sports of his degraded companions;
oftener, perhaps, being regarded simply as a burdensome property, he
was slain in his cradle; so we may reasonably conjecture, when we
notice that no blind man is ever signalised among the clan of freedmen
as having worked his way to liberty by his talent. How is it that
the blind, if they were allowed to live, did not manifest, as in our
days, that general and constant aptitude for music, which forms one of
the distinctive traits of their organisation; how is it that no skilful
performer on the flute or lyre is found, recommended by his very condition to the notice of writers? Moreover, to suppose the deliberate
destruction of children afflicted with an important organic defect, is
not to calumniate antiquity. At Sparta they were thrown into the
Eurotas; and we know that, even at the present day, among some
Eastern nations, infirm infants newly born pass at once from life to
death."

An argument, every clause of which is introduced by a
"peut-être," a "sans doute," or a "conjecture à bon droit,"
fails of cogency. The inference from Sparta to Rome, from
the destruction of free-born children on the Eurotas to that of
blind-born slaves on the Tiber, and from existing practices in
Eastern nations to the conduct of the nations of classical antiquity, involves a logical leap in which we cannot follow the
author. But even if the facts he states did warrant the conclusion
(in the absence of distinct testimony) that Roman slaves born
blind were habitually put to death in their cradles, this circumstance would help M. Dufau but little. The great majority of
blind persons (slaves no less than others) become blind in adult
age; very few indeed before their eighth year; while no one
(according to M. Dufau) is ever, strictly speaking, born blind.*
The destruction of all slaves who lost their sight in early childhood would not materially have diminished the total number of
blind slaves. Considering, moreover, that the younger among
the blind would almost necessarily—from the inapplicability of
the ordinary means of culture, and the non-existence of any
special system of training—be intellectually less advanced

---

* "Il n'y a pas d'aveugles-nés, à proprement parler, c'est à dire d'enfants
sortant aveugles du sein de leur mère, par suite de l'état spécial de l'appareil
visuel."—*Des Aveugles*, p. 1.

than those whose sight was lost at a maturer age, it is not among the former that we should expect to find a talent capable of working its way to freedom. With regard to the fact that no mention is made, in any classical author, of slaves acquiring celebrity by musical talent, it is worth noting that music does not seem to have been among the liberal or semi-liberal arts, which slaves were sometimes encouraged to cultivate. There were *servi literati*, literary slaves, who acted as readers, amanuenses, copiers for booksellers, secretaries, short-hand writers; but we find no mention of a class of musical slaves, corresponding to the *anagnostæ* and *librarii*. The tradition which represented Homer as blind, and the description given in the Odyssey of the Phæacian bard Demodocus—

> τὸν πέρι Μοῦσ᾽ ἐφίλησε, δίδου δ᾽ ἀγαθόν τε κακόν τε
> ὀφθαλμῶν μὲν ἄμερσε, δίδου δ᾽ ἡδεῖαν ἀοιδήν *—

point distinctly to a sympathy with the blind, as at once chastened by and loved of the gods, to whom, as they are

> " from the cheerful ways of men
> Cut off, and for the book of knowledge fair
> Presented with a universal blank
> Of Nature's works, ...
> So much the rather the celestial light
> Shines inward, and the mind through all her powers
> Irradiates . . . .
> . . . . . that they may see and tell
> Of things invisible to mortal sight."

In the *Œdipus at Colonus*, no doubt other elements of tragic emotion are predominant; but no reader can be insensible to the degree in which the blindness of the dethroned and wandering monarch is made to add to the pathos of the character and the situation.

---

* *Odyssey*, viii. 63:
> " Dear to the Muse who gave his days to flow,
> With mighty blessings mixed with mighty woe,
> In clouds and darkness quenched his visual ray,
> Yet gave him power to raise the lofty lay." *Pope.*

The philosophers, mentioned by Diogenes Laertius—among them Democritus—who put out their eyes in order to concentrate their attention on the abstractions with which they were engaged ; and the more trustworthy allusions in many of Cicero's writings to his old teacher Diodotus, whose loss of sight did not interfere with his skill in teaching geometry,—are, as far as we know, the principal documents in relation to blindness to be found in the classical writers of heathendom.

Turning to the East, there is evidence that music was an art especially cultivated in Egypt by the blind. " Among the mural tablets of the ancient Egyptians," says Dr. Kitto, "there is one, copied by Rossellini and Sir J. G. Wilkinson, which is among the very few exhibiting anything of character or sentiment, or able to inspire any emotion. It is from the tombs of Alabastron, and represents a blind harper, sitting cross-legged on the ground, attended by seven other blind men similarly seated, who sing and beat time with their hands. They are clearly professional musicians ; and from this we learn that music was a source of employment in Egypt to the blind, who in that country have always been frightfully numerous. That it was no less a source of enjoyment is manifest in their countenances, lighted up with animation and interest in their work ; while the artist has contrived that not only the eyes, but every feature of the face, and the position of the heads, express the *blindness* of their condition."*

In more modern times, Chardin's account of the blind Persian princes at Ispahan, whose mathematical attainments and methods of study he describes, and the more questionable stories told by Charlevoix of the college of blind men in Japan, to whose memory the public records of the empire are confided, are the chief records of this class in the East.

It would be an endless and useless task to enumerate even the names of those who, since the Christian era, have, notwithstanding the absence of what is ordinarily deemed the most essential

---

* Kitto, p. 171.

of the inlets of knowledge, been distinguished by proficiency in the various departments of intellectual culture and research. A tolerably complete list of these will be found in the article on the Instruction of the Blind in the original edition of the *Penny Cyclopædia*. It presents us with votaries of the mathematical and physico-mathematical sciences, the sciences of observation and experiment ;—chemistry and natural history, speculative philosophy, law, medicine, and divinity, politics and history, poetry, music, and sculpture, and the various arts of mechanical construction. Unfortunately the names of those who thus pursued knowledge under difficulties, and the fact of their achievements, are all that is recorded. Stupid indifference and neglect, or scarcely more intelligent wonder (as at the tricks of trained animals, or at striking displays of untrained animal instinct), with its unfailing accompaniment of exaggeration, do not seem to have given place to any more worthy curiosity. It was not until the middle of the eighteenth century that an attempt was made to realise the intellectual and moral condition of the blind. Diderot's *Lettre sur les Aveugles, à l'usage de ceux qui voient* ("Letter on the Blind, for the use of those who see"), published in 1749, first distinctly suggested and exemplified the manner in which the study of the experience and feelings of the blind might be made to throw light upon some of the most interesting problems of mental science. If it can be ascertained that the blind are, as a rule, without, or possess only in an inferior degree and undeveloped condition, ideas and perceptions which are the common property of those who see ; if certain otherwise universal emotions and feelings are absent from their minds, or only feebly present to them ; if a marked mental tendency, a certain cast of character differencing them as a class from other human beings, can be detected—an important aid is gained towards the determination of the part which the faculty of vision plays in the acquisition of knowledge, the training of the intellect, and the formation of the tastes, affections, and moral dispositions. This essay of Diderot's and a subsequent production of the same author, *Lettre sur les Sourds et Muets, à l'usage de ceux qui entendent et qui parlent* ("Letter on Deaf Mutes, for the use of those who hear and speak"), published in 1751, occupy an important place in the history, not only of the literature of our present subject, but of philosophy in France, and, through France, in Europe. They suggested the method of exposition and illustration which Condillac made use of in his *Traité des Sensations*. Speculation in France, since the publication of that work, and until the reaction during the closing years of Napoleon's reign, was simply the explanation and development of the doctrines then laid down. In it, as is well known, Condillac supposes a "statue endowed with an interior organisation like our own, but with a mind totally destitute of ideas." He further "supposes that the exterior, consisting entirely of marble, does not allow it the use of any of the senses; and reserves to himself the liberty of opening them at discretion to the different impressions of which they are susceptible." By gifting it at first with each sense separately, and then with all the possible combinations of the different senses, he endeavours to determine the feelings and conceptions due to their action, first in isolation, and secondly in conjunction.

"The idea," say the editors of the Brussels edition (1825) of Diderot's *Philosophical Works*,—"the idea of *decomposing* a man to ascertain what he derives from each of the senses which he possesses, and that of a company of five persons each endowed with only one sense, evidently gave birth to the *Statue organisée intérieurement comme nous*, which Condillac has placed in his *Traité des Sensations*, published three years after the *Lettre sur les Sourds et Muets*.* In his *Réponse à un reproche qui m'a été fait sur le projet exécuté dans le Traité des Sensations*, Condillac has not succeeded in exculpating himself; and the *Biographie Universelle* is in error in saying, 'it is alleged that this work is contained in the Letters on the Blind and on Deaf Mutes. . . . Condillac felt the imputation; he cited two fragments from Diderot, and it is clear that the latter was not

---

* The *Lettre sur les Sourds et Muets* was published in 1751.

the author of Condillac's treatise ; ' but everyone acknowledges that Condillac drew from Diderot the idea of his *Statue*. *Suum cuique*."

It is not to the credit of English thinkers that the first really philosophical work on what Diderot calls " la morale et la métaphysique des aveugles " should have proceeded from a French writer, since his materials and his method of dealing with them certainly came from England. The doctrine which he aimed to enforce was derived (whether by a correct interpretation or not) from Locke. His method of inquiry was that of Bacon, of whose *Novum Organon* Diderot was the first French expounder. Special circumstances would seem likely to have directed attention in England to the condition of the blind, and to the various problems on which an examination of that condition might be expected to throw light. In Locke's *Essay on the Human Understanding*, published in 1690, the question was mooted, whether a blind man restored to sight would be able to recognise by his eye, and without handling them, geometrical figures which he had known during his blindness by touch. Hobbes afterwards, we believe, discussed the same question. In 1709, Berkeley published his *Theory of Vision*. In 1728, Cheselden contributed to the *Philosophical Transactions* his celebrated report entitled, " Account of some Observations made by a young gentleman who was born blind, or lost his sight so early that he had no remembrance of ever having seen, and was couched between thirteen and fourteen years of age." Dr. Saunderson, who died in 1739, had presented the extraordinary spectacle of a man totally blind from his first year filling with distinction the office of Mathematical Professor at Cambridge, and instructing those who saw in the laws of light. Yet all these favouring circumstances failed to incite to intelligent curiosity. Diderot himself administered a well-deserved rebuke to this sluggish indifference : " England," he says, "is the country of philosophers, of inquirers, of men of system ; nevertheless, except for Mr. Incheliff, we should have known of Saunderson only what the most ordinary men could have told us ; for example, that he recognised places into which he had once been introduced by the echo from the walls and pavements, and a hundred other things of the same kind which were common to him with nearly all blind men. What, then ! are blind men of Saunderson's merit so frequently to be met with in England ? and are people to be found there every day who have never seen, and who lecture on optics ? " (p. 176).

The subject opened out in Diderot's letter does not appear to have been followed up. Excepting its influence on Condillac, its only effect was one personal to the author. The heterodox opinions broached in it procured him a *lettre de cachet* and three months' imprisonment in the Bastille, of which twenty-nine days were spent in solitary confinement, without books or light. As he refused, however, to give up the name of his printer, and as his services were required for the forthcoming *Encyclopædia*, he was at length released.

To another Frenchman we owe the foundation of the first institution for the education of the blind. The success of the Abbé Epée as a teacher of the deaf and dumb suggested to Valentine Haüy (the brother of the discoverer of the derivative forms of crystals) the " idea of communicating to another class of unfortunates, hitherto not less neglected, the benefit of instruction."

" But if this generous thought became henceforth fixed in his mind, an accidental and whimsical circumstance was needed to determine him to realise it. Haüy has himself related it in the following terms : ' Many years ago, a novelty of a singular character attracted a crowd of people at the entrance of one of those public walks where honest citizens are wont to take relaxation at the fall of day: eight or ten blind men, with spectacles on nose, posted behind a desk, with music-books before them, performed a discordant symphony, which seemed very much to delight the standers-by. A feeling of quite a different kind took possession of my mind ; and I conceived at that moment the possibility of turning to account for their benefit the means of which they made a pretended and ridiculous use. " Does not the blind man," I said to myself, " recognise objects by the diversity of their forms? Is he ever mistaken as to the value of a piece of money? Why should he not distinguish an *ut* from a *sol*, an *a* from a *g*, if

these characters were made palpable?"' Such was the origin of the
method of special instruction created by Haüy" [by means of works
printed in relief].*

Having proved its practicability in the case of a single pupil,
who up to this time had begged at church doors, and whom he
paid for receiving his instruction, Haüy obtained the co-operation, first of the "Philanthropic Society," and then of the
government, for the purpose of experiments on a large scale.
The result was the foundation of the School for the Young Blind,
from which arose the National (now probably the Imperial)
Institution for the Blind at Paris. In 1806, he visited St.
Petersburg, at the invitation of the Russian Government, in
order to superintend the establishment of an institution of a
similar character in that city. In this task he spent eleven years,
and returned to France in 1817. The asylums and schools for the
blind which now exist in almost every capital and populous town
of Europe and the United States, are as certainly, if less directly,
founded by Valentine Haüy as those of Paris and St. Petersburg.
The systematic attention which, since the beginning of the present
century, has been paid in these establishments to the condition
of the blind has been naturally directed more to the practical
amelioration of their lot in life than to systematic inquiry into
the points of scientific interest which their privation presents;
in other words (unlike Diderot's *Lettre*), it has had for its end,
not "the use of those who see," but the benefit of those who do
not see. The training provided in the schools for the blind,
especially those in England and in the United States, is chiefly
industrial. Only the most rudimentary general education is
imparted. The inmates, belonging mostly to the indigent classes,
are taught such trades as they can exercise with reasonable hope
of supporting themselves when they quit the asylum. In many
of the continental schools, on the other hand, notably in that at
Paris, a higher intellectual training is aimed at. It is this circumstance, probably, which has given to the works of foreign

---

* Dufau, *Des Aveugles*, pp. 305, 306.

writers a higher value and a wider scope than can in general be predicated of those of their English and American *collaborateurs.* The latter, no doubt, contain many valuable facts and suggestions; but they seldom rise above details, and are generally too much devoted to the technicalities of what a German writer, with true German love of an imposing terminology, calls *typhlopädagogik*, to be very profitable, except to professional teachers or others practically concerned in the administration of institutions for the blind. The books, again, which address the general public are almost purely anecdotical, not to say gossiping. Many French and German works are of a higher order. Among these, the treatise of M. Dufau stands pre-eminent for the evidence which it presents of exhaustive knowledge of his subject, both in its theoretic and practical aspects, for the philosophic method and powers of generalisation it displays, as well as the insight it gives into the many interesting questions of psychology to which the study of the mental life of the blind introduces us. The blind are treated of in his essay as "at once objects of social beneficence and of scientific observation"; and in either relation with equal skill. It is in the latter aspect that we propose now to view them. But before proceeding to this part of our subject, we desire to gather together such scanty statistics of blindness as have been collected. They are far from being either extensive or exact enough to warrant any very positive conclusions on the points to the clearing-up of which attention should be drawn. Among these, M. Dufau, to whom (except when another authority is expressly cited) we are indebted for the details about to be stated, enumerates the "relative extent to which blindness prevails in town and country, in agricultural and manufacturing districts, dry and marshy lands; the various degrees of blindness; the age at which, in each case, it has supervened; the rank in life of the sufferers," &c.

The following figures convey the proportion which the blind hold, in the undermentioned countries, to the entire population. The average of three censuses, taken in Prussia in the years 1831, 1834, and 1837, gives one blind person among 1401 inhabitants.

In Belgium, in 1831, the proportion was rather higher, being one in 1316. As regards France, no reliable information appears to exist. M. Dufau, comparing it with the two neighbouring countries, states that in 1836, supposing the proportion of blind the same as in Prussia, there would have been 23,862 of this class in France ; and if the ratio were equal to that of Belgium, 25,487 ; or, taking a mean, 24,675. In an English book published this year, *Realities of Paris Life*, the number of blind in France is estimated at 50,000. But this is mere guess-work. Among the subjects of Queen Victoria, according to Mr. Johns, the ratio is one in 1000, there being 30,000 blind among 30,000,000 who see. In Ireland one in 870 is blind ; in Sweden one in 1091 ; in Norway one in 566. In Spain the number of blind persons is very great. In Egypt and Morocco they are rudely estimated in the ratio of one to every hundred of the population. Of the white inhabitants of the United States, one in 2824 is blind ; among the coloured population the proportion is nearly twice as great, being one in 1465.* In Africa, on the other hand, the white population is said to suffer more than the black from ophthalmic affections. Dr. Zeune, of Berlin, has drawn up a table representing the manner in which, as he believes, blindness varies according to degrees of latitude :

Latitude	20° to	30°	1 blind in	100	individuals.
„	30 „	40	1 . „	300	„
„	40 „	50	1 „	800	„
„	50 „	60	1 „	1400	„
„	60 „	70	1 „	1000	„

It is evident, however, that a definite numerical statement of this kind is as yet (to say the least) premature. Some of the details

---

* Dufau, p. 217. The partial identity of these numbers with those given by Mr. Johns respecting Pennsylvania alone, makes it possible that we have, in one case or the other, an inaccurate form of the same statement. "There are some points of detail connected with the statistics of blindness in America of which we can offer our readers no satisfactory explanation. For example, why should the free and independent drab-coated men of Pennsylvania,

already cited conflict with it. Dr. Zeune's general principle is, however, true, that "the number of the blind, considerable in the more northern parts of the globe, diminishes in the temperate zones, and then increases more rapidly as we approach the equator, where it is at its maximum." Still it is impossible at present to draw lines of equal blindness, like the lines of equal heat which physical geographers have laid down ; and it is clear that the former would, just as little as the latter, correspond exactly with the parallels of latitude. Conditions of climate, soil, and employment ; social arrangements—sanitary, economical, and others ; and many other circumstances which do not vary as the distances from the equator, are no doubt causes which, as they affect the physical organisation for good or ill, tend to promote or check blindness. There seems some reason to believe that mountainous districts are more favourable to the preservation of sight than flat tracts of country. In the canton of Berne, a return made in 1840 gave few blind—one in 1570. In the three more elevated provinces of Prussia the blind were one in 1613 ; in the ten lower and more level provinces, one in 1308.

As regards the age at which blindness occurs, it seems established that comparatively few cases occur in childhood, or even adolescence. " In Prussia, in 1831, it was calculated that out of 9212 blind persons of every age, 846, or nearly one-eleventh, were between one and fifteen years of age ; while in Sweden, in 1840, on a total number of 2790 blind, only 138, or one-twentieth, belonged to this category." In the duchy of Brunswick, out of 286 blind persons, 14, or one-twentieth, were under seven years

---

having white skins, suffer only to the amount of one in 2842; *negroes in a state of freedom*, to that of one in 370 ; while if they do *not* survive sugar-hoeing, and never emerge into free life, blindness attacks only one in 2645? If the statistics be true,—and we quote on the best authority,—great must be the virtues of sugar-planting and hoeing, and gross, we fear, the excesses into which liberty too often leads the free and emancipated negro :—Mrs. H. B. Stowe nevertheless and notwithstanding" (*Land of Darkness*, pp. 99, 100). If the same figures were cited of Roman bondsmen and *liberti*, they would furnish a more powerful argument than any M. Dufau has been able to bring forward to show that Roman masters were in the habit of destroying their blind slaves ;—and yet an entirely false one.

of age ; 18, or one-fifteenth, under fifteen years of age. Dr. Bull sets down 2500 out of 30,000 (that is, one-twelfth of the whole) as born blind in England ; by which he means blind before their eighth year. In America, the adolescent blind apparently furnish a much larger percentage of a much smaller number of blind. " From a recent report of the Pennsylvania Blind-School," says Mr. Johns, "we find that there are 10,000 blind persons in the United States ; of whom 8000 are under thirty-five years of age, 4000 blind at birth, or before the third year, and 5500 [including, of course, the 4000 just named] before the tenth year." * In France, in Prussia, and in Belgium, the greater number of the blind belong to the male sex.

As regards the hereditary transmission of blindness, the solitary fact stated by M. Dufau, and that without much confidence in its accuracy, is that in England such cases are four per cent. The proportion, he thinks, is probably higher. A single fact conveys the only statement we can give as to the relative prevalence of different degrees of blindness. "In the duchy of Brunswick, in 1842, of 277 [accounted] blind persons, three saw moderately (*avaient un œil médiocre*), six saw confusedly (*jouissaient d'une vue confuse*), fifty-one had what is called a point of view (*avaient ce qu'on appelle un point de vue*), the blindness of the remaining 217 was complete." †

We have now quoted all the facts on which we could lay our hands, at the risk of wearying the reader, to show the inadequacy of the existing knowledge on the subject as the basis of any but the most provisional generalisations and inferences as to the causes of blindness, and to justify our abstinence from any inquiry into those causes, which at present stand in need of more facts and less speculation on them. On most of the points referred to,—the geographical distribution of the blind ; the relative numbers of blind children, adolescents, and adults ; of men and women ; the age at which vision disappeared ; the comparative prevalence of blindness in different ranks in life, as

---

* *Land of Darkness*, p. 99. † Dufau, p. 222.

indicated by the employments of the parents or of the sufferers themselves,—it would be quite easy in England to collect a body of exact and authentic information on the occasion of the next census. If proper explanations were offered, few would object to make the requisite returns, which could scarcely be made other than voluntarily. Information on some of these heads was, in fact, asked for and obtained in Ireland on occasion of the last census.

In considering the characteristics of the blind as a class, we begin with their physical nature, to which Bloomfield's imaginative description of the life of the blind boy may serve as an introduction :

> " Where's the blind boy, so admirably fair,
> With guileless dimples, and with flaxen hair
> That waves in every breeze? He's often seen
> Beyond yon cottage-wall, or on the green,
> With others match'd in spirit and in size,
> Health on their cheeks and rapture in their eyes.
> That full expanse of voice, to children dear,
> Soul of their sports, is duly cherished here.
> And hark! that laugh is his,—that jovial cry—
> He hears the ball and trundling hoop brush by,
> And runs the giddy course with all his might,—
> A very child in everything but sight ;
> With circumscribed but not abated powers,
> Play the great object of his infant hours.
> In many a game he takes a noisy part,
> And shows the native gladness of his heart."

Dr. Bull, who quotes this fancy sketch, says that the picture which it contains is " touchingly and most truthfully delineated." " Foremost among his young companions in their pleasant pastime," says the Doctor in his own person, " he [the blind child] pursues his sport as active and daring as any, guided and guarded by the exquisite keenness of the perceptions of hearing and touch."* There are instances familiar to every one, which both Bloomfield's and Dr. Bull's language very faintly

---

* *Sense [of Vision] Denied and Lost,* p. 37.

and inadequately portray. Such is that of John Metcalf (or, as he was called, "Blind Jack"), celebrated as a lad for his boldness in swimming, diving, fox-hunting, and all daring and athletic amusements.* So far, however, is it from being true that blind children ordinarily manifest the same bodily energy, that M. Dufau points out in them a tendency to inaction and repose which is in remarkable contrast with the incessant and restless mobility of children who see. Instead of "running the giddy course with all their might," a "more or less rapid walk, according as the place in which they may be is more or less known to them, is generally the only exercise they take." There are children who arrive at the age of reason without ever having run. "Their games," says the same authority, "are seldom animated." At work, their immobility is even more striking. "At most one

---

* As we may afterwards have to refer to the case of Metcalf, it may be well to give some account of him here.

John Metcalf was born at Knaresborough, in 1716. He lost his sight through smallpox, when he was six years of age. At fifteen he was employed to dive for the bodies of two drowned men in the river Nid, and succeeded in bringing one of them up. He also dived for, and brought up, two packs of yarn, which were sunk in twenty-one feet of water. He rode and won a race, on his own horse; and enlisting in 1745 in Thornton's troop, fought at Culloden and elsewhere. He afterwards acted as a guide for belated travellers, and drove a stage-waggon between York and Knaresborough. After studying mensuration and engineering, "we soon find him engaged," says Dr. Bull, from whom we have abridged the foregoing statement, "as a projector and surveyor of roads and bridges. Amongst other works, he built Boroughbridge, and made roads through Yorkshire, Lancashire, Derbyshire, and Cheshire. Dr. Bew, the intimate friend of Dr. Moyse, was well acquainted with Metcalf, and thus speaks of him : ' With the assistance only of a long staff, I have several times seen this man traversing the roads, ascending precipices, exploring valleys, and investigating their several extents, forms, and situations, so as to further his projects in the best manner. . . . . Most of the roads over the Peak in Derbyshire have been altered by his directions, particularly those in the vicinity of Buxton. . . . . I afterwards made some inquiries respecting a new road he was making. It was really astonishing to hear with what accuracy he described the courses, and the nature of the different soils through which it was conducted. Having mentioned a boggy piece of ground it passed through, he observed that it was the only place he had doubts about, and that he was apprehensive they had, contrary to his directions, been too sparing of their materials. This extraordinary man lived to the advanced age of eighty-five, possessed of his mental faculties to the last, and died in 1802.' " (Bull's *Sense Denied*, pp. 103-7.)

sees a hand noiselessly seeking its neighbour hand : the words *Tenez-vous tranquille,* which are elsewhere always in the master's mouth, are here rarely used ; it is very common to see young people, who have reached the time of life at which an ardent activity develops itself in us, remaining for a quarter of an hour at a time perfectly motionless : their closed eyes, their grave foreheads, their countenances, in which the soul fails to be reflected, then present the appearance of the calmest sleep. When their features are good, you might think them antique busts, the models of which had been borrowed from the school of Zeno." *

This picture of the young blind is, no doubt, from M. Dufau's extensive opportunities of observation, the true one. The indisposition which he remarks in them to active exercises is not to be attributed merely to the hesitation and constraint attendant upon their darkness ; it must be sought for in physiological considerations. In persons whose blindness is due to a paralysis of the optic nerve, the brain and nervous system generally are often impaired. That superabundant vital energy, therefore, the spontaneous overflowings of which seem to prompt the purposeless gambols of young animals, does not exist in them. The feeble " nerve-force " (whatever it may be) gives but a feeble stimulus from within to muscular action. Again, the influence of *light* upon the nervous system is necessary to its healthy tone, as the experiments of Dr. Edwards in regard to its effects upon animal organisation conclusively show. Tadpoles excluded from the light, while they grew in size, did not change into frogs ; other tadpoles, subjected to precisely the same treatment in every respect excepting the exclusion of light, went through the proper metamorphosis at the usual time. Dr. Edwards also observes, that those nations among whom the fashion of dress leaves a considerable surface of the body exposed to the action of light, exhibit forms more gracefully rounded and of better muscular development than are to be found elsewhere.

---

* Dufau, pp. 2, 3.

Miners, on the other hand, and those who live much in the dark, are generally misshapen, and of "pale and leaden" hue.* *Anhæmia* (want of blood) is a consequence of their mode of living. According to M. Dufau's description, the condition of the blind bears much resemblance to this. He compares their appearance to that of pale etiolated plants which have grown up in the shade. He speaks of their imperfect sanguification, and their awkward attitudes and gestures. He further points out that of the blind those who have some imperfect visual sense are more vivacious and active than those whose darkness is total. Of the latter class, those whose blindness is due to paralysis of the optic nerve, or affection of the brain, are less inclined to movement than those in whom the visual apparatus merely is disordered. These circumstances seem to show that, independently of its effect as the cause of vision, the action of light on the eye is a powerful and healthy stimulus, through the optic nerve, of the entire nervous system, and that its action upon the surface of the body, though less effectual, is real and beneficial. When either of the factors is diminished or impaired,—when the light acts on a feebler organisation, or less light finds access to an organisation of equal vigour,—the result is a diminished nervous force and muscular activity.

While we are speaking of the physical influence of light, we may refer to a question connected with this subject which has been made a matter of controversy among the blind themselves; viz. whether those who are totally destitute of vision have any sense whatever of the presence or absence of the luminous fluid. M. Knie, who has translated into German, with notes of his own, the treatise of M. Dufau, affirms that, "in spite of his state of complete blindness, he has a feeling of the light." M. Rodenbach, who also is blind, affirms, on the other hand, that the blind man whose eye has altogether wasted away can have no sensation except of the degree of heat, moisture, &c., which coincides with the presence of the luminous ray. M. Zeune is of the same

---

* See *Encyclopædia Britannica*, 8th edition, art. "Light."

opinion. M. Dufau seems to incline to the opposite view. The question was first started by Diderot, who relates the following incident of Saunderson :

"It is said that, during some astronomical observations which were one day being made in a garden in his presence, the clouds which from time to time hid the disk of the sun from the observers occasioned a change in the action of the rays upon his face, which was sufficiently sensible to him to enable him to mark the moments which were favourable for observations, and the contrary. You may perhaps suppose that some agitation capable of informing him of the presence of light, but not of the presence of objects, occurred in his eyes. I should have thought so too, if it were not certain that Saunderson had lost not only sight, but the organs of sight. Saunderson, therefore, saw by means of his skin."

As clouds would intercept heat as well as light, this instance is not conclusive. M. Dufau relates others ; but they do not necessarily show more than that the blind are cognisant of a difference between day and night. This, however, may be due to the change of temperature, and of atmospheric conditions, rather than to any distinct and immediate perception of the luminous fluid itself. Nevertheless, considering that the solar rays which convey heat are different from those which convey light, and that the necessity of the *latter* to healthy organic life, vegetable and animal, is clearly established, it may very well be the case that their action upon the nerves of the skin, of which the effect probably is to quicken and exalt the vital activity, is attended with a peculiar feeling, which, like most vague and obscure sensations, escapes those who have a better clue to the presence of the object from which it proceeds. The physical (as distinguished from visual) sense of the absence of light, in a slackened energy and torpor of the entire organisation, is perhaps expressed in the complaint which Milton transfers from himself to the hero of the *Samson Agonistes :*

"Since light so necessary is to life,
And almost life itself, ...
. . . . why was the sight
To such a tender ball as the eye confined,
So obvious and so easy to be quenched?

And not, like feeling, through all parts diffused,
That she might look at will through every pore?
Then had I not been thus exiled from light,
To live a life half-dead, a living death,
And buried; but oh, yet more miserable,
Myself my sepulchre, a living tomb!"

From the influence of blindness on the physical constitution generally, we pass to the effects of the absence of vision upon the remaining senses. Its well-known tendency to increase their range and quicken their susceptibility is expressed in the often-quoted lines of Rochester, which tell us,

"That if one sense should be suppressed,
It but retires into the rest;"

from which the inference would be that the perception of colours, which alone is proper to sight, is possible without it. The meaning intended to be conveyed is, however, clear and true,—that the knowledge of outward objects and their laws, which the seeing gain by the examination of one set of their qualities, the blind may acquire as certainly and accurately by attention to another. This part of our subject has been abundantly illustrated by anecdotical writers. It is the most piquant and interesting; and it would be unfair to our readers to omit it, and to confine them entirely to those more abstract and drier topics which have preceded and will follow it. Indeed, the intellectual and moral characteristics of the blind as a class are so intimately connected with, and are to a large extent so clearly the consequence of, the peculiarities of their organisation and sensibility, that some consideration of the latter is essential to the understanding of the former.

Taking the several senses in succession, we begin, for several reasons, with the *Muscular Sense*, or the feelings attending the muscular motions; the claims of which to rank as a sixth sense are now pretty generally recognised by writers on physiology and mental science. The new-born infant, in obedience, it may be probably conjectured, to an impulse from within, to a spontaneous discharge of the nervous force proceeding from its centres in the brain and spinal ganglia to the muscles, moves and tosses his limbs long before he shows any sign of being affected by impressions from without. These movements are attended with certain feelings peculiar to them, often of a very pleasurable kind, as is shown by the delight taken by children in active games, by the young of animals in their gambols, and by men of vigorous health, "muscular Christians" and others, in athletic exercises. To be incapable of this pleasure, to have a distaste for the exertions which procure it, is justly deemed a proof of a disordered or languid organisation. We have seen that this is, as a rule, the case with the blind. The chief physical enjoyments connected with the muscular systems are for them those of conscious repose, resembling probably the agreeable sensations of rest after moderate fatigue. A slight feeling of fatigue may be considered as their ordinary condition, in regard at least to this part of their nature. Their delight in bodily inaction, or in slow and measured movements, is like that of the weak eye in a shaded light, or its preference of the milder green rays to "the common light of day." It is easy to see how this state of feeling re-acts upon the intellectual character. Rapidity of mere physical motion produces a certain rapidity and intensity of mental action. Many instances of this might be adduced. The student is often compelled to stimulate the sluggish flow of thought by a rapid walk up and down his chamber. Douglas Jerrold is said to have composed in this way. The violent gestures of the popular orator are often quite evidently assumed, in the first instance, to rouse in him the vehemence which they seem to express, and of which they may afterwards become the unconscious expression. Slow movements, on the other hand, have a contrary effect ; they calm and soothe rather than stimulate. What is true of them in their action on special occasions, is of course equally true of them as a life-long influence. It is in harmony with these observations that the blind, as a class, are seldom characterised by that rapidity and intensity of mental action, that keenness of penetration, which pierces at once to the very heart of a matter,—that *vivida vis animi* which

is the characteristic of the highest genius. Their intellects are
in general cautious, calm, deliberative, slow, distinguished rather
by soundness than by brilliancy. The force which they apply is
accumulative rather than instantaneous. We do not mean that
all these qualities are to be attributed exclusively to the single
source which we have indicated, or even that all the said qualities are to be found in all blind people. What is asserted is
that the *tendency* of the condition of the muscular sensibility in
the blind is to produce the characteristics acknowledged, though
with many exceptions and in various degrees, to belong to them
as an order. The fact that their attachments are generally of a
calm and equable kind, formed on judgment and " right reason,"
rather than upon those inexplicable attractions which so often
bind others together; the infrequency with which they seem to
give way to strong impulses of affection, and a certain want of
geniality and expansiveness which has often been noted in them,
—may also, no doubt, in part be attributed to the same cause.
Vividness of sensation, and clearness of perception, exist always
in an inverse ratio; or, as Sir William Hamilton, to whom we
believe the first statement of this law of mind is due, expresses
it : " Above a certain point, the stronger the sensation, the weaker
the perception ; and the distincter the perception, the less obtru-
sive the sensation." Vision, which is the clearest of our modes
of objective perception, is ordinarily attended with scarcely any
subjective feeling ; taste and smell, which give us hardly any
knowledge of objects, appeal forcibly to the passive sensibility.
Intense light dazzles the eye, excessive sound deafens the ear ;
and both prevent clear perception. The feebleness of the muscular sensations in the blind does not, therefore, by any means
imply indistinctness in the corresponding perceptions. These
are, among others, the discrimination of degrees in the weight,
in the hardness and softness, the elasticity and inelasticity, of
objects, as estimated by the resistance they offer to pressure,
and the consequent muscular tension needed to withstand or
overcome this resistance. Without, perhaps, being peculiar to
this sense, the cognition of space, and its several modes and

diversities—that is to say, the magnitude, the distance and direction (which, taken together, gives the position) of objects, their form, &c.—may no doubt be gained by consciousness of differences in the sweep and contraction of the muscular movements. The nicety of discrimination acquired by the blind in regard to these qualities has received many illustrations. Diderot says of the celebrated blind man of Puesseaux, a visit to whom occasioned his *Lettre sur les Aveugles :* "He appreciates with wonderful accuracy the weights of bodies and the capacities of vessels ; and he has made of his arms balances so exact, and of his fingers compasses so well tested, that on occasions on which this sort of static is called into play, I would always back our blind man against twenty who see." The lady patient of Sir Hans Sloane, who became blind, deaf, and dumb, through confluent small-pox, manifested the same fineness of muscular sensibility. "To amuse herself in the mournful and perpetual solitude and darkness to which her disorder had reduced her, she used to work much at her needle ; and it is remarkable that her needlework was uncommonly neat and exact. . . . . . She used also sometimes to write ; and her writing was yet more extraordinary than her needlework ; it was executed with the same regularity and exactness ; the character was very pretty, the lines were all even, and the letters placed at equal distances from each other : but the most astonishing particular of all, with respect to her writing, is that she could by some means discover when a letter had by some mistake been omitted, and would place it over that part of the word where it should have been inserted, with a *caret* under it."*

This last-mentioned circumstance requires stronger faith or stronger testimony than we possess to convince us of the fact. There is nothing improbable in the other assertions. The blind in general, indeed, are obliged to have recourse to a special apparatus in writing, to prevent the pen from wandering over the paper. But the case of the American girl, Laura Bridgman

---

* *Encyclopædia Britannica*, original edition, art. "Blind."

(blind, deaf, and dumb), as well as that of Sir Hans Sloane's patient, proves that the muscular sense may be brought to a degree of perfection which enables it to dispense with artificial aids. Mr. Dickens, in his *American Notes*, says of Laura Bridgman, who wrote in his presence : "No line was indicated by any contrivance ; but she wrote straight and freely." Laura Bridgman appears to have used one set of muscular movements to watch over, and correct if needful, the set in action. "I observed," says Mr. Dickens, that she kept her left hand always touching and following up her right, in which of course she held the pen." The left hand in this way discharged for her the functions of superintendence and control, which with the seeing are rendered by the eye. John Metcalf (of whom an account has already been given) must in his surveying expeditions have relied principally upon the same sense. From the direction and degree of inclination of his staff, and the various amounts of resistance it encountered, he drew his inferences as to the physical features and soil of the districts he examined ; and he could only know the position of the staff by the experience of the muscular tension and contraction consequent upon its changes as he shifted it about. The great number of blind persons who have been able to practise with success various manual trades and mechanical arts, from shoemaking and plain carpentry up to the making of watches and the manufacture of organs and pianos, and the pupils in almost every blind-school in which useful handicrafts are taught, are all dependent on the same faculty. Only from it can they learn the right mode of handling their tools, and the proper range, direction, and force to be given to their movements.

From the muscular feelings we proceed to the *Sense of Touch*. We assign it the second place among the modes of external perception, not only on account of its close connection with the muscular sensations (which until recently were confounded with it, and are so still by "popular" writers), but because, while any or all of the remaining senses may be lost, we cannot conceive touch absent from a sentient organism. Beings who possess *only* this sense and the muscular feelings have existed, and do exist; but the entire paralysis of the nervous system which would be necessary to destroy tactile feeling could scarcely be distinguished from death. According to Cabanis, whose doctrine on this point is adopted by Sir William Hamilton, and his able disciple and expositor Mr. Mansel, all the commonly admitted five senses may be resolved into modifications of touch. This sense is diffused over the entire surface of the body, and has its seat in the *papillæ* of the skin. The exquisite sensibility which it habitually attains in the blind, is perhaps the best-known feature of their condition. Many, however, of the phenomena commonly attributed to it really belong to the muscular sense. That the two orders of feeling are distinct is shown by the fact, that the susceptibility of the former is often very faint, when that of the latter is most keen and discriminating. This is the case with most handicraft labourers, the skin of whose hands is generally hard and callous, while their perceptions of weight, distance, figure, &c., are wonderfully delicate and exact. An example, if one is needed, is presented by the blind deaf-mute Edward Meyster. Before entering the Blind Asylum at Lausanne, he had been employed in cutting wood, in consequence of which "his fingers never acquired the delicacy of touch of the other pupils."[*] Nevertheless he excelled all his companions in mechanical skill, and was unusually dexterous in the use of the turning-lathe.

One of the most remarkable instances of the power which this sense may acquire is presented in the history of John Gough, who lost his sight through small-pox when in his third year. He devoted himself with great ardour to the study of natural history, and made considerable progress both in zoology and botany, especially in the latter science. The sensibility of touch in his fingers was sufficient to enable him to recognise, classify, and arrange ordinary plants. "It is mentioned, that towards the end of his life a rare plant was put into his hands, which he

---

[*] Bull, p. 182.

very soon called by its name, observing that he had never met with more than one specimen of it, and that was fifty years ago." When he failed to recognise a plant by his fingers, he used to apply it to his lips and tongue; and was generally able in this way to identify it, or refer it to its botanical order. The explanation of this expedient is as follows. The experiments of Weber have shown that the tactile sensibility of the skin varies in different parts. Placing the points of a pair of compasses, blunted with sealing-wax, on the tip of the tongue, he found that the points could be recognised as different at the distance of the twentieth part of an English inch; on the lower surface of the finger, they required to be widened to the tenth part of an inch in order to be distinguished. The tactile discrimination of the tongue is, therefore, twice as great as that of the finger-ends; an object placed on the former appears twice as great as it does when examined by the fingers. Gough's use of his tongue corresponded strictly to the use of a glass of double magnifying power by the seeing.

' "The *lips*," says Dr. Bull, "are almost as liberally supplied with the nerves of touch as the tips of the fingers [Weber's experiments show that they have greater tactile discrimination than the fingers, and very nearly as great as that of the tongue], and in one instance have done good service to a fellow-sufferer. A poor blind girl, residing in one of the provinces of France, had for many years, as her greatest comfort, perused her embossed Bible with her finger; getting out of health, and becoming partially paralysed, the hand also was affected, and gradually all power of touch was lost. Her agony of mind at her deprivation was great, and in a moment of despair she took up her Bible, bent down her head, and kissed the open leaf, by way, as she supposed, of a last farewell. In the act of doing so, to her great surprise and sudden joy, she felt the letters distinctly with her lips; and from that day this poor child has thus been reading in the Word of God, 'words more precious to her than silver or gold—even fine gold.'" (p. 68.)

The discriminating sensibility of the fingers may, however, be indefinitely improved by practice. It varies very much in individuals. In the interesting account of Mdlle. de Salignac,

which forms the postscript of Diderot's *Lettre sur les Aveugles*
(and was, indeed, written more than thirty years after), several
illustrations of this are given. She could read books in the
ordinary type (embossed printing had not then been invented),
which were printed on only one side of the page. We have also
heard of a blind German who was able to read books printed on
the coarse rough paper used in that country. Mdlle de Salignac's
nicety of touch enabled her to play at cards with perfect
accuracy. Marks were made on each card, which she was able
to distinguish, though they escaped both the eye and touch of
those who saw. Dr. Guillié gives an account of a blind Dutchman who could recognise the differences of the figures on cards
without this aid ; the different textures of the colours, black and
red, and the different forms of club and spade, heart and
diamond, were palpable to his feeling. In consequence, whenever he dealt he always won. Touching all the cards of the
pack as he gave them out, he had virtually seen his opponent's
hands. The evidence of this power possessed by some of the
blind to discern differences of colours is, indeed, irresistible : Sir
Hans Sloane's patient,* the blind Highland tailor Maguire
(mentioned in the *Philosophical Transactions*), who made tartan
(parti-coloured) dresses without mistake, Madam von Paradis,
the Dutchman alluded to by Leibnitz and the Count of Mans-
feldt, of whom Keckermann gives an account, are instances. A
more recent example is given by Dr. Bull, on the testimony of

---

* " She could distinguish the different colours of silk and flowers. . . .
A lady who was nearly related to her having an apron on that was em-
broidered with silk of different colours, asked her, in the manner which has
been described, if she could tell what colour it was; and after applying her
fingers attentively to the figures of the embroidery, she replied, that it was
red, blue, and green, which was true. The same lady having a pink-coloured
ribbon on her head, and being willing still further to satisfy her curiosity
and her doubts, asked what colour that was. Her cousin, after feeling some
time, answered that it was pink. Her answer was yet more astonishing,
because it showed not only a power of distinguishing different colours, but
different kinds of the same colour ; the ribbon was discovered not only to be
red, but the red was discovered to be of the pale kind called pink."—*Encyc.
Britan.*, article " Blind."

a friend.* Two eminent blind men, Dr. Blacklock and M. Rodenbach, have declared themselves totally destitute of this power,
and sceptical as to its existence. But the fact that most blind
people are without it, does not prove that some few do not
possess it. It is not pretended that it is anything but an
exceptional faculty. Mr. Johns's remark, that " if the testimony
of all the inmates of the largest blind school in Europe is to be
believed, they have not the least power of detecting colour,"
does not prove much. The pupils in the Southwark school, to
which he refers, are habitually employed in handicraft trades,
the effect of which is to harden and blunt the sensibility of the
skin. M. Dufau mentions that the blind have often complained
to him, that the sensibility of the finger-ends diminishes as they
grow up, and renders reading and similar tasks more difficult
to them ; and he wisely insists on the necessity of the blind
guarding their touch from injury as carefully as the seeing
do their eyes.†

---

* "Visiting, in 1847, some friends in Gloucestershire, one morning a man
about 25, perfectly blind, for the eyes were entirely gone, called to return
thanks for his admission into a blind asylum, in which he had been residing
for some years past. In giving an account of what he had learnt there, he
mentioned the power of distinguishing colours by the touch, and begged
those present to try him. I made him feel my dress, a French merino, and
he replied, ' I should say this is a reddish-brown,' which it was. The next
given him was one of the Rob-Roy tartan ; he said, ' This is a material of
two colours, red and black.' Another person made him feel her blue gauze
veil. ' This is blue, but a very thin dress for the time of the year,' was the
reply. The only other trial to which he was put was a printed cotton, which
he pronounced to be of various colours. Being asked how he attained this
power, he replied, ' A piece of cloth was given me, and its colour named,
which I felt till quite familiar with it ; then another, which I continued to
examine until I could correctly distinguish one from the other ; and so on
until I knew all the colours,' and as it seemed to us, even shades of some.
The darkest colours appeared to him to have most body in them. He said it
required a very sensitive touch, and great patience and perseverance, and
that consequently very few attain the power " (Bull, pp. 54, 55).

† M. Rodenbach relates that, while at the Musée des Aveugles in Paris,
M. Fournier and he, in order to develop their sense of touch, procured some
pumice-stone, with which they rubbed the index-finger, taking care to wear
on the finger a covering of fine leather (*un doigtier de peau*). In the *Annual
Report of the Boston Institution for* 1842 (p. 20), it is said that "an old blind

Other examples of tactile sensibility in the blind to which we may briefly refer are the power possessed by Dr. Saunderson and Madame Paradis of distinguishing false from genuine Roman medals, which connoisseurs with eyes were unable to do ; and the still more astonishing circumstance related of Dr. Moyse, who with his fingers measured the length of a stroke, which was invisible to the eye, made by an etching tool on a plate of steel. Even in the case of the seeing, minute inequalities of surface not cognisable by vision may be discerned by the touch. When the movement of the fingers is called into play, in the recognition of the forms of objects, such as the larger plants, animals, and shells,—still more in ascertaining the dimensions and shapes of rooms, &c.,—the muscular sense aids the merely tactile perceptions.

" The world of the blind," says Mr. Prescott, " is circumscribed by the little circle which they can span with their own arms. All beyond has for them no real existence " (*Essays*, p. 47). This remark is by no means true even of the blind who are confined to touch for their knowledge of the outer world. It is still less so of those who can hear also, as we shall show when we come to speak of the sense of hearing. Blind guides, like Metcalf and Simon Moyser,* and indeed all those who are able

---

soldier, in order to render the hardened skin of his fingers capable of perceiving characters in relief, applied blisters to them on several occasions." The following passage from M. Dufau's *Souvenirs d'une Aveugle-née* may be added : " Every substance likely to injure the delicate susceptibility of the epidermis was withdrawn from my habitual contact; and my hands even were usually covered with a fine and supple skin-glove, which preserved their tactile envelope without hindering free movement. This expedient took the place with me of the glasses worn by those who wish to take precautions against the loss or enfeeblement of their sight. Had not nature, in fact, in my case placed my eyes at my finger-ends? " (p. 19).

* " Simon Moyser, who was born among the Alps of Tyrol, lost his sight at two years of age: he devoted himself to so patient an exploration of the surrounding mountain-tops, that he was soon capable of directing thither the steps of all those who visited them. Carried away by a sort of passion for travelling, he pushed his excursions further and further, betook himself to Gratz, and became a messenger, carrying letters and money in these mountainous countries, in which scarcely any other method of communication is

without eyes to find their own way from place to place, must, it is
obvious, have some perception of objects lying beyond the "little
circle which they can span with their own arms." The currents
of air as they meet the face report with exactitude the direction,
the proximity, the size, and the character of the objects which
partially intercept and modify them, enabling the blind traveller
to recognise, as he passes them, houses, trees, hedgerows, gates,
posts, bridges, and other objects to be avoided or approached.
Dr. Bull, who became blind in mature life, states that this faculty
developed itself in him after his blindness to a degree which
astonished himself, though far inferior to that in which it exists
in those born blind.

"Sight and hearing," says Mr. Morell, "have been termed
by some the *objective*, by others the *theoretic*, senses. These
names are merely employed to designate the fact, that they
stand more closely connected than others do with the intellectual powers ; that they fix the mind's attention more directly
upon the *object* affecting them ; and that they make us less sensible than the rest of the corporeal affection apart from the
objective cause." * The associated feelings of touch and movement have surely an equal claim to be ranked among the theoretic and objective sensations. By their means alone, as the
cases of Saunderson, of Moyse, and of Gough† prove, the entire
circle of studies which are included in a knowledge of the external
universe may be mastered. The mathematical and physico-
mathematical sciences, chemistry, and natural history in its various
branches, were respectively cultivated by these philosophers, the

possible. In 1818, when he was thirty-three years of age, he perished in a
torrent in which several seeing persons had lost their lives before him"
(Dufau, p. 97).

* *Elements of Psychology*, part i. p. 112.

† We do not refer to the still more distinguished names of Euler and Huber,
because the former, who lost his sight when he was fifty-nine years of age,
no doubt made use of the conceptions derived from sight in his subsequent
mathematical investigations ; and because the latter, who became blind at
seventeen, availed himself of the eyes of others in his studies of bees, directing
their observations, and forming his own conclusions from their reports, and
did not employ any of his remaining senses.

first of whom lost his sight before he was a year old, and the two last when they were only three years of age. None of them retained the slightest memory of ever having seen, or any conception derived from sight. It is impossible for us to realise the world in which they lived—a world consisting of harder or softer, rougher or smoother impressions on the skin, and of more or less resistance offered to the muscles. The degree in which the impressions of any sense can be made to serve the purposes of intelligence and knowledge depends on the facility and distinctness with which it is possible to revive the idea of them in the absence of the object which first occasioned them. This it is easy to do in the case of sight—" our eyes see visions when they are shut ; " easy also in the case of sounds, though not so easy,—

> " Music, when soft voices die,
> Vibrates in the memory ;"

almost impossible to most persons with regard to muscular or tactile feelings. The idea of an absent weight or touch does not generally body itself forth as a living reality to the imagination, hanging a load on the muscles, or exciting a tingling in the finger-ends. Yet it must do so in the case of the blind, or comparison, the clear discernment of resemblances and differences, and the knowledge which depends upon it, would be impossible. "If," says Diderot, "the memory [of tactile sensations] is very transient in us, if we can scarcely form an idea of the manner in which the man born blind fixes, recalls, and combines the sensations of touch, it is in consequence of our habit, adopted from the eyes, of realising everything in our imagination by means of colours. It has nevertheless happened to myself, in the agitation of violent passion, to experience a *frissonnement* all over my hand, to feel the impression of bodies which I had touched a long time since revive as vividly as if they had been still present to my grasp, and to perceive very distinctly that the limits of the sensation coincided precisely with those of the absent bodies." "We cannot," he says again, "make the blind man understand how the imagination presents absent objects to us as if they were present ; but we may very well recognise in ourselves the faculty of feeling at the end of a finger a body which is no longer there. For this purpose, press the index-finger against the thumb ; close your eyes ; separate your fingers ; examine immediately after this separation what passes within you, and tell me if the sensation does not last some time after the compression has ceased." We have only to suppose this power of recalling a perished, and perpetuating a present sensation of touch, indefinitely extended by cultivation and brought into dependence upon the will, in order to realise the physical conceptions of the blind.

The success of the blind as geometers sufficiently disproves Mr. Johns's preposterous assertion, that they have no idea whatever of space ; and even the more qualified doctrine of Sir William Hamilton, that sight is necessary to the prompt and precise perception of the relations of extension, magnitude, and figure. To enter upon this question, however, would involve a discussion of one of the most controverted points of mental philosophy : we will only say, that the confusion which has arisen from unskilful questioning of the blind, and from the difficulty which they naturally experience in translating ideas derived from one sense into the language of another, has been the cause of a mistake of which the theoretic refutation may be found in many treatises on psychology, and to which the labours of Saunderson afford a practical answer like that with which the cynic controverted the proof of the impossibility of motion. Cases of the restoration of the blind to sight are interesting in connection with many controverted points of the theory of vision, but do not fall within the limits of our present subject.

We have seen that the scientific acquirements of the blind are gained principally by touch. To the peculiar conditions under which this sense operates, some of the peculiarities of their intellectual character may be traced. The prevailing *analytic* tendency of their minds, and the slowness, caution, and accuracy of their procedure, are thus explained by M. Dufau :

" In fact, their means of arriving at a knowledge of objects, if more certain, are also, it is evident, less prompt and rapid than our own ;

only by observing objects with care, by studying them part by part, in short, by analysing them, can they attain to a knowledge of them. To convince oneself of the justice of this distinction, we need only compare the mode in which the blind and the seeing acquire their knowledge of any object; for example, of a plant. The former casts a glance upon it, embraces it as a whole, envelops it with a look, and his task is done; he has a general idea of it, with which he usually contents himself, because it is sufficient to enable him to recognise and to name the object. The blind man, on the contrary, is obliged to examine, to touch with the utmost care, the stalk, the branches, the leaves; to acquire, in short, a complete and detailed idea of the plant, without which it would be impossible for him to distinguish it from others. Thus it is that necessity makes analysis a habit to him, which retards his acquisition of knowledge, but at the same time renders it more positive and more certain."[*]

We come now to the sense of hearing; to which principally, though not exclusively, the blind owe their conception of objects which lie beyond the " narrow circle which they can span with their own arms."

" Dr. Saunderson, by the reverberation of his tread, could judge with wonderful accuracy as to the character of objects from five to twenty yards' distance. Thus he was enabled to distinguish a tree from a post at the distance of five yards, a fence from a house at fifteen or twenty yards. The sound of his footfall in a room enabled him to judge of the dimensions and character of the apartment. Having once crossed a threshold, so distinct was his individualisation of every locality, that he would at once know it again, even after the lapse of many years."[†]

Dr. Moyse had the same faculty. "A person," says Dr. Kitto, "who knew him relates, that whenever he entered a room he remained for some time silent. The sound directed his judgment as to the dimensions of the room, and the different voices and number of persons in it. His distinctions in these respects were very accurate; and his memory so retentive, that he was seldom mistaken."[‡]

" A young blind man told me one day," says M. Dufau, "that in his walks . . . he at once perceived a wall, a hedge, a

---

* Dufau, p. 43.   † Bull, p. 208.   ‡ Kitto, p. 209.

mountain, any obstacle, in short, which might be before him. 'When I find myself in a vast plain,' he added, raising his hand to his ear, with a very expressive gesture, 'it seems to me that I am *à perte d'ouïe.*' This remarkable expression, imitated from our *à perte de vue* in an analogous situation, enlightened me much as to the importance of this sense to the blind." * By means of a light cry, or a gentle tap with the foot, at the entrance of an apartment, the blind are able to tell whether anyone is present in it or not, its extent, the nature of, and any alteration in, the furniture.† "There is now living in the city of York," says Mr. Johns, "a gentleman of fortune, who, though totally blind, is an expert archer ; so expert," says our informant (who knows him well), "that out of twenty shots with the long-bow, he was far my superior. His sense of hearing was so keen, that when a boy behind the target rang a bell, the blind archer knew precisely how to aim the shaft." ‡ Diderot tells a tale of the blind man of Puisaux, who, in anger at one of his brothers, occasioned by some boyish dispute, threw a stone at him with such exact aim, that it struck him in the middle of the forehead, and levelled him with the ground.§

As a practical guide through the dark ways of their life, hearing is more valuable to the blind than touch, though inferior to it as an instrument of scientific research. It is, perhaps, most important to them as the basis of their judgments in regard to character. Their personal prepossessions and prejudices are founded on the tones and cadences of the voice, and are at least not oftener unjust than those which we derive from the general appearance and physiognomy of men. Their judgment of the physical characteristics of a speaker, his age, height, health, &c., are wonderfully exact. "The blind easily recognise hump-backed people " (as M. Rodenbach, himself blind, avers) " by the sound of their voices. He relates that at a *soirée* in Brussels, a blind man succeeded in stating with precision, according to their

---

* Dufau, p. 71.   † Ibid.   ‡ Johns, p. 103.
§ Diderot, p. 136.

voices, the ages of all the persons present. His only *mistakes* were with regard to some ladies, who were not displeased at his inexactitude." * The ability which the blind possess of recognising a voice once heard after an interval of years, in spite of attempted disguise, is as well attested as any of their peculiar powers.

As a medium of social intercourse, hearing is to the blind much what it is to the seeing ; or rather, it is more to the blind than it is to us, since they seek in the tones of the voice that commentary on the bare meaning of the words which we find in the play of features and gesture. But it is most important as being the sole inlet of emotion which they possess. Feelings of solemnity and awe, of grief and joy, of physical pleasure and pain, can only be conveyed to them through the modulation of sound. This is one reason, no doubt, of their passionate attachment to music. Notwithstanding the ingenious distinction of a German philosopher, who, with some show of truth, characterises "sight as the clearest, and hearing as the deepest of the senses," the one appealing to intellectual conviction, the other penetrating to the heart, and more deeply stirring the entire nature,—it is a fact, that the understanding of the blind is far better developed than their emotional nature. They excel in science ; but no blind man has ever attained eminence in poetry.† Blind Harry, Dr. Blacklock, Miss Frances Brown, among English writers, and one or two French and Italian authors mentioned by M. Dufau, exhaust the list of the blind-born who have cultivated poetry; but they do not rise above the level of smooth and agreeable versifiers. What is remarkable in them is, that their writings abound in attempted descriptions of visual scenery, made up, often very ingeniously, and with a clever avoidance of the errors to which we should suppose them liable, of epithets and phrases, derived from the works of those who saw, but unmeaning to them. Poetry is in their case strictly,

---

* Dufau, p. 69.

† Poets have become blind, as Milton; but this is very different from a blind man becoming a poet.

as Aristotle called it, an imitative art. The metaphysical poetry, so popular in our day, which paints human emotions and dwells on the inner life of the soul,—to which we should suppose them, from their introspective, meditative, and self-centred turn of mind, particularly prone,—is quite remote from the spirit of their verse. As little does the "beauty born of murmuring sound" find any echo or expression there. No such effects (we speak of kind, and not of degree) as Tennyson's bugle-song can be quoted from any blind poet. And yet there is not a line, and only a phrase, in it which the blind man is not as competent as the seeing, or even more competent, vividly to realise :

> " Blow, bugle, blow, set the wild echoes flying;
> Blow, bugle, answer echoes dying, dying, dying.
> O hark, O hear! how thin and clear,
>   And thinner, clearer, farther going!
> O sweet and far, from cliff and scar
>   The horns of elfland faintly blowing.
> Blow, let us hear, the purple glens replying;
> Blow, bugle, answer echoes dying, dying, dying."

The phrase "purple glens" is the only one in these exquisite lines which would be unintelligible to the blind ; and yet it is the only one which reminds us of the "poetry" which they are in the habit of writing. "Azure distances," "yellow corn," "dewy greens," &c., are the stock images of blind versifiers. It would appear as if, on the one hand, the merely sensuous feelings (which respond to music), and, on the other, the purely intellectual apprehensions, existed in their full force in the blind, but that the emotions in which thought and feeling blend were but feebly present to them. The dislike (which is said to show itself in many ways among them) of appearing different from the seeing, no doubt leads them to parody the description of "coloured nature" which they find in ordinary works. There is also some kind of mysterious attraction to them, perhaps, in realities from the knowledge of which they are excluded.

It is not necessary to say anything of the remaining senses, *smell* and *taste*. They do not often present any peculiarities in the merely blind ; though the former of them is often marvellously developed in blind and deaf mutes, especially, it would appear, when the reason is somewhat weakened. It seems then to acquire something of the fineness and discrimination which it has in the lower animal races. In speaking of the special senses, we have somewhat anticipated the subject of the intellectual qualities which the absence of sight seems to foster. A remarkable power of concentrated attention, natural in those whose minds are not solicited by the attractions of the multifarious objects of vision, is the fundamental quality of their understanding. To this may be attributed the strength of memory for which as a class they are celebrated. Attention and memory are the two constituents of the faculty of comparison, or the discernment of resemblances and differences, on which all knowledge depends. We have already, in quoting from M. Dufau, shown how the successive apprehension of the several properties and parts of a complete object, alone possible to the sense of touch, favours habits of abstraction and analysis. These are just the qualities needful for success in science, and just the qualities fatal to poetry and imagination, which deal not with constituent elements, but with concrete and living wholes, and which have their source with the intuitive rather than the discursive faculties of the mind.

Of the moral qualities which generally accompany blindness it is less easy to speak with decision. Diderot attributes to them a deficiency in modesty, and also in compassionate feeling. His reasons for the latter deficiency are worth giving :

"Since of all the exterior demonstrations which arouse in us commiseration and the idea of pain, the blind are affected only by the cry of grief, I suspect them, as a general rule, of inhumanity. . . . . Do not we ourselves cease to feel compassion when the distance or the smallness of objects produces in us the same effects that the privation of sight does in the blind? so much do our virtues depend on the mode of our sensations, and on the degree in which exterior things affect us. I have no doubt, therefore, that, except for the fear of chastisement, many people would have less pain in killing a man at a distance, which made him appear no larger than a swallow, than they would have in cutting the throat of an ox with their own hands. If we have compassion for a suffering horse, and if we crush an ant without any scruple, is it not the same principle which sways us?"

To this (rather by way of compliment than of accusation) he adds an insinuation of irreligion.

Dr. Guillié expresses himself much to the same effect. He echoes Diderot's charge of want of modesty on the part of the blind ; decides that they are very imperfectly acquainted with the emotions which draw us one to another, and decide our affections and attachments ; and though he acquits them of atheism, is unable "altogether to justify them from the reproach of impiety, which, with some foundation, has been urged against them. . . . Conscience, in short," he sums up by saying, "has not the influence over their actions which it has over ours. . . . The moral world does not exist for the blind ; . . . . he acts as if he alone existed, he refers everything to himself. . . . Their situation, which compels them to keep on their guard against all mankind, often leads them to rank in the same category their benefactors and their enemies, and, perhaps without intending it, to show themselves ungrateful." Immodesty, inhumanity, selfishness, irreligion, and ingratitude, are the attributes which Dr. Guillié assigns to those whom he elsewhere calls " his poor adopted children " (*ces infortunés, mes enfants adoptifs*). His authority is deservedly so high on every point connected with the blind, that we are glad to find his testimony on this matter contradicted by an observer entitled to even greater deference—M. Dufau, who strenuously combats the injurious estimates of his predecessor in the Institution at Paris. The reserved, self-contained nature of the blind ; their undemonstrative character ; their aversion to mere sentimental effusion ; and want of attention on the observers' part to the very different way in which the same feelings will express themselves in the blind and in the seeing,— have led, according to M. Dufau, to the errors of Diderot and Dr. Guillié. With regard to the first charge against them, the sense of modesty " passe chez eux de la vue à l'ouïe. . . . Cette chasteté

E

d'oreille exclut en général de leur langage les paroles légères et
les équivoques sans décence ; il en resulte aussi que des traits qui
ne sont que gais pour nous dans quelqu'uns de nos meilleurs
écrivains, dans nos anciens comiques, par exemple, deviennent
inconvenans pour eux ; si leur âme est pure, ils n'en rient pas, et
restent parfois déconcertés et mal à l'aise " (p. 20). M. Rodenbach, himself a very distinguished blind man,* pronounces that
three-fourths of the blind men whom he has known have felt
more strongly than others the need of religious consolations, and
have been remarkably alive to religious feeling. The accusations
of inhumanity and ingratitude are rebutted by M. Dufau, and the
mistake, which has led to their being preferred, pointed out.
There is probably this amount of foundation for the charges of
Diderot and Dr. Guillié, that the suspicion and timidity which
M. Dufau acknowledges to belong very frequently to the blind,
and which may be referred to the sense of disadvantage under
which they labour in regard to the seeing, do, *so far as they alone
operate*, tend to produce the defects which have been too absolutely
laid to their charge. And further, an isolated self-centred life is
unfavourable to the development of the social qualities. Free
expression of feeling is needful to the vitality and freshness of
feeling. As regards religion, though the logical argument exists

---

* " Alexander Rodenbach, born at Roulers (West Flanders) in 1786, lost
his sight when he was eleven years of age. He entered the *Musée des Aveugles*,
then under the direction of Haüy, and soon became one of his most distinguished
pupils. On returning home he gave himself up to profound inquiries into
different questions of public interest, which he afterwards discussed in several
publications, which attracted to him the attention of his fellow-citizens. A
lively opposition to the tendencies impressed on the country by the House of
Nassau was formed. M. Rodenbach joined the ranks of the periodical press,
in order to give his support to this opposition, and became one of the most
active promoters of the revolution from which the Belgian nationality sprang.
He was elected a member of Congress in 1830, and has ever since continued
to sit in the Chamber of Representatives, where he has distinguished himself
on several occasions by the soundness of his views as well as by an animated
and ready style of elocution. M. Rodenbach has been elected burgomaster
of the commune where he lives, near Roulers. He is member of several
academies, Knight of the Order of St. Leopold, and has been decorated with
the Iron Cross " (Dufau, *Des Aveugles*, pp. xxiii. xxiv.).

in all its force for the blind, the appeal to wonder and awe made by " the two infinities," as Pascal calls them, that surround us, and which are revealed by the telescope and the microscope, is silent for those without " eyes to see." Moreover, the prevailingly *intellectual* character of the blind presents religion to them rather on its dogmatic than on its emotional side. The same circumstance leads them to base their affections on judgment and calm preference rather than on an impulse. So far from " conscience having less effect on their actions than it has on ours," a profound sense of justice and equity is remarked by M. Dufau as a strikingly prominent feature of their characters.

Our exhausted space warns us to bring these remarks to a close. We have freely used the materials presented in the works named at the head of this article, always, we hope, with adequate acknowledgment. We shall be glad if what has been said tends in any way to awaken philanthropic and scientific interest in the condition of that large class (calculated at nearly a million over the entire earth) who journey through this world, like Virgil's travellers " through Pluto's empty mansions and shadowy kingdoms,"

> " Obscuri sola sub nocte per umbram
>
> .   .   .   .   .   .
>
> Qualem per incertam lunam sub luce maligna
> Est iter in sylvis, ubi cœlum condidit umbrâ
> Juppiter, et rebus nox abstulit atra colorem."

LONDON:
PRINTED BY WILLIAM CLOWES AND SONS, Limited,
STAMFORD STREET AND CHARING CROSS.

A GUIDE

TO THE PROPER

MANAGEMENT AND EDUCATION

OF

BLIND CHILDREN

DURING THEIR EARLIER YEARS

(Whether in their own family, in public schools, or under private teachers)

By J. G. KNIE

Director of the School for the Blind at Breslau, Member of the Silesian Society for National Improvement, and to whom was awarded the Medal of Merit, given by the Grand Duke at Weimar

TRANSLATED BY

THE REV. WILLIAM TAYLOR

S C.L., F.R.S., F.R.A.S., M.R.I., Hon. Mem. R.S.S.A., Hon. Mem. R.S.S., Paris, &c.

Who has added an Introduction and an Appendix

NEW EDITION

———

" Wie süss, wie schön ist es sie abzuwischen
Die Zähre, die des Dulder's Aug enstürzt "

KLEIN

———

LONDON : SIMPKIN, MARSHALL & CO
WORCESTER : DEIGHTON & SON, 53, HIGH STREET
PRINTERS AND PUBLISHERS
1851

LONDON
SAMPSON LOW, MARSTON & COMPANY
LIMITED
St. Dunstan's House
FETTER LANE, FLEET STREET, E.C.
1894

A GUIDE

TO THE PROPER

MANAGEMENT AND EDUCATION

OF

BLIND CHILDREN

DURING THEIR EARLIER YEARS

(*Whether in their own family, in public schools, or under private teachers*)

By J. G. KNIE

Director of the School for the Blind at Breslau, Member of the Silesian Society for National Improvement, and to whom was awarded the Medal of Merit, given by the Grand Duke at Weimar

TRANSLATED BY

THE REV. WILLIAM TAYLOR

S.C.L., F.R.S., F.R.A.S., M.R.I., Hon. Mem. R.S.S.A., Hon. Mem. R.S.S., Paris, &c.

Who has added an Introduction and an Appendix

NEW EDITION

———

" Wie süss, wie schön ist es sie abzuwischen
Die Zähre, die des Dulder's Aug enstürzt "

KLEIN

———

LONDON: SIMPKIN, MARSHALL & CO
WORCESTER: DEIGHTON & SON, 53, HIGH STREET
PRINTERS AND PUBLISHERS
1851

LONDON
SAMPSON LOW, MARSTON & COMPANY
LIMITED
St. Dunstan's House
FETTER LANE, FLEET STREET, E.C.
1894

NOTICE.

As I have, for more than forty years, paid particular attention to the education and general treatment of the Blind, and, during that time visited many of the principal Blind Schools in Europe, I have had opportunity of examining their systems and management, and of ascertaining their practical results; and I am bound, in candour, to acknowledge that, in some respects, they are superior to most of the Institutions of a similar kind in England. On this subject many very valuable works have been published, both in French and German, but, I am sorry to say, that nothing of a practical nature has yet appeared in English (except a translation of Dr. Guillie's very useful book, "ESSAI SUR L'INSTRUCTION DES AVEUGLES"). This induced me to undertake the following Translation, which might have been more ably done by many others; but, as they have not done it, I thought it better to do it, even imperfectly, than that information so valuable and useful should not be made available in this country. The work is a little abridged, and some parts slightly altered to accord with our customs. And should this humble attempt to discharge a duty to the Blind (by publishing, in English, KNIE'S useful little work) induce others, more qualified, to take up their cause, I shall feel that I have not laboured in vain; and I trust that the importance of the subject may, in some degree, atone for the imperfect manner in which it is now brought before the British public.

W. T.

1861.

TRANSLATOR'S INTRODUCTION.

" So lang der Blinde mit und unter Sehende lebt, muss man suchen, ihn in
" seinem eigenen, Benehmen, und in der Behandlung, so viel es nur möglich
" its, den Sehenden näher zu bringen, um ihm manchen Anstoss und manche
" schmerzhafte Erinnerung an seinen Zustand zu ersparen."

KLEIN.

The human race seems to have been subject to Blindness at all
times and in all countries. The enthroned Monarch is no more
exempt from it than the humblest of his subjects, for it spares
neither age, sex, nor condition. To-day we gaze with delight
upon the beauties of nature—to-morrow we may be deprived of
that pleasure, and doomed to perpetual darkness,—even " amidst
the blaze of noon."

What pen can describe the pang that rends a father's heart,
when first he finds his child is blind ? Who can tell the feelings
with which a tender mother presses to her heaving breast her
sightless offspring ? She may weep o'er her babe, but her tears
are not regarded—she may smile upon it, but her smile is not
returned—her fond attempts to attract its notice fail ! 'Tis then
the sting with greatest force is felt !

The Blind may be divided into two classes—those who were
born blind, and those who have become blind after having seen.
Very few are *born blind,* but numbers lose their sight in the early
stages of their existence. Soon after birth infants are liable to
inflammation of the eyes, and, formerly, many of those cases
terminated in partial or total blindness, but, since the introduction
of Vaccination and the improved mode of treatment, as well as to
the increased facility with which the poorer classes can obtain
Medical assistance, the cases of loss of sight have been greatly
diminished. Still, in this country, upwards of 30,000 Blind
persons were registered in the last Census ! Of this number no
inconsiderable portion will, of course, be found amongst the
wealthier classes ; but as they seldom move about, except in
carriages, or under the guidance of friends, they are not so readily
recognized as those who are led by a dog, or have to grope their
way by help of a stick. This has given rise to the idea that very
few blind are to be found among the rich. Doubtless the larger
proportion occurs among the poor, as they are more exposed to
accidents in factories, &c., and can less afford to seek the aid of
the Oculist, than those in better circumstances.

When parents are unfortunate enough to have a blind child
they seldom know what to do with it. The first impression is

B 2

that it will never be able to do anything for itself, but will be a burden to them as long as it lives, and greatly mar their future happiness. When this case occurs to *poor* parents, who are, perhaps, engaged all day in the fields, or other employment from home, and cannot attend to their sightless offspring, it is often left, confined in a chair, throwing its legs and arms about, making grimaces, and acquiring habits which it will be difficult to eradicate, and which tend to give strangers an unfavourable opinion of its state of intellect. Whereas, if it were properly treated, and, when old enough, sent to any common school, it would improve in manner, and gather much information ; its mental faculties would have some chance of developing themselves, and it would be better prepared to receive further instruction. When the case happens to *rich* parents, *they*, likewise, are at a loss to know how to proceed with their little blind charge. The same dread of its being burthensome to them and a draw-back upon their happiness occurs to *them*, as it does to the poor ; and, indeed, with greater force ; since, for the *indigent* blind, there are many schools, where they may be taught to earn much, if not the whole, of their own livelihood ; whilst for those in the *wealthier* classes, there is, in this country, unfortunately, no place where they can receive an education, suitable to their station in life, and experienced Tutors of the Blind are seldom to be procured. No wonder, then, that parents—whether rich or poor—who have blind children, should, at first, be a little cast down at the prospect before them. But it is the object of the following pages to enliven those prospects, and to console and cheer such parents, by furnishing them with a few plain instructions to guide them in the treatment of their blind children, at least during the first years of their life. It would be well for those parents to visit Schools for the Blind, and see what is there done by the pupils. And if they would read the accounts of some of the numerous blind persons who have arrived at the highest eminence in science and literature, and have been not only a credit to themselves, but a comfort to their friends, and valuable members of society (see Appendix), it would afford them great consolation, and encourage them to regard, with resignation and composure, their little blind charge, and to watch, with affectionate interest, the development of its mental and bodily powers. And should it, hereafter, eminently distinguish itself, as so many have done, how sweet would, then, be the reward for all their parental care and anxiety ! This little work is not merely a statement of theoretical speculations, but the result of long experience and close observation. KNIE (the Author), who is himself blind, is highly educated, and has been Director of the Institution for the Blind, at Breslau, since the year 1821. His School is so admirably and advantageously conducted, that it is looked upon as a *model* School for the country round it, even to the distance of many leagues, and is greatly patronized by the neighbouring Powers.

Till within about seventy or eighty years, the blind were thought to be incapable of acquiring any great degree of useful knowledge ; now, however, experience has shewn that there is scarcely any branch of education beyond their reach. All Blind persons—except idiots—may be taught enough to lessen their affliction, if not to make them useful and happy. And by help of embossed printing, and the many ingenious contrivances used in teaching the Blind, the difference, between them and their seeing brethren, is now reduced almost to a minimum.

The Blind, as well as others, have an undoubted claim to be educated, but the amount of their education must depend upon many things. Formerly it was thought they could be taught only in schools for the blind, where proper tools and teachers are provided for them, but, now the subject is better understood, they may be partially, if not entirely, educated in their own family circle.

Many people, when they are in company where there is a Blind person, often keep aloof from him, not from any want of kindly feeling, but merely from not knowing how to address him. They would do well to talk to him, just as if he had his sight,—not ask him if he has *heard* such and such a book read, &c., as that would remind him of his misfortune, and give him pain ; but say, " Have you *read* such and such a book ? Have you *seen* Mr. B— to-day ?" and such like. This mode of addressing him gives him the comfortable feeling that there is nothing, so very peculiar, about him as to remind them that he is blind. In short, " Treat him, as far as possible, in the same manner as you would those possessing sight." Zöllner says (" *Unterhaltung ueber die Erde*," &c., Band v., S. 576), " I have never yet known a Blind person who had been respectably brought up, and tolerably educated, whose character was not amiable, and in whose society I did not feel pleasure."—KNIE is a good classical scholar and tolerable mathematician, and has translated into his own language (German) several works from the Latin, French, Italian, &c. A young man in London (Fred. Clark) has, with his own hand, and his own press, printed, in relief and in the common Roman letter, a Latin Dictionary, for the use of the Blind ; but, unfortunately, only seven copies were struck off, so that the work must be very scarce, and may be looked upon as a literary curiosity. He has since gone to America, where he hopes to obtain employment in giving lessons in Mathematics, even up to the Differential Calculus ! Such a case has not occurred, in this country, since the time of Saunderson, who, though Blind, was Professor of Mathematics in the University of Cambridge, and recommended to that office by Sir I. Newton.

It is to be regretted that there is, in the English language, no *practical* treatise on the education and general management of the Blind, except a translation of Dr. Guillie's admirable work, "*Essai sur l'Instruction des Aveugles.*" This circumstance will contribute much towards rendering KNIE'S book acceptable, as containing, in a small space, much valuable information, which cannot fail to be highly useful to those who have the care of Blind children, and who may never have seen *how* or *what* they are taught, in the various schools for the Blind, or what they are capable of learning. Tracts, containing information of this kind, are distributed, gratis, in Prussia, Austria, &c., and greatly tend to rescue many a sightless sufferer from a life of indolence and misery, and to relieve the parents from the painful feeling that their Blind child must be a burden to them through life.

Jäger says ("*Ueber die Behandlung, welche blinden und taubstummen Kindern, hauptsaechlich bis zu ihrem achten Lebensjahre, in Kreise ihrer Familien an ihren Wohnorten ueberhaupt zu theile werden sollte*"), "No greater benefit can be done to a Blind child than to accustom him, as soon as possible, to do everything he can for himself ; and first of all to move alone, from one place to another."

Much has been said about the loss of one sense being compensated for by the improvement of the remaining ones. No doubt, where *four* senses have to do the duty of *five*, they must be more frequently called into action, and thus improved, or rendered more acute, by practice. A Blind man (Jacob Birrer) was asked if he thought, when one sense was lost, that the others were proportionately strengthened ? To which he answered, "If there are five pipes conveying water from a fountain, and you stop one of them, will the water flow any more readily through the other four ? "

There is a very common notion that the Blind can "*feel* colours.*" No doubt they can tell the difference between a basket twig that is not coloured and one that is, where the colouring matter has caused the surface to feel more or less rough. Also, some colours render cloth more harsh to the touch than others, and sometimes have a peculiar smell, and the Blind make great use of their olfactories in distinguishing one thing from another. But if you give them glass, feathers, petals of flowers, &c., they can tell nothing about the colour of them. Spread a silk handkerchief upon the table, and let them put their hands upon it, and ask them if it is of *one* colour or of *many* ? If they say "many," ask what they are, and request them to trace, with the finger, the boundary of each (which they can easily do, *if they can distinguish one colour from another, by the touch*), and you will soon discover that "feeling colours" is altogether a fallacy. Their hands have been placed in coloured water, but in no case did they tell what the colour was. Care must be taken, in these experiments, to bandage well their eyes, for, if they have the least glimmer of sight, they can distinguish *colours*, though not *forms*. They will sometimes undertake to tell colours by the touch, even in a dark room, where there can be no colour. I mention this because there are disreputable Blind persons who, for the sake of obtaining money, endeavour to impose upon the unsuspecting by pretending to distinguish colours by the touch. Some years ago, a girl undertook to tell the colour of bits of silk, cloth, &c., when put into a bottle, she only feeling the outside of it. And, strange to say, there were persons who paid their own power of investigation so ill a compliment as to believe it!! A clever Blind young man, at Zurich, when asked if he could feel colours, answered, "No!— it is impossible for a Blind person to *feel colours*. The colouring matter sometimes makes the surface of the thing coloured more or less rough, and *that* we can feel, but more than one colour may produce the same degree of roughness."

Those who are interested in the treatment and education of the Blind will do well to consult the various works mentioned in the Appendix, as they afford every information relating to this subject, especially the "*Lehrbuch zum Unterrichte der Blinden*," by Klein, of Vienna, whose penetration, sound judgment, and fifty years' experience must give great weight to his opinion.

In pursuing this subject, I now come to a case which cannot fail to touch every feeling heart, and excite the compassion of every humane mind—I mean the case, which not unfrequently occurs, of a child being born, or becoming, not only *Blind*, but also *Deaf*, and, consequently, *Dumb*—there being no case recorded (as far as I know) of congenital deafness being unaccompanied by the consequent want of speech.—Reader, I ask you to pause and contemplate so lamentable a case. A human being doomed to drag out his existence in perpetual darkness and perpetual silence, never to see an approving smile—never to hear a consoling word! But, even in this extreme case, there is a ray of comfort for the afflicted parents. For by the embossed printing, the various and ingenious contrivances for facilitating the education of the Blind, and the improved methods of instruction, even these unfortunates are often taught to read, write, to do work of various kinds, and, apparently, to feel comfortable, if not happy! Let those who have children, blessed with all their senses, consider this, and be thankful.

It is much more difficult, in these cases, for parents to know what to do, or how to ascertain the best mode of treating such helpless objects. Many persons are acquainted with the case of Laura Bridgeman, Deaf and Dumb, and Blind, who has long been under the care of that talented and excellent friend to the sightless, Dr. Howe, at Boston, U.S. She has, through his skilful management and judicious instruction, acquired so much information, on various subjects, as to astonish all who have seen her. Other cases of this kind occur at Philadelphia, Bruges, Lausanne, Stuttgart, &c., and also in Great Britain. The one at Bruges is a female, in the Institution which the judicious and indefatigable Abbé Carton directs, with so much credit to himself and benefit to the pupils. In a very few months she learned to knit, even fancy knitting, and was able to distinguish the letters of the alphabet embossed on paper or card. When I saw her she appeared very happy, and always seemed pleased when the Abbé took hold of her hand. The sense of *touch* may be said to be the only inlet through which information or instruction can be conveyed to beings so unfortunately circumstanced. How desirable, then, is it so to cultivate that sense, as to make it a means of communicating such information to these afflicted objects, as may, in some degree at least, associate them with their seeing brethren!

Much has been said and done (in this country chiefly, for it is very little patronized on the Continent or in America) respecting *Arbitrary* Alphabets in embossing books for the use of the Blind. Unfortunately we have, in Great Britain, several such alphabets in use in different Institutions, and the advocates of one system oppose those of others, with a hostility which is neither complimentary to their judgment nor to their benevolence. For whatever tends (as all arbitrary alphabets do when used as a means of education) to separate the Blind from the seeing, in their social intercourse with them, must, of necessity, be hostile to their best interests, because it lessens their opportunities of obtaining assistance from others. Fancy a fellow creature enshrouded in perpetual darkness, deaf to every sound, and unable to give utterance either to his feelings or his wants, and then say whether he should be taught the common alphabet, known to all, or an arbitrary character, known only to a very few? This point I may safely leave to any unprejudiced person. The Blind should be EDUCATED *by means of the alphabet in common use with those who see*, and afterwards they may, for amusement or information, learn any alphabet invented for them. As opinion should always give way to fact, take the case of one blind and deaf and dumb. How can information be conveyed to him except through the sense of touch? If he has been taught the common alphabet, any one, by writing with the finger upon his hand or back, may communicate some cheerful sentence to relieve the monotony of his gloomy existence, but, if he has been taught only an *arbitrary* character, no one, who has not learnt it, can communicate with him; and as he may probably, after leaving the school, never meet with any one who understands his system, he is, therefore, deprived of that advantage which a knowledge of the common alphabet would afford him. This is a cruelty we have no moral right to inflict.

In the report of the Jurors at the Great Exhibition, vol. ii., page 918, is the following :—" *Mr. Friedlander repeats the* UNANSWERABLE *arguments against the adoption of arbitrary characters and stenographic or phonetic systems, and strongly recommends the use of our own alphabet.*"

PREFATORY REMARKS,

BY THE AUTHOR.

As I have written no particular Preface, I feel it necessary here to remark that the following (fourth) edition of this work (as well as the first and second) is printed at the cost of the Prussian Authorities, and that is the reason why it has not appeared in the shops of the booksellers.

In drawing up several of the sections of this fourth edition, especially that relating to music, I have thankfully availed myself of the very valuable remarks of my friends, Ernest Koblitz and Albert Kienel.

J. K.

Note—the words between [   ] and the foot-notes are by the Translator.

Some passages, on account of their importance, occur twice, such as the articles mentioned in page 28, which are nearly repeated in page 40; but the one is in Knie's work and the other in the Appendix.

A GUIDE

MANAGEMENT AND INSTRUCTION

OF

BLIND CHILDREN.

Section I.

THE erroneous idea which many, who have their sight, entertain, that children who are born blind, or who have lost their sight at a very early age, are incapable of receiving instruction, has frequently occasioned either the most culpable neglect or the most absurd treatment of such unfortunate children, and when they are afterwards received into Schools for the Blind, sometimes presents, to the teachers, greater difficulties than even the blindness itself, and not unfrequently prevents the accomplishment of the object in view, or, at least, renders it painfully tedious. Hence, about the year 1830, the Silesian Association for Instructing the Blind, felt it their duty, to the parents and teachers of blind children, to print and distribute, gratis, throughout Silesia, a short Guide, or instructions, for the use of such as might have the management or education of those sightless unfortunates. The happy results of this step have clearly shown themselves in the progress made in learning, by such pupils, when afterwards received into our Institutions for the Blind; whereas, on the other hand, many Blind children, whose parents had no knowledge of these Instructions, were found in the most deplorable state of ignorance when brought to the schools, even at seventeen or eighteen years of age. In 1837 a member of the Prussian Government caused, at his own cost, a new and enlarged edition to be distributed, gratis, through the Prussian provinces. In 1839 a third edition was published and distributed, at the cost of the State. But, as the parents and relations of Blind children, for whose benefit they are intended, belong, for the most part, to the humbler classes, and therefore seldom read such things, it is particularly requested that all who have it in their power—especially the clergy—in places where there are Blind children, will not only call the attention of those who have the care of them to these instructions, but also endeavour to explain and enforce them in such manner as to render them as serviceable as possible in promoting the welfare of a class of our fellow creatures who have so large a claim upon the sympathy and assistance of their more fortunate brethren.

Section II.—The Treatment of Infants.

THE mind of a child is capable, at a very early period of its life, of receiving impressions and forming ideas of external objects through the sense of vision. Even in the mother's arms it soon distinguishes her smile, and gives expressions of joy or dislike at the things it *sees*. But very few of these operations of the mind evince themselves in a blind child, the parents of which look in vain for it to smile upon them, or shew any desire to take hold of things presented to it. [Oh ! who can tell the pang which rends the father's heart on discovering that his child is blind ? Who can describe the feelings with which the fond mother presses to her heaving bosom her sightless offspring ? or who can conceive a yearning parent's anxieties for its future welfare ?] In bringing up blind children the remaining senses should be most carefully cultivated, in order to compensate, as far as possible, for the one which they have not ; and this can now, through the help of the many ingenious contrivances for facilitating the education of the Blind, be done to a great extent by the sense of touch, which, in things that can be handled, will go far to supply the loss of sight. The Blind must *handle* objects, in order to acquire a knowledge of their form, &c., and for this purpose the *ends* of the fingers serve best. The *colours* of various substances can be known by the *sight alone*. Therefore the parents of blind children, in order to prevent their faculties or mind remaining inactive, should especially attend to the senses of *touch* and *hearing*, and put into the hands of their children all such things as they may handle and examine without danger. Things differing in form and quality should be constantly given and exchanged, one for the other, and the characteristic differences pointed out. At one time give them *rough* things, at another *smooth, angled, round, hard, soft, &c.* For example, wood, fruit, cloth, money, children's playthings, especially bells, rattles, drums, trumpets, &c., afterwards models of animals, machines and such like. At the same time they should be conversed with and instructed in a mild and kind manner. Children who have their sight perceive the love of their parents in their looks and gestures—the Blind become sensible of it from the tone of the voice, but not in lamentation over their misfortune. It is a cruel sympathy for the Blind, who do not know the extent of their deprivation, to be constantly reminding them of it by useless expressions of pity and compassion. Furthermore, it is advisable to sing to them, and when an instrument can be had, to play to them some simple, soft, and pleasing melody ; for thereby the *ear* is formed and a taste for music awakened in the child before it can utter a note or musical sound. In this manner the organs of speech and the power of thinking will be as readily developed in a blind child as in one who can see.

Section III.—Treatment after the first Year or two.

Now comes the rule to be observed, THAT BLIND CHILDREN SHOULD BE TREATED, AS FAR AS POSSIBLE, IN THE SAME WAY AS THOSE WHO HAVE THEIR SIGHT,—except in some few particulars peculiar to their situation.

They should be taught to understand and name the different parts of the body and limbs, and the uses of them. To this knowledge of themselves should be added that of the furniture in the room, &c. They must not be allowed to pass their time in sitting still or being idle, for thereby they lose the opportunity of acquiring any knowledge of the objects around them, or of learning to move cleverly and cautiously from place to place. It is a mistaken kindness to carry blind children about, more than those who have their sight, or to guide them farther or beyond what is necessary ; for when they come to walk or play, and expect direction or assistance from others (no one, perhaps, being present), they may injure themselves or the things around them. To be constantly inactive is injurious both to their mind and body.

Section IV.—Learning to walk, &c.

BLIND children learn to walk as soon as those who see, but it is necessary, at first, to guide them a little more, and shew them how high to lift their feet, &c., for they often get a habit either of lifting them very high or scarcely lifting them at all. Attention should also be paid to their turning out their toes properly, for which purpose it will be well, every day, to make them stand awhile in the proper position, as soldiers do at drill. Furthermore, it is necessary to accustom them, in going about, to hold one hand (the left generally) across before their breast, in order to guard them against danger from open doors, &c., the other feeling below for such things as tables, chairs, &c. The body should be erect and the head well up, in no wise to lean forward, as is often the case with the *neglected* Blind, who, at first, from timidity, frequently confine their movements to turning round in nearly the same spot. They should, therefore, be taught to go about the room and examine such of the furniture, &c., as may be in it, and left *as much as possible to shift for themselves.* Place them in one part of the room and direct them to make their way to some other, endeavouring to guard *themselves* against injury from such things as may arrest their progress. This will teach them caution. When the child has become acquainted with the room he generally inhabits, take him, by degrees, to other parts of the house, and even to the garden or neighbouring places, and let him endeavour to find his way back to the place he had left, and with as little assistance as possible. With very young children it is best, in teaching them to go about, first to lead them by the hand; afterwards, let them take hold of one end of a *stick*, the teacher holding the other—this tends to increase their confidence. Then do the same by a *string*, which, from its flexibility, is not so good a guide as the stick, and consequently teaches them to depend more upon themselves. Next let them try to follow the teacher about by listening to the sound of his feet, and then they will soon be able to move carefully without any assistance. Going up and down stairs requires particular attention. He should be directed not to change his feet upon the same step, but to place the moving foot upon the next step, and to hold fast by the rail or banister. It is not good—except for very young children—to give signals to guide them, because they would feel the want of them when they went to strange places, where none would be given. By moving about *slowly* at first they acquire confidence, and thereby the sooner become able to go more quickly, according to the old proverb, "Eile mit weile,"—"Hasten slowly."—If in difficulty or doubt, when they are walking, the safest way is to set the toe down first, and then the heel, making good each step before taking another. In the same cautious manner he should be taught, as he gets older, to find his way to the house of some neighbour, to some field, &c., and then it will be well for him to carry in his hand a light switch or walking stick, with which to feel his way and prevent his falling into a pit or ditch; or going against anything that may hurt him, or over which he might stumble. When a blind person is taken to places or roads, with which he is *not well* acquainted, let him take hold of the guide's arm,—not the guide his—keeping a quarter of a step, as it were, behind him. He will thus feel the motion of his leader, and should be taught to "keep step with him." In crossing water by narrow bridges or planks, the guide should go first, holding him by one hand, directing him to examine, with his stick, the breadth of the bridge as he proceeds, always keeping his stick touching one side, and he will thus pass over safely. (This and the following rules apply also to those who have become blind in later life, who, through timidity, are often more helpless than those who were born blind.)

When a blind person attempts to sit down, he should first feel the seat with his hand, not only to ascertain its true position, but, also, to discover if anything be upon it, which he should carefully remove, and then sit slowly down. When he bows or stoops down, it is best first to draw back one foot a little, in order to stand firm, and then place one hand before his chin to prevent his coming in contact with a table, the back of a chair, &c., which he may not be aware of. By practice and observation a blind person will be able, by the impulse of the air upon his face, &c., or by the difference in the sound of his feet, to ascertain when he approaches any person, or thing as large as, or larger than himself, and even to form some idea of its size.

Section V.—*The Use of the Hands and Sense of Touch.*

THE *hands* of a blind person must, in numerous cases, serve him for *eyes*, therefore a *skilful use of them* is of the greatest importance. Should this be neglected in early years it is often impossible to *acquire* it afterwards. The hands which have long been unaccustomed to do anything become weak and soft, the bones thin, and the fingers so loose, as it were, that they might in some cases be turned back to touch the wrist, because the flexor muscles have never been called into strong action. Such neglected children are not only unfit for *hand work*, or mechanical operations, but also, from not being accustomed to make any good use of the sense of touch, are scarcely capable of applying it to feeling embossed maps, to reading from raised letters, &c., without very great labour and patience on the part of the teacher. And this difficulty is often increased by the neglected state of the *mind*, which is, generally, in such children, equal to that of the *body*, although they may possess first-rate abilities, which, for want of development, lie useless. It is, therefore, highly necessary that blind children should, from their earliest years, be well accustomed to the use of their hands and of their powers of observation. For this purpose let them have all sorts of toys, &c., and think not that the Blind have no pleasure in such things, because they do not *see* them. In this way they first learn the use of their hands, and by dressing and undressing dolls, girls learn to dress and undress themselves, and to understand the different parts of their dress. Let them have an opportunity of feeling different sorts of fruits, vegetables, &c., and as they are changed, one for another, the difference pointed out, such as their shape, hardness or softness, weight, roughness, or smoothness, taste, smell, &c. Such things, in a dry state, should be kept in little boxes, where they can often be referred to. Amongst these should be several things of the same *form* but differing in *material*, others of the same *material* but differing in *form*. Such a collection should contain something of all sorts—balls and dice, of glass, ivory, wood, metal, &c.—wire of various kinds and sizes ; things made of horn, leather, pasteboard, &c.—seeds of plants, flowers (such as will dry), pieces of wood of different kinds. Cloth of silk, linen, cotton, woollen, &c. Feathers, hair, fur, bristles, scales of fishes, when not too small ; cord, buttons, hooks, bits of iron, brass, lead, tin, copper, zinc, &c., rough and polished ; also coins of various kinds. The child should be taught to select some of these according to their *form*, others according to their *material*, and that may be done by way of amusement. Something relating to their use, substance, construction, &c., should, at the same time, be stated by the teacher, and afterwards required of the pupil.

When children show an enquiring mind, they should in no way be checked, but, on the contrary, encouraged by the teacher to ask numerous questions, although he may sometimes be under the necessity of giving for answer, " I, myself, do not exactly know." Should he be detected in pretending to know things, which he really does not, or in giving evasive answers to conceal his ignorance, he will lose the confidence of his blind pupil. The child must be well practised in counting from 1 to 100, forwards and backwards (let not this latter be neglected), and in the multiplication table ; also in mental arithmetic, which is a most valuable exercise for the mind. He should be taught to measure the length, breadth, and depth of various things ; and till he can use a rule with notches or pins to mark the divisions, a string with knots of different sizes, half-an-inch or an inch apart, may be employed. Also he should be taught the weight of things, and the use of scales, steelyards, &c. He would learn that things of the same weight and form might differ in size, on account of the nature of the substance of which they are made, &c. As scales and weights can be found in almost every house, it will not be necessary to shew how they may be explained (when not at hand) by a stick, balanced in the middle, between the thumb and finger, &c. The thickness and strength of string, thread, &c., should not be omitted. Models, of houses, churches, mills, carriages, ships, &c., and of other things too large to be examined by the hand ; also of ferocious animals, venomous reptiles, &c., should be plentifully supplied. By frequent and close examination of these things, his touch will become more certain in its indications, and his fingers acquire that strength and activity, which to him are indispensable. It is desirable to preserve the ends of the fingers as much as possible from injury, as they are to supply, as far as may be, the place of eyes. That the Blind can distinguish colours by the touch is altogether an erroneous idea. Colour is the effect of the rays of light, and therefore not perceivable by the touch. In the dark there is no colour. Certain things may be distinguished by the Blind, according to the colour, when the colouring matter has altered the nature of the surface or texture of the thing coloured ; but for this distinction they are indebted to the roughness, smoothness, harshness, &c., caused by the pigment, and not to the reflected rays of light. Thus the Blind easily deceive themselves by taking that for colour which is really not so.

Section VI.—*Use of the Taste and Smell.*

NOT only the sense of touch, or feeling by the finger end, is to be practised by the Blind, but also the senses of Taste and Smell, so that they may be able, not merely to say this or that thing tastes sweet or sour, salt or bitter ; and that others smell agreeably or unpleasantly, are fragrant or pungent ; but should be able so far to distinguish things, as to say, at once, this is sugar, vinegar, lemon, wine, beer, honey, sulphur, tobacco, snuff, soap, wax, tallow, cheese, &c. Further, their attention should be directed to the *taste* of different metals, such as gold, silver, copper, tin, &c., and to such things as clay, which, when unburnt, will adhere to the tongue, and when breathed upon, emit a faint odour, &c.

Section VII.—*The use of the Sense of Hearing.*

THE sense of Hearing, in the Blind, must be *particularly* cultivated. Not every blind child has so much discernment as, of itself, to distinguish the sounds of different things, such as that of a knife, money, wood, stone, &c., when it falls to the ground, but he will soon learn to distinguish the value of different pieces of money by the sound. The sound of things sliding upon, or rubbing against others, also the buzzing of various insects, the noises of domestic and other animals, birds, etc., should be noticed. The possession of a singing bird is generally interesting and amusing to the Blind, and not altogether useless. There is a sprightliness in the singing of a bird which cheers them. Attention should be directed to the noise made by the *movement* of animals, persons, &c., and that it is different in small and large rooms. The size of any room may be well judged of, by speaking in it, also its height, length, and breadth, and whether furnished or not. Also the distance of a speaker, by the sound of the voice.—This can be practised by removing to different distances from the speaker, &c. A well-educated ear will enable the Blind, not only to guess the height of a person who speaks to him, but to form some—not unfrequently, correct—idea of his character. As the *countenance* is the " mirror of the mind," to those who see, so is the *voice* to the Blind. But far different from the cultivation of the ear, for general purposes, is that training of it for *music*, since the talent or taste for that art is not possessed in the same degree by all. Playing or singing to Blind children simple airs, as was before stated, will best suit for the beginning, but for the further development of that talent, methodical and regular musical instruction will be necessary.

Section VIII.—*On Dressing and Undressing, Feeding themselves, &c.*

THE blind child should be taught, as soon as possible, to dress and undress himself, to button, tie knots of various kinds, both fast and slip, or loop knots, and if this be well practised daily, for about a quarter of an hour or so, it will soon prove to be no waste of time, as some unthinking parents suppose, who for years together, through mistaken kindness, dress and undress their blind children, instead of teaching them to do it for themselves, and then complain that God has laid upon them so heavy an affliction, while the fault, in *this particular*, at least, is their own, and the remedy within their power. The clothing, especially of the girls, should be made in the plainest and simplest manner, so that nothing should be tied or fastened on the *back*, as that greatly increases the difficulty of putting them on and off without assistance, and hooks or buttons should be used rather than pins. The folding of neckcloths, pocket-handkerchiefs, aprons, and other linen may be first taught by practising upon paper. The clothes, when taken off, should always be carefully laid one upon another, so that they may be readily found when they are again to be put on. *In these and all other operations, the greatest order should be strongly inculcated*, for that which is desirable in all, is doubly necessary and beneficial for the Blind. Even so should the child be taught to feed himself with a spoon, then with a fork, and, lastly, with a knife, in addition ; and to observe the greatest cleanliness possible. First a deep plate or dish should be used, which must be held by the edge in the left hand, or rather the hand laid upon the flat edge, to prevent the contents being pushed off it by the spoon, fork, or knife, which he must hold in the right hand. And when the plate is nearly empty, it must, by the left hand, be raised a little on one side, and the fragments gathered together with the spoon or fork in the right, so as to be more easily found and taken up. Clever children can easily be taught to use dexterously the spoon, fork, and knife. It is much to be recommended that a small plate or saucer be placed near, on which bones, stones of fruit, &c., may be put, as it is not easy for the Blind to avoid taking them up a second time, when left upon the same plate ; nor can they easily, as the seeing do, place them round the edge of their plate. The Blind may be readily taught to help themselves to such drinkables as are *cold*, for as they pour them into a glass, they will feel the cold increase upwards as the glass fills : moreover, the weight and sound of the liquor, as it gets nearer to the top, will assist much, if attended to. The Blind should be taught to serve themselves, as much as possible, *in everything*. In many of these necessary manipulations they will often receive assistance from those around them, and when any one, who has his sight, is about to teach the Blind, he would often derive considerable advantage by first trying the experiment with his own eyes shut.

Section IX.—*The use of the Memory and of the Intellect.*

THE exercise of the memory should be neglected in no child, but especially in the *Blind*, for *they* cannot, like those who see, have recourse to books, or written memorandums to assist them. Also, a naturally weak memory can, by practice, become tolerably strong, retentive and exact. In order to accomplish this end in the Blind, the memory must be gradually and accurately led on, from things well known, to things unknown, else that evil—a dislike to learning—will arise, especially in the young. It is also necessary that they be taught the right use and meaning of words ; for, if children acquire a bad pronunciation, or wrong meaning of a word, it will not easily be corrected. Interesting anecdotes, and well-selected poetry, may be constantly read or related to them, with great advantage, but what is called " nonsense " should be avoided. Something new should be taught every day, and some of the former day's lessons repeated. More extended repetitions should be made weekly, and, perhaps, monthly. The proverb that " Repetition is the mother of knowledge," used to be considered a golden rule ; and a *quick* memory can become a *retentive* and *true* one, only by repetition.

In beginning to exercise the memory, the teacher should choose short and easily understood sentences, which may be made to operate beneficially upon the heart and mind, and may be illustrated by fit examples and simple narratives. Verses or sentences out of the Bible, or Prayer Book, may be selected ; also fables, parables, histories, &c., especially such as are in rhyme, as they are more easily fixed in the memory. Preference should be given to such passages as inculcate trust in the providence of God, contentment under His dispensations, the advantages of virtuous conduct, and a stedfast hope in a better life after this. These should be impressed upon the memory by frequent repetition. It is doubly important that the Blind should have their minds well stored with religious maxims and subjects, as they have not the same advantage of referring to books as they have who see, and therefore need it the more. Ballads and epic poems are generally interesting and instructive. For the understanding of more refined language, the best plan is to read to the pupils short narratives and descriptions, only from point to point, they repeating each portion read, till the whole shall have been gone through, then read the whole again, without interruption. Avoid setting before the Blind things which, on account of their age, or state, would be beyond their comprehension, and let all explanations be clear and understood, lest a wrong impression be formed. It is by no means necessary to guard against such subjects or expressions as may relate immediately to their loss of sight ; on the contrary, it is better to use such as they occur, without any

c 2

remark. Blind persons, who have been well-accustomed to the use of their other senses, acquire thereby such a knowledge of things in general,—colours excepted,—that they are as able to converse upon them as those who have their sight.

The Blind, even those who are born so, very commonly, in their conversation, use the verb to "see," such as "I saw Mr. M., I have seen a cocoa nut, &c.," and call different colours by their names, which they have learnt by their intercourse with those who have their sight. Therefore it is best to speak to them of colours as you would to others, especially the colours of common things, that they may have less difficulty in conversing about them with those who see. In this way the child's memory will not only be much strengthened, but also well stored with a fund of various branches of knowledge, which will lead his reflecting mind and fertile imagination to higher things, and develope the powers of his understanding. Should he shew an inquisitive mind or a desire for knowledge, check it not, but carefully encourage it. Should he evince little or no such desire, then try, by easy questions, to awaken his attention and reflection. Ask him to describe, in his own way, any thing that he is well acquainted with, or describe something to him and let him say what the thing is, which you are describing, &c. Easy riddles, puzzles, and such things, are good practice ; and asking his *unreserved* opinion on various subjects and occurrences, with which he is familiar, will lead to some knowledge of his moral tendencies—a point of no small importance.

Section X.—Attending School, and School Instruction.

A LARGE portion of what has been said applies not only to a *home education*, but also to *school instruction ;* for a blind child, after it has arrived at six or eight years of age, can attend any common elementary school, for those who have their sight, with considerable benefit, if the teacher will only make proper allowance for the disadvantage under which his pupil labours. Indeed, seeing children might, on such opportunities, be taught some good moral lessons, if the teacher will call their attention to the misfortune of their blind companion, and the various means employed for relieving it. Every little friendly attention they show to him— whether it be by assisting him in his lesson, or by contributing to his amusement, in the hours of recreation—will exercise some of the best feelings of their nature, and make so strong an impression upon their minds that, in after life, they will, probably, look back upon it with satisfaction and delight.

If we go further into the different branches of school routine we shall find that the blind child will be quite as capable of learning mental arithmetic, and spelling, when it is orally taught, as any of his seeing schoolfellows. The form of the figures and letters is easily learnt by books which are embossed for the use of the Blind, and when the letters are not too large, they will be readily distinguished by a single touch of the finger. If no such books are at hand, the letters may be written, the wrong way (that is towards the left hand), and of moderate size, upon a sheet of thick paper, then let them be closely punctured, through the paper, with a pin or needle, and they will form letters, raised on the other side, so as to be readily legible by the touch. A third method of *writing*, for the Blind to read, by feel, is this :—Put into some gum water as much powdered chalk or magnesia, or lamp-black, as it will bear, without being too thick to flow. Dip a pen into this and write, as with ink—it may be made black by the addition of ink. If it be not sufficiently raised, at first, to be read by the touch, it may be gone over again as often as necessary, The blind child should have the fore-finger of the right hand directed over the letters, as if he were forming them, and he will thereby acquire a knowledge of their shape, &c. Letters may be made on separate bits of pasteboard, and a quantity of them put into different cells in a box. They may then be taken and placed in a frame with channels to fit them, to form words for learning to spell, &c. [Metal types, which are better for this purpose, may be had of Reed and Fox, type founders, London.] The advantage of such exercise, in improving the touch and fixing the attention, is greater than at first may be supposed.

For beginners in arithmetic the apparatus called the " Russian reckoning frame " will be found very serviceable, even for those who see, as well as the blind, and every teacher should be acquainted with its use. It may be procured at most toy shops. To use the frame or machine place it horizontally, so that the wires may lie with one end towards you ; then the beads (9 of which will be on each wire) on the right hand wire will represent the units, up to nine ; those on the second, represent the tens ; the third the hundreds ; the fourth the thousands, &c. Each wire being at least as long again as is necessary to hold the beads. Place all the beads at the farther ends, then bring down, on each wire, as many beads as will represent the number belonging to that wire, thus to represent 1861, bring down 1 on the right hand wire, 6 on the next, 8 on the third, and 1 on the fourth from the right hand ; when a cypher occurs, none are brought down, &c. With this machine, in the hands of a skilful teacher, amusement may be combined with instruction. Some use it with the wires placed horizontally, when the frame may be upright or lie flat : in that case the units will be on the upper wire, or the one farthest from you.

When anything is to be committed to memory, the Blind (if it be read to them) will equal, if not surpass those who see, in getting it off.

Religious Instruction.—The mind of a blind person is very readily impressed with a pious belief, and turns with gratitude to any one who will kindly unfold to him the truths of religion, to guide and console him in his dark passage through this life, and cheer him with the prospect of a better hereafter. If, in the school which he attends, the elements of Geometry should be taught, he will be able, by the touch, to comprehend, as well as those who have their sight, the forms of the various bodies presented to him, and the diagrams may be drawn on paper and punctured with a needle from the other side. Triangles, squares, &c., cut out of paper or pasteboard, will answer the purpose exceedingly well, or the paper may be laid upon something soft, as cloth, &c., and the figures drawn the reverse way with a stile or blunt point, which will raise them on the other side. Should there be instruction in Natural History, illustrated by the exhibition of natural products, he will be found fully capable of examining and understanding even the more delicate parts of plants, flowers, and living creatures, or stuffed specimens. Geography is also within the reach of the Blind, and will interest them much. Maps may be rendered available by puncturing the division lines, &c., as recommended for letters or geometrical figures. A large puncture for a city, finer ones for smaller towns, and a pressure with a blunt instrument for hills, &c. ; or some of this may be done with the thickened gum water. Rivers or roads may be traced with a blunt point as before mentioned. A dotting wheel, such as is generally supplied in cases of drawing instruments, run over the lines on the back of the paper, will beautifully emboss diagrams, letters, maps, &c.

History is a very proper, interesting, and well-adapted, subject for the Blind, as it serves to enrich the memory and the understanding, and requires no other help for the study of it than a close attention. Should the parents of the blind child be in circumstances to enable them, out of school hours, to give him a little private instruction, by way of preparation for the school, they will thereby find his progress in learning much facilitated and increased. Of course all this should, as far as possible, have respect to his great inlet for information—*the sense of touch.*

Arithmetic * forms an important branch of education for the Blind, and it may be taught—to any extent—by means of boards full of holes, into which little pegs are to be placed, to represent the figures. The holes and pegs are pentangular, in some ; square or octangular in others. Each peg has a small pointed projection at one end and two such projections at the other, and, as it can be placed, in the pentagonal holes, five different ways, with the one

---

* The plans here described for teaching Arithmetic are such as are in use in England, those described by Knie being more cumbrous and expensive, and not so fit for general use.

end up, and five with the other, every peg can thus be made to represent any one of the nine figures, and the cypher. These various boards may be seen and procured at most schools for the Blind, and can be better understood by inspection. Those with *octagonal* holes have square pegs, each of which can be placed in 16 distinct positions, consequently 16 different characters can be represented by them, enabling the pupil to perform operations in Algebra, involving not more than three unknown quantities. [These boards are made of gutta-percha, with type metal pegs, and may be had of Messrs. Pope and Son, 80, Edgware Road, London.] But it will always be desirable to practise the Blind in *mental* arithmetic, to some extent, before putting the board and pegs into their hands. One great object is to give to the Blind a clear notion of the mode pursued in teaching arithmetic to those who have their sight, and to explain fully to them the terms and expressions used in so doing. Arithmetic is an admirable exercise for the mind. Not less important is it, in some cases, to teach the Blind to *write*, in the common way, which is easily done with a black-lead-pencil between two raised lines, or, which is better, by laying a piece of black tracing paper upon the other and writing with a blunt point, by which means the letters will be formed on the white paper and remain permanent. Yet sometimes the Blind will not make much use of this acquirement, merely because they are not able to read what they have written. Stamps for making the aforesaid punctured letters are to be had at most of the Blind Schools in Germany, and at some in England. KNIE has contrived a convenient apparatus, of this kind, fitted up with the requisite letters, signs, &c., and it may be obtained at the School for the Blind, at Breslau, for 5 thalers—[about 15s. English].

For instruction in geography, the terrestrial globes of Dr. Zeune, of Berlin, are to be recommended. On these the land is represented higher than the water, and the hills still higher, so as to be very distinguishable by the touch. The same kind of globes, and also maps in the same embossed way, are to be had of Mr. Kummer, in Berlin, either with or without the addition of the names of places, &c. Lest the names should crowd these maps so as to render them difficult to make out, it is advisable to make a knot upon a piece of strong thread or string, and, with a needle pass it through the map, where any town may be, and on the back of the map, tie to the string a bit of card or parchment, with the name stamped upon it, in the punctured manner before named, so as to be legible by the touch. If only a *few* names are required on a large map, they may be pasted on the face near to the hole, and even when they are very numerous, if tied to the threads, the name wanted may be easily found, by placing the left hand on the face of the map, and the right hand under amongst the names. Then by drawing up the knot representing any town, the name attached to it on the back will readily be found, with the right hand, and may then be read.

Some knowledge of geometry is highly advantageous to blind persons, and should be taught in all cases, where it is practicable, not merely because it beneficially exercises and sharpens the mental faculties, but also because it furnishes the mind with useful information, supplies matter for contemplation, and is the best means of enabling the blind to understand descriptions of such bodies as may be either too large, or too small, to be examined by the touch.

The diagrams and figures in plain geometry may be made by drawing them on strong paper, and puncturing them through, from the back, in the same way as for letters, &c., or they may be drawn with the thickened gum-water before-mentioned. For solid geometry, as well as for spherical trigonometry, the author has contrived a collection of figures, &c., which suit equally for the blind and the seeing, and may be had for thirty thalers [about £4 10s. English]. But it should be particularly stated whether they are for the blind or those who see, as, when made for the latter only, the figures are not raised, or distinguishable by the touch, and therefore can only be used by such as have their sight. If, in the school, there should no instruction be given, in mechanical or natural knowledge, these things will serve for private education ; and, even with females, this sort of information should, by no means, be altogether neglected. In teaching history, &c., the names of places, dates, and such like may be impressed, (by the before-described stamps for letters,) either by the tutor or pupil, by way of exercise or repetition.

The Blind very readily acquire foreign languages, and the more they are taught the better,—provided they be well grounded in them,—as they can in after life become excellent teachers, not only of the Blind, but also of those who have their sight, and thereby earn a livelihood as tutors or governesses. Even so can they teach mental arithmetic, history, religion, and (by help of various ingenious contrivances) geography, geometry, mechanics, &c. One of the best Latin schools in Saxony is kept by a blind man, who is famed for well grounding his pupils in that language. Should there be a gymnasium (college) in the town, a clever blind person may visit or attend it, with advantage ; and if his friends are in circumstances to afford to let him have one or two boys who see (if of his own class the better), to read and write for him, he will benefit more than if he has only a tutor who could not spare much time to read to him, &c. For the wealthy blind, mental or intellectual acquirements are most suitable ; for the poor, mechanical operations. Music is desirable for both.

Section XI.—Instruction in Music.

BLINDNESS seems to produce, what might be termed, a natural delight in music ; yet it is not every blind person who has a natural talent for learning it. Those who have their sight often fail to accomplish it, but the blind, *in general*, very readily acquire considerable proficiency in that art, from which they derive so much pleasure. The best test or proof of musical talent, in a blind child, is the practice of singing, by which it will soon be ascertained, whether or not he has a voice, or at least an ear for music. First sing to the child (if he has not already of himself begun to sing) some single note within the compass of his voice, (or give the note from some instrument,) sustaining it, and at the same time endeavour to cause the child to imitate it : should he fail to do so, but yet produce some other note, then let the teacher take *that* note, and sustain it, till his pupil has correctly sung it several times in succession. After this, two notes may be sounded, one after the other, and the child required to say which is the higher or lower. In this practice the notes should always be near to each other, as 2nd, 3rd, 4th, &c. If two notes (which differ only a whole or a half-tone) be sounded in succession, and the child can readily say which is the higher, or which is the lower, there is good ground for supposing that he has some ear for music, and likely to make progress in it.

NOTE.—A musical ear, like most other senses, is capable of great improvement by judicious treatment. Pupils who at first could not distinguish between two notes, a third apart, have, afterwards, as experience has shewn, been able to judge to the eighth part of a note or tone. Care must be taken not to over-strain the voice by attempting, at first, to reach very high notes.

The following observations and advice respecting the names and effects of single tones, the various scales, chords, &c., must be as strictly observed by the Blind as by those who have their sight. The blind pupil should be first made acquainted with the notes, and different keys in music, and this can be easily done by help of the thickened gum water, &c., by which notes may be made so as to be readily distinguished by the touch.* The "time" also must be taught, and the value of crotchets, quavers, &c., thoroughly understood. In each exercise, before proceeding to another, the pupil must know, and at once be able to name, each note, its value, &c. Particular care should be taken to form the notes correctly. Sometimes it happens that the child may have no voice for singing and yet possess a good ear for music ; such children will readily distinguish between notes played or sung by others, or

* In Glasgow several music books are published in embossed notes, which answer far better than making the notes of thickened gum water, &c. Also a selection of embossed Psalm tunes, with a table of the musical characters, notes, &c. To be had of Marsh, York.

imitate them by whistling, and thus evince their turn for *instrumental* music. If you find that your pupil has an ear for music, endeavour to teach him to play on some instrument. First make him well acquainted with his instrument and its different parts, and then shew him how the different notes are produced upon it—repeat to him the scale, and explain how it relates to that particular instrument. Let him practice the scale in the different keys, and neglect nothing that may tend to ground him well in the theory. In choosing a music master seek one that is not merely a good musician, but one who has also some idea of *method*, in his teaching, and able and inclined to enter into full explanations, for he should remember that his blind pupil has a *mind*, as well as hands and ears, to be instructed.

In teaching the blind, tunes, pieces of music, &c., there are two methods employed, the one is to *read* the notes to them, giving their names, value, place upon the stave, &c., the other is to *play* the notes to them on an instrument. The former takes more time, therefore, the latter is more generally used, for they acquire thereby a knowledge of the tone as well as the name of the note, and also of the time. In long pieces it is best to take only a few bars at once, and when these are learnt, to go on to a few more, till the whole be gone through. A little patience will, in this way, accomplish much. Of course, at first, very easy things should be chosen, and played over, in portions, to the pupil, as often as is necessary, for him to remember them. Great speed in learning is not desirable, at first. And, that playing by ear may not become a mere mechanical operation, let the pupil, after he has acquired any portion, give, orally, some account of the "time," value of the notes, &c., or try to sing them, if his voice will admit of it. This should be particularly attended to, and, if the teacher be not afraid of a little trouble, he will find the effect very satisfactory, as the pupil will thus acquire such a knowledge of the piece as to enable him to sing it over, as it were, in his mind, and to retain it.

It is not uncommon for the blind to be defective in "time." This arises chiefly from their having the piece in their memory, on which account the notes occur to them more readily than if they had to read them from paper, and therefore they, imperceptibly, quicken in playing, as those who have their sight generally do, when they play what they have "learnt by heart." This fault must be especially guarded against, and a correct idea of time or measure taught as early as possible. Let them be accustomed to compare crotchets with quavers, semiquavers, &c., and where the instrument will admit of it, to play them together as bass and treble, &c., and thus commence the practice of harmony. The before-mentioned naming and singing the notes (sol-fa-ing,) in the mind, as it were, will, here, have good effect. Transposition, or change from one key to another, should by no means be neglected, when the pupil is sufficiently advanced to perform this necessary exercise. It gives a knowledge of the keys, scales, &c., and affords an agreeable and useful practice. Begin with transposing single scales and chords, and practise this till the pupil can easily play or sing any short examples. This will be the time to explain something of the relations and connections of chords, &c. In learning instrumental music, the pupil should, where it can be done, begin with the piano. The fixed tones or notes of this instrument operate beneficially in educating a musical ear. Playing in full harmony gives a taste and feeling for the relations and connections of chords, &c. The great compass of this instrument affords the pupil an opportunity of practising the strength and activity of his fingers. In short, the piano is the best instrument for making a complete musician. In learning other instruments the following observations should be attended to :—If, in addition to a good ear, the pupil should possess physical activity, he may learn the violin, violoncello, &c., the bowing and fingering of which instruments require considerable dexterity. Should he not be so endowed he may choose a wind instrument, of wood or brass ; but, in that case, he should have good lungs and well-formed lips. And in these instruments he must learn to "tongue" certain notes, and when to take breath, which is very important. The *quality* of the tone should be studied ; and the mode of holding the instrument, as well as the position of the body, should in no case be neglected, more especially with the Blind, who have not the advantage of studying attitude or position by observing it in others. To give them grace and elegance requires particular and peculiar attention, but it is important. Where it is possible, let the tutor play to the pupil the piece to be learned, upon the instrument he has chosen and devoted himself to. Execution cannot be expected till the mechanical difficulties of the instrument are overcome. Unmeaning passages and pieces should never be chosen for exercise, as they mislead the imagination, and injure the musical taste of the pupil. Classical compositions will at all times serve to warm and exalt the feelings, and give a turn for the sublime and beautiful. When several blind pupils are to be taught together, such pieces and exercises should be chosen as include little solos upon each one's particular voice or instrument, as solo playing or singing gives the pupil confidence, and an opportunity of showing his taste and skill by playing.

Teachers who use irregular or unscientific accompaniments, do unpardonable mischief to their pupils, for the rules in music to be observed by the seeing are equally applicable to those without sight. The Blind may become organists, tuners of pianos ; teachers of singing, and of such instruments as they themselves have learnt to play upon. Also, members of quadrille bands, chorus singers, glee singers, &c. Boys may learn various sorts of instruments, but girls seldom play upon anything except the piano, organ, harp, guitar, or concertina. For the *poor* blind, music is somewhat dangerous, if they have not, with it, been taught some trade, or had their minds well cultivated, as it often leads them into bad company, or to go about as beggars. Even as respectable glee singers they are exposed to the temptation of drinking and other moral digressions. On account of this tendency to encourage vagrancy and irregular modes of living, in the dissolute and idle, music should be taught only as an amusement, or as a help towards a maintenance, in situations and societies, where the morals of the blind will be least in danger. That a good musical education ennobles the mind, ameliorates the feelings of the heart, and, at the same time, conduces, in some cases, to bodily exertion, in others, to manual dexterity, cannot be denied. Therefore musical instruction is to the blind, as it were, a sort of connecting link or medium between his intellectual and his mechanical education.

Section XII.—Handicraft peculiarly adapted for the Blind.

Not only to themselves (as shewn in sections 3 to 8), but also to others, the blind can become highly useful. The girls (when young), in such things as winding yarn, fetching things for the use of the house, where this can be done without danger ; shelling peas and beans, paring potatoes and turnips, washing dishes, &c. When strong enough, they may make beds, and do other household work. The boys may fodder cattle, churn butter, pump water, &c. More opportunities of this kind occur in the country than in towns. Girls of delicate and feeble constitutions may plait straw, thread, whale-bone, hair, &c. ; spin, with spindle, and with the wheel ; knit with two or more needles ; also sewing may be done by them. Hesitate not to make blind boys (as you would the seeing) acquainted with knives, scissors, files, hammers, chisels ; and let them use them in making toys, &c.,—it will prepare them for using them afterwards in more important operations, as a means of subsistence. In most Institutions or Schools for the Blind the following branches have been carried to great extent, and have also been profitable :—Spinning, knitting in all its branches,— crochet work, making doileys, &c. ; netting of all kinds, in silk and other materials ; plaiting hair, ribbon weaving, making sash- line, list and leather shoes and boots ; straw plaiting, mats for dishes, ditto for the feet ; beehives, and mattresses of all kinds ; pasteboard boxes, of various sorts, basket work, from the coarsest to the finest kinds, in fancy patterns ; wood-turning, joinery, coopering, sawing, planing, &c. ; chairs bottomed with willows, reeds, cane, &c. ; brushes of various kinds ; whips, straps, twine, ropes ; clasps, hooks and eyes, wire covers for dishes, lattice, flower stands, file cutting, &c. Even more difficult work has been done by some clever blind persons, such as making clocks, musical instruments, cutting and polishing precious stones, carving in wood, &c. [In all these operations a leather finger-stall will be of great advantage if placed on one finger (usually the forefinger of the right hand) to protect it, and keep the touch as delicate as possible, for the purpose of feeling small things and reading embossed books.] Let teachers of the Blind remember that those who have their sight learn much from *seeing* their masters, or more clever companions, at work—this advantage the Blind are deprived of—everything must be *explained to them* in a peculiar manner. First shew them the article you are about to teach them to make in a complete state, together with the raw material ; explain the different parts of it, also the tools and manner of using them : then proceed, step by step, till you accomplish your object. This must be done by *guiding the hand* in every operation ; but the person guiding often holds it so fast that the Blind cannot perceive the effect he is producing either by his hand or the tool in it. This should be guarded against. Let the teacher (whether he has his sight or not) perform very slowly some work, and let the Blind lay his hand upon that of the teacher and examine and mark every movement of it, as well as of any instrument used in it, as he goes on, and he will soon be able to do the like himself. The instruction of the Blind in works of handicraft is at first difficult, and requires patience and thought, but the difficulty soon vanishes. In order to accomplish some of the before-named works, many peculiar plans have been devised, and many machines and implements contrived, which are in use in most schools for the Blind—others are done by the Blind in the same way as by the seeing. Basket makers, rope makers, &c., who have their sight, may, if they have heads and hearts in the right place, safely take blind boys as apprentices, if they have first been instructed in the elements of their trade in some blind school, as before directed. They would find them faithful and industrious labourers, and grateful pupils. This difficulty in teaching the blind ought by no means to deter persons from undertaking it, for, if they will only consider the importance of it, they will be encouraged to come forward in so good a work, not merely on account of any pecuniary advantage, but for the sake of the religious and moral influence which their precepts and instructions might have in promoting the future welfare of their sightless pupils. The Blind who have learnt a trade are thereby rendered the more cheerful, from a feeling that they can, in some degree, contribute to their own support ; are more reconciled to their fate, and more submissive to the will of God. The greatest act of charity you can do to needy blind children is to teach them a trade ; for by so doing you may save them from becoming common beggars, or a burthen to their friends. To " eat the labour of their own hands " is, to the

Blind, most gratifying and encouraging. You parents who have blind children, and suffer them, through neglect, to continue in idleness or fall into a state which may lead, perhaps, to beggary and immorality, forget not that you will have to give an account to God for a breach of duty to children who have a more than common claim upon your parental care and affection, which, if timely and properly applied, might prevent consequences deeply to be deplored. You who think that blind persons are incapable of learning to become useful members of society, read the accounts of remarkable blind persons, or visit schools for the blind, and you will soon see cause to change your opinion, and no longer remain in an error which must be injurious to your afflicted offspring. As an example of the mode of teaching here alluded to, take the threading of a needle. At first take a large bodkin, through the eye of which a small string will readily pass. Let the child take the string, with the end cut *short off*, and place it between the left thumb and forefinger, so that the end of the string may not come quite to the ends of his thumb and finger ; then let the child take with the right hand the bodkin, about a finger's breadth from the eye ; cause the eye to touch the thumb nail of the left hand (in order to ascertain its exact position) ; open a little the thumb and finger, between which the end of the string or thread is held ; press the eye of the bodkin between them against the end of the string, which will easily enter it ; open the thumb and finger a little more and thrust the string forwards, then close the thumb and finger of the left hand so as to hold the bodkin, while the string is drawn through, by the right thumb and finger. With very dull or unskilful children a wire may be at first used instead of a string, and a piece of wood or bone, with a somewhat larger hole bored through it. Instead of a bodkin they may put the string through large beads, buttons, &c. By degrees, with frequent trials, they may change the string for coarse thread, and the bodkin for a darning needle, and afterwards finer thread and needle as they become more expert. [Some thread needles No. 8 or 9, with the tongue !]

Knitting requires little apparatus and little room, and can be learned in any town or village. At first the child or pupil should use very strong needles somewhat pointed, and a thick flexible string or yarn. Let the teacher take two needles, and with them " cast on " 12 or 15 stitches and knit a few rounds, during which the blind girl should lay her hands upon those of the teacher and examine carefully, by feel, what she is doing and how she does it. Of course she must knit very slowly, and describe every part and movement as she proceeds, which the pupil should closely attend to. Then let the pupil try, holding one needle in each hand, and the thread over, and once round, the fore-finger of the right hand, and between the other fingers. The use of this will afterwards appear. Having done this let the pupil, with the left thumb-nail, separate from the rest the stitch nearest the end of the needle, or the last made, then slantingly, from the inside towards the outside, thrust the needle she has in her right hand through the stitch, and under the other needle ; now let her put the thread over the end of the needle (thus thrust through from the left towards the right), and draw the needle back, through the stitch, with the thread upon it, pointing it a little downwards to prevent the thread slipping off,—draw the stitch, which was first separated from the others, off the end of the left-hand needle, and a stitch is completed. This operation must be repeated for every stitch. By a little practice it will be easy to knit with four or five needles, and the most intricate work may be performed by the blind as well as by those who have their sight. Beads of various sorts may also be knitted in, with good effect, but they must be put upon the yarn before the knitting is begun. It is, perhaps, easier to knit with a sheath fastened to the waist, into which the near end of the needle with which the stitch is made is to be put, when three or more needles are to be used. Round knitting may then be taught without difficulty. Plaiting straw, &c., may also be taught by any one acquainted with the art.

Section XIII.—A few Games at which the Blind may play, and even join in them with the seeing.

Dice and Dominoes.—In these games the spots must be raised, by having small round-headed nails driven into the dice or dominoes, or the latter may be cut out of thick paste-board, and the dots punctured with a needle, which will raise a burr on the other side, easily distinguishable by the touch. Or, when very large, the dots or spots may be *sunk*, as in common cases, and yet be easily felt.

Draughts.—The draught board must have all the white squares raised about the twentieth of an inch. Half of the men have, in the middle, a little peg, which projects about a quarter of an inch ; the other half have holes in the middle, into which the pegs go, when "kings" are made, as, without the pegs, the upper one would be liable to be displaced by the blind, in feeling the state of the game.

Chess may be played on the same board ; but, for this purpose, each square must have a hole in the centre for the reception of a peg at the bottom of each piece. The white men or pieces are all pointed on the top, and the black ones rounded. The form in other respects may be according to taste.*

* There is, at present, a blind chess player who can play six games at once (that is, with six different players), without touching any board. He knows the situation of every piece upon each of the boards, so that, should either of the boards, in any part of the game, be accidentally upset, the pieces can all be again put into their proper places, under his direction.

Throwing the Ring.

Skittles or Nine Pins.—A favourite game with the Blind.

Cards.—A pack of cards must be prepared for the blind, in the following manner. With a *fine* needle, pierce them through from the back, thus : for the *suit*, the punctures must be in the middle of the top ; one for hearts, two for spades, three for clubs, and four for diamonds. For the *value*, the right hand corner, at the top, must be pierced with dots in the form that counters or coins are placed to reckon the tricks at whist. For an ace, one dot or puncture. For a duce, two placed horizontally. For a trey, three dots placed horizontally. For the four, four dots placed horizontally. For the five, two horizontal and one over them, forming a triangle. For the six, three horizontal dots and one over the middle one. For the seven, two horizontal and one under (the five reversed). For the eight, three horizontal dots, with one under the middle one (the six reversed). For the nine, four dots in the form of a square. Ten, four dots in the form of a lozenge. Knave, two dots placed perpendicularly. Queen, three perpendicular dots. King, four perpendicular dots. Thus :—

1	2	3	4	5	6	7	8	9	10	K	Q	Kg

Blind-man's Buff, Hide and Seek, Riding a Spring Horse, Swinging, &c. Riddles, Charades, &c., &c., &c.

Section XIV.—Particular views and observations relating to the Treatment and Education of the Blind, and to the care for their welfare.

BLIND children should be taught to be very particular in attending to everything which demeanour, custom, or modesty, requires or forbids. But, as loss of sight shuts them out from many advantages, and makes divers plain and simple things, at first, difficult to comprehend, they require more patience and attention, on the part of the teacher, than those who see. Therefore, teach them how to dress and undress themselves ; how to attend to their various wants ; how to address people and express their obligations ; how to behave, at Church, at table, in company, &c. For example—When they speak to any one, they should always turn their face towards him ; when they yawn or cough, always put a handkerchief, or at least the hand, before their mouth, &c. Further, it is highly necessary that the Blind be taught not to sit in a crooked posture ; not to move about awkwardly ; not to keep their bodies, nor any part thereof in constant unnecessary motion ; not to have their heads drawn down between their shoulders ; not to keep the mouth open, when attending to anything; not to make unseemly distortions of the features—not to thrust the finger into the eye-sockets,—a custom very common with the Blind. All these, and other bad habits, must be early attended to, and particularly guarded against—for it is misplaced indulgence, and false kindness, in parents to allow these things, as they tend to render their blind children, if not objects of ridicule to the thoughtless, at least less agreeable to their friends. Therefore let such habits be checked in the beginning, for it is much easier to prevent than to correct them. Since the Blind are deprived of such enjoyments as depend upon sight, it is not to be wondered at that they should, sometimes, have recourse to other and less desirable means of amusing themselves. Regular exercise and occupation are the most likely to prevent many disagreeable and perhaps injurious practices. Idleness (the beginning of most evils) will, if indulged in, produce and encourage habits which may affect their morals and mar their happiness. The Blind have less to distract their attention than others, consequently things take a deeper hold upon their minds, on which account it is doubly important to watch closely all their conduct, and guard against everything which may be hostile to good manners or to a virtuous course of life. They should be kept from all places where they would hear bad language, or bad sentiments, for their good memories will not only retain what they hear, but their lively and active imaginations will work upon it, so as, often, to endanger their principles. * * * * Many persons, with the kindest motive, but not aware of its effect, will express pity for the Blind in their hearing. This ought especially to be avoided, as it painfully reminds them of their misfortune. Those who have been born blind, or have lost their sight at a very early age, are ignorant of many of the pleasures and advantages which they are deprived of, by want of sight—therefore it is most desirable, in their presence, not to speak of their situation as *unfortunate*, not to commiserate, *aloud*, their affliction. Through such misplaced sympathy many blind persons are rendered dissatisfied with their lot, and become morose, who would, otherwise, be contented and happy. Those, who *see*, should never forget that blindness excludes very few *mental* enjoyments or advantages; it is nearly confined to exterior ones, therefore such expressions of pity should be avoided, as no one likes to be constantly reminded of that which he would gladly forget. Expressions of this kind betray want of thought, if not of feeling.

It is a painful thing, to the Blind, to be laughed at on account of any little mistake they may make through want of sight,—this the young feel more than the old, and are more injured by it, as it discourages them from asking for information, or expressing their sentiments, with that freedom which is so necessary to their comfort and advantage; no benevolent person will be guilty of it.

D

Great injury is often done by *undue and injudicious praise*, and by (what appears to the informed blind absurd) the wonder and astonishment, so frequently expressed by those who have their sight, at their accomplishing many little works which are, to them, not really difficult, and if done by the seeing would be considered merely as ordinary operations. Such praise does harm, for it gives the better informed blind the idea that those, who see, think meanly of them and their capabilities, by praising mere trifles. This injudicious praise more especially affects the *young* and inexperienced blind, and frequently induces them to fancy that they are unusually clever ; thus they become vain, and dissatisfied, if they are not lauded for every trifling operation they perform. The blind have much need of *patience and perseverance* to enable them to overcome the difficulties which, on account of their deprivation, beset them on every side. To both these they should be well accustomed from their early years ; and neither, in their lessons nor in their work, should they be allowed to go to any new thing, till they well understand that which they are then about ; therefore it is most desirable (at first, at least,) not to put them to do anything which they are not likely to accomplish, for to have to give up things, as above their skill, only serves to discourage them. Furthermore, they should be accustomed to govern their passions and inclinations, and not let the allurements of sin take too deep hold upon their minds. Contentment, discreet openness towards others, readiness to oblige, becoming modesty, and faithfulness to any trust reposed in them, should be constantly inculcated. The character of the blind is, generally speaking, amiable and cheerful, often marked by stedfastness, justice, a great desire for knowledge, and a love of truth. When it is otherwise, it not unfrequently arises from the cold, and sometimes unkind, treatment which they occasionally experience from unthinking, or unfeeling, persons, who have their sight.

Should there be some ground to hope that the blind child might hereafter, by an operation, or otherwise, be restored to sight, it will still be desirable to educate him as if there were no such hope. For should a cure not be effected, he will then be in a worse condition than other blind children, who had been regularly trained to encounter the difficulties connected with their situation. Even in case of a successful operation he will, for want of education, be more backward than other seeing children ; for that which has been neglected in early years can seldom, if ever, be made up afterwards. It is *generally* more difficult to educate one who is born blind, or who became so at a very early period, than one who loses his sight at the age of eight or ten, or perhaps later, and retains a clear recollection of what he had been accustomed to see : for his knowledge of external objects will enable him to understand many explanations and descriptions, which those who are born blind can but imperfectly comprehend. Most of the observations in the foregoing sections will be equally applicable to blind adults, in learning trades, &c.—The erroneous notion that the blind are incapable of acquiring useful knowledge, is the chief cause of their being so often neglected in their childhood and youth ; and yet the direct contrary is little less dangerous to their welfare. For some people suppose that the Blind, *in consequence* of their misfortune, are endowed with extraordinary capabilities, and vainly think that, if they are educated in some one branch only, such as music, for example, they must, necessarily, be able to attain perfection in any other. This has already misled many teachers of the blind, even in public Institutions, where one branch of education predominates, and induced them to attempt too much, with pupils of only moderate abilities. The fault here manifestly arises from not well considering what the talents of the pupil are equal to,—whether he is likely to arrive at eminence in any particular branch, so as to do credit to himself, or gain a livelihood thereby. Sometimes, in public schools attention is chiefly paid to the affluent, or to the highly gifted, while those of only moderate abilities, or the poor, are culpably neglected. This ought not to be the case, for it is not right to develope the extraordinary talents of one, at the expense of numbers, who are only moderately endowed. The former are likely to become conceited, the latter discouraged.

There are many Asylums in which the Blind are provided for, during their whole life, but it is impossible that such Institutions can receive all who are fit objects for them. The care for a blind child does not cease with his youth. His parents—unless they are amongst the wealthy—must always feel great anxiety lest, in case he should survive them, they should not be able so to provide for him, as to ensure to him a comfortable subsistence, or at least to keep him from want. Those who can afford it, would do well to purchase for him an Annuity, which, at a comparatively small outlay, would afford him a maintenance, and secure him from being burdensome to his friends. This, in the case of blind daughters, is most desirable, in addition to what they may enjoy from any little testamentary bequest, official salary, or the profits of manual labour.

APPENDIX.

Short Biographical Sketches of some remarkable persons who were born Blind, or became so in their early years, selected, chiefly, from Klein's " Lehrbuch."

Jacob Brown, born at Bruck, in Lower Austria, 1795, was the son of a carpenter, and lost his sight at three years old, by small pox. He was Klein's first pupil, and, in consequence of the progress he made in learning. the school at Vienna was founded in 1806. He learnt to read from raised letters, and to write, played the harp, acquired a good knowledge of geography, history, natural history, natural philosophy, and several other branches of education. He could knit, net, weave, make baskets, turn on the lathe, and was so expert a carpenter that he made tables, chairs, bed-teads, wardrobes, and other kinds of household furniture. He modelled animals and other things in wax (of a reduced size), and made himself a plate electrical machine, with which he amused himself. He arranged all his household affairs; sowed seeds in his garden, planted and grafted trees; gave instructions to other blind young men, in various occupations, and was so fully employed, all day, that time never hung heavy on his hands.

Corsepius, born at Passenheim, in E. Prussia, lost his sight when six years old, by the small pox. He modelled in wax, and made many machines, both in wood and metal.

Frederick Gottlieb Funk, of Nodau, in Switzerland, was born 1780, and, went quite blind at seven years old. He, without much assistance from others acquired sufficient knowledge, on various subjects, to enable him to become a teacher, not only of those who were blind, but also of those who had their sight. He contrived several methods and devised divers means of facilitating the education of the blind; amongst which were an arithmetic board, with holes, and pegs on the top of which the figures are worked in points, &c. Also, a writing-table, and a simple instrument for embossing letters, by which he could make all the Roman capitals on paper. He was a good musician, turned on the lathe, worked in wood and metals, in a way calculated to astonish those who saw him. For five years he was tutor to the children of a neighbouring clergyman, and in 1809 he was appointed a teacher in the blind school at Zurich, where his talents, patience, and industry, produced surprising effects upon his pupils. He may be looked upon as an example of what a blind man can effect, by his own perseverance and a little help from others.

Joseph Gattermeyer, born at Obritz, in Austria, in 1758, became blind in his third year. He foddered the cattle, drew water, cut wood, cleaned the house, and, for amusement, made children's waggons, bird-cages, &c. He worked in the field and vineyard, could thatch, hedge, make bricks, mend his shoes, and thread a needle. He made all the chairs, tables, &c., in his house; bought everything for his family, such as food, clothing, &c. Looked after the cellars of his brother, who was a wine and spirit merchant, and often acted as guide to strangers in the neighbourhood. He was a married man.

Francis Gregor, born blind, at Sternberg, in Moravia, in 1802, was a great proficient upon the harp, on which he played in public, when he was so young that it was necessary to set him and his harp upon a table, in order that he might be seen. He made great progress in different branches of knowledge, as well as in the theory and practice of music.

Blind Jacob,—his surname and time of birth not known,—was born at Netra, a Hessian village, and lost his sight, in the eighteenth month of his age, by the small pox. He acquired much knowledge in the village school when a boy, and, afterwards, endeavoured to compensate for his loss of sight by various simple contrivances, among which the following was one of his most important : He took staves of wood, about 30 inches long, and half-an-inch square, along these he cut, with a knife, certain marks or notches, which served him instead of letters or words. Each of these staves was thus notched, or written upon, as it were, on two sides, and recorded what he wished to remember, of what he had heard read or spoken. He cut these notches with great quickness, and from them he could read as from a book. All the staves which belonged to the same subject he tied together, forming, as it were, volumes, and distinguished them by certain signs, so that he could, at once, lay his hand upon the bundle he wanted to consult. Thus he formed a library of such bundles or volumes ; and when any book was mentioned which he had heard read, he could immediately take up the bundle containing his remarks upon it, and read them off quite fluently. He died in 1779. His curious staves fell into the hands of his relatives, who, not knowing their use or value, destroyed them.

Joseph Kleinhanns, born in 1777, lost his sight by small pox at 4½ years old. He was remarkable as a carver in wood. He made busts and statues from one foot high to the size of life. At the request of his countrymen he carved the figure of a Tyrolese soldier, 18 inches high, and gave such expression to the countenance as would have done credit to a *seeing* artist.

Johann Knie—[Author of the little work here translated]—was born at Erfurt in 1794, and was totally blinded, by the small pox, in his tenth year. He acquired much knowledge, in various branches of education, by attending schools for the seeing ; and at the age of 15 he entered the blind school at Berlin ; there, under the management and tuition of that able and benevolent man, Dr. Zeune, he made unusual progress, in learning, during the five years which he passed in that institution. He felt so great a desire to benefit his companions in misfortune, that he determined to devote himself to the education of the Blind. And, in order to fit himself for the task of teaching, he went to the University at Breslau, where for three years he studied, with great success, Mathematics, History, Geography, and whatever was necessary for the instruction of youth. His extraordinary memory was of the greatest use to him in acquiring the dead languages, which he did with great facility. He could repeat, almost verbatim, any lecture he had heard. In 1818 he prevailed upon twelve gentlemen to form themselves into a committee for establishing, in Breslau, a school for the Blind, which was opened in 1819, and in 1821 he became the director of it, and has continued to hold that appointment ever since, with credit to himself and advantage to the institution. His mild disposition and irreproachable conduct, together with his great acquirements, eminently qualify him for the discharge of the important duties which he has undertaken. He has translated several works connected with the blind, from different languages. He travelled, alone, through the greatest part of Prussia, Germany, &c., for the purpose of visiting the various schools and asylums for the blind, as well as other public institutions, and published an account of his journey in a very interesting 8vo. volume, entitled, " *Paedagogische Reise durch Deutschland, &c. in* 1847."

John Kaferle was born at Weiblingen, Würtemberg, in 1768. In his fourth year he became quite blind, from an arrow which struck him, whilst looking at archers practising. He soon showed extraordinary talents especially for Music and Mechanics. When he was five years old, some one gave him a common toy fiddle, on which he was soon able to play all the melodies with which he was acquainted. He then learned to play the guitar, and in a very short time surpassed his teacher. At 13 years old he made various implements, machines, and pieces of furniture, with such skill as to excite the admiration of all who saw them. In later years he made clocks, and invented a machine by which he could readily make the wheels, &c. At the age of 22 he made a piano-forte. Shortly after this his father's mill was burnt down by lightning, and when it was re-built he made most of the wheels, &c. He invented a peculiar kind of air-gun, but it was prohibited by the police. To relate all the extraordinary things which this wonderful man was able to perform would exceed the limits of this sketch, and appear almost incredible.

John Fred. Niendorfer, born in 1757, lost his sight by the small pox when he was three years old. He could not only clean but repair clocks, watches, and even repeaters!

— *Bunau*, daughter of a civil officer in Roda, was born about the year 1770, and may be looked upon as a pattern or example of all those who share her misfortune. She was blinded by the small pox in her third year. Her mental qualities were of a high kind, and she possessed superior natural talents, which she exercised in various ways, to lessen the severity of her misfortune, by useful occupation and innocent amusement. In order to communicate with her distant friends, she caused a large quantity of bits of paper, to be cut of the same size, and the letters of the alphabet written singly upon them. These she kept in a box of cells or divisions, like those in which printers put their types. When she wanted to write to any one, she took a needle and thread, and put upon it the different letters, in the order of the words she wished to communicate, putting a blank bit between every word. The receiver of this communication had only to draw the papers a little apart, and read them in the order in which they are placed upon the thread. She afterwards learnt to write with a pencil, of which she made great use; and she became unusually expert in various feminine occupations, as well as several mechanical ones. She was very poetical.

Maria Theresia von Paradies, born in 1759, lost her sight at three years of age. Her parents were persons of rank and fortune, and they spared no expense in cultivating her extraordinary talents, and procuring for her the various ingenious contrivances then known for facilitating the education of the Blind. She was a distinguished Musician, and as such visited nearly all the capitals and principal towns of Europe. Her disposition was mild and cheerful, her character altogether most amiable, and her manners easy and pleasing. She thought the opinion of the *seeing*, as to what was beautiful, could not be of much value, as so few of them agreed on that point. When she was at Paris she corresponded with her highly-educated blind friend Weissenberg, of Manheim. This becoming known to the never-to-be-forgotten Valentine Haüy, gave him the first idea of establishing a school for the general instruction of those deprived of sight, and hence arose that great and valuable Institution for the Blind, which does credit to Paris and to the French nation. M. T. von Paradies became an expert Arithmetician, through the use of the table or apparatus invented by the great Saunderson, the blind Professor of Mathematics in Cambridge. The Empress, Maria Theresa, was her godmother, and allowed her a yearly pension of 200 florins.

Le Sueur, born at Paris in 1776, was the first pupil of the first school for the blind,—the Paris School,—of which he afterwards became the manager.

Von Golz, blind at 13 years old, was a doctor of law, and professor in Königsberg.

Paingeon, born blind. Professor of Mathematics in Paris.

Pfeffel, the renowned poet, blind from his youth, was principal of the military school at Colmar, and afterwards established and conducted a school for those who had their sight.

Schoenberger, lost his sight at three years old, was born at Königsberg, and understood many of the living and dead languages; gave instructions in them, and discussed, with acuteness, many subjects, both in mathematics and philosophy.

Griesinger, of Worms, lost his sight at three years old; understood eight different languages, and was a popular preacher in Königsberg.

Rolli, born in Rome, studied science, especially physics and the higher mathematics.

To give even a short sketch of all the remarkable blind persons, of both sexes, would require a large volume. I have not given any account of the extraordinary blind persons in *England*, such as Moyes, Blacklock, Melcalf, Gough, Saunderson, Stanley, Strong, Lucas, Milton, &c., as they have been made known to the public by Wilson and others; but I hope the few I have noticed will be sufficient to encourage parents, who may have blind children, to give them the best education they can, and not to look upon them as burthensome, or a drawback upon their happiness, but regard their charge as a sacred duty, to those for whom God especially cares, inasmuch as he has pronounced a curse upon him who maketh the blind to " wander out of the way."—Deut. xxvii. 18.

Additional Remarks.

NOTE.—Many poor persons who have blind children often endure great privations rather than seek parochial relief for their sightless offspring, under an impression that they shall, thereby, become *paupers* and lose certain privileges; but there is a clause in an Act passed in the reign of Wm. IV.,* which authorises parents to receive parish relief for blind, or deaf and dumb children, under sixteen years of age, without thereby becoming paupers, or forfeiting any privileges. This ought to be generally known, as it may prevent much unnecessary suffering.

Gymnastic exercises are very desirable for the blind, and they may enjoy the pleasure of running " at full stretch "—without danger.—in the following way : Let a post be fixed firmly in the centre of some grass plat; let the one end of a long cord be fastened to a ring, which turns round the post, and let the blind person take hold of the other end, and run round the post, keeping the cord tight. Perhaps it would be better if a long pole, like a capstan, were attached to the post, as in that case several may take hold of it, and run at the same time, the smaller ones being nearer to the centre.

A board of cork is very useful : Pins may be stuck in it, and a thread passed round them, so as to represent right-lined geometrical, and other figures, &c.

The blind acquire much information by attending common schools for the seeing. [See biography of Blind Jacob, page 36]

It is desirable that the blind, in doing rough work, should wear a " finger-stall," upon the finger they chiefly use in reading embossed books, examining minute objects, &c.. in order to preserve, as much as possible, the delicacy of touch. In reading it is best to use the fore-finger of the right hand to decipher the letters, while the others may be employed in ascertaining the length of the word, and whether (in the common alphabet) it ends with a letter which goes above the line, as b, d, l, &c., or one which goes below, as g, y, p, &c., as this will greatly facilitate the making out of the word, and enable the pupil to read more quickly. When the blind do not succeed in reading, in any alphabet, the fault is oftener with the teacher than the pupil. The blind are the best teachers of the blind in all things not requiring sight. In reading embossed books, it is desirable to place a piece of pasteboard between the page being read and the next, to prevent the letters of the under one being felt through the paper of the upper, which would produce confusion. With this the books get less injured, and last longer.

The blind often feel interested in reading inscriptions and epitaphs on grave-stones. Of course only those who have learnt the *common* letters.

Reading to the blind is always acceptable and profitable to them.

Hientzsch has given the following interesting table of the blind in Prussia ,

* 4th and 5th Wm. IV. c. 76, s. 56.

in the years 1846 and 1849, shewing the general decrease of the malady in that country in three years:—

	Children under 15 years of age.		Between 15 and 30.		Above 30 years of age.		Total.
	Males.	Females.	Males.	Females.	Males.	Females.	
1846. .	451	371	706	674	4,015	3,788	10,005
1849. .	441	326	770	635	3,900	3,507	9,579
Result.	10	45	64	39	115	281	426

Head-work for the Blind.

THEY may be taught reading, writing, cyphering, geography, algebra, geometry, and other branches of the mathematics, with the sciences founded upon them; such as astronomy, mechanics, hydraulics, &c., also history, natural history, theology, metaphysics, logic, grammar, languages, and philosophy, both natural and moral; may lecture in literature and science; study chemistry, modelling in clay, wax, &c.; teach schools, be parish clerks, conduct psalmody and other singing, &c.

Hand-work which the Blind are capable of doing.

VARIOUS kinds of housework, such as making beds, washing, baking, rubbing furniture, turning mangles, carrying water, wood, &c.; churning, shelling peas, beans, &c.; taking care of linen; knitting, netting, sewing, crochet, lace, plaiting straw, hair, &c.; making doileys, mats for dishes, paper boxes, shoes, of list or leather; brush-making, wire-working, cutting files, sawing wood, drilling and filing iron, brass, &c.; joinering, turning, coopering, blowing bellows, ringing bells, playing organs, or other instruments; weaving cloth, mats, hearth-rugs, girths, &c.; making sash-line, whips, hooks and eyes, glass bugles, bead-work; make bricks, tiles, &c.; grind malt, coffee, pepper, colours, &c.; fringe-making, rope-making, spinning thread; tuning pianos; pounding in mortars; pumping water, cutting straw for horses, crushing beans, slicing turnips, carrots, &c., for cattle; basket-making, &c.

A few general Rules which may be useful to those who have the care of Blind Children.

IT is of the greatest importance that blind children be religiously brought up; for, as they are deprived of many advantages which are open to those who have their sight, they stand in greater need of the promises and consolations of religion, which alone can afford them real comfort under their affliction, and enable them to bear it with patience and resignation. In giving religious instruction the greatest care should be taken that every portion they are taught be fully and clearly explained to them, for, if left in doubt, they are very likely to fall into superstition on the one hand, or into scepticism on the other.

They should be treated in all things as much like the *seeing*, as circumstances will admit of, in order to render social intercourse with them agreeable and beneficial; for, as they have to live amongst those who see, they should have as many things in common with them as possible.

They should be accustomed to *activity* from their childhood, even if it be only for amusement. It, in a great measure, prevents their brooding over their misfortune, which not only injures their health, but unfits them for any useful exertion, either of mind or body.

Never assist them further than is necessary, in order to teach them to depend upon themselves. Jäger says "you cannot do a greater benefit to a blind child than to accustom him, as soon as may be, to do everything for himself as far as possible."

Encourage them to examine, carefully, everything which comes in their way, and not to be afraid of asking questions.

You need not be much concerned about any little hurt they may receive, from running against chairs, tables, &c., or in using certain instruments or tools, as such trifling accidents prevent greater, by teaching them caution.

In moving about a room, &c., should they take a wrong direction, it will be well to set them right *privately*, and to avoid as much as possible, where others are present, doing or saying anything to make them feel their dependence upon those who have their sight.

Amongst the many ingenious contrivances for facilitating the education of the blind, make choice of the *simplest*, and, as far as possible, such as are in use among those who see, when they are sufficient for your purpose; *and never depart from the common or beaten track, when that will lead to the object you have in view.*

Avoid giving utterance to feelings of pity or commiseration for the blind, in their presence, as it reminds them of their misfortune and gives them pain. Von Baczko (blind), relates the following anecdote:—"I was once sitting on a public seat, when a neighbour, whom I knew to have what is called a hunchback, joined me, and began to pity my misfortune, and to tell me of the pleasure I lost on account of my blindness, &c. I said Yes, it is a misfortune to be unlike other people. Possibly *you*, sometimes, have the unpleasantness of hearing unfeeling remarks made upon your deformity.—I had proceeded no further, when my crook-backed neighbour got up and, muttering some dissatisfaction, walked away."

When you meet blind persons whom you intend to address, always make yourself known to them, by mentioning your name, unless your voice is familiar to them,—it spares them the unpleasantness of doubt, as to who you are, and, to some extent, guides them in what they have to say in return.—Where there are several together, always make it known which of them you speak to, either by touching their hand or shoulder, or by mentioning their name, if you know it. For if they do not know which is spoken to, neither of them will venture to give an answer; and this often makes strangers go away with an unfavourable opinion of them,—perhaps thinking them stupid,—whereas the fault lies with themselves. A touch of the finger on the hand or arm is, to a blind person, what a smile is, to one who can see.

When you ask a blind person a question, and you receive an answer, always signify your agreement with it, or dissent from; for if you go away in silence, you leave him in doubt whether or not his answer may have displeased you.

Do not ask blind persons if they have *heard* such and such a book read, but say, "have you *read* such and such a book, or have you *seen* Mr. A. or Mr. B., &c." It gives them the comfortable feeling that there is nothing so remarkable in their appearance as to direct attention to their misfortune.

Be careful how you *watch* blind persons,—unperceived, as you may suppose,—lest by smelling, hearing, or by feeling an impulse of the air, they detect your presence; in that case you will forfeit their good opinion. Also be very careful never, intentionally, to *deceive* them, even though you should think it for their good, for, if they find it out, it will tend to render them suspicious, and you will lose their confidence, never to regain it. Besides, it is not so easy to deceive them, as some may imagine; for as they have to depend upon *four* senses to do the duty of *five*, their discernment acquires an unusual degree of acuteness, which is extremely valuable to them, not only in their intercourse with others, but also in their education.

It is not necessary, in conversing with the blind, to avoid such subjects as relate to vision, &c., for, from frequently hearing things described, they will

E

form very good notions of them, and their lively imagination will supply useful representations of them.

Give them every possible opportunity of examining natural and artificial objects. Among the former may be reckoned specimens in geology, zoology, conchology, crystalography, metals, seeds, plants, flowers, fruits, wood, &c. Among the latter, various instruments, machines, money, weights, measures, cloth, articles of various manufactures, regular solids, such as cones, cubes, spheres, cylinders, &c.

When young, store their minds with extracts from the best authors, and especially from the Scriptures.

Never keep a pupil puzzling over things which he does not understand,—it only tends to make him less inclined to encounter difficulties. Always explain to him fully and clearly the *principles* on which he is acting, and lead him on by questions which he can easily answer, to those which are more difficult. *Success* will encourage him to greater efforts, but *defeat* will damp his ardour, and perhaps produce in him a dislike to learning.

Never praise him for *great talents*, but for industry, attention, perseverance, good conduct, and such other things as are under his control.

Contemplations on the Blind.

Who can read the annals of the Blind, or witness their privation, without the deepest interest in their welfare? Who can shut his ear against their rightful claims for succour and support? Or who, that is now blest with sight, can feel secure that he may never have to share their lot? To them, the outer world is all a blank! Their mortal life is veil'd in one perpetual night, and all around them pitchy darkness—"Dark amidst the blaze of noon!" Yet not in wrath has God thus closed one inlet to the mind, but in His wisdom, and for ends unknown to man. The blind do not behold the hand that administers to their relief; nor do they see the tear of sympathy which flows at their misfortune: but, when the voice of kindness or affection falls upon their ear, their hearts will bound with joy and turn, in grateful love, to that Almighty Being, "who tempers the wind to the shorn lamb." Though they cannot perceive the golden morn advance upon the mountains, nor mark the shades of night retiring from the vales, yet they listen to the matins of the lark, as though it were a voice from Heaven, inviting them to enter upon the new-born day, by lifting up their hearts in prayer to God who takes them under his peculiar care.* They look not upon the verdant landscape, bounded by the distant hills, and studded with "cloud-capt towers" or "heaven-directed spires," yet they can hear the hum of busy life—can feel the influence of the cooling breeze, and muse in calm enjoyment! They see not how the still evening closes on the drowsy world; they gaze not upon the brightness of the starry host, nor watch the fleeting clouds progressing through the moon's pale beams. Yet, though their outward senses are diminished, their minds are free to wander through the boundless realms of space, and open to receive the knowledge of that benignant God "whose goodness extends to every creature" and "whose tender mercies are over all His works."† The Blind, as well as those who have their sight, can ponder with delight upon the mighty operations of Nature, which their lively imaginations present, "to the mind's eye," in all their grandeur and perfection. Their hearts can glow with all the better feelings of humanity; they are capable of entering into social converse and enjoyments; can take their stand as useful members of society, and well sustain their part among their seeing brethren. At times, indeed, they, from

* Deut. xxvii. 18. Isaiah xlii. 16.
† Psalm cxlv.

the neighbouring steeple, hear the solemn knell, as if it were the voice of friends departed, calling them to serious thoughts and holy contemplations. This oftentimes produces, in the Blind, a tranquil resignation and points to that true, clear, and inward, light, which cannot fail to animate their hopes, and cheer their weary journey through this mortal life, to that all-glorious land, where " they will rest from their labours," where their " sorrows will be turned into joy," and where their eyes will be opened to behold their God !

T.

" Geniesse, was dir Gott beschieden.
Entbehre gern, was du nicht hast,
Ein jeder Stand hat seinen Frieden,
Ein jeder Stand hat seine Last."

GELLERT.

BOOKS, ON THIS SUBJECT, IN ENGLISH.

Biography of the Blind. By James Wilson.

The Land of Silence and the Land of Darkness. By the Rev. B. G. Johns, Chaplain of the Blind School, St. George's Fields.

The Sense Denied and Lost. By Thos. Bull, M.D. Edited by the Rev. B. G. Johns, Chaplain of the Blind School, St. George's Fields.

Tangible Typography : or How the Blind Read. By Edmund C. Johnson, Member of the Committee of the School for the Indigent Blind, &c.

The Blind of London. By E. C. Johnson, Esq.

Dr. Guillie's Work on the Blind, translated into English from the French.

Reports of the School for the Blind at Boston, U.S. By Dr. S. Howe.

Reports of the School for the Blind at Philadelphia. By Friedlander.

There is also, at Philadelphia, an English Dictionary, in 3 vols., 4to., Embossed in the common or Roman Letters, for the Use of the Blind. Published by the Directors of the Blind School at Philadelphia, under the superintendence of Professor Dunglison, M.D.

The Blind : their Capabilities, Condition, and Claims. By Alexander Mitchell (himself blind). Honorary Secretary to the Society for Improving the Social Position of the Blind. Wilton House, Walworth Road, London.

By the Translator. Diagrams of the first book of Euclid ; Embossed for the Blind.

——— Selection of Psalm Tunes ; Embossed for the Blind.

——— Report on different Alphabets proposed for the use of the Blind, written at the request of the Royal Scotch Society of Arts, Edinburgh, and published in their Transactions.

——— Report on Printing for the Blind. Published in the Transactions of the British Association for the Advancement of Science, &c.

——— Lecture on the education of the Blind, delivered at the Royal Institution of Great Britain, an abstract of which is published in their Transactions.

——— Paper on the Education of the Blind, and on the establishment of a College for those of the opulent classes, read at the meeting of the Social Science Society, at Liverpool.

By the Translator. A short sketch (translated from the German) of the Life of J. W. Klein, Founder and Director of the Blind School at Vienna.
———— The Relation of the Blind to the World around them. (Translated from the German.)

It is to be regretted that the following works have not been rendered available in England by translation, as the excellent matter they contain will afford every necessary information and instruction for the guidance of those who have the management and education of the Blind.

Klein. Lehrbuch zum Unterricht der Blinden.
———— Geschichte des Blinden Unterrichtes.
———— Anleitung Blinden Kindern, &c.
———— Jakob Braun.
———— Anstalten für Blinde.
———— Blinden Lieder.
———— Beschreibung eines gelungenen Versuches Blinden Kinder zur Burg : Brauchbarkeit zu Bilden.
Rotermund. Nachrichten v. einigen Blindgebornen, &c.
Daniel. An Regierungen, Eltern, und Lehrer, &c.
Jäger. Ueber die Behandlung welche Blinden Kindern, &c.
Orell. Blinden Anstalt in Zürich.
Carton. Le Sourd-Muet et l'Aveugle.
Didero. Lettres sur les Aveugles.
Dolezálek. Ansichten über die Erziehung der Zölinge eines Blinden Anstalt, &c.
Hienzsch. Ueber die Erziehung und den Unterricht der Blinden, &c.
Georgi. Geschichte der K. S. Blinden Anstalt zu Dresden.
Struve. Kurzer Unterricht für Eltern und Lehrer der Blinden.
Zeune. Belisar, oder über Blinde und Blinden Anstalten.
Freudenberg. Gründliche Hülfe für Blinde, &c.
Baczko. Ueber mich selbst und meine Unglücks-gefährten, die Blinden.

Also the works of *Knie, Düfau, Müller, Niboyet, Hirzel, Nageli, Koch, Wolke, Altorfer, Neudegg, Lachmann, Braille, &c. &c.*

LONDON : PRINTED BY WILLIAM CLOWES AND SONS, LIMITED,
STAMFORD STREET AND CHARING CROSS.

www.ingramcontent.com/pod-product-compliance
Lightning Source LLC
Chambersburg PA
CBHW031348290326
41932CB00044B/432